Controlled Drug Bioavailability

Controlled Drug Bioavailability

VOLUME 1

DRUG PRODUCT DESIGN AND PERFORMANCE

Edited by

VICTOR F. SMOLEN
PharmaControl Corporation
Englewood Cliffs, New Jersey

LUANN BALL
Ciba-Geigy Corporation
Summit, New Jersey

A Wiley-Interscience Publication

JOHN WILEY & SONS

New York • Chichester • Brisbane • Toronto • Singapore

Library of Congress Cataloging in Publication Data:

Main entry under title:

Drug product design and performance.

(Controlled drug bioavailability; v. 1)
"A Wiley-Interscience publication."
Includes index.
Contents: Optimally controlled drug bioavailability in theory and products/Victor F. Smolen—Applied biodynamic analysis of drugs/Victor F. Smolen—Pharmacokinetic analysis of drug-responding systems/David J. Cutler—[etc.]
1. Bipharmaceutics. 2. Pharmacokinetics. 3. Structure-activity relationship (Pharmacology) I. Smolen, Victor F. II. Ball, LuAnn. III. Series.

RM301.4.D78 1983 615′.7 83-6726
ISBN 0-471-05732-0

Printed in the United States of America

10 9 8 7 6 5 4 3 2 1

Contributors

Virgil L. Anderson, Department of Statistics, Purdue University, West Lafayette, Indiana

Joseph V. Bondi, Merck Sharp and Dohme Research Laboratories, West Point, Pennsylvania

David J. Cutler, The School of Pharmacy, Brunswick Square, University of London, England. *Present address:* Department of Pharmacy, University of Sydney, Sydney, Australia

T. Deutsch, Computer Center, Chinoin Pharmaceutical and Chemical Works, Budapest, Hungary

John P. Matheu, Vice-President, Pfizer, Inc., New York, New York

Robert A. McLean, Department of Statistics, Purdue University, West Lafayette, Indiana. Present address: Department of Statistics, University of Tennessee, Knoxville, Tennessee

Nicolaos A. Peppas, School of Chemical Engineering, Purdue University, West Lafayette, Indiana

M. Schulz, Computer Center, Chinoin Pharmaceutical and Chemical Works, Budapest, Hungary. *Present address:* Biomedical Research, Hospital for Sick Children, Toronto, Canada

Victor F. Smolen, PharmaControl Corporation, Englewood Cliffs, New Jersey

G. Tamás, Jr., Computer Center, Chinoin Pharmaceutical and Chemical Works, Budapest, Hungary

Robert D. Tanner, Chemical Engineering Department, Vanderbilt University, Nashville, Tennessee

Donald Vaughan, Department of Pharmacy, Sunderland Polytechnic, Sunderland, Tyne & Wear, United Kingdom

P. G. Walton, Department of Mathematics, Sunderland Polytechnic, Sunderland, Tyne & Wear, United Kingdom

Series Preface

The purpose of this newly established continuing series of monographs is to provide a forum to disseminate current knowledge that contributes to expediting the design, development, evaluation, manufacture, control, marketing, and clinical use of increasingly safer and more effective drug products at lower costs. A critical problem with the entire health care industry is the high and rapidly escalating costs. A significant contribution to this problem is the cost of drugs. Not only is the research for the development of drug products expensive, but so is the process for the establishment of their quality, safety, effectiveness, and manner of use. It has been estimated that it presently takes an average of seven years and in excess of $50 million to gain approval of a single new drug in the United States by the Food and Drug Administration (FDA). Briefly, a promising new drug must first be tested in up to thousands of animals to assess its possible toxicity. That done, it must then be used in multiphasic tests before the dosage form(s) and dose levels, safety, effectiveness, and possible side effects can be determined. These human subjects must be under the almost constant surveillance of high-priced specialists, and the results of all these studies must be analyzed by statisticians and reported. Finally, this mass of data must be reviewed and approved by drug regulatory agencies such as the FDA before permission to market the drug can be given. It is obviously imperative that the most current knowledge be effectively applied to reduce the costs of drug product development and accelerate the availability of new therapies and improved products to the patients needing them.

In all approaches to drug development it cannot be overlooked that drugs are never used as the pure chemical substances whose molecular structures are responsible for their intrinsic pharmacological activities. Drugs are always put into delivery systems, such as liquids to be injected by mechanical or electromechanical devices, or are formulated into dosage forms such as tablets, capsules, suppositories, and so on, and recently even into patches placed on the skin's surface; such dosage forms become the marketed drug products themselves. In practice, the dynamics of the manner by which a dosage form releases its drug to become available to its site(s) of action in the body is equally as important in determining the safety and effectiveness of the course of drug therapy as is the intrinsic pharmacological activity of the chemical substance that the drug product contains.

The formulation and manufacture of drug dosage forms, as well as how drug delivery devices are designed and operated, has a profound influence on the manner in which drugs access their sites(s) of action. In recent years it has become widely recognized among pharmaceutical scientists, clinicians, and government regulatory agencies that drug bioavailability, defined as the time course of the rates and extents of drug entrance into the body or release to its sites of absorption prior to entering into the body, is of the most fundamental importance to the design, development, evaluation, and clinical use of drug products. This importance becomes apparent from simply considering that once a drug enters into the body (i.e., becomes bioavailable), the course of its therapeutic and toxic effects becomes entirely determined by the intrinsic dynamics of the drug's disposition and actions in the body. Since targeting of drug molecules to specific sites of action is not yet achieved, there is presently virtually nothing that can be routinely and effectively done to alter the course of these effects. Therefore, selection of or otherwise affecting the manner in which the drug is allowed to enter the body in the first place (i.e., the bioavailability input of the drug) provides the only practical means to control, or inadvertently alter, the safety and effectiveness of drug products. A potential basis for drug product design and development must, therefore, always consider the relationship between the drug bioavailability inputs that a product will deliver and the resulting time course of pharmacological effects and body fluid drug levels that ensue. Products having the same bioavailability inputs can be considered bioequivalent. Pharmacokinetics, defined as what the body does to the drug (i.e., absorb, distribute, metabolize, and eliminate it), and pharmacodynamics, defined as what the drug does to the body (i.e., elicit pharmacological effects), provide the theoretical and computationally practical means of relating drug bioavailability inputs to the drug level and pharmacological responses that underlie the safety and clinical effectiveness of a drug's usage.

Even though the development of new clinical drug entities—which was incipient and flourished after World War II—continues to produce new and exciting progress, there is presently a rapidly increasing awareness that the drug industry has entered a new era of even greater precision in drug therapy based on controlled drug bioavailability. As is the case with all trends in our society, circumstances of politics, law, and economics, in addition to developments in science and pharmaceutical technology, are providing a strong impetus to the growth of precisely controlled bioavailability. This can be understood from considering the regulatory law requirements and economics of new drug entity development relative to the inordinately lower costs of developing and marketing better drug delivery systems for generic drugs whose intrinsic safety and effectiveness have already been well established.

Generic drugs are those for which patent protection has expired, allowing them to be sold by other manufacturers in competition with the original patenting pharmaceutical company. In 1979 the U.S. market in generic drugs was an estimated $4.37 billion, representing 43% of the total pharmaceutical drug market in that year. A recent Frost and Sullivan report on the generic drugs market forecasts generic drug sales to reach nearly $10 billion by 1989 in the United States alone. Others forecast $10 billion generic sales to be reached by 1985. Significant factors in this growth are the expiration of patents of 48 of the major pharmaceuticals (which had combined sales in the United States of $2.2 billion in 1979) and the time, difficulty, and expense of developing new ethical, patented drugs. Therefore, the competition by both ethical and generic drug companies to retain and capture market shares can be projected to become increasingly fierce. Successful competitors can be expected to offer superior drug products that provide therapeutic advantages. The leveling of competition between multisource suppliers of the same generic drug entity should provide the economic impetus to develop drug products that are not merely satisfactory but have a therapeutically optimal, controlled drug bioavailability. The development of such products would contribute to even more rapidly advancing the pharmaceutical sciences as well as being of obvious benefit to drug-consuming patients. It is to these objectives that this series of monographs is dedicated, through presenting current information relating to the theory and practice of controlled drug bioavailability.

The present and subsequent volumes are devoted primarily to those topical areas whose interaction is requisite to the development of drug products of optimal therapeutic benefit. Most broadly, these topics include (1) pharmacokinetics and pharmacodynamics that provide the theoretical and computational means necessary to relate the dynamic manner in which a drug must be allowed to enter the body to elicit optimally sought pharmacological effects (the performance criteria, on which to design the drug release dynamics of drug products to achieve optimal therapeutic benefits can be determined); (2) methodologies and drug regulatory considerations for the bioavailability–bioequivalency requirements and the evaluation of drug delivery systems; (3) the specific design, development, properties, manufacture, control, and factors that affect the bioavailability of particular types of drug delivery system that most broadly are chemical, mechanical, or electromechanical devices; and (4) the marketing and promotion of drug products. The projected market success of a controlled-release drug product is of course the initiating factor for its development. The manner of promoting a uniquely new product will include a need to educate the physician, pharmacist, nurse, and patient in order to gain its acceptance; therefore, the promotion of a new and novel drug delivery system is even more important than the otherwise unrealized potential therapeutic benefits such products can provide. For example, there is clearly a need for controlled-release drug products that allow for a once-a-day dosing schedule to always be maintained for all the drugs a patient is taking in order to achieve maximum patient compliance and therapeutic benefits. This must be done while permitting the dosage for many of the most important drugs to be readily adjusted to a patient's individualized needs. These objectives would necessitate that the drugs be supplied in unconventional forms. The marketing and promotion of new drug product forms would require the application of both a clinical pharmacokinetic and educational support program to ensure the proper and most successful usage of such products. This example serves to illustrate the need for the integration of all the relevant topics and themes of this series to deliver a maximum therapeutic benefit to patients in what is envisaged to continue to be an era of increasing improvements in controlled drug bioavailability.

VICTOR F. SMOLEN
LUANN BALL

Englewood Cliffs, New Jersey
Summit, New Jersey
August 1983

Preface

The pharmaceutical sciences have firmly entered an era of achieving optimally controlled drug bioavailability from drug products that are thereby designed to elicit maximum therapeutic benefits. The importance to the pharmaceutical industry in the 1980s of optimally designing drug delivery systems to this purpose can be clearly projected from the economic and marketing considerations concerning both new and old (generic) drugs as discussed in Chapter 9 of this first volume and the series preface that introduces this new series of monographs. In this context, the theoretical basis and computational approaches to solving the problems of establishing therapeutic performance criteria for optimally controlled drug delivery systems becomes of critical, practical, and economic significance. The first volume in this continuing series on controlled drug bioavailability is of particular value to the pharmacokineticist with the task of providing "state of the science" guidance to drug delivery system developers to achieve optimally acceptable therapeutic objectives for their products. The most basically important link between the time course of the manner in which a drug product releases its drug contents and the therapeutic benefits achieved is a recurring theme. Chapter 1 elaborates on this theme and provides a broad perspective of the utility and manner of application of drug bioavailability input–output response relationships to two fundamental categories of controlled drug delivery systems based on differences in the operational approaches that are best utilized in their development; these are termed *in-vitro programmable* and *in-vivo unpredictable* and are exemplified by new and novel and more conventional types of controlled-release drug delivery system, respectively. These "open-loop" systems are described and contrasted to the ultimate in therapeutic performance that will be achieved from "closed-loop" controlled drug delivery systems in the near future. Chapter 2, on the topic of applied biodynamic analysis of drugs, presents an overview of the various methods of describing the kinetic behavior of drug responding systems that are further elaborated in detail in Chapter 3. Chapter 4 takes up the theme of drug bioavailability input–output relationships relative to achieving an optimization of a drug's performance. Optimization of drug inputs is further exemplified by an administration strategy for insulin described in Chapter 5. The important topic of time-dependent, nonlinear drug kinetics often seen in biosystems is treated in Chapter 6 by the methods of kinetic hysteresis analysis. Chapter 7 focuses attention away from the biosystem in which the drug product must perform and places it on the mathematical analysis of the drug delivery system whose dynamic drug-release properties must be controlled and predicted to achieve a desired in-vivo performance. Chapter 8 describes experimental designs and the statistical basis for bioavailability evaluations of drug products.

VICTOR F. SMOLEN
LUANN BALL

Englewood Cliffs, New Jersey
Summit, New Jersey
August 1983

Contents

CHAPTER 1

Optimally Controlled Drug Bioavailability in Theory and Products

VICTOR F. SMOLEN

PharmaControl Corporation
Englewood Cliffs, New Jersey

CONTENTS

It has become well recognized that the rates and extents to which a given drug entity accesses its sites of action in the body (biophase) is as important to the safety and effectiveness of the drug therapy as the chemical structures of the drug itself from which the drug derives its intrinsic pharmacological activities. Ideally, it would be most desirable to specifically target a drug to selected sites in the body and eliminate unwanted effects that would occur at other sites and thereby limit the drug's actions to only those manifest in sought-after (desired) therapeutic responses. Research on such targeted drug delivery systems is in progress; by taking advantage of ferromagnetic drug-containing particles, one can guide the drug to its sites of action with externally applied magnetic fields. The incorporation of cell-specific antibodies into surfaces of microencapsulated drug systems can direct them to specific tissue sites (e.g., tumors) in the body. However, such modern "magic bullets" have not yet been translated into marketable drug products, although exciting progress has indeed been made in the commercialization of "new and novel" drug delivery systems.

Except for the yet unavailable site-specific targeted drug delivery systems of the near future, it is fundamentally important to recognize that once a drug has been allowed to enter the body, there is nothing that can be done in a necessarily routine manner to further affect the time course of the drug's therapeutic or toxic effects. Such necessary control can be accomplished only through preprogramming or continuously readjusting the rate(s) at which the drug enters the systemic circulation or is released at its sites of absorption into the body. This control function is accomplished by drug bioavailability systems that have been intelligently designed to accomplish a maximal therapeutic benefit for the patient. The great majority of drug delivery systems—including what are commonly referred to as *controlled-release*, *prolonged-release*, *sustained-action*, and *timed-release systems*—which presently constitute marketed drug products, have not been optimally preprogrammed to achieve a maximum therapeutic utility.

1. DRUG DELIVERY SYSTEMS

In general, drug delivery systems have been broadly defined as chemical, mechanical, or electromechanical devices designed to input drugs to the systemic circulation or to specific target sites in the body at predetermined, controlled rates (1, 2). If the drug input is not obtained at a predetermined, controlled rate, however, the drug delivery system can best be described as a drug dump system. Most drug products currently on the market fall into the latter category in that the time course of their release (e.g., through dissolution from a tablet) is generally fortuitous rather than being predetermined or designed on the basis of rational pharmacological criteria (1, 2). Despite extensive research and development efforts, very few chemical drug delivery systems readily lend themselves to predetermined and controlled rates of drug release in vivo. In all cases, drug-release rates depend on the kinetic processes of dissolution, diffusion, and/or chemical reaction (hydrolysis), all of which are difficult to predict or control in the complex and often uncertain biologic environment within which drug delivery systems must perform. Therefore, rigorously controlled drug release is relatively difficult to attain by means of most chemical systems; up to the present time, such systems have been only partially successful. However, many promising approaches (e.g., osmotic pumps, transdermal drug delivery devices, biodegradable polymer drug systems, and implants) hold definite promise (3–6). The ultimate control of drug bioavailability that can be achieved is not provided by such systems, but by closed-loop systems for the automatic feedback (computer)-controlled administration of drugs (SAFCAD) (7) as compared to open-loop, conventional systems. This chapter discusses the properties and approaches to the expeditious development of optimal open- and closed loop drug delivery systems.

1.1 Closed-Loop Controlled Drug Bioavailability Systems

Drug products as we commonly know them are chemical systems (e.g., tablets, capsules, ointments, and liquids) whose release and subsequent activity, once the dose has been administered, are (1) predetermined by the product's formulation and (2) uncontrollable after the drug has been introduced into the body. Such open-loop (i.e., not feedback-controlled) drug delivery systems can be designed to elicit optimal therapeutic response behavior in the median, or "average patient." Because of high interpatient drug-response variability, dosages for potent drugs must be adjusted by trial and error; in this manner the undershoot or overshoot of dosage can be successively adjusted until the patient has been "titrated" to an individual dosage regimen. Some drugs, such as intravenous anesthetics, hypotensive agents, and insulin, can require continuous readjustment of dose rates in response to the development of tolerances or hypersensitivities, or in accordance with changing pathophysiological conditions or dietary factors. Such individualized dosage adjustment is especially important for rapidly acting drugs that have a narrow therapeutic range. In theory, what is needed to solve the problem of interpatient drug-response variability are closed-loop, feedback-controlled drug products that release drugs in response to the patient's momentary therapeutic needs rather than drug products that merely release quantities of drugs at standard rates that are predetermined by the product's design and formulation for the average patient.

Such a drug delivery system (i.e., one that continuously monitors the patient's moment-to-moment needs) can take the form of a miniaturized electromechanical analytic device implanted in the body. This approach has been taken in the development of an electrochemical sensor that monitors blood glucose, thus functioning as a component of an artificial pancreatic system for automatic administration of insulin (14, 15). However, the glucose sensor has presented difficulties in clinical application; in general, many problems remain to be resolved before such implantable, biocompatible, chemical-specific, miniaturized analytic devices can be developed for monitoring blood or tissue levels of drugs in vivo. One problem is that tissue growth surrounding the semipermeable membranes of the glucose sensor retards that sensor's response to changes in blood glucose. In light of the advances that are constantly being made in biologic surface chemistry and in analytic instrumentation, it would seem that these problems may eventually be surmounted.

An approach to the development of electromechanical drug delivery systems that can immediately be applied because it obviates chemical sensors is shown in Figure 1, which contains a block diagram describing the manner in which all drugs are used. In each case, a desired level of drug–effect output is sought. In some cases, the level of effect can be readily determined [e.g., by blood pressure (BP) monitoring], whereas in others, sophisticated signal data processing is necessary [e.g., to quantitate levels of anesthesia on the basis of on-line computerized analysis of EEG signals (2, 7, 16)]. In any event, the level of effect actually being elicited by the patient is compared to the level of response being sought, and the difference is described as the error signal. The error signal is then fed into a controller that readjusts the drug dose rate to attain a level of effect that more closely approximates the level of response being sought from the patient. For long-acting, relatively safe drugs, the function of the controller can be performed by a clinician in the

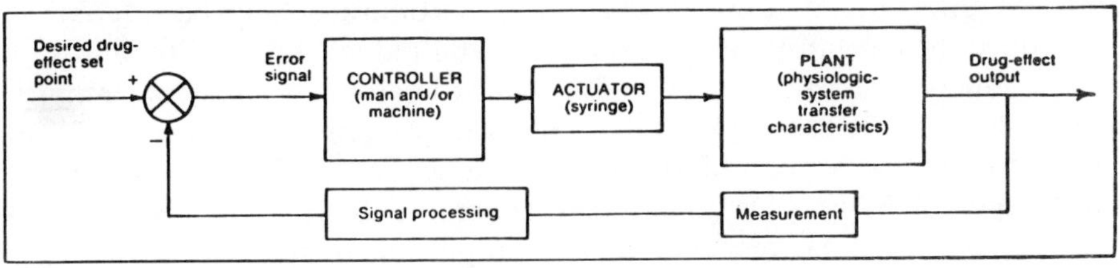

Figure 1. General block diagram of a feedback-controlled, automatic drug delivery system Reprinted with permission from V. F. Smolen. Practical Pharmacodynamic Engineering in the Design, Development and Evaluation of Optimal Drug Products. In H. S. Bean, A. H. Backett, and J. E. Canless (eds.), *Advances in Pharmaceutical Sciences*, Vol. 5, Academic Press, London, 1981, pp. 115–198.

hospital ward. For short-acting, potent drugs, however, this function is best accomplished by a mechanical device. With monitoring of the intensity of pharmacological response(s) to a drug rather than monitoring body fluid levels, current technology can be used to achieve automatic drug administration. Once a satisfactory means of monitoring drug levels or pharmacological effects has been developed, automatic controllers can be used to actuate drug-infusion pumps, thereby directing the rates of drug administration into the body. Published reports by the present author (2, 8–10) and others (14, 15, 17–26) have described the operation of such systems. Chapter 5 in the present volume deals with insulin–glucose systems, and Chapter 3 in Volume 3 of this series describes and reviews SAFCAD systems in general. In addition to insulin, the majority of the present work and interest in the development of marketable SAFCAD products appears as being directed to sodium nitroprusside, lidocaine, surgical anesthetics, and thiopental sodium. The thiopental–SAFCAD system is of particular interest in that it utilizes an optimal-adaptive, closed-loop, control system algorithm that causes the controller to automatically sense changes in the patient's responsivity to the drug (i.e., changes in the dynamic relationship between the rates the drug is input to the patient and the time variations in the changes in pharmacological responses that ensue). It then reprograms itself to always maintain a maximum therapeutic benefit to the patient from the drug's usage by minimizing any overshoot and undershoot of the therapeutic response from the set-point level (16). In application to thiopental sodium, the system continuously monitors EEG activity and performs an on-line computerized analysis of the EEG signal to extract quantitative measures of the degree of CNS depression induced by the drug at any time. In addition to its use as an anesthetic, anticonvulsant, and narcosynthesitic agent, thiopental is being increasingly used to very effectively treat conditions where cerebral ischemia causes cerebral hypertension due to cerebral edema. These highly morbid conditions arise following head injury, stroke, and vascular surgery. In head injuries, thiopental and other rapid acting barbiturates have been reported to reduce the mortality rate by up to 65% and reduce the severity of loss of brain function in survivors (27–29). Unfortunately, the patients require meticulous monitoring by skilled medical personnel because they can remain comatose for periods of weeks at a time. This problem will be solved by thiopental–SAFCADs systems that render this highly effective barbiturate therapy practical and very economically applicable on a broad scale.

Closed-loop, optimal adaptive drug bioavailability systems can be described as the ultimate in precision and accuracy that can be achieved only through the application of electronic, computer control. Because of their obvious therapeutic advantages and the rapid advances that are continuing to be made in electronics miniaturization and computer science, the development of such electromechanical drug delivery devices can be envisaged to be applied to an increasing number of drugs. Since the technology already exists, it is not difficult to envisage SAFCAD to someday take forms somewhat similar to the bandagelike transdermal drug delivery systems that have recently been successfully marketed for scopolamine and nitroglycerin, thereby combining the advantages of transdermal drug delivery, relative to oral and parenteral administration, and the precision of closed-loop feedback control.

1.2 Open-Loop Controlled Drug Bioavailability Systems

All drug products must conform to acceptable levels of performance in accordance with criteria such as (1) chemical stability of the drug and adjuvants, (2) physical stability of the product, (3) pharmaceutical elegance, patient acceptance, and other marketing considerations, (4) chemical purity and freedom from contamination particularly in the case of parenterals by microbes, particulates, and pyrogens, (5) feasibility and cost of large-scale manufacturing and quality control of production, (6) toxicity of all components, and especially (7) the time course of the rate(s) and extent of the drug's bioavailability. Each of these criteria must remain within preselected specifications during the useful life of the product. Suitably accurate and precise methodologies must be available to establish and assess these performance criteria. In the present increasingly emerging era of precisely controlled drug bioavailability from dosage forms, the determination of optimal drug bioavailability–time profiles that are consistent with providing maximum therapeutic performance for the product, and the means by which such bioavailability criteria can be programmed into the design of drug delivery systems, takes on practical importance tantamount to any of the other performance criteria that are noted. Failure in areas of any of the other seven criteria renders a drug delivery system impractical to market. Failure in achieving optimally controlled rather than merely satisfactory bioavailability dynamics can be envisaged to render a product noncompetitive. This is especially the case with the multisource, generic drug market that is now rapidly developing. Therefore, from a practical, product development standpoint it will become increasingly important to categorize controlled drug delivery systems as "in-vitro programmable" and "in-vivo unpredictable" as is done below.

2. IN-VITRO PROGRAMMABLE OPEN-LOOP DRUG DELIVERY SYSTEMS

In-vitro programmable systems are those whose in-vivo bioavailability performance can be designed and predicted from entirely theoretical considerations and/or quite simple in-vitro tests. This category obviously includes constant-rate or preprogrammable variable-rate intravenous drug infusion equipment and some of the new and novel therapeutic systems such as those patented by the Alza Corporation. These are discussed in Chapters 2 and 6 of Volume 3 of this series. In all these cases the rates of drug bioavailability are either entirely independent of the biological environment to which the drug delivery system is subjected (e.g., an intravenous infusion pump) or relatively unaffected by the biological conditions that are encountered. The latter case is best exemplified by transdermal drug delivery systems in which a constant rate of drug penetration through the skin to reach the systemic circulation is predetermined by the permeability of a rate-controlling membrane interposed between the absorbing skin surface and the drug reservoir. Transdermal drug delivery systems of this and alternate designs are discussed in Chapters 2, 4, and 5 of Volume 3. Osmotic pumps for oral and parenteral drug delivery are another example where the in-vivo bioavailability can be computationally predicted a priori by use of mathematical expressions relating drug release rates to adjustable design parameters of the dosage form. The drug release rates of such products are largely unaffected by the conditions of the biological environment into which they are placed except for the osmotic pressure of the fluids by which they become surrounded. The osmotic pressure of tissue and gastrointestinal fluids for this purpose can be considered as a constant, unvarying condition affecting the osmotic pump's drug release dynamics. Although the rates of drug release for orally administered osmotic pumps may be predictable in computationally designed systems and can be confirmed in simple in-vitro drug release kinetic experiments, the extent of the drug's bioavailability could still be simply influenced by diet, position, exercise, disease conditions, and other factors that can cause inter- and intrapatient variation in gastrointestinal transit times. This would be particularly important for dosage forms designed for once or twice daily administration; of course, it is assumed for this type of system that the rate-limited process in the bioavailability of the drug is its release from the dosage form and that any differences in the intrinsic absorption or stability of the drug in different regions of the gastrointestinal tract are not a factor. Such complications aside, the essential feature of programmable, open-loop drug delivery systems is that their in-vivo drug release dynamics can be predicted with acceptable accuracy and precision from theoretical considerations and in-vitro experimentation.

3. IN-VIVO UNPREDICTABLE OPEN-LOOP DRUG DELIVERY SYSTEMS

This second category of drug delivery systems includes most conventional types of dosage form whose in-vivo drug bioavailability dynamics often result from a complex interaction of formulation and processing variables with the conditions attendant to the biological environment(s) in which they release the drug contents. The complexity of the operative biological, physical, and chemical processes affecting the drug's release behavior effectively precludes the development of accurate and reliable mathematical models to interrelate their in-vivo bioavailability dynamics to dosage form design parameters. When this is the case and there is no reliably predictive in-vitro test available, a trial–error product development approach must be implemented to develop an acceptable formulation through performing a minimum of costly in-vivo human or animal bioavailability tests to screen successive candidate formulations. This disadvantage of developing conventionally constituted controlled drug delivery systems with a predetermined desired bioavailability through what can be an inordinate amount of costly and time-consuming human testing may be entirely outweighed by the other performance criteria listed above. For example, new and novel drug delivery systems may require new and novel production facilities to be constructed and processess to be developed to manufacture them; their manufacture may be too costly or otherwise not feasible to implement on a necessary large production scale. The savings gained in the initial design and development of such systems may become entirely dissipated in the additional costs and efforts required to produce it as well as to educate and promote it to medical practitioners and patient markets unfamiliar with and unaccustomed to the use of such new systems. In addition, there are always the inevitable problems that were not foreseen because of a lack of previous experience with any such similar, newly designed, product that must be solved. In contrast, conventionally constituted dosage forms will utilize the same preexisting production and quality control facilities in most drug firms that are used for their other products of essentially similar form. The risk of product development failure, for causes other than achieving an optimally sought bioavailability behavior, is nearly negligible with conventional dosage forms relative to the uncertainties to be overcome with new and novel drug delivery systems. Another consideration is that such new and novel systems have usually been patented and a license for the patent rights may not be available or too costly to be economical. An optimal, conventionally constituted formulation for a specific drug can in most cases be patented by its inventor.

The likely need to perform extensive human bioavailability testing is the chief drawback to the development of controlled-release conventional-type drug products. This objection, however, can be minimized or eliminated by the development and use of predictive, in-vitro drug product bioavailability testing methods. Such testing methods must be very rapid and negligibly expensive as compared to human testing, while providing results that reliably substitute for the use of panels of human subjects. Of the many types of dissolution testing apparatus and methods developed over the last 3 decades, feedback controlled dissolution testing appears as the most promising for general application (1, 2, 28, 29). This technique and apparatus of in-vitro drug product bioavailability testing is further discussed below and in Chapter 5 in Volume 2 of the present series.

4. ESTABLISHMENT OF CONTROLLED DRUG BIOAVAILABILITY PERFORMANCE CRITERIA IN PRODUCT DEVELOPMENT

4.1 Definition of the Therapeutic Objective

The drug release dynamics of a dosage form determines the time course of pharmacological effects and thus the therapeutic benefit that ensues from its administration. Details of computational methods for directly determining time-optimal drug bioavailability inputs from pharmacological data—which correspond to the elicitation of a maximum therapeutic benefit for a desired duration of time—have been reported by the author (2, 30–37) and are briefly treated in subsequent chapters of this present volume. Most generally and simply, a constant zero-order rate of drug bioavailability is most commonly sought that on repeated dosing with the delivery system will maintain levels of drug at its site(s) of action that are within the drug's desired therapeutic range. These therapeutic levels are usually, but not always, reflected in plasma drug levels. The author has described methods for determining optimal drug bioavailability input profiles using pharmacological response intensities directly (1, 2, 30, 31). However, for the purposes of illustration it will here be assumed, as is often the case, that a therapeutic range of plasma level has been established as exemplified for theophylline in Figure 2. It is then generally the objective of the drug therapy to develop therapeutic plasma levels of the drug as soon as feasible after single and repeated dosing with the controlled drug delivery system and maintain drug levels in this range thereafter for the duration of the treatment; this is exemplified by the plasma-level profiles shown in Figure 3. It can occur that definitive statistical data on a patient population relating the incidence of occurrence of dose-relative toxicity and therapeutic failure to a therapeutic range of average plasma levels (as shown in Figure 2) may not be directly available for a particular drug of interest at the time it is required to develop a controlled-release dosage form. However, the therapeutic window of plasma levels can in this case be surmised as the average difference between the sawtooth pattern of peaks and nadirs in the steady-state plasma level–time profile observed after repetitive dosing with the drug in, for

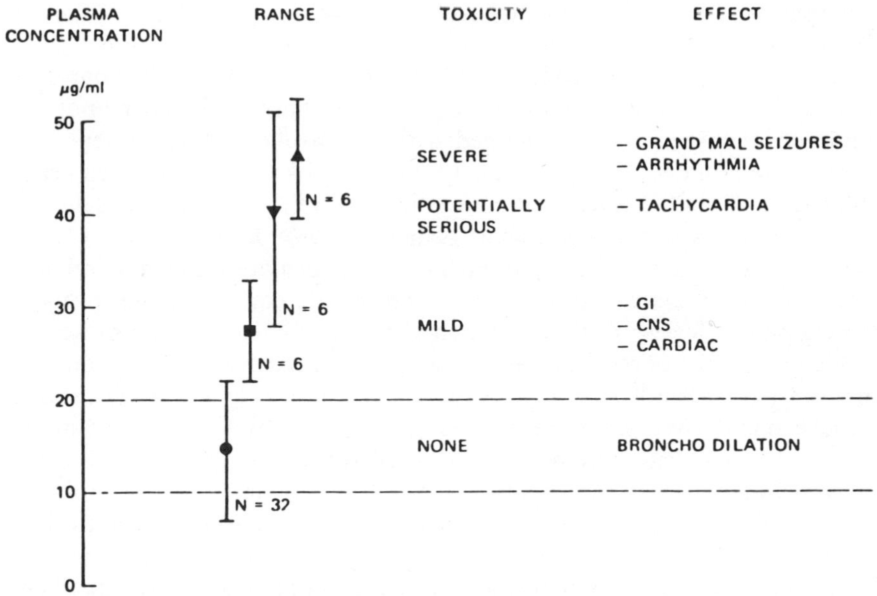

Figure 2. Plasma concentrations of theophylline related directly to the appearance of adverse reactions. Bronchodilation is the therapeutic effect of this drug.

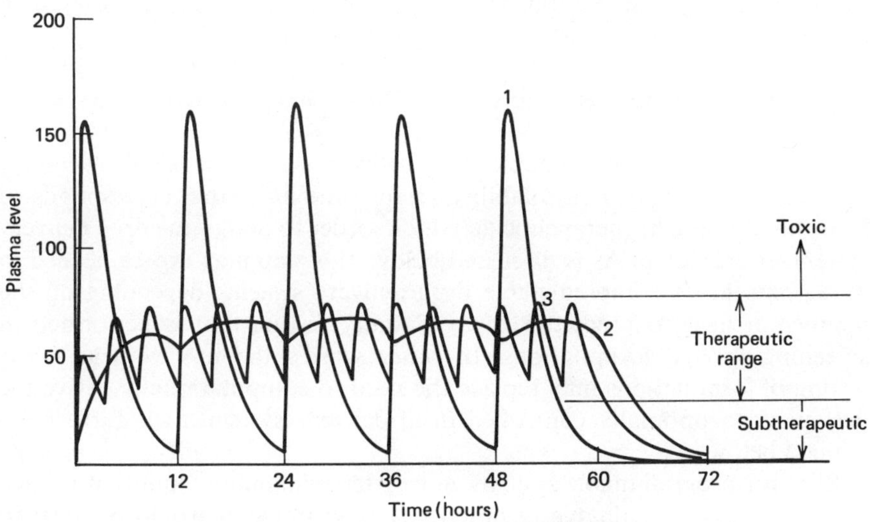

Figure 3. Predicted plasma levels of drug. Curve 1, 100-mg tablet every 12 hours; curve 2, 100-mg controlled-release system every 12 hours; curve 3, 33.3-mg oral tablet every 4 hours.

example, the form of an immediate-release oral capsule, a tablet or a liquid. The therapeutic range is defined in this manner as shown in Figure 2. With reference to Figure 2, the administration of the entire 100-mg, 12-hour dose at one time would overshoot the upper toxic limit and undershoot the minimum therapeutic level obtained with a controlled-release system. The improvement in decreasing the magnitude of the oscillations between peaks and nadirs of plasma levels that maintains the levels relatively well centered within the therapeutic range (while achieving twice daily, compared to six times daily dosing) is quite apparent. The ability of a dosage form to reliably deliver its drug content at a preprogrammed rate corresponding to maintaining plasma levels in a desired narrow therapeutic window diminishes the incidence of adverse reactions as well as what can be even more hazardous, that is, subtherapeutic activity; it also permits a targeting of delivery rates to achieve singularly desired effects among a multiplicity of pharmacological activities that a drug may be capable of eliciting that correspond to other different plasma level, therapeutic windows. The targeting of the bioavailability rate of scopolamine from a transdermal drug delivery system to elicit antinausea activity, while effectively preventing the overshoot in plasma levels that is attendant to undesirable side effects of this drug, is an excellent example of maximizing the therapeutic utility of a drug through controlling its bioavailability rates; this example is discussed in Chapters 2 and 4 of Volume 3. The Ocusert® systems for pilocarpine also discussed in Chapter 2 of Volume 3 presents another example. In addition to therapeutic advantages, the increase in patient compliance with a less frequent need for dosing with controlled (prolonged) release is also a most distinct benefit.

4.2 Drug Bioavailability Input–Output Response Relationships

Even for in-vitro programmable drug delivery systems it is still necessary to compute the drug bioavailability versus time input that corresponds to an optimally sought therapeutic activity in order to design the drug delivery system to provide it. As is discussed below, this step may not be needed in developing in-vivo unpredictable drug delivery systems depending on the manner of in-vitro predictive bioavailability testing that is performed in screening in-vivo formulations. In other words, the in-vitro trial–error testing of formulations may replace the need to computationally derive the design of an optimally controlled drug delivery system, as is further explained below.

Even for programmable systems, a drug bioavailability input that is ideal in theory is not obtainable in practice. For example, it would be ideal to achieve a plasma profile that resembles a pulse with the pulse height being in the middle of the therapeutic range and the pulse duration ideally set at, for example, 24 hours for once-a-day dosing. Although this may be ideal, real systems cannot be made to behave in this manner since the initial rate of drug input would in theory have to be infinitely rapid, abruptly change to a desired zero-order constant rate, and abruptly complete its delivery after 24 hours. Although this can be approximated by a bolus intravenous dose followed by a constant-rate infusion, the drug levels will still decline exponentially after the termination of infusion as a result of elimination of the drug from the body being slower than instantaneous. What can be practically achieved with oral dosage forms is still much further constrained by the practical considerations of their design, construction, and mode of operation. The elementary osmotic pump (3), although it is a most notable advance in drug delivery systems, still provides an example of such constraints and how they can be minimized. Although this pump is discussed in Chapters 2 and 6 of Volume 3, it is useful for the purposes of this example to briefly describe the mode of operation of elementary osmotic pumps.

5. PROGRAMMING BIOAVAILABILITY INPUTS FROM AN OSMOTIC PUMP DRUG DELIVERY SYSTEM

The elementary osmotic pump as diagrammed in Figure 4 consists of an osmotic core (which contains the drug) surrounded by a semipermeable membrane with a delivery orifice. When the system is exposed to water, water enters the core at a rate that is dependent on the osmotic pressure of the core formulation and the permeability of the membrane to water. Once inside, the core dissolves. As long as there is excess solid present, a saturated solution is formed. If the internal volume of the system remains constant, this saturated solution is released from the delivery orifice at the same rate that water enters, leading to a zero-order rate of drug delivery. The delivery

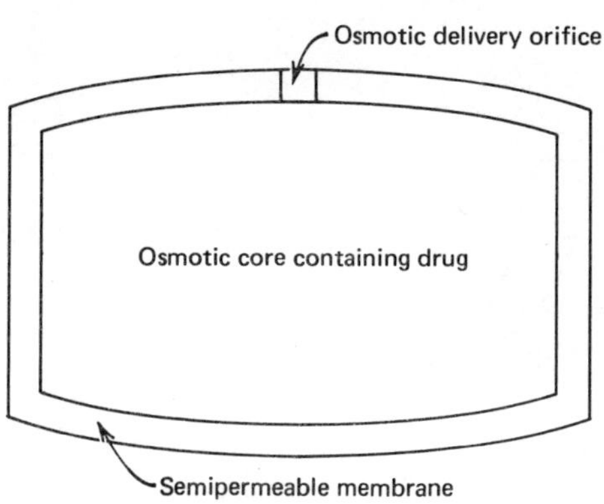

Figure 4. Elementary osmotic pump cross section.

rate declines parabolically to zero once the solution formed within the core is no longer saturated. The amount of drug delivered at this nonzero rate is the amount that just fills the core volume with a saturated solution. The larger the amount of drug needed to form a saturated solution, the smaller the percentage of total drug to be delivered by zero order. Therefore, a compound with greater solubility will have a smaller percentage of total delivered by zero order since a larger amount of drug is needed to form a saturated solution. Similarly, the greater the density of the core, the greater is the percentage delivered by zero order since more drug will fit into the core volume.

Figure 5 shows the calculated release rate–time profiles from four different elementary osmotic pump systems. The dose in all four cases is the same, as is the time over which 90% of the dose is administered. The fraction of dose administered by non-zero-order rates varies from 10 to 40% of total. The greater the percentage delivered by zero order, the longer the zero-order delivery time and the lower the zero-order rate.

The zero-order delivery rate is independent of pH of the surrounding medium since the membrane is not readily permeable to ions. The delivery rate is also independent of agitation of the medium. Therefore, in-vivo release rates can be predicted to be similar to in-vitro release rates. The most significant feature of this programmable system is, of course, that both the in-vitro and in-vivo release rates can be computationally predicted and achieved by the selection of design parameters of the dosage form such as the

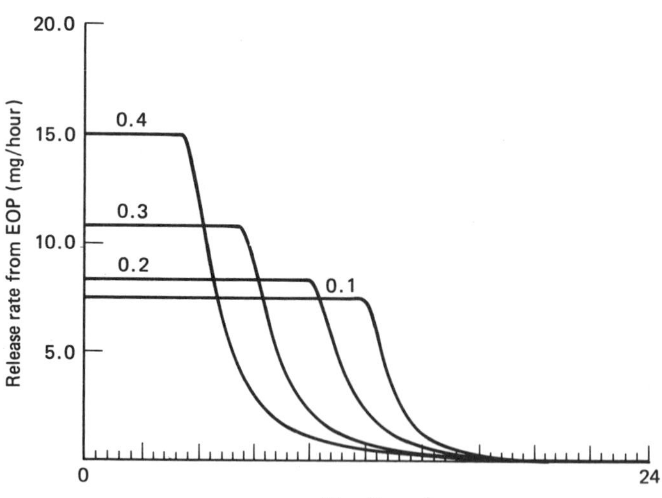

Figure 5. Calculated release rates from four elementary osmotic pump systems.

permeability of the membrane, the diameter of the osmotic delivery orifice, and the inclusion of osmotic agents in preselected quantities to affect the osmotic pumping gradient and rates. Knowing that the in-vitro and in-vivo drug release rates are the same and can be programmed by the design of the system, one can use in-vitro release information from an elementary osmotic pump to predict plasma levels and/or pharmacological response profiles in humans. First, however, the relationship between in-vivo release and plasma levels for a given drug must be known or established.

As discussed in Chapter 2 of this volume, the author has developed and demonstrated their fidelity and has reported (1, 2, 30–37) generalized, model independent methods of interrelating drug bioavailability inputs to either pharmacological or body fluid level response outputs. As these 'black-box' approaches are quite general, they are independent of the route of administration and can be applied to drug-responding systems that manifest nonlinear kinetics due to capacity limited metabolic or other dynamic processes (1, 2). For the purpose of the present example, the input–output relationship may be simply described, as diagrammed in Figure 6, in terms of a transfer function in the complex frequency domain (34) or weighting function in the time domain (35). For the purpose of this example, the weighting function could be experimentally determined as the observed dose-normalized plasma level–time profile resulting from an instantaneous (impulse) input of drug into the gastrointestinal tract from which the drug becomes subsequently absorbed, distributed, and eliminated from the systemic blood. In practice, an impulse input, for which the input function, $A(\omega)$ is equal to one, may be approximated by the oral administration of a solution dose of the drug. It must be assumed, however, that the absorption properties of drug everywhere along the gastrointestinal tract from which the drug will be absorbed from the controlled-release dosage form, are the same as the region of the gastrointestinal tract (mostly the stomach) from which the solution dose becomes absorbed. The validity of this assumption will, of course, vary with specific

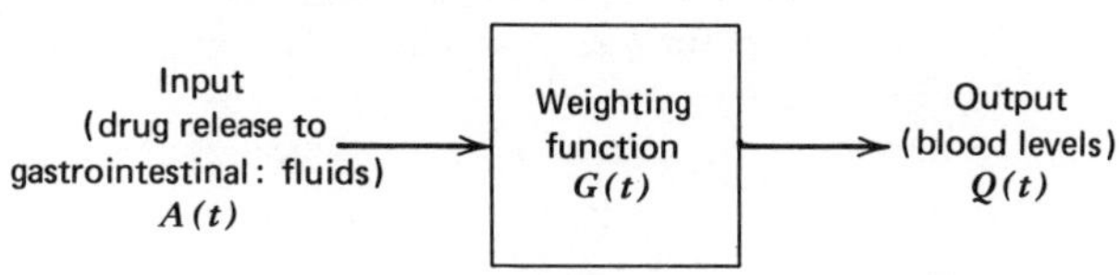

$$\frac{Q(\omega)}{\dot{A}(\omega)} = G(\omega)$$

$G(\omega)$= transfer function

Figure 6. Weighting function and transfer function between plasma level and in-vivo drug release.

drugs and depends on the bioavailability being at all times rate limited by the drug's release from the dosage form.

Drug input–output response computations can be performed numerically by the operations of convolution and deconvolution (33) as described in Chapters 2 and 3 of this volume and Chapter 4 of Volume 2; a program written in BASIC for this purpose, which runs on an Apple II+ computer, is available from the PharmaControl Corporation in Englewood Cliffs, New Jersey. Since the computations can be done numerically, it is unnecessary to perform any curve fitting of the experimentally observed, plasma-level data. However, fitting a multiexponential expression to the observed data would in the simplest case of first-order absorption and elimination result in an expression given by equation 1, where parameter A is related to a hypothetical volume of distribution and the fraction of dose absorbed; $t_{1/2,e}$ and $t_{1/2,a}$ are the elimination and absorption half-lives, respectively.

$$C_p = A\left[\exp\left(\frac{0.693t}{-t_{1/2,e}}\right) + \exp\left(\frac{0.693t}{-t_{1/2,e}}\right)\right] \tag{1}$$

With the use of this simplest of methods, the weighting functions corresponding to hypothetical drugs with the half-lives shown in Table 1 are graphically presented in Figure 7. They would experimentally result from the administration of unit oral doses of drug solution. Figure 8 shows the results of predicting single-dose plasma levels for drug A. Curve 1 is the weighting function $G(t)$, and curve 2 is the calculated in-vitro release rate from an elementary osmotic pump designed to have 20% of a 100-mg dose being delivered by non-zero-order rate y and 90% of the dose being administered in 14 hours. These two functions, when convolved, yield curve 3—the predicted plasma level profile for a 100-mg elementary osmotic pump dose of drug A. Predicted multiple-dose plasma-level profiles can be obtained by the numerical superposition (35, 36) of single-dose response profiles.

Table 1. Absorption and Elimination Parameters for Four Hypothetical Drugs

Drug	$t_{1/2,a}$ (hours)	$t_{1/2,e}$ (hours)
A	0.5	2.0
B	0.5	6.0
C	1.0	0.5
D	1.0	8.0
E	0.3	1.45

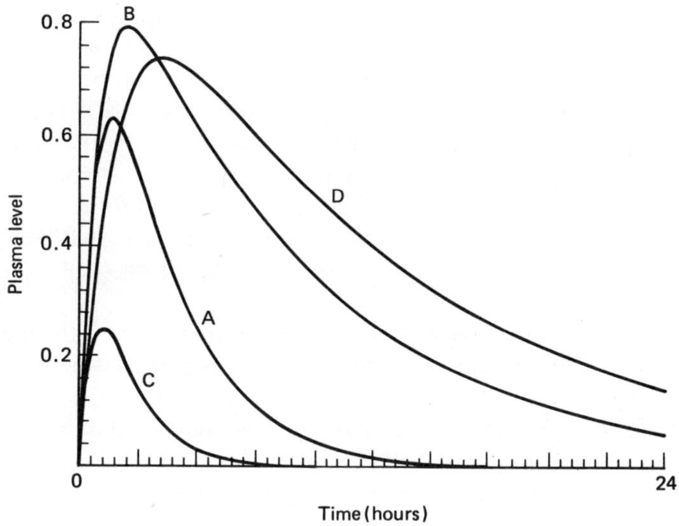

Figure 7. Weighting functions for four hypothetical drugs.

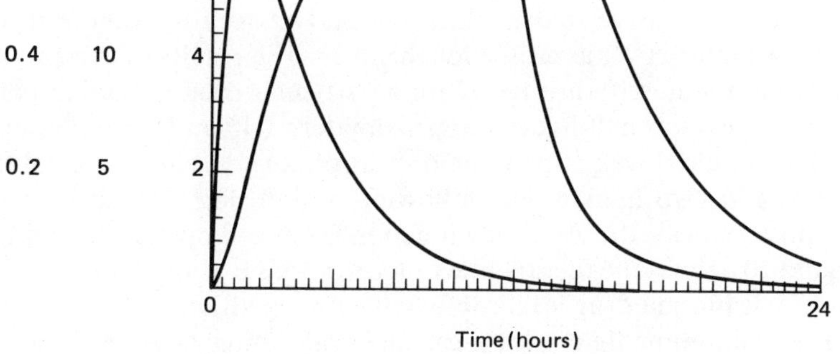

Figure 8. Predicted plasma levels for drug A when administered by an elementary osmotic pump. Curve 1, weighting function $G(t)$; curve 2, in-vitro release rate from an elementary osmotic pump $\dot{A}(t)$ ($y=0.2$, $t_{90}=14$ hours, dose $=100$ mg); curve 3, predicted plasma level $Q(t)$.

Figure 3, already discussed above, shows the multiple-dose plasma-level profiles as curve 1 for 100-mg oral solution doses and as curve 2 for 100-mg elementary osmotic pump doses for drug A. It can again be noted how the large peaks and valleys seen with solution dosing are greatly reduced when the same drug is administered at the same dose and at the same dosing interval by an elementary osmotic pump drug delivery system. If the dosage regimen for the solution is changed to 33.3 mg every 4 hours, the peaks and valleys are reduced but are still more prominent than with elementary osmotic pump dosing. Similar results can be seen for drugs B, C, and D in Figure 9.

If a desired optimum plasma profile of a drug is known, the elementary osmotic pump release rate necessary to yield plasma levels in a desired therapeutic window can be calculated. Referring back to the mathematical definition of a transfer function in Figure 6, it can be seen that by rearranging the equation, the drug input ($\dot{A}(t)$) can be calculated by dividing the plasma level $Q(\omega)$ by the transfer function $G(\omega)$ and converting back to the time domain. These operations in practice can be performed numerically either in the time t or frequency (ω) domain (33, 34).

In programming a drug delivery system, the formulator must be cognizant of the characteristics and limitations on the release dynamics of the system imposed by its design and the mechanism(s) of its operation. Since the in-vivo release dynamics can be mathematically expressed and are predicted in the present example of the osmotic pump, an optimal design of the system to achieve the most satisfactory plasma-level profile could be obtained as a mathematical solution to a constrained optimization problem, using, for example, the Lagrangian method (38) or simply even a statistical, least-squares, curve-fitting program such as SPSS-21 (39). As an example, this program was implemented to provide a set of drug delivery system design parameters that represent a drug release rate–time profile that corresponds to a plasma-level curve that in turn is a best fit to a hypothetical ideally desired plasma level–time profile for the drug. The results of this procedure are shown in Figures 10 through 12 for a particular drug E that has elimination and absorption half-lives of approximately 1.45 and 0.3 hours, respectively. The required weighting function was obtained as an empirical fit (34) to observed in-vivo human data following oral dosing with an immediate-release dosage form; the weighting function is defined by the curve in Figure 13. Figure 10 defines the therapeutic range for drug E as the range of effective and nontoxic plasma drug levels obtained with repetitive, every-4-hour (q4h) dosing with an immediate-release capsule oral dosage form. Also shown in Figure 10 is what can be described as an ideally sought but realistic estimate of a plasma-level curve that would be desirable to achieve by a once-a-day dosing with an osmotic pump delivery system for this drug. Deconvolving (34)

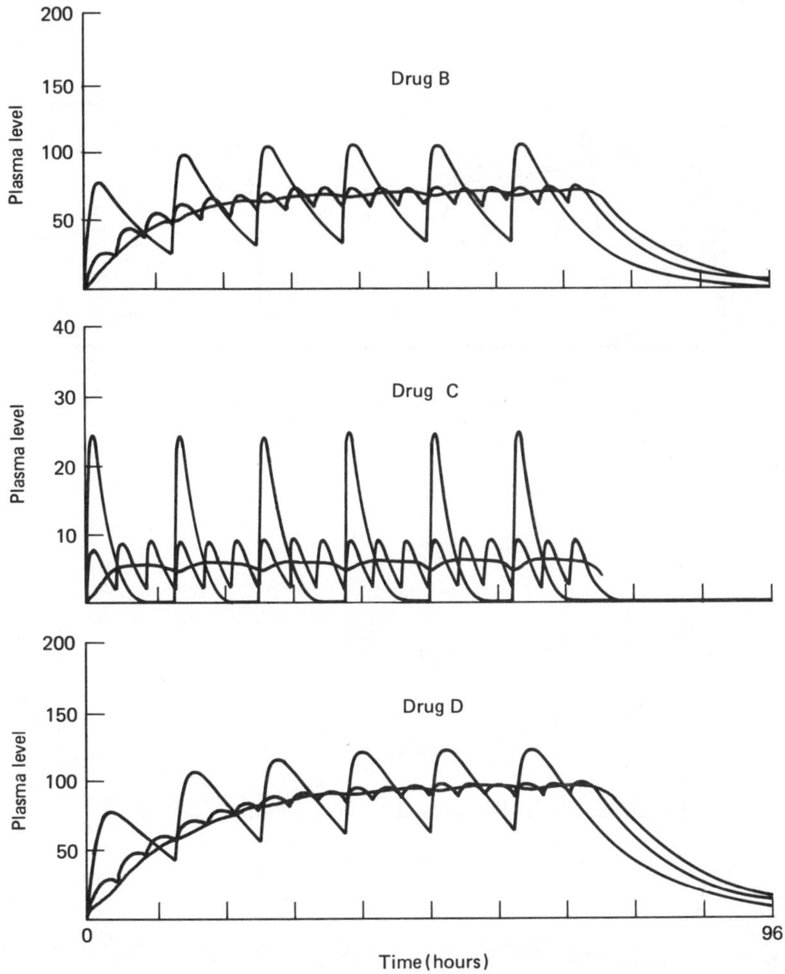

Figure 9. Plasma levels for drugs B, C, and D resulting from 100-mg elementary osmotic pump dosing every 12 hours, 100-mg oral solution dosing every 12 hours, and 33.3 mg oral solution dosing every 4 hours.

the weighting function with the idealized plasma-level curve produces the input rate–time profile plotted in Figure 11 that corresponds to the plasma level curve. Also shown in Figure 11 is a best-fit input rate profile that can readily be obtained from the programming of an osmotic pump delivery system. Such a best-fit input-rate profile can be computed from the use of a computer program such as the SPSS-21 mentioned above, to vary the parameters of the osmotic pump's design to obtain a best fit to the ideally

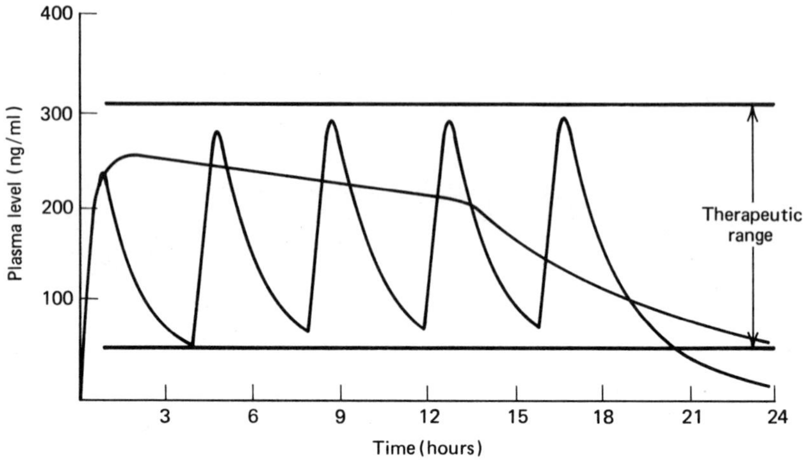

Figure 10. Ideally sought plasma level compared with 37.5-mg capsule dosing every 4 hours.

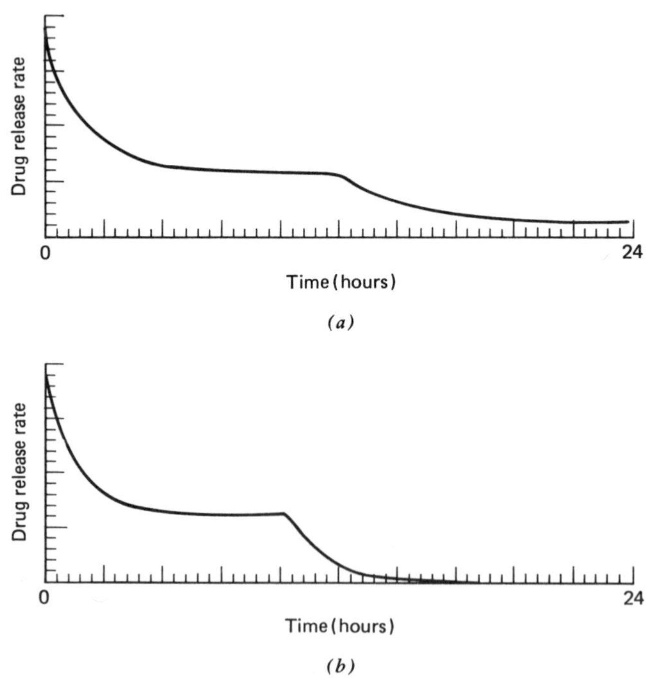

Figure 11. In-vitro release rates from an elementary osmotic pump: (*a*) ideal drug release rate; (*b*) easily attainable drug release rate.

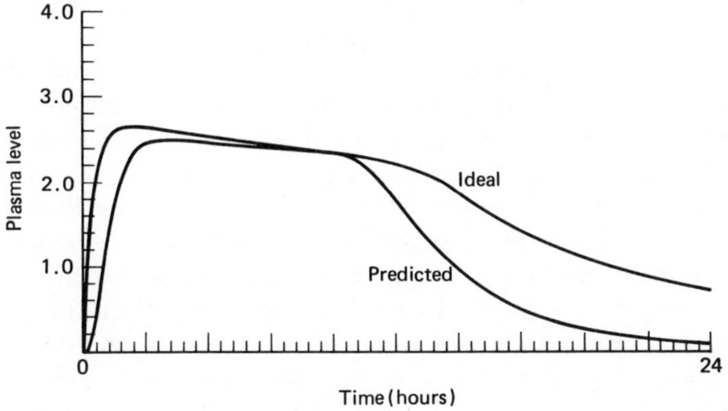

Figure 12. Ideal versus predicted plasma levels from a once-a-day dosing, elementary osmotic pump drug delivery system.

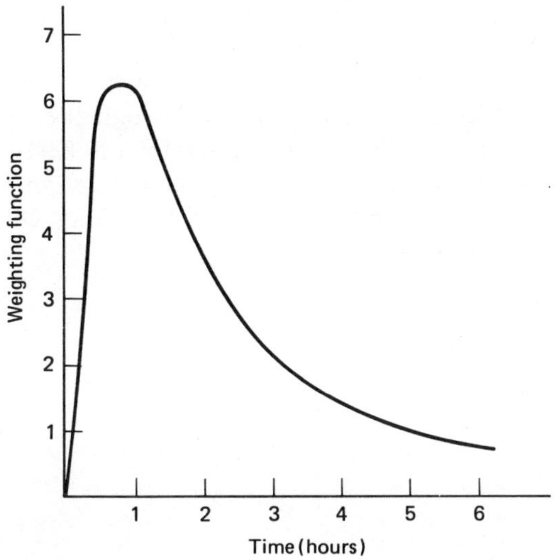

Figure 13. Weighting function for drug E.

desired system. As described in Chapters 2 and 4 of Volume 3, the osmotic pump can be constructed to correspond to obtaining in-vivo drug-release parameters such as the duration of time over which the drug is delivered at a zero-order rate, the zero-order delivery rate, and the fraction of the dose that is delivered at a zero- or non-zero-order rate.

In addition to the drug that is released from the interior of the osmotic pump, parameters for the release of drug that is coated or compressed on or around the surface of the osmotic pump tablet can be defined. For example, a first-order rate constant for this immediately available drug as well as the fraction of the total dose of the drug that constitutes this priming dose placed on the surface of the osmotic pump can be chosen as design parameters. Therefore, five independent parameters can be readily adjusted and optimized to affect the shape of the drug release input-rate profile obtainable from the osmotic pump delivery system under consideration. The lower curve in Figure 11 presents an input-rate profile that can be easily attained from the osmotic pump by adjusting its drug release parameters and thereby resembles the ideally sought input profile. Figure 12 compares the ideally but reasonably sought plasma-level profile (which remains within the therapeutic range for 24 hours after a single dose of drug E) with the plasma level profile that can be predicted to be attained from an osmotic pump with its drug release parameters selected to approach the ideal. It can be seen that the predicted, attainable profile does not provide the required plasma levels of drug over the entire 24-hour period as sought. However, the profile that can be readily attained from the optimized osmotic pump can be judged to be remarkably good for a drug with as short an elimination half-life as 1.5 hours. It can be seen that although once-a-day dosing is not feasible, twice-daily dosing is quite a practical objective to be achieved through the use of an osmotic pump to deliver this drug. Figure 14 illustrates the best results that were found by using the SPSS-21 computer to adjust the design parameters of the osmotic pump with and without the use of a priming dose to provide an initial rapid release of the drug.

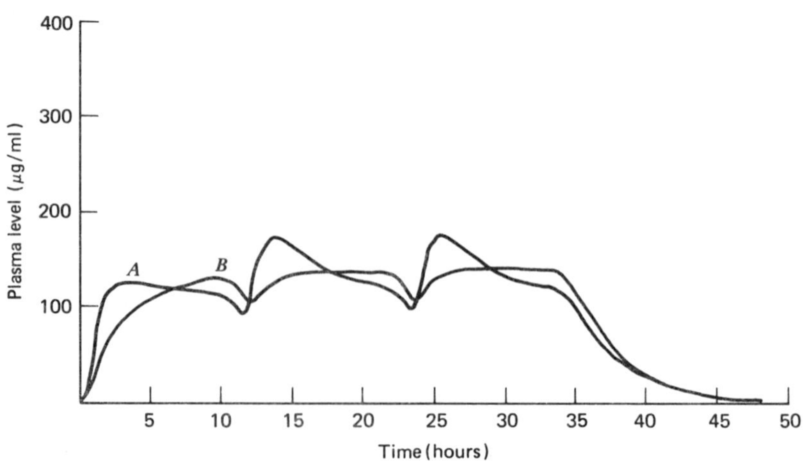

Figure 14. Comparison of plasma levels resulting from equal elementary osmotic pump doses with (curve *A*) and without (curve *B*) a priming dose.

6. IN-VIVO UNPREDICTABLE, OPTIMAL DRUG DELIVERY SYSTEM DEVELOPMENT

In contrast to programmable drug delivery systems such as osmotic pumps, it is indeed rare that the in-vivo bioavailability of more conventional-type dosage forms can be predicted from mathematical manipulation such as described above. Fixed permeability of membranes and mechanical control by, for example, the osmotic expansion of hypertonic salt solutions as in osmotic pumps most commonly provide the mechanisms of programmable controlled drug delivery. Membrane control in one form or another has been most successful in achieving zero-order drug release from both programmable and "unpredictable" categories of dosage forms. In more conventional oral-dosage-form types, however, the permeability of the membranes around, for example, beads that have a drug-containing core surrounded by cellulosic or fatty membrane coatings is not a priori known, constant, or predictable. In addition, the drug can also be released simultaneously in the same formulation by dissolution, erosion, and diffusion from a matrix that is undergoing erosion and/or swelling. Although the drug release kinetics can be mathematically described (as in Chapter 7 of this volume) for relatively simple systems under controlled conditions, the complexity of factors involved and their interaction with the biological environment render it quite difficult and impractical to a priori computationally predict in-vivo drug release profiles that will result from the composition and mode of processing of a particular formulation. However, once a desired in-vivo release profile is obtained from such a conventionally constructed delivery system, its reliability can be as good as any programmable type of system, in addition to possessing the other advantages of manufacturability, quality control, acceptance, and other factors discussed above. The relative inability to predict the in-vivo bioavailability of conventionally constituted systems is a disadvantage only in the time and expense that may be necessary to develop such systems through trial–error human bioavailability testing. This drawback can be overcome through the development of in-vitro laboratory test methods that are predictive of in-vivo bioavailability.

6.1 Predictive In-Vitro Drug Product Bioavailability Testing

For drugs to become bioavailable through gaining access to their sites of absorption, they must first be in a solution state. Therefore, from all the various physical and chemical tests that can be performed in-vitro on a drug product formulation, dissolution testing is the most closely related to drug bioavailability. Over the last nearly 3 decades there have been more than 100 different dissolution testing apparatuses and methods proposed, with each claiming some advantage of one over the rest. The majority of such apparatuses are now museum pieces, and the apparatuses and methodologies that have survived and are presently official in the *United States Pharmacopeia* still have the problem of biorelevence associated with them. In general, it is entirely impractical to perform the extensive and expensive human testing of drug products that is needed to (1) optimize the bioavailability dynamics of formulations of new drugs to develop products having a maximum therapeutic utility and attain a desired duration of action, (2) assure the bioequivalency of generic drug products or develop improved formulations for old drugs, (3) assure bioequivalency through lot-to-lot reproducibility testing—bioirrelevent dissolution tests can cause economic losses through the rejection of drug product lots whose in-vitro results are overly sensitive although the in-vivo performance is in fact satisfactory, and (4) assure satisfactory bioavailability of drug products through to their expiry dates. The use of in-vivo irrelevant tests can indicate that reductions in bioavailability have occurred through apparent physical instability, whereas in fact such changes may be entirely irrelevant to biological performance; needless product recalls and early expiry dating can be the results. What is required in every case is an in-vivo relevant, in-vitro test that can be rapidly and easily performed to produce results that are optimally predictive of a drug product's performance in vivo. A computerized feedback-controlled, drug product dissolution testing apparatus has been described (1, 2, 39–44) that is initially programmed with a minimum amount of in-vivo drug-response data (e.g., blood level, urinary recovery rate, or pharmacological response–time profiles) obtained from a panel of human subjects for a reference dosage form(s). The apparatus subsequently functions to generate dissolution rate profiles for drug products undergoing the test that are predictive of the average response–time curves that would be obtained from the same panel of human subjects from which the in-vivo data used to program the apparatus were originally obtained. The apparatus operates in a feedback, closed-loop automatic control mode that continuously, over time, simultaneously adjusts up to four dissolution test process variables: (1) dissolution media composition; (2) total flow rate through the dissolution cell chamber; (3) recycle flow of the media back into the chamber to vary sink conditions around the dissolving solids; and (4) stirring rates. The process variables are automatically controlled by the computer in such a manner as to generate a dissolution rate–time profile that reproduces the in-vivo response–time profile, which has been properly time and amplitude scaled, for the reference dosage form. The signals controlling the process variables developed during this simulative, closed-loop, mode of operation with the reference dosage form are continuously tapped off to other dissolution cells operating simultaneously as they are generated. In this way,

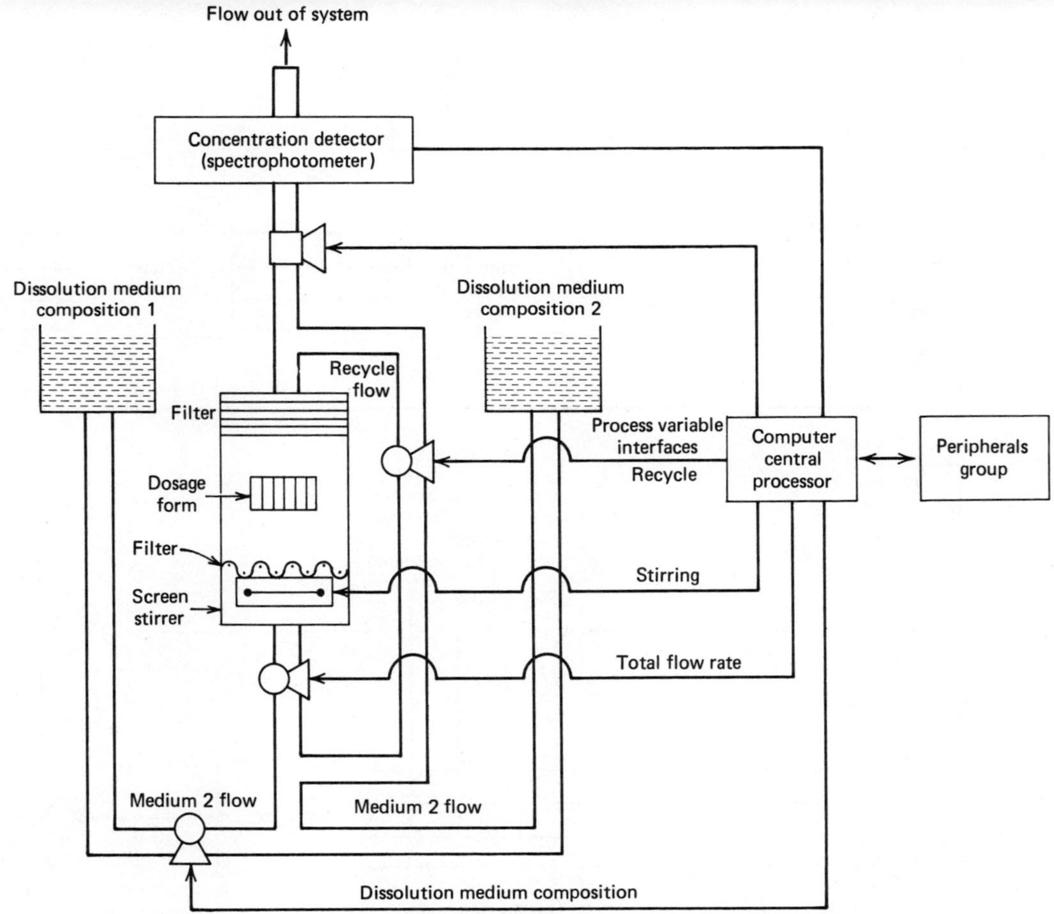

Figure 15. Schematic diagram of the biopredictor dissolution–permeation testing system.

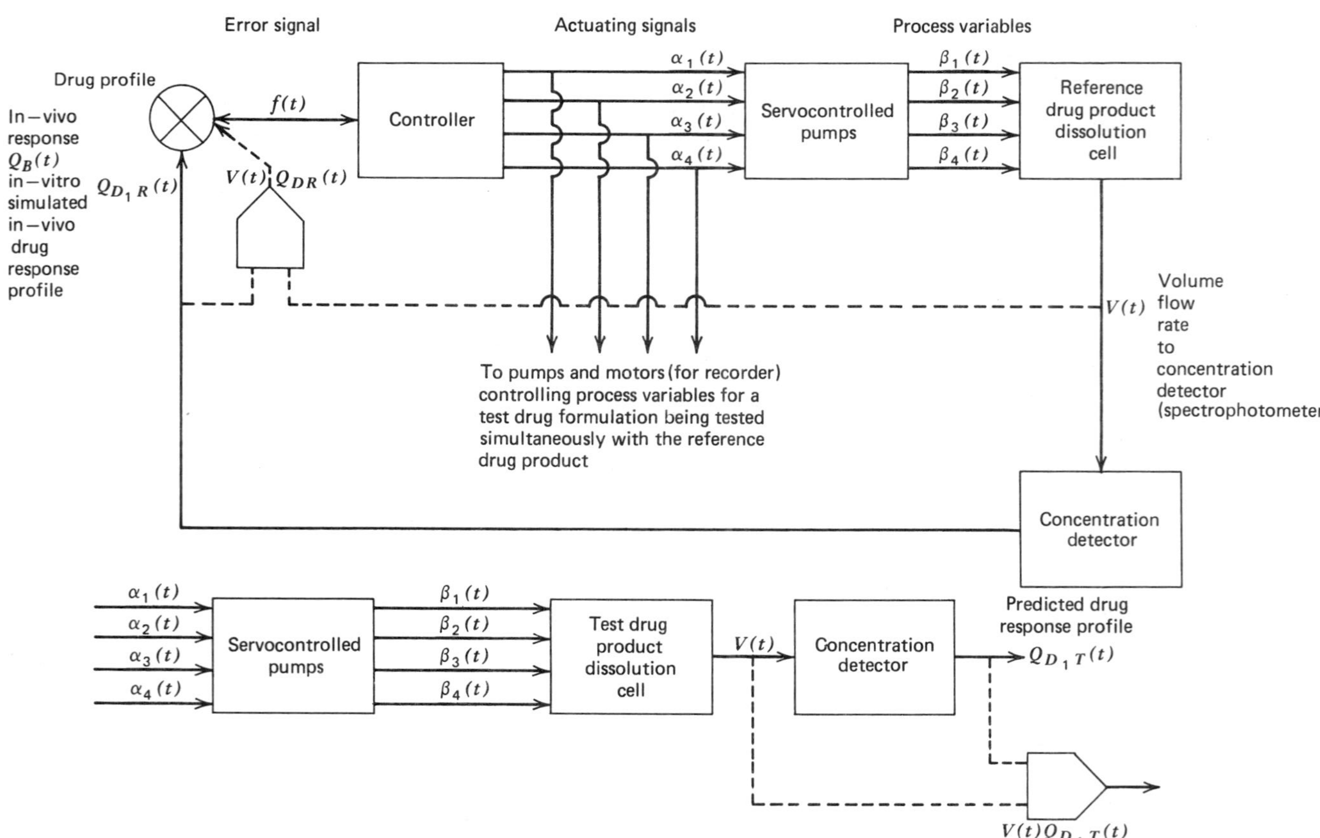

Figure 16. Block diagram describing the closed-loop and open-loop operation of the biopredictor dissolution–permeation testing system.

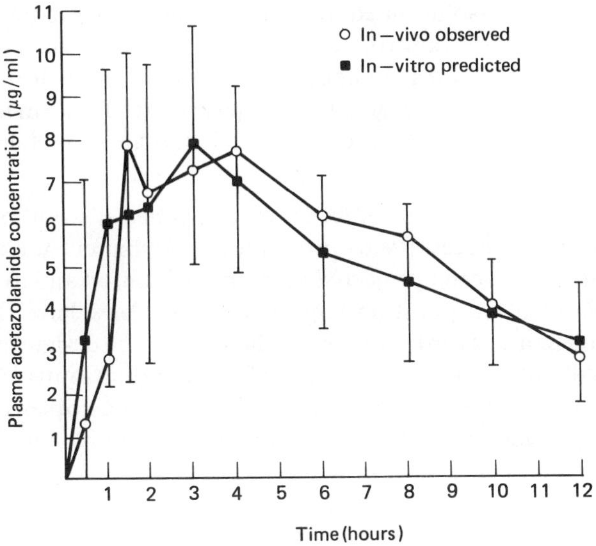

Figure 17. Comparison of in-vivo observed average plasma levels of acetazolamide tablet B with the in-vitro predicted plasma-level curve obtained by the feedback-controlled apparatus using a proportional controller and continuous control of recycle flow. The in-vivo values are plotted with their standard deviations indicated. Reprinted with permission from V. F. Smolen, L. Ball, and M. Scheffler. Predicting the time course of in vivo bioavailability from in vitro dissolution tests: Control systems engineering approaches. *Pharm. Technol.* **3**: 88–102 (1979).

identical process variable conditions are provided to up to 48 other dosage forms undergoing simultaneous testing in an open-loop, predictive mode of operation. The dissolution rate–time profiles developed for these test dosage forms are predictive of their in-vivo response–time profiles. The use of computer, feedback control in this approach to dissolution testing solves three of the most important problems concerning the dissolution testing of drug products:

1. The setting of dissolution standards. With the use of feedback control, in-vivo relevant dissolution standards are nonarbitrarily established and defined by the in-vivo response–time profile for the reference dosage form.
2. The selection of process variable conditions for dissolution tests. The process variables are automatically generated by feedback control during the course of each run.

3. Calibration of dissolution equipment and the reproducibility of results. Through feedback control, the apparatus calibrates itself for each experimental run and is unaffected by changes in environmental conditions or laboratory personnel. The reference dosage form functions in a manner analogous to the use of internal standards in chemical assays.

The instrumentation to perform feedback controlled dissolution testing, as well as the software necessary to program the equipment for each specific drug application, has been projected to be manufactured and available from the PharmaControl Corporation Englewood Cliffs, New Jersey by mid-1983 under the tradename of BioPredictor ®. Diagrams of the design and operation of the BioPredictor taken with permission from PharmaControl Corporation Product literature are shown as Figures 15 and 16. Examples of the ability of a relatively crude apparatus, and computer programs, for prediction of in-vivo blood level curves are shown in Figures 17–19.

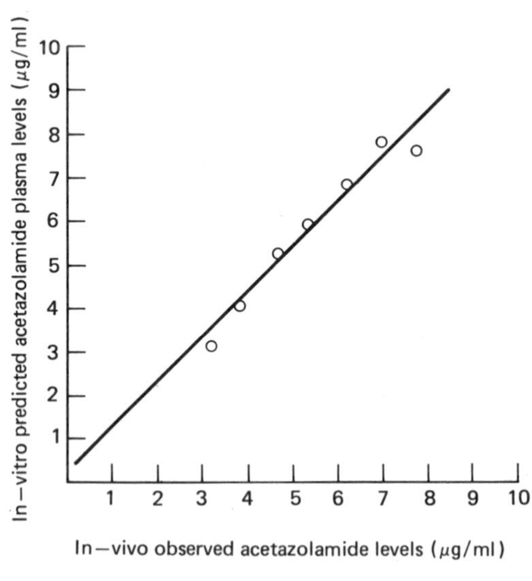

Figure 18. Linear least-squares comparison of acetazolamide plasma concentrations for tablet B observed in-vivo with values predicted at corresponding times from the results of a feedback-controlled apparatus using a proportional controller and varying recycle flow. The least-squares regression line is given by $Y = 1.01X + 0.28$. The linear regression coefficient is 0.97. Reprinted with permission from V. F. Smolen, L. Ball, and M. Scheffler. Predicting the time course of in-vivo bioavailability from in-vitro dissolution tests: Control systems engineering approaches. *Pharm. Technol.* **3**: 88–102 (1979).

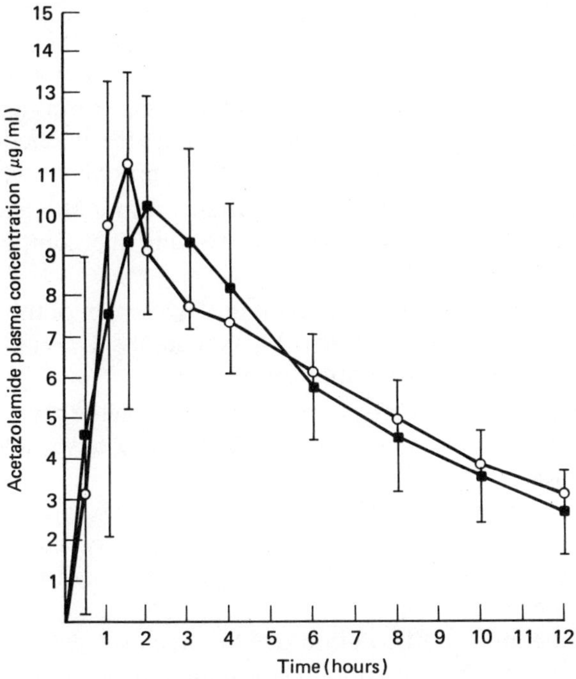

Figure 19. Comparison of in-vivo observed with in-vitro predicted plasma-level curve for acetazolamide tablet D obtained by the flow-through apparatus with continuous control of the dissolution medium pH. A proportional integral controller was used to operate the apparatus in the feedback-controlled mode with reference tablet C. The in-vivo data points are plotted with their standard deviations indicated by bars. The linear correlation coefficient between the observed and predicted values is 0.96. Reprinted with permission from V. F. Smolen, L. Ball, and M. Scheffler. Predicting the time course of in-vivo bioavailability from in-vitro dissolution tests: Control systems engineering approaches. *Pharm. Technol.* **3**: 88–102 (1979).

6.2 Steps in Expeditious Development of Optimal, In-Vivo Unpredictable Drug Bioavailability Systems

Step 1. From the pharmacokinetic–pharmacodynamic properties of the drug, establish what a practical form of a drug response (pharmacological responses or body fluid levels)–time (bioavailability) profile should optimally be to achieve a maximum therapeutic benefit for a desired duration of effects (i.e., 12, 24, or 72 hours).

Step 2. Collect in-vivo bioavailability data (e.g., plasma-level curves obtained on drug product formulations that are as similar to the product to be developed) as may be available. These data, and the dosage form(s) to which they correspond, are used to program computer-controlled, dissolution testing instrumentation to, in effect, function as a substitute for a panel of human subjects in predicting in-vivo drug response–time profiles of experimental formulations. Depending on the dosage forms and the quality of the data used to accomplish the programming, the predictions obtained at this stage may not be the best, but only first approximations.

Step 3. Prepare laboratory batches of product formulations with differing drug release dynamics by systematically varying the composition of the formulations.

Step 4. Apply the dissolution test as an in-vitro screen of the formulations in Step 3 for their predicted in-vivo bioavailability. Develop a first "best shot" controlled-release formulation on this basis.

Step 5. Perform an actual in-vivo bioavailability on the "best shot" dosage form in Step 4 and a second formulation made to have different in-vivo release dynamics.

Step 6. If the "best shot" formulation is found not to be optimal, reprogram the dissolution test apparatus by using the results of the bioavailability study and validate its in-vivo predictive capability using the second dosage form.

Step 7. Use the in-vitro dissolution test to screen successive dosage forms selected in accordance with an optimal experimental design to vary formulation variables and most rapidly, iteratively, converge to developing the optimal drug product. The optimal experimental design, whereby each successive experiment is guided by the results of preceding experiments, minimizes the number of formulations that must be prepared and tested to obtain the optimal product.

Step 8. Perform an in-vivo human bioavailability study to validate the in-vivo response profile produced by the in-vitro testing of the optimal drug product.

Step 9. Utilize the in-vitro test to validate the in-vivo bioavailability performance of the "scaled-up for production" product and other dosage strengths of the optimal formulation.

Step 10. File a new drug application for the product and obtain premarket approval. The validated, biorelevant in-vitro test method can henceforth be utilized for quality control of the manufacture of the product.

The resulting controlled-release drug product could probably be produced and sold very competitively since the drug delivery system is not just adequate, but optimal in providing therapeutic benefits for the drug. If a procedure such as that outlined above is followed, the development of an in-vivo unpredictable controlled-release drug product could be accelerated in time and minimized in expense through the use of dissolution testing to eliminate the need for what could otherwise be a large and impractical number of human bioavailability studies on experimental formulations. Therefore, advances in in-vitro drug dissolution testing can hold the key to the practical development of conventional in-vivo unpredictable, drug delivery systems that can be quite competitive with in-vitro programmable systems in providing optimal therapeutic benefits.

7. CONTROLLED DRUG BIOAVAILABILITY SYSTEMS OF THE FUTURE

It is certainly an exciting time to speculate on the prospects for controlled drug delivery systems of the future. Considering the rapid advances that are occurring in electronics miniaturization and computer sciences, it has become entirely feasible to apply the same engineering principles of control theory, signals and systems analysis, and optimization that permitted directing spacecraft to the moon, Mars, and even beyond our solar system to the development of revolutionary new drug bioavailability systems. Obviously, SAFCADs will continue to benefit from the further transfer of technologies from the electronics, computer, and aerospace industries. It can be readily envisaged that with presently available technology, small implantable SAFCAD systems are entirely feasible. It can be further projected that SAFCAD technology can be sufficiently miniaturized and incorporated into transdermal drug delivery systems designed as small bandagelike adhesive patches attached to the skin surface at convenient locations on the body. Considering that sensors for physiological signals can be wired throughout the body somewhat in the manner of the leads to cardiac pacemakers, it is quite conceivable that the physiological monitoring needed to precisely feedback control the administration of drugs can be directed to a microcontroller constituted by a computer chip incorporated in the transdermal patch. Physiological signals most often required to control the rates of drug administration (electrocardiographic, echocardiographic, plethysmographic, electroencephalographic, electromyographic, etc.) can be obtained noninvasively from the relatively simple placement of skin surface electrodes and transducers. The precision of computer, feedback-controlled drug administration can be achieved by iontophoretically driving drugs through intact skin for drugs that are ionizable into charged chemical species by either their inherent or modified (prodrug) chemical structure; uncharged drugs could be administered through the skin under pressure through what could be called a *microsyringe pad* placed onto the skin. Such pads have been mentioned in several patents and could generally be described as an array of microneedles sufficient in length to penetrate the barrier layers of the skin. Small quantities of drug would enter through the microneedles at depths beneath the stratum corneum or epidermis to enter subcutaneously through each needle-like projection in the microsyringe pad but noninjuriously spread over a relatively large area. The rate of drug delivery can simply be controlled by varying the area of active microneedles beneath a drug reservoir maintained at a relatively constant pressure by, for example, an elastomeric polymer.

In addition to the engineering sciences, the advances being rapidly made in immunology and the "new biology" most certainly hold exciting prospects for the development of controlled drug delivery systems that may become practical for marketing within the present century. The discovery and identification of cell-membrane-bound antigens and the large-scale ability to produce antibodies to such antigens by hybridoma or recombinant DNA methods suggests the practical capability of directing drugs transiently coupled to the antibodies to specific target cell sites in the body. The "drugs" could be comprised by cytotoxic antitumor agents, enzymes, hormonal-regulatory peptides, or polynucleotides carrying genetic codes for the transformation of specific cell types. By this means it becomes possible to create the "magic bullet" to affect specific beneficial changes in diseased, as well as normal, tissues of the body. The coupling between drug and antibody may be accomplished through chemical bonding between them or the attachment of the antibodies to the surface of microcapsules that release their drug contents at their antibody-directed, cell-specific, target sites. Related to the rapidly emerging microencapsulation technologies is cell replacement therapy; in this case the drug, which is an endogenously produced hormone such as insulin, is generated by cells (e.g., pancreatic beta cells) that are encapsulated within a membrane that protects them from immunologic destruction when implanted in the body. Although the large protein antibodies and white cells cannot penetrate the protective membrane to destroy the foreign cells, the membrane permits the entrance of smaller-sized molecules, such as glucose, and the release of regulatory hormone(s) produced by the cells as they naturally operate as a biological feedback control system similar to electromechanical SAFCADs; in this case, however, the cells synthesize, in addition to metering out, the drug in response to the patient's needs.

The far-reaching prospects of what drug delivery systems could ultimately become as a consequence of a salutary merging of advanced engineering and new biology technologies is highly intriguing but for the present almost too incredible to speculate. For the more immediate future it can be expected that transdermal drug delivery devices will certainly expand to be successfully marketed for additional drugs, besides nitroglycerin and scopolamine, and especially for drugs that have a narrow therapeutic range, undergo extensive first-pass metabolic degradation when given orally and are effective in relatively low parenteral doses. Osmotic pump oral drug delivery systems will likely be marketed for once-a-day dosing of an increasing number of drugs whose development is presently under way. Progress is being made to meet the need for controlled release of parenterally administered drugs that are often quite toxic, and/or unabsorbable when administered by other than injection into a depot from which they must subsequently become released at preprogrammed rates. Chapters in Volume 3 of this series discuss various approaches to accomplish such drug release programming for prolonged periods of time. What is required is a biologically inactive, polymeric, biocompatible system that can be generally applied to different drugs and through bioerosion, permeation through rate controlling membranes, osmotic pumping, or biodegradation of covalent drug–polymer linkages, release the drug in a predetermined dynamic manner. Although no single, generally applicable, controlled-release parenteral drug delivery system has yet proved to have the required characteristics in broad practice, the use of entirely biodegradable, nontoxic, polymer systems composed of endogenously occurring monomers such as lactic acid holds considerable promise.

REFERENCES

1. V. F. Smolen. Bioavailability and pharmacokinetic analysis of drug responding systems. *Ann. Rev. Pharmacol. Toxicol.* **18**: 495–522 (1978).
2. V. F. Smolen. Practical pharmacodynamic engineering in the Design, Development, and Evaluation of Optimal Drug Products. In H. S. Bean, A. H. Backett, and J. E. Canless (eds.), *Advances In Pharmaceutical Sciences*, Vol. 5, Academic Press, London, 1981, pp. 115–198.
3. F. Theeuwees. Elementary osmotic pump. *J. Pharm. Sci.* **64**: 1987–1991 (1975).
4. A. Zaffaroni. Therapeutic implications of controlled drug delivery. *Clin. Pharmacol.* **5**: 53–61 (1975).
5. S. Yolles, J. Eldridge, R. Leafe, J. A. R. Woodland, and F. Meyer. Long-Acting Delivery Systems for Narcotic Antagonists. In A. C. Tanguary and R. E. Lacey (eds.), *Controlled Release of Biologically Active Agents*, Plenum Press, New York, 1974.
6. R. Langer and J. Falkman. The use of polymers for the sustained release of proteins and other macromolecules. *Polymer Preprints* **18**: 379–384 (1977).
7. V. F. Smolen, R. G. Barile, and D. J. Carr. Design and operation of a system for automatic feedback-controlled administration of drugs. *J. Med. Device Diagn. Ind.* **1**: 50–69 (1979).
8. A. J. Koivo, V. F. Smolen, and R. G. Barile. An automated drug administration system to control blood pressure in rabbits. *Math. Biosci.* **38**: 46–56 (1978).
9. V. F. Smolen, R. G. Barile, T. A. Friermood, W. D. Stoltman, and W. A. Weigand. Automated biofeedback-controlled administration of a hypotensive drug. *Acad. Pharm. Sci.*, August 8, 1974 (abstract).

10. V. F. Smolen, R. G. Barile, and D. J. Carr. Automatic feedback control of blood pressure in rabbits and dogs. *Acad. Pharm. Sci.*, May 18, 1978 (abstract).

11. R. J. Cosgrove and V. F. Smolen. Systems for the Automatic Feedback-Controlled Administration of Drugs: Analog and Digital Optimal-Adaptive Control of Thiopental Anesthesia. In J. Martin (ed.), *Innovations in Biomedicine: Proceedings Of The San Diego Biomedical Symposium*, Western Periodicals, North Hollywood, Calif., 1978.

12. T. A. Friermood. *Automatic Feedback Control of Blood Pressure*. M.S. thesis, Purdue University, West Lafayette, Ind.

13. D. J. Carr. *Automatic Feedback Control of Blood Pressure in Dogs*. M.S. thesis, Purdue University, West Lafayette, Ind.

14. A. M. Albisser, B. S. Leibel, B. Zinman, F. T. Murray, W. Zingg, C. K. Botz, A. Denoga, and E. B. Marliss. Studies with an artificial endocrine pancreas. *Arch. Intern. Med.* **137**: 639–649 (1977).

15. W. J. Spencer. For diabetes: An electronic pancreas. *IEEE Spectrum* **15**: 38–42 (1978).

16. R. J. Cosgrove and V. F. Smolen. United States Patent No. 4,280,494. *Systems For The Automatic Feedback-Controlled Administration Of Drugs*, July 28, 1981.

17. R. C. Arzbaecher, S. Collins, R. L. Novotney, and R. R. Dean. Control system dynamics in antiarrhythmic therapy. *Proc. San Diego Biomedical Symp.* **13**: 301–306 (1974).

18. S. Collins and R. C. Arzbaecher. Automated intravenous antiarrhythmic drug infusion. In *Computers in Cardiology, Long Beach, California, IEEE Computer Society*, 1977, p. 55.

19. A. Faulconer, Jr. and R. G. Bickford. *Electroencephalography in Anesthesiology*, Thomas, Springfield, Ill., 1960.

20. D. E. Soltero, A. Faulconer, Jr., and R. G. Bickford. The clinical application of automatic anesthesia. *Anesthesiology* **12**: 574–582 (1951).

21. D. K. Kiersey, A. Faulconer, Jr., and R. G. Bickford. Automatic EEG control of thiopental anesthesia. *Anesthesiology* **15**: 356–364 (1954).

22. V. H. Muller and M. Stauch. A blood-pressure-controlled infusion machine. *Z. Biologie* **116**: 288–298 (1969).

23. C. M. Schade. An automatic therapeutic control system for regulating blood pressure. *Proc. San Diego Biomed. Symp.* **12**: 47–52 (1973).

24. Y. Fukui, R. A. Fleming, and N. T. Smith. Digital and sampled-data control of arterial BP during halothane anesthesia. *Proc. San Diego Biomed. Symp.* **13**: 273–278 (1974).

25. L. C. Sheppard, N. T. Kouchoukos, J. F. Shotts, and F. D. Wallace. Regulation of Mean Arterial Pressure by Computer Control of Vasoactive Agents in Postoperative Patients. In *Computers in Cardiology, Long Beach, California, IEEE Computer Society*, 1975, pp. 91–94.

26. R. T. McNally, K. Engelman, A. Noordergraaf, and M. Edwards, Jr. A device for the precise regulation of blood pressure in patients during surgery and hypertensive crises. *Proc. San Diego Biomed. Symp.* **16**: 419–424 (1977).

27. H. M. Shapiro, A. Galino, S. R. Wyte, et al. Rapid inoperative reduction of intracranial hypertension with thiopentone. *Br. J. Anaesth.* **45**: 1057–1062 (1973).

28. M. L. Marsh, L. R. Marshall, and H. M. Shapiro. Neurological intensive care. *Anesthesiology* **47**: 149–163 (1977).

29. M. Clark and B. Gastel. Saving coma victims. *Newsweek*, September 4, p. 54 (1973).

30. V. F. Smolen, B. D. Turrie, and W. A. Weigand. Drug input optimization: Bioavailability effected time optimal control of multiple simultaneous pharmacological effects and their interrelationships. *J. Pharm. Sci.* **61**: 1941–1952 (1972).

31. V. F. Smolen, E. J. Williams, and P. B. Kuehn. Idealized approach to the optimal design, development, and evaluation of drug delivery systems I. Drug bioavailability input/pharmacological response output relationships. *Drug Dev. Commun.* **1**: 143–172 (1974–1975).

32. V. F. Smolen, E. J. Williams, and P. B. Kuehn. Idealized approach to the optimal design, development, and evaluation of drug delivery systems. II. Optimization of drug bioavailability input and in-vitro release testing. *Drug Dev. Commun.* **1**: 231–258 (1974–1975).

33. V. F. Smolen. A Frequency Response Method for Pharmacokinetic Model Identification. In L. Endrenyi (ed.), *Kinetic Data Analysis*, Plenum Press, New York, 1981, pp. 209–233.

34. V. F. Smolen. A Generalized Numerical Deconvolution Procedure for Computing Absolute Bioavailability–Time Profiles. In L. Endrenyi (ed.), *Kinetic Data Analysis*, Plenum Press, New York, 1981, pp. 375–389.

35. V. F. Smolen. Theoretical and computational basis for drug bioavailability determinations using pharmacological data. I. General considerations and procedures. *J. Pharmacokinet. Biopharm.* **4**: 337–353 (1976).

36. V. F. Smolen. Theoretical and computational basis for drug bioavailability determinations using pharmacological data. II. Drug input/response relationships. *J. Pharmacokinet. Biopharm.* **4**: 355–375 (1976).

37. V. F. Smolen. Pharmacokinetic engineering approach to drug delivery system design and the optimization of drug effects. *IEEE Proc. Internatl. Conf. Cybern. Soc.* Washington, D.C., pp. 340–356, November 1–3, 1976.

38. J. B. Schwartz. Optimization Techniques in Pharmaceutical Formulation and Processing. In G. S. Banker and C. T. Rhodes (eds.), *Modern Pharmaceutics: Drugs and the Pharmaceutical Sciences*, Vol. 7, Marcel Dekker, New York, 1979, pp. 711–734.

39. V. F. Smolen and W. A. Weigand. Optimally predictive in vitro drug dissolution testing for in vivo bioavailability. *J. Pharm. Sci.* **65**: 1718–1724 (1976).

40. V. F. Smolen and W. A. Weigand. In vitro drug product dissolution tests as substitutes for bioavailability studies in human subjects. *Acta Pharmaceutica Suecica* **15**: 309–311 (1979).

41. V. F. Smolen. In vitro drug product bioequivalency requirements: What can they become? *J. Pharm. Technol.* **1**: 27–31 (1977).

42. V. F. Smolen, L. Ball, and M. Scheffler. Predicting the time course of in vivo bioavailability from in vitro dissolution tests: Control systems engineering approaches. *Pharm. Technol.* **3**: 88–102 (1979).

43. V. F. Smolen. United States Patent No. 4,335,438. *Method And Apparatus For Automatic Dissolution Testing Of Products*, June 15, 1982.

44. V. F. Smolen. United States Patent No. 4,279,860. *Multiple Injector Flow Through Dissolution Cell For Dissolution Testing Apparatus*, July 21, 1981.

CHAPTER 2

Applied Biodynamic Analysis of Drugs

VICTOR F. SMOLEN

PharmaControl Corporation
Englewood Cliffs, New Jersey

CONTENTS

Clinical studies with humans, as well as the animal experimentation that must proceed them, are costly and time consuming to perform; therefore, such studies should always be designed, executed, and analyzed to obtain the greatest abundance of useful information possible. In addition to elucidating dose ranges, incidence of toxicities, and the overall pharmacological behavior of drugs, the most quantitative data generated most commonly consist of parent drug and/or metabolite levels in body fluids monitored over time following single or chronic dosing of humans or animals. In addition, the results of concomitantly or separately monitoring the time variation of the intensity of pharmacological effects, elicited by the single drugs themselves and/or in combination with other agents, may be monitored. On the basis of such data, the objectives of its biodynamic analysis are to (1) extract as much information and develop as many generalizations from such pharmacokinetic and pharmacological data as can be obtained, (2) assess the reliability of the developed mathematical models with regard to the fidelity of their predictive capabilities and the accuracy of generalizations concerning the drug's and biosystem's dynamic (time varying) behavior—the predictions are resolved through the mathematical and statistical treatment of the data for each drug and drug combination studied, and (3) apply the results of the biodynamic analysis of the data to the development of drug products and the determination of the manner of their clinical usage that elicits a maximum therapeutic benefit to the individual patient.

1. BIODYNAMIC MODELS

Alfred North Whitehead has been quoted as saying, "To see what is general in what is particular and what is permanent in what is transitory is the aim of scientific thought." James Clerk Maxwell has stated that "The first process in the effectual study of the science must be one of simplification and reduction of previous investigations to a form in which the mind can grasp them ...." Both quotations express the need for simplication and generalizations of data derived from experimental investigations; numbers are not enough! To be of conceptual and thus lasting and predictive value, the results of experimentation must be interpreted in terms of hypothetical constructs called "models." This is in essence an expression of the scientific method and models are the basic tools of science.

A model may be defined as a simplified representation of a real system that simulates and abstracts the essential features of the real system and allows predictions of the real system to be made from operations performed on the model system. This definition may be summarized by stating that useful models must be (1) descriptive, (2) simulative, and especially (3) predictive of the behavior of the real system being modeled.

Models are developed from a combination of physical laws and mathematical principles that describe the behavior of a system's components and the interactions between them. Models permit the characterization of a system through the computation of parameters that can be generalized from the results of experimental measurements. In this way, they provide the framework and the mathematical means to systematize seemingly unrelated data resulting from experimental observations of a biosystem's behavior and develop the conceptualized understanding necessary to effectively design new experiments from which such understanding is further enhanced. Replicas (model airplanes, anatomical dolls, etc.) are distinguished from models in that although they may be descriptive and even simulative to a degree, replicas are incapable of predicting the behavior of the real system under previously untried, new conditions.

1.1 Biophysical versus Phenomenological Models

Pharmacokinetics (herein defined as what the body does to the drug, such as absorb, metabolize, distribute, and eliminate it) and pharmacodynamics (defined as what the drug does to the body, i.e., the physiological changes it induces), both rely on the use of mathematical models to describe the temporal behavior or drug-responding systems. Such models can be broadly categorized as (1) biophysical and (2) phenomenological. In all cases experimental data (numbers) are fitted to an equation or a system of mathematical expressions that serve to reduce and generalize the numbers in terms of equation parameters that best represent the observations in a condensed form. The equations utilized in the development of biophysical models are chosen on the basis of known or hypothetically inferred information concerning the biophysical mechanisms responsible for the experimentally observed behavior of the biosystem. For example, the shapes of drug blood level–time curves may suggest that the drug is eliminated by a capacity-limited metabolic process; it may be further known from perfused liver studies that a saturable biotransformation process could indeed be operative. Such information would suggest the incorporation of Michaelis–Menten-type enzyme kinetic expressions into the model and the interpretation of at least two of the model parameters in terms of a Michaelis constant and a maximum reaction velocity for the involved hepatic enzyme system. A danger in the development of biophysical models is the bias that can be introduced in interpreting and constraining the observed data to fit some preferred hypothesis rather than develop hypotheses and models that rigorously conform to the observations. This difficulty is not encountered in phenomenological modeling in that the only purpose here is to obtain an empirical, mathematical representation of the behavior of the system that is as simple as it can be made and still possesses an acceptable fidelity in simulating and predicting the system's time-varying behavior under prescribed conditions. In this case the equation parameters are merely empirically determined values that best (statistically) describe the average behavior of the system. Generally such empirical equation parameters can, when there is justification to do so, be related to system parameters of biophysical significance. For example, drug blood level(Q)–time(t) curves can most often be empirically fitted to multiexponential expressions of the type given by equation 1, where the A_i and m_i values are empirical equation parameters obtained by least squares, best fits to the observed data. Most commonly, one to three exponential terms are sufficient to fit a set of data:

$$Q = A_1e^{-m_1t} + A_2e^{-m_2t} + A_3e^{-m_3t} \tag{1}$$

If there is a theoretical basis for postulation of a compartment model (1–3) to describe the rate processes occurring in the system, parameters such as first-order rate constants for absorption and disposition of the drug and the volumes of the postulated compartments in the model (to which some biophysical significance may be ascribed such as plasma volume, fat, muscle, CNS tissue space, etc.) are computed from the empirically determined equation parameters. Again, care must be exercised so as not to distort the empirical representation of the data for the sake of assumed, hypothetical, biophysical mechanisms (4).

Biophysical models, such as compartmented representations (see Figure 1), serve to integrate pharmacokinetic and pharmacodynamic processes and are quite valuable as conceptual tools to further the understanding of the biosystem behavior. Such models should always be evolved when there is a sufficient background of information and understanding of the system available to justify the effort. However, for all practical pharmacokinetic and pharmacodynamic purposes, phenomenological models that relate the dynamic manner in which the drug enters the body [or is released at its site(s) of absorption] to the resulting time course of the levels of drug and its metabolites at the sites in the body where they are sampled and/or to the time course of the intensity of pharmacological effects, is all that is required (2, 5–8). Phenomenological equations to interrelate and computationally predict the time variation of drug and metabolite levels or intensities of pharmacological effects from measurements of any other drug, metabolite, or pharmacological response can also be developed without the need for a mechanistic understanding of the biophysical processes underlying the empirical relationships (9). As knowledge of the involved biophysical processes and their operative mechanisms develops, the parameters of the empirical equations can become understood in terms of biophysically meaningful parameters. In the meantime, the phenomenological models

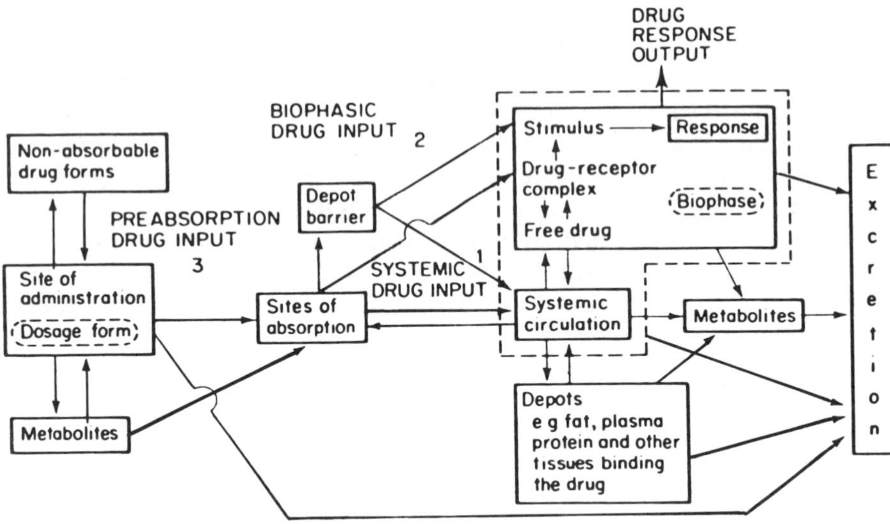

Figure 1. Simplified compartmental representation of the processes influencing drug response characteristics. The various processes operating to determine the characteristics of a drug effect are depicted, showing the familiar type of representation of the body as a compartmented system; the compartments are represented by the rectangles, and the various drug transport processes are described by the arrows. The heavy arrows indicate drug inputs and a response output. In such models compartments are analogous to well-stirred tanks and represent spaces into which the drug can enter, or a chemical entry into which it can be metabolically transformed. The biophase is a compartment into which the drug enters to induce its effects. The broken lines enclosing the systemic circulation and biophase compartments signify that these compartments may not be kinetically distinguishable; this depends on the rapidity with which the drug can pass between them. The three types of drug input are depicted: (1) the drug enters the systemic circulation before being distributed to its biophase (this is what occurs with oral or parenteral dosing); (2) the drug is absorbed into its biophase prior to entering the systemic circulation (e.g., as when a localized effect of the drug is sought by means of ophthalmic dosing, topical application to the skin, or intrauterine or vaginal implantation; in this case, the presence of the drug in the blood is undesirable); (3) the preabsorption bioavailability of the drug is shown as the drug released from its dosage form to its sites of absorption.

can be implemented to the solution of practical problems dealing with the simulation and prediction of the biosystem's behavior in response to the introduction of drugs and the dynamic manner of their input (2, 5). For example, as shown in Figure 1, the time course of the rates and extent of a drug's release from a drug delivery system to become available to (1) site(s) of absorption in the body (preabsorption bioavailability), (2) the systemic circulation (systemic bioavailability), and/or (3) its sites of action in the body (biophasic availability) can be computed, using phenomenological models, from the results of monitoring drug or metabolite body fluid levels or pharmacological effects (9). Conversely, when the dynamic manner in which the drug becomes available is known (drug input), the time course of the response(s) to the drug can be computationally predicted without knowledge of the involved mechanisms. However, the value of a mechanistic understanding of the system cannot be overemphasized even though such an understanding may be slow to develop. Phenomenological models thus provide an interim means of approaching problems of practical concern without the need to wait for the accumulation of the knowledge required to develop biophysical models.

1.2 Functional Analysis

Depending on the nature of the data, the resulting models could, at one extreme, merely involve the development of quite conventional single or multiple compartment models and describe the time course of drug levels in terms of volumes of distribution and rate constants for distribution and elimination; nonlinear elements could be introduced into the models as required. On the other hand, if there are data of sufficient quantity and quality to justify the mathematical complexity and computational effort involved, a functional analysis treatment of the data may be implemented. This powerful and general approach has been applied (9) to the computation of time optimal drug dosage inputs that most rapidly achieve a desired level of therapeutic response without exceeding prescribed levels of simultaneously occurring toxic side effects. Functional analysis is a branch of mathematics that generalizes the concepts of classical analysis (including calculus, algebra, and geometry) from variables. Relationships that deal with point functions [i.e., $y = f(x)$] are replaced by more general types of function, called *functionals* or *operators*, wherein the function depends on another function rather than on point values. Functional analysis provides a unified framework for considering problems in which variables are not just numbers but time functions. This powerful functional analysis approach (9–12) is well suited for pharmacokinetic purposes. This technique possesses several important advantages relative to other less general mathematical methods that are more commonly applied to control engineering, optimization, and biokinetic problems. In addition to relative computational and theoretical simplicity, the approach possesses:

1. The capability to accommodate multiple drug inputs. This feature is important in that it permits the quantitative treatment of multiple, pharmacological response or drug level–time data resulting from the simultaneous administration of the same or different drugs by different or the same routes and modes of administration. This is an important

capability for the simulation and prediction of the pharmacological and/or drug-level response behavior elicited from acute and chronic administration of a single drug or interacting drug combinations.

2. A capability to treat system behavior using system differential equations of seventh or higher order (i.e., models corresponding to seven or more compartments for each pharmacological or drug level response are readily constructed). This capability is more than sufficient for the treatment of the dynamic systems behavior which is commonly encountered.
3. The capability to treat adaptive system nonlinearities such as those that can mechanistically arise from the occurrence of threshold and saturation phenomena affecting drug plasma and tissue binding, drug transport and metabolic processes, and dose–effect relationships (13). Drug-interaction-induced time variations in dynamic model parameters resulting from the coadministration of drugs in combination can also be effectively managed. An example of the application of this technique is described in reference 9.

Despite the elegance and generality of the functional analysis approach, the specific approaches to be implemented with a given drug and a set of data must obviously depend on the specific objectives of the data analysis as well as the nature, quality, and quantity of the data. Keeping in mind the "law of parsimony" (i.e., of not multiplying entities without necessity), analysts must draw on their repertories of mathematical modeling and computational techniques to obtain the simplest mathematical model that is consistent with the available data and the goals of the analysis.

As already mentioned, all that may be sought is a linear compartmental analysis of the data. In other cases it may be necessary to include provisions for observed nonlinearities in the system's dynamics. When developing models that integrate both temporal pharmacological data and blood levels of the drug and metabolites, it may be necessary to provide for nonlinearities such as threshold and saturation behavior in the pharmacological response and compensate for time variations in the model parameters; such variations can be anticipated to occur as a result of the development of tolerances. Compensation for the development of tolerances is of particular importance, for example, when dealing with the pharmacological activities of opiate narcotics.

1.3 Black-Box Analysis of Pharmacodynamic Data

The most practical objective of biodynamic data analysis is to computationally predict the drug bioavailability input (as determined by the drug release characteristics of drug formulations, the dose size, and the dosing schedule) required to achieve and maintain a desired level of drug, metabolite(s), or pharmacological activity (or antagonism to the pharmacological activity of another drug). For this purpose, an entirely general and simple method of establishing and verifying drug bioavailability input–pharmacological response and/or drug level relationships can be appropriately implemented as diagrammed in Figure 2. This is a phenomenological method developed by the author (2, 5, 13) that can be applied to almost any system without requiring any knowledge of the involved biophysical mechanisms underlying the observed phenomenon; the results of its application can in fact serve to elucidate such mechanisms (8).

The approach, as diagrammed in Figure 2, is equally applicable to biophasic, preabsorption, and in-vitro predicted (13, 14) absolute bioavailability determinations in addition to computing systemic bioavailability

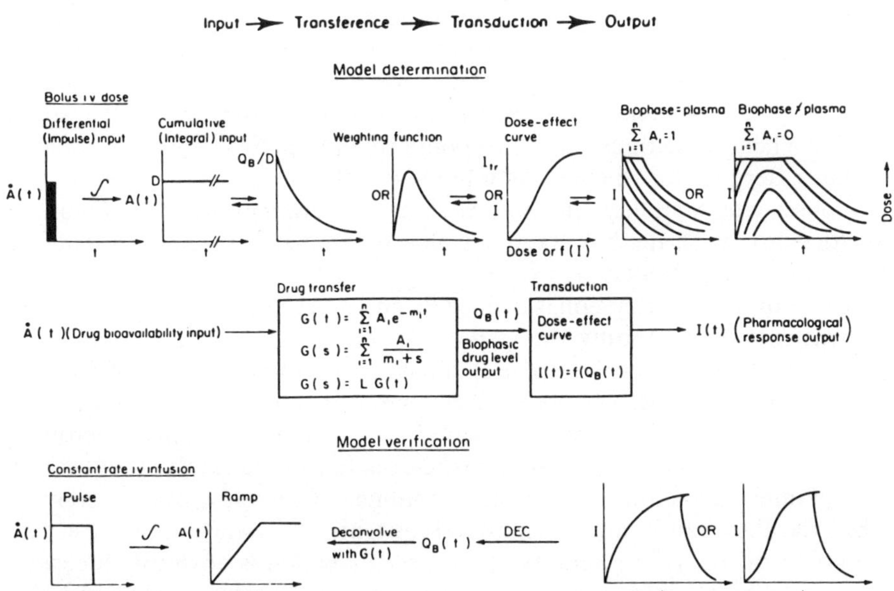

Figure 2. Drug input⇌pharmacological response output relationships. The upper curves illustrate the process of determining a weighting function (in the time domain *t*) or transfer function model (in the complex frequency domain *s*) as defined by the relative dose *D* normalized biophasic drug level $Q_B(t)/D - t$ response curve to an impulse (bolus intravenous dose) input. The $Q_B(t)$ values are obtained by conversion of observed pharmacological response intensities *I* by the use of the dose effect curve (DEC). The weighting function model is verified for use in bioavailability computations by comparisons of an experimentally known, for example, constant rate intravenous infusion inputs, with the inputs computed from the observed *I–t* output curves, which are converted to $Q_B(t)$ and deconvolved with $G(t)$. The DEC is constructed as a plot of *I* (observed at a constant time *t* after dosing) versus dose.

from either pharmacological, blood, or urine-level data. The blocks in the diagram in Figure 2 signify weighting and transduction mathematical functions that interrelate a drug input with each pharmacological response output. When direct assay data are used or the dose–effect curve for pharmacological response is a straight line, the transduction function is not needed (2, 5). The functions are experimentally determined from the observed response to known drug inputs. Although any type of known input can be used, it is most simple to use impulse inputs. In this case, the biophasic drug level or direct assay drug-level response–time profile observed for an impulse input directly defines the weighting function. The weighting function then, in general, provides the relationship between any drug input entering the site of the impulse input and the observed response output. When the systemic bioavailability is of interest, the impulse input would in practice be constituted by a bolus intravenous dose; the weighting function then relates the rate–time profile for the drug entering the systemic circulation from the site of injection when it is given by any other route or dosage form. Similarly, the weighting function resulting from the administration of a bolus of solution given orally or into the eye relates preabsorption bioavailability input rates into the gastrointestinal contents or the fluids of the eye (8, 13), respectively. Whether the time of peak response to an impulse occurs at time zero or later, depends on whether the input site is the same compartment as the response data sampling site; this is shown diagrammatically in Figure 1 for the case when the biophase and plasma compartment are the same or different compartments.

The transduction function is defined by an observed dose–effect curve that is constructed by plotting the response intensity observed at a consistent time (usually time of peak response) following the administration of doses of increasing magnitude. The dose–effect curve is then used in the manner of a calibration curve to convert observed pharmacological response intensities into their corresponding biophasic (site-of-action) drug levels. Their use in this manner is analogous to using a nonlinear Beer's law plot to convert observed absorbances into plasma-level concentrations when using a spectrophotometric assay. The validity of the Beer's law plot is obviously independent of the route and mode of administration as well as the time at which the plasma sample being analyzed is collected. This is also the case for the use of the dose–effect curve to convert observed pharmacological responses into biophasic drug levels. This is, therefore, a quite general method by which nonlinear, observed pharmacological response variables can be converted into biophasic drug levels that can then be treated by linear mathematics. Since the transduction function is experimentally determined, as the dose–effect curve, it is independent of the assumption of any particular drug–receptor site interaction model (15, 16), as discussed below.

When the dose–effect curve is linear, observed pharmacological response intensities can be used directly in computations just like results of a chemical assay. This has been found to be the case with pupilometric and intraocular pressure lowering responses to oral and intravenous doses of chlorpromazine in human subjects (7, 8). Generally, however, this is not the case, and the conversion of pharmacological data by means of a dose–effect curve into biophasic drug levels is performed to simplify the construction of pharmacokinetic models and their use for the computation of bioavailability. The theoretical basis for these transformations has been described (5, 6, 18). Briefly, the method is predicted on two major assumptions:

Assumption 1. "The dynamics of the drug's disposition are linear." (A generalized, nonlinear correction approach is discussed below). This means that dose-dependent (capacity-limited) processes are not operable in the dosing range of interest. When this assumption is valid, the time variation of the quantity of the drug Q_B in a biophase compartment following bolus intravenous dosing (or administration by any other route where the absorption of the drug is a linear process) is described by a sum of exponentials where the A_i and m_i values are constants, t is the time after dosing, and D denotes the dose:

$$Q_B = D \sum_{i=1}^{n} A_i e^{-m_i t} \tag{2}$$

At any arbitrarily chosen constant time t_r, Q_B will be directly proportional to the dose since the sum of the exponentials in equation 2 will be constant and defined by

$$\sum_{i=1}^{n} A_i e^{-m_i t_r} = B_{t_r} = \text{constant} \tag{3}$$

Substitution of B_{t_r} into equation 2 yields

$$Q_B = DB_{t_r} \tag{4}$$

Equation 4 merely expresses the direct relationship between biophasic drug levels and dose at a constant time after dosing. It is shown by equations 4 and 5 that the dose is a relative biophasic drug level since B_{t_r} is constant and D is directly proportional to Q_B. The units of Q_B are the same as the dose, and A_i are dimensionless:

$$D = \frac{Q_B}{B_{t_r}} = f(I) \tag{5}$$

The dose, or relative biophasic drug level, is denoted in equation 5 as $f(I)$ to emphasize its functional relationship to the pharmacological response intensity I; the I is usually expressed as a drug-induced physiological change ΔR relative to its predrug level; R_0 thus

$$I = \frac{\Delta R}{R_0} \tag{6}$$

The functional relationship between Q_B/B_{t_r} and I [i.e., $f(I)$] is defined by plotting the intensity of response observed at an arbitrary reference time t_r as a function of dose.

For practical reasons, t_r is chosen as the time of maximum response. When the maximum response intensity occurs at time zero, following bolus intravenous dosing, then

$$B_{t_r} = \sum_{i=1}^{n} A_i = 1 \quad \text{and} \quad D = Q_B = f(I) \tag{7}$$

This is the case when the exchange of drug between plasma and biophase (site of action) is so rapid that these tissues may always be regarded in equilibrium and can mathematically be treated as the same compartment. Most commonly, drug effects manifest their maxima some time after the dose is given. In such cases

$$\sum_{i=1}^{n} A_i = 0, \quad t_{\max} > 0, \quad \text{and} \quad B_{t_r} < 1 \tag{8}$$

Response–time profiles following bolus intravenous dosing are exemplified in Figure 2 for the cases of $B_{t_r} = 1$ and $B_{t_r} > 0$ where the central and systemic compartments are the same and different, respectively, from the biophase compartment.

Assumption 2. "The intensity of pharmacological response is a single-valued function of biophasic drug levels." This assumption is implicit in all drug-receptor site interaction models. It may be invalid in cases where a tolerance to the drug rapidly develops or possibly for some indirect effects. In the latter case, the validity of the assumption will depend on the manner in which the response to the drug is defined. For any particular response to a drug, the validity of both Assumptions 1 and 2 is often apparent by mere inspection of the drug response data.

When Assumption 2 is valid, only one value of a biophasic or relative biophasic drug level, shown above to equal the dose, corresponds to any given intensity of response. Therefore, the dose–effect curve must define this single-valued relationship; it is then only necessary to relabel the dose axis as Q_B/B_{t_r} or $f(I)$ and drop the t_r subscript on the I_{t_r} axis and relabel it simply as I to obtain a calibration curve. The resulting calibration curve can then be used to convert I values, observed at any time following dosing by any route, into corresponding biophasic or relative biophasic drug levels [i.e., $f(I)$ values].

The top portion of Figure 2 graphically illustrates the method of determining a pharmacokinetic model to describe the relationship between systemic drug inputs and pharmacological response outputs. The graphs at the bottom of the figure illustrate the procedure used for verifying the model. The fidelity of the determined model is evaluated from the results of comparing experimentally known, usually slow intravenous infusion, drug inputs with the drug inputs computed and predicted from the results of monitoring the pharmacological responses to the known inputs. The model previously determined from bolus intravenous doses is used for the computations. Therefore, whether the method applies in any particular case is determined from pharmacological data alone, and this approach can be applied with drugs for which chemical assays do not exist or whose exact chemical composition or active constituent may not even be known. It has been demonstrated that neither the mathematical form of the weighting or transduction function need be known or explicitly defined in order to compute drug inputs and outputs from one another; the computations can be performed entirely numerically and in the frequency rather than time domain (19, 20). The only assumption involved is that the disposition kinetics of the drug in the body behave at least approximately linear, in the sense that the superposition principle applies, over the range of drug inputs considered.

Three problems can be encountered with this generalized approach. The first problem arises when response profiles have multiple peaks without any well-defined maximum occurring at a consistent time that can be used to plot a dose–effect curve. In this case the area under the response curve (AUC) is plotted against dose instead. The resulting plot is linearized by finding some function of the AUC that when plotted against dose yields a straight line. It is a simple matter to show mathematically that the same function that linearizes AUC–dose plots also linearizes plots of maximum response intensity versus dose. Therefore, when this function is applied to observed intensities of response, it converts them into the relative biophasic drug levels needed for linear pharmacokinetic analysis. The second problem is the occurrence of dose–effect curves that are not monotonic increasing with dose; this causes the difficulty of response intensities corresponding to more than one biophasic drug level. This problem is solved by utilizing a time-tracking program to select the correct values of biophasic drug levels for any observed response intensity (21). The third problem arises when the disposition kinetics of the system are nonlinear as described below.

1.4 Generalized Black-Box Drug Bioavailability Analysis of Nonlinear Systems

A complication in the implementation of the drug input–output response scheme depicted in Figure 2 arises when the disposition kinetics of the system appear to be nonlinear (13). A trend with dose, in the time of peak pharmacological response intensities, can indicate that this is the case (8, 13). Such a trend is observable in the hypothermic response profiles for chlorpromazine shown in Figure 3. A general, piecewise linear approach to circumventing this problem that can always be applied involves the following: (1) constructing the usual dose–effect curve by plotting maximum intensities of response against dose irrespective of the time of their occurrence and using it to convert the pharmacological response intensity I profiles observed for each dose, into corresponding biophasic drug levels Q_B and (2) fitting a sum of exponential expressions to each of the Q_B–time profiles obtained for each impulse input dose as given by equation 2. Alternatively, any other empirical expression, such as a polynomial, could be used. In any case, these results define dose-dependent weighting functions. Plotting of the parameters of the dose-dependent weighting functions versus time-averaged values $\bar{Q}_B$ corresponding to each dose, as can be defined by equation 2, where there are k observations of $Q_{B,p}$ recorded at each pth time interval following the jth dose, is given by equation 9:

$$Q_{B,j} = \sum_{p=1}^{k} Q_{B,p} \tag{9}$$

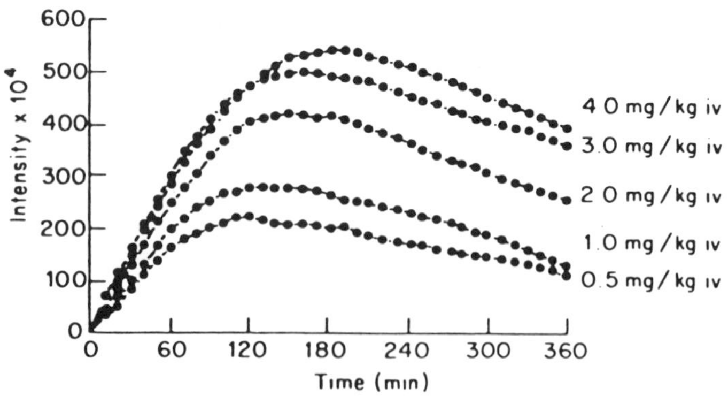

Figure 3. Intensity of rectal temperature depression in rabbits at 20°C recorded as a function of five bolus intravenous doses of chlorpromazine. Reprinted with permission from V. F. Smolen. Practical Pharmacodynamic Engineering in the Design, Development, and Evaluation of Optimal Drug Products. In H. S. Bean, A. H. Backett, and J. E. Canless (eds.), *Advances in Pharmaceutical Sciences*, Vol. 5, Academic Press, London, 1981, pp. 115–198.

In this manner, the dependence of the parameters of the weighting function on the intensity of the response output is established. (1) Selection of a set of weighting-function parameters from the plots constructed in step 3 that correspond to each of the Q_B data points of a Q_B–time profile observed to result from the absolute bioavailability input profile that is to be determined by computation. The weighting-function parameters are then used to calculate weighting-function values that correspond to each of the Q_B values for which the corresponding absolute bioavailability input is being sought. In this manner the weighting function is continuously adjusted to compensate for its dependence on the magnitude of the Q_B response output at any time. (2) Computation of the desired absolute bioavailability input by numerical deconvolution (13, 19, 20) of the output-adjusted values of the weighting function with their corresponding output response values; this produces the desired absolute bioavailability rate–time profile. The extent of absolute bioavailability–time profile is obtained by integration of the rate profile. Step 1 in this procedure can be omitted and I values used instead of Q_B values. However, the partial compensation for nonlinearity in the gain of the systems (2) that results from the dose–effect curve conversion of I into Q_B values will generally contribute appreciably to the accuracy of the computed absolute bioavailability profiles. That this is the case for the hypothermic response to chlorpromazine in rabbits is demonstrated by the results shown in Figures 4–7. Figure 4 contains averaged hypothermic

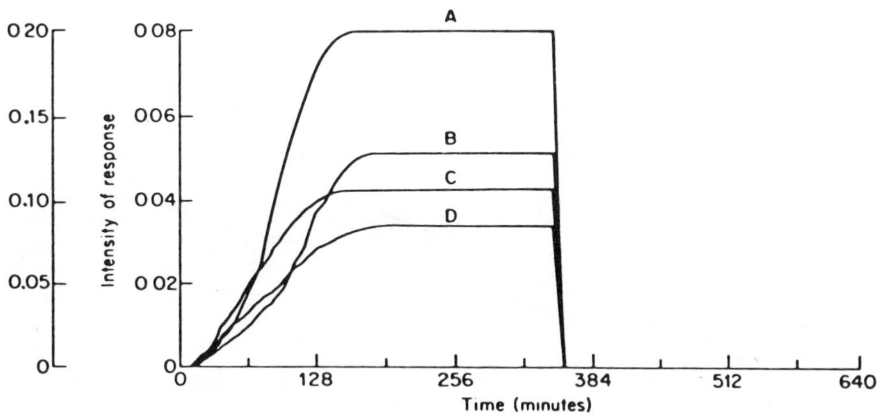

Figure 4. Plots of I and $f(I)$ versus time for 0.50 and 0.75 mg/(kg/hour) infusions: (A) $f(I)$ for 0.75 mg(kg/hour); (B) $f(I)$ for 0.50 mg/(kg/hour); (C) I for 0.75 mg/(kg/hour); (D) I for 0.50 mg/(kg/hour). Reprinted with permission from V. F. Smolen. Practical Pharmacodynamic Engineering in the Design, Development, and Evaluation of Optimal Drug Products. In H. S. Bean, A. H. Backett, and J. E. Canless (eds.), *Advances in Pharmaceutical Sciences*, Vol. 5, Academic Press, London, 1981, pp. 115–198.

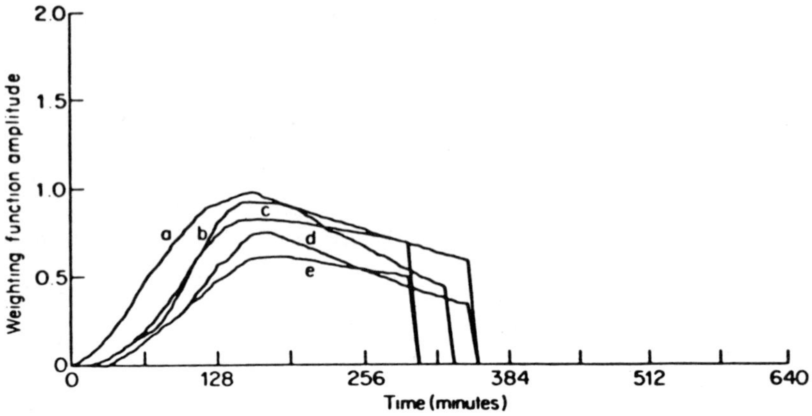

Figure 5. Weighting function for chlorpromazine temperature depression in rabbits: (*a*) average triexponential model; (*b*) generalized nonlinear model for *f*(*I*) at 0.75 mg/(kg/hour); (*c*) generalized nonlinear model for intensity response at 0.75 mg/(kg/hour); (*d*) generalized nonlinear model for *f*(*I*) at 0.50 mg/(kg/hour); (*e*) generalized nonlinear model for intensity response at 0.50 mg/(kg/hour). Reprinted with permission from V. F. Smolen. Practical Pharmacodynamic Engineering in the Design, Development, and Evaluation of Optimal Drug Products. In H. S. Bean, A. H. Backett, and J. E. Canless (eds.), *Advances in Pharmaceutical Sciences*, Vol. 5, Academic Press, London, 1981, pp. 115–198.

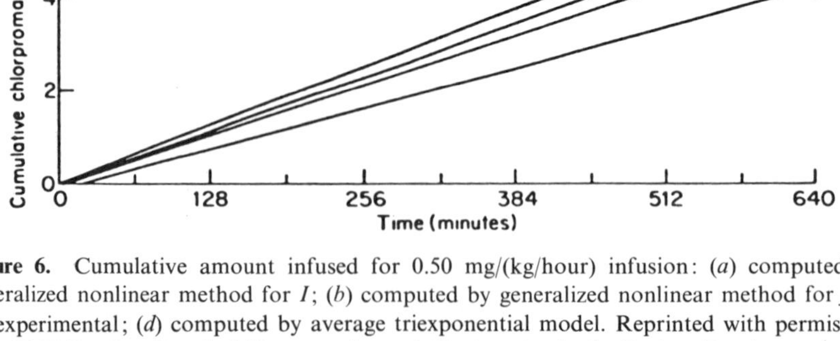

Figure 6. Cumulative amount infused for 0.50 mg/(kg/hour) infusion: (*a*) computed by generalized nonlinear method for *I*; (*b*) computed by generalized nonlinear method for *f*(*I*); (*c*) experimental; (*d*) computed by average triexponential model. Reprinted with permission from V. F. Smolen. Practical Pharmacodynamic Engineering in the Design, Development, and Evaluation of Optimal Drug Products. In H. S. Bean, A. H. Backett, and J. E. Canless (eds.), *Advances in Pharmaceutical Sciences*, Vol. 5, Academic Press, London, 1981, pp. 115–198.

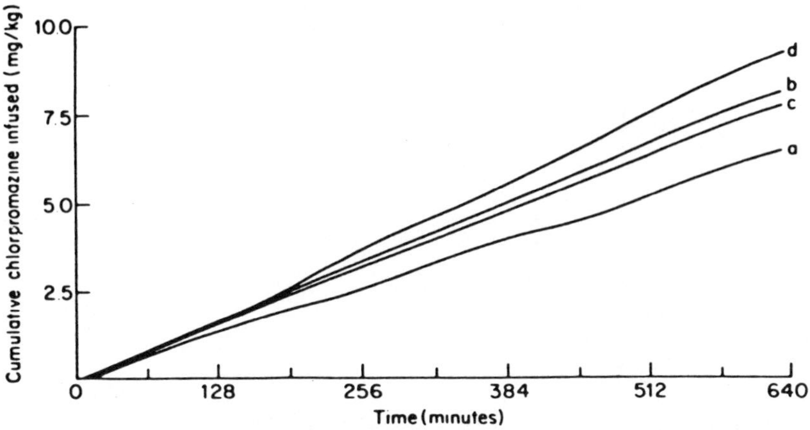

Figure 7. Cumulative amount infused for 0.75 mg/(kg/hour) infusion: (*a*) computed by generalized nonlinear method for I; (*b*) computed by generalized nonlinear method for $f(I)$; (*c*) experimental; (*d*) computed by average triexponential model. Reprinted with permission from V. F. Smolen. Practical Pharmacodynamic Engineering in the Design, Development, and Evaluation of Optimal Drug Products. In H. S. Bean, A. H. Backett, and J. E. Canless (eds.), *Advances in Pharmaceutical Sciences*, Vol. 5, Academic Press, London, 1981, pp. 115–198.

response intensity profiles observed in nine rabbits administered the drug by constant-rate intravenous infusion of 0.50 and 0.75 mg/kg/hour; these profiles are labeled *D* and *C*, respectively. The curves labeled *A* and *B* are the results of transforming the *C* and *D* curves into corresponding biophasic drug levels symbolized as $f(I)$ by means of the hypothermic response dose–effect curve for chlorpromazine given in Figure 8. Figure 5 presents weighting functions specifically determined in the above-described manner for each of the response profiles shown in Figure 4. The weighting functions corrected for nonlinearity, labeled *b–e*, are seen to differ appreciably from the uncorrected triexponential weighting function obtained merely as a least-squares best fit to the averaged, dose-normalized relative biophasic drug levels designated in Figure 5 as *a*. Figures 6 and 7 display the cumulative input–time profiles computed by numerically deconvolving each weighting function shown in Figure 5 for which, except for the uncorrected *a* weighting function, they were specifically constructed. It can be seen in Figures 6 and 7 that the cumulative input profiles computed by use of the relative biophasic drug level $f(I)$ weighting functions corrected for nonlinearities provided the best results in each case as judged from a comparison of the computed profiles, designated as *b* with the experimentally known input profiles designated as *c* in Figures 6 and 7. The results obtained with the direct use of intensity I values were not as good as when the I values were converted to $f(I)$ values despite the weighting function having been cor-

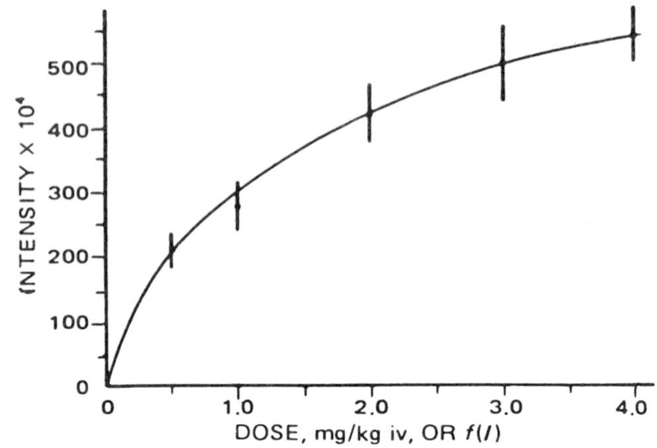

Figure 8. Intravenous dose–effect curve for chlorpromazine-induced rectal temperature depression in rabbits constructed from the maximum intensities of temperature depression in Figure 1, with the standard error of the mean indicated for each value. The abscissa is relabeled $f(I)$, which corresponds to a relative biophasic drug level.

rected for nonlinearity. The worst result was obtained with the averaged, uncorrected for nonlinearity, weighting function.

The considerable significance of the above-described approach to performing drug input–output response computations lies in the fact that it is generally applicable and requires no knowledge or assumptions concerning the mechanisms responsible for the observed nonlinear behavior of the system. Therefore, this method can always be applied and permits nonlinear systems to be treated with the generality of linear systems mathematics.

1.5 Other Approaches to Nonlinear Systems Analysis

The occurrence of variable coefficients and/or nonlinear terms is also commonly encountered in chemical rate processes of interest in chemical engineering. A method alternative to the one described above that is used to approach the modeling of such systems is also directly applicable to biosystems. One common approach, when the functional form of the time-varying or nonlinear terms is known, is to linearize the differential equation by expansion in Taylor series. The resulting linearized differential equation then has coefficients that are dependent on the operating conditions (the state) around which the Taylor series expansion was made. If this approach were applied to a pharmacokinetic model, the variable coefficients would be mathematically related to the time-varying drug levels that occur during the course of bioavailability calculations. In this way a set of piecewise linear approximations can be made to the nonlinear system and the solutions for these approximations could be combined to describe the response over a broad range of drug levels where nonlinear effects are operationally significant. This approach could lead to analytical solutions in some cases.

Other means borrowed from engineering practice to treat the dynamics of nonlinear chemical processes can also be useful. For example, one means of approximating the dynamics of distillation columns operating to produce high-purity products (a very nonlinear process) is the concept of inventory time (24). In essence, this concept relates the approximate time constant of the system to the mass flow rates in and out and the mass holdup in the system. In addition to a strong dependence of the time constants of this type of system on the magnitude of the input, it is also found that the direction of the input is important. For example, the speed of response to a position input may be much slower than the response going back to the initial condition when the input is removed. Such behavior has been observed in biological systems (25). This technique, and others, could be applied to the modeling of drug systems if strong asymetric behavior is found as discussed for drug–enzyme kinetics in Chapter 6 of the present volume.

The above discussions have dealt with the analysis of nonlinear systems by using linear approximations of one type of another. In many cases the most useful approach would be to integrate the nonlinear system equations directly by using, say, a fourth-order Runge–Kutta scheme with a variable step size option. This method was used to integrate unsteady-state mass balance equations with Michaelis–Menten kinetics (26). It can also be used to check the accuracy of the approximate solutions when linearization can be used.

The analysis of the controlled and uncontrolled stability behavior of complex nonlinear systems has been the subject of investigations of reactors described in the chemical engineering literature (27–30). Although rather theoretical, the concepts and methods of such work could lead to productive new areas of research on drug dynamics and controlled drug administration in the future. For example, nonlinear system stability analysis techniques have been applied to the problem of the control of a microbial reactor (26) in order to permit operation at an unstable operating point. Similar techniques may be applicable to predicting and controlling the pharmacological response stability of biological systems that have been affected by the combined administration of two or more interacting drugs.

2. PHYSIOLOGICAL–PHARMACOKINETIC MODELS AND ANIMAL SCALE-UP

It is often the objective of the biodynamic analysis of experimental results to develop a capability to predict the time dependency of the accumulation, distribution, and elimination of selected compounds, as well as their significant metabolites, when introduced into humans. Because of the often serious, morbific properties of such substances as xenobiotics (e.g., PCBs and some anticancer drugs), direct human experimentation with these substances is precluded or limited to clinical cases of accidental contamination and terminally ill patients. However, the qualitative prediction of the disposition kinetics of these substances in humans can be approached through the construction and extrapolation (scale-up) to humans of biomathematical models developed to simulate the observed kinetic behavior of the compounds in animals. Although many exceptions occur, generally animal models can qualitatively describe the dynamic behavior of the same drugs in humans. However, because of species differences in size and specificity in metabolic, distributive, and excretory pathways, these models seldom translate quantitatively to humans. Fortunately, it is sometimes feasible to adjust the model parameters, such as metabolic and renal clearances and plasma- and tissue-binding affinities, to compensate for species differences. The information required to extrapolate the applicability of animal models to humans may, in these cases, be obtained from considerations of body mass and relative values of physiological parameters, such as blood flow rates perfusing tissues and organs; when appropriate, the results of in-vitro experiments performed to elucidate the binding and metabolism of the compounds in excised animal and human tissue may also be used to predict in-vivo physiological model parameters. Such approaches to interspecies scaling of physiological kinetic models of in-vivo drug disposition have been described and successfully applied (32, 33). Except for data deriving from accidental contaminations, it will not generally be feasible to verify the "scale-up" model in humans. However, some degree of confidence in the approach taken to the scale-up models in humans may be obtained by first scaling up to dogs or preferably higher primates and making direct comparisons of observed data—for example, plasma level–time curves and selected tissue levels of parent compounds and metabolites—with the same results computationally predicted from the scaled-up dog or primate models.

When the substance being studied is sufficiently safe to allow the same type of data to be recorded in both an animal and a human, weighting (transfer) function relationships can be developed that permit drug level or pharmacological response–time profiles in humans to be computationally predicted from the results of experiments performed in animals. The required computational technique is identical to that developed and applied (8, 13, 14, 19, 20) to computationally predict in-vivo blood level profiles from in-vitro drug product dissolution curves. Nonlinearities (8, 13) in the kinetics of the system can also in general be handled as described above.

3. RANDOM-INPUT MODELING (RIM)

Many pharmacologically responding biologic systems exhibit nonlinear dynamic behavior; the response of such systems then depends on the magnitude and type of input stimulus used to evoke a system response. For example, the same dose of a drug given as an impulse input (intravenous bolus dose) or as a pulse input (constant-rate intravenous infusion) can elicit different weighting (transfer) functions; such functions also vary with the magnitude of the administered dose.

The preferred type of input from which to obtain a weighting-function relationship between drug bioavailability inputs and drug-response outputs is provided by a Gaussian–white-noise stimulus; if the stimulus is provided for a sufficiently long time period, there is a finite probability that any given stimulus wave form will be represented by some sample of the white-noise signal. In this way a particularly rich stimulus is provided for use in system identification; in addition, the results are, for the most part, unaffected by contaminating noise. Determination of the weighting function is also made more accurately and in a shorter period of experimental time than would be the case if other stimuli (e.g., sinusoidal types) were used. Since the white-noise input can be superimposed onto the normal actuating signal (in this case, the voltage of a servo-controlled drug-infusion pump), the system weighting function can be identified on line during a normal closed-loop operation; the amplitude can be maintained close to the normal operating level, and the average drug input resulting from the white-noise signal remains zero. Therefore, the system is not significantly disturbed at any time during the identification process.

Random input system identification, or modeling, is a well-known technique in mechanical process and electronic systems analysis. Briefly, the method involves driving a system with a white-noise input signal whose bandwidth is at least 10 times larger than the system response bandwidth. It should be noted that band-limited white noise has all frequencies up to the bandwidth present at equal amplitude. Thus the power spectrum of white noise is flat to W_B, the bandwidth, as shown in Figure 9. It can be shown that the cross-correlation of any input x and output y is the convolution of the autocorrelation of x (35, 36) and the system weighting function (impulse response):

$$R_{xy}(\tau) = \int_0^{\infty} R_x(\tau - \lambda)h(\lambda)d(\lambda) \tag{10}$$

where R_x is the autocorrelation of $x(t)$ and R_{xy} is the cross-correlation of $x(t)$ and $y(t)$.

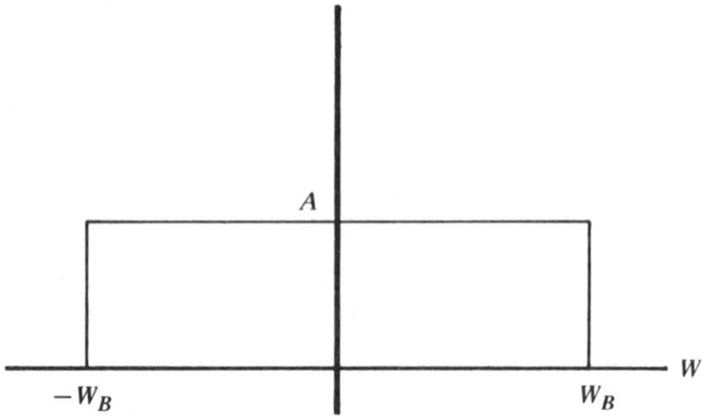

Figure 9. Power spectrum of white noise with bandwidth W_B and amplitude A.

For a white-noise input where S is the spectral density of white noise, the result is even simpler:

$$R_x(\tau) = S_0\delta \tag{11}$$

$$R_{xy}(\tau) = \int_0^{\infty} S_0\delta(\tau - \lambda)h(\lambda)d(\lambda) = \begin{cases} S_0 h(\tau) & \tau \geqslant 0 \\ 0 & \tau < 0 \end{cases} \tag{12}$$

This leads to a simple method of obtaining the transfer function by allowing τ to vary and low-pass filtering to reconstruct the signal.

Random-input modeling was applied by the author (34) to obtain the weighting-function relationships between the rate(s) of thiopental sodium infusion and the dynamics of the effect of the drug or pharmacological response variables derived from an on-line power spectral density analysis of the electroencephalogram (EEG). In this case, random-input thiopental flow rates were generated by a syringe pump driven by a pseudorandom binary signal (PRBS), which was generated, in turn, by the computer. A PRBS must be filtered to produce a random signal. Generally, the rule of thumb is that the maximum binary frequency should be approximately 20 times the cutoff frequency of the filter. In this case the syringe pump itself adequately filtered the PRBS.

The application of RIM to describe the hemodynamics of sodium nitroprusside (SN) in dogs performed by the author demonstrates this approach. A PRBS was generated by use of a Hewlett-Packard 5451B-Fourier analyzer system with a minimum pulse width of 0.32 seconds. Since the animal responds much more slowly than the syringe pump, the bandwidth criterion for the random signal was fully satisfied. Random input modeling was performed by superimposing the appropriate PRBS on a step input of nitroprusside. For example, a dog was given a step input of 15 mg SN, and 5 minutes after a steady state was achieved, a PRBS—calculated to give a response twice the standard deviation of the step input response—was initiated. The duration of the PRBS input was 10 minutes. The input PRBS and output were recorded, digitized, and analyzed on the Hewlett-Packard, 5451B Fourier analyzer/2100S computer system. To obtain meaningful results, the average value of both input and output was subtracted before correlations were performed.

Figure 10 depicts the mean arterial pressure response in a dog subjected to a constant-rate intravenous infusion of SN superimposed by PRBS signals. The actual PRBS input recorded over a period of 10 minutes is shown in the lower section of Figure 11, which corresponds to the recorded blood pressure response above it in the same figure. Figure 12 shows that the autocorrelation of the PRBS input is an impulse function at time zero. The cross correlation, shown at the bottom of Figure 12, between the PRBS input and BP response output thus provides the weighting function for the system as the impulse response. The computed impulse response in Figure 12 shows a 1-minute time lag and a broad peak with a maximum at 3.5–4 minutes. Similar results of another experiment carried out over 5 minutes are shown in Figure 13. In both cases the short half-life of the BP response to the drug is quite apparent. The author has found that the BP, weighting-

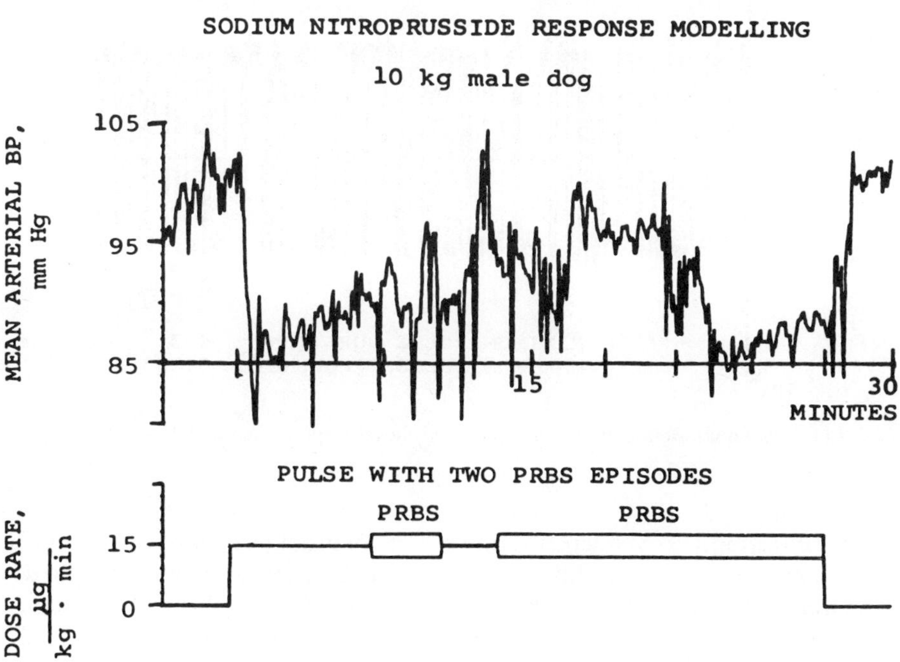

Figure 10. Sodium nitroprusside response modeling for a 10-kg male dog.

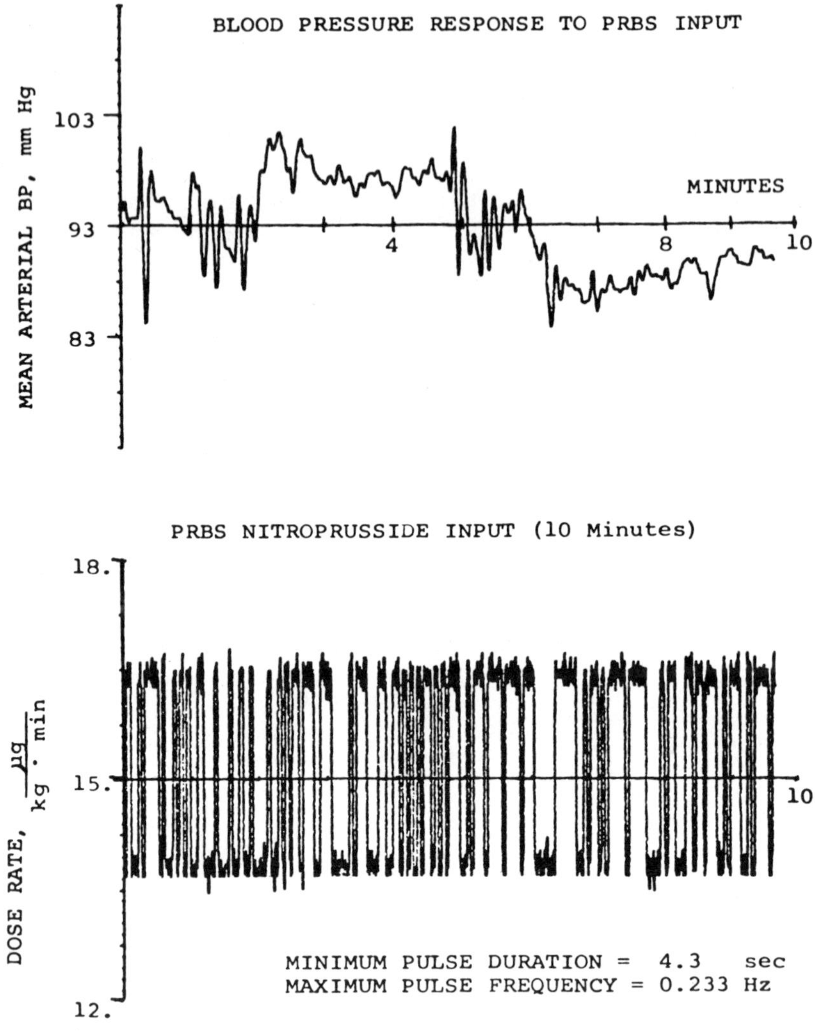

Figure 11. Pseudorandom binary signal input and the corresponding blood pressure response output.

function response to SN depends on the type of input (e.g., impulse or pulse) as well as the magnitude of the input and the duration of time it is applied. The weighting function is also hysteretic and time varying. When the system dynamics are this complex and rapid, the best characterization is obtained by RIM at any given time following the initiation of the drug's administration. This also has the advantage that the system is not appreciably disturbed

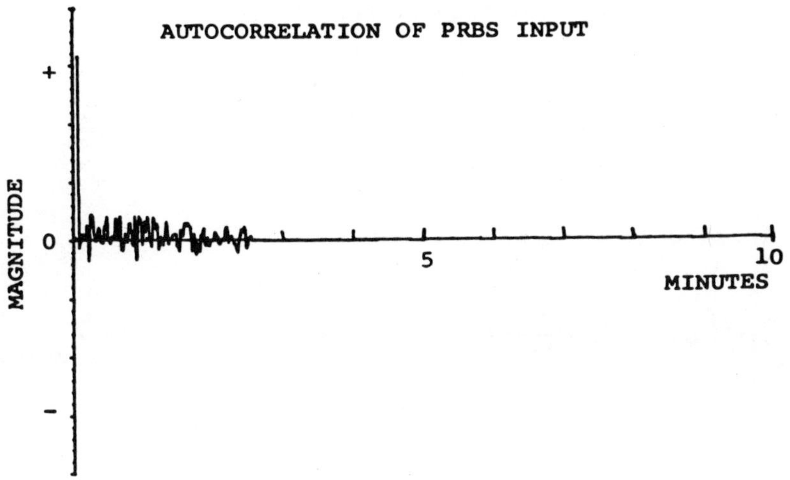

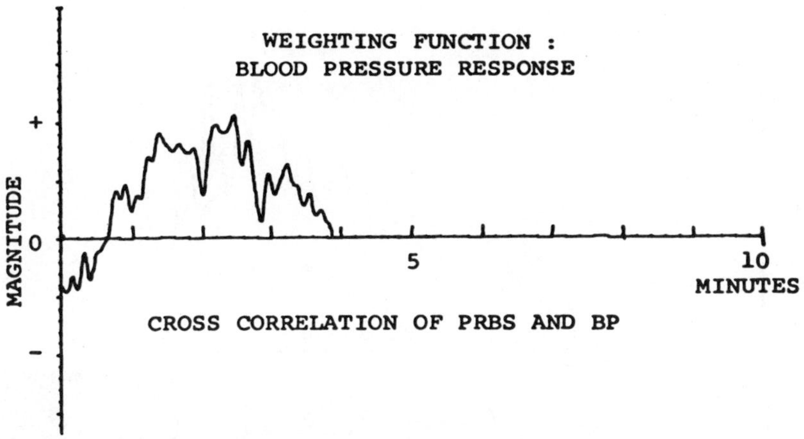

Figure 12. Autocorrelation of PRBS input and weighting function for sodium nitroprusside administered to a dog.

from its operating level while its dynamics are being identified. For practical purposes, this permits the closed-loop, feedback-controlled administration of rapid-acting drugs such as thiopental and SN to be accomplished by using an optimal adaptive control action where the controller is periodically updated from the results of reidentifying and modeling the drug-responding system's dynamics. Except for such work described by the author (13, 34), the powerful utility of RIM (36) in pharmacokinetics has not yet been realized and applied in clinical pharmacokinetics.

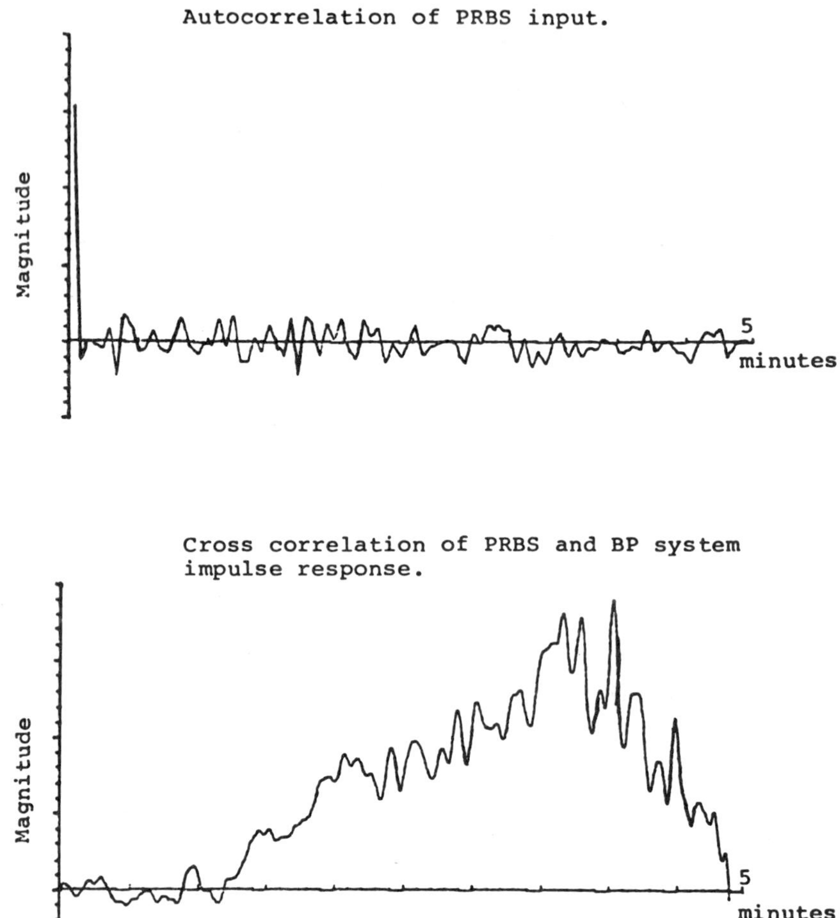

Figure 13. (*a*) Autocorrelation of PRBS input; (*b*) cross-correlation of PRBS and BP system impulse response.

4. COMPUTER CURVE FITTING AND SYSTEM IDENTIFICATION

Drug input–output response computations are of the greatest practical value to drug product development. With the use of phenomenological models, such computations can be performed entirely by numerical computational techniques without any need for expressing the input–output relationships by analytical expressions that require the estimation of equation (model) parameters; data smoothing may be all that is required in the way of curve fitting. Details of both time-domain and frequency-domain computational methods for performing the operations of convolution and deconvolution required for system identification and input–output relationships have been published by the author (19, 20). By use of such methods, the results can be obtained entirely in graphical and/or tabular form.

However, it can be of interest and use to employ methods of computerized curve fitting of data and/or systems identification to obtain the best statistical estimates of equation and model parameters. Commonly used computer programs, include SAAM, MIMIC, AUTOAN, BMDX-85, SPSS-21, and NONLIN for the performance of curvilinear, least-squares, regression, and compartment modeling. The author has developed a program called MULTIFIT that can also be used to perform weighted, least-squares, multiexponential curve fitting of experimental data. The MULTIFIT program has some advantages over most other curvilinear regression programs in that it computes its own and thus does not require initial estimates for the A and m values that appear in the resulting sum of exponentials $\sum_{i=1}^{n} A_i e^{-m_i t}$ as equation parameters. The MULTIFIT program utilizes an iterative systematized search technique that minimizes the chance of merely converging to a local minimum. However, it requires a relatively large amount of computer time for execution; the actual computer time in any particular case depends on the number of data points, the number of exponentials chosen for inclusion in the summation, and the extent to which the iterative refinement of the initial estimates of equation parameters is carried out. To conserve computer time, the MULTIFIT program can be used to provide initial estimates of parameters and then refine these values by using a less computer-time-consuming curvilinear regression program such as SPSS-21.

Initial estimates of the equation parameters can also be obtained from a pulse-testing (PLTEST) program (20) developed by the author. The PLTEST program utilizes a frequency-response method. Such methods are widely used in engineering analysis for system identification [i.e., transfer (weighting) function determination]. Traditionally, system identification by frequency response analysis is done by subjecting a system to a series of sinusoidal inputs of various frequencies. Alternatively, the system can be stimulated by injecting a known pulse input into the system. The latter method has the advantage that the system under investigation need be perturbed only a single time. In actuality, a pulse excites the system at all frequencies at once because it has a continuous frequency spectrum whereas a sine wave has only a particular frequency associated with it. Essentially, the pulse testing program takes the input pulse into, and the output data from, a system and computes their individual Fourier transforms. Using complex numbers, one can divide the Fourier-transformed output data by the Fourier-transformed input pulse to yield the transfer function of the system:

$$\frac{Y(j\omega)}{X(j\omega)}=G(j\omega)$$

The actual output from the program is in the form of frequency:amplitude ratio and the frequency–phase angle; the gain of the process is also computed and printed out.

The digital computation of the Fourier transforms is accomplished by use of a fast Fourier-transform (FFT) algorithm. A log–log plot of amplitude ratio versus frequency results in a conventional Bode diagram. Examination of the Bode diagram along with the phase-angle plot yields the transfer function of the system. Asymptotes to the curve drawn at successive slopes of 6 dB/octave are used to approximate the Bode plot. Intersections of successive asymptotes yields the parameters for the transfer function from which a multiexponential representation of the system may be obtained. The PLTEST program can be applied to identify a system responding to any input (other than a pulse) and has a provision for computing least-squares estimates of system parameters from the Bode diagram. Because this is a frequency-domain approach, it has the advantages over all time-domain curve-fitting techniques that (1) all the data points contribute to the estimation of all the system parameters and (2) no assumptions concerning the dynamics of the system's behavior need be made. For example, the order of the system (and thus the number of compartments), the existence of time delays, recycling between compartments (damped oscillations), and nonlinearities in the system's dynamics are directly indicated by the properties of the Bode diagram and need not be assumed.

REFERENCES

1. J. G. Wagner. Do you need a pharmacokinetic model, and if so, which one? *J. Pharmacokinet. Biopharm.* **3**: 457–478 (1975).
2. V. F. Smolen. Theoretical and computational basis for drug bioavailability determination using pharmacological data. II. Drug input/response relationships. *J. Pharmacokinet. Biopharm.* **4**: 355–375 (1976).
3. A. Rescigno and G. Segre. *Drug And Tracer Kinetics*, Blaisdell, Waltham, Mass., 1966, pp. 24–74.
4. V. F. Smolen. Quantitative determination of drug bioavailability and biokinetic behavior from pharmacological data for ophthalmic and oral administration of a mydriatic drug. *J. Pharm. Sci.* **60**: 354–365 (1971).
5. V. F. Smolen. Theoretical and computational basis for drug bioavailability determinations

using pharmacological data. I. General considerations and procedures. *J. Pharmacokinet. Biopharm.* **4**: 337–353 (1976).

6. V. F. Smolen, R. G. Barile, and T. G. Theophanous. Relationship between dose, effect, time, and biophasic drug levels. *J. Pharm. Sci.* **61**: 467–470 (1972).

7. V. F. Smolen, E. J. Williams, and P. B. Kuehn. Bioavailability and pharmacokinetic analysis of chlorpromazine in humans and animals using pharmacological data. *Can J. Pharm. Sci.* **10**: 95–106 (1975).

8. V. F. Smolen. Bioavailability and pharmacokinetic analysis of drug responding systems. *Ann. Rev. Pharmacol. Toxicol.* **18**: 495–523 (1978).

9. V. F. Smolen, B. D. Turrie, and W. A. Weigand. Drug input optimization: Bioavailability effected time optimal control of multiple simultaneous pharmacological effects and their interrelationships. *J. Pharm. Sci.* **61**: 1941–1952 (1972).

10. S. J. Citron. *Elements of Optimal Control*, Holt, Rinehart and Winston, New York, 1969, pp. 1–16.

11. E. Kreindler and P. E. Sarachik. On the Concepts of Controllability and Observability of Linear Systems. *IEEE Transactions on Automatic Control*, Vol. 1, Butterworths, London, 1960, pp. 481–492.

12. L. S. Pontryagin et al. *The Mathematical Theory of Optimal Processes*, Wiley-Interscience, New York, 1962.

13. V. F. Smolen. Practical Pharmacodynamic Engineering in the Design, Development, and Evaluation of Optimal Drug Products. In H. S. Bean, A. H. Backett, and J. E. Canless (eds.), *Advances In Pharmaceutical Sciences*, Vol. 5, Academic Press, London, 1981, pp. 115–198.

14. V. F. Smolen and R. J. Erb. The predictive conversion of in-vitro drug dissolution data into in-vivo drug response vs. time profiles exemplified for plasma levels of warfarin. *J. Pharm. Sci.* **66**: 297–304 (1977).

15. G. Levy. Relationship Between Pharmacological Effects and Plasma or Tissue Concentration of Drugs in Man. In D. S. Davies and B. N. C. Pritchard (eds.), *Biological Effects of Drugs in Relation to Their Plasma Concentrations*, University Park Press, Baltimore, Md., 1973, pp. 84–95.

16. G. Levy and M. Gibaldi. Pharmacokinetics of Drug Action. In A. W. Elliot, R. Okun, and R. George (eds.), *Ann. Rev. Pharmacol., Ann. Reviews Inc.*, Palo Alto, Calif., 1972, pp. 85–98.

17. V. F. Smolen, H. R. Murdock, and E. J. Williams. Bioavailability analysis of chlorpromazine from pupilometric data. *J. Pharmacol. Exp. Ther.* **195**: 404–415 (1975).

18. W. A. Weigand and A. K. Jhawar. Dose–effect and relative biophasic drug levels: Elucidation of these concepts and the illustration of their use for the determination of bioavailability, rate of absorption, and time course of pharmacological effects. *J. Pharmacokinet. Biopharm.* **4**: 67–80 (1976).

19. V. F. Smolen. A Frequency Response Method for Pharmacokinetic Model Identification. In L. Endrenyi (ed.), *Kinetic Data Analysis*, Plenum Press, New York, 1981, pp. 209–233.

20. V. F. Smolen. A Generalized Numerical Deconvolution Procedure for Computing Absolute Bioavailability–Time Profiles. In L. Endrenyi (ed.), *Kinetic Data Analysis*, Plenum Press, New York, 1981, pp. 375–389.

21. R. J. Erb. *Pharmacokinetics of the Development and Evaluation of a Prolonged Acting Drug Delivery System for the Treatment of Glaucoma*. Ph.D. thesis, Purdue University, West Lafayette, Ind., 1977.

22. D. S. Riggs. *Control Theory And Physiological Feedback Mechanisms*, Williams and Wilkins, Baltimore, Md., 1970, pp. 23–26.

23. J. A. Jacquez. *Compartmental Analysis in Biology and Medicine*, American Elsevier, New York, 1972, pp. 1–12.

24. W. A. Weigand, A. K. Jhawar, and T. J. Williams. Calculation method for the response time to step inputs for approximate dynamic models of distillation columns. *AIChE J.* **18**: 1234–1252 (1972).

25. M. Clynes. Toward a View of Man. In M. Clynes and J. H. Milsum (eds.), *Biomedical Engineering Systems*, McGraw Hill, New York, 1970, pp. 272–358.

26. D. DiBiasio, H. C. Lim, W. A. Weigand, and G. T. Tsao. Phase-plane analysis of feedback control of unstable steady states in a biological reactor. *AIChE J.* **24**: 686–692 (1978).

27. C. T. Liou, H. C. Lim, and W. A. Weigand. Sufficient condition for uniqueness and local asymptotic stability of adiabatic tubular reactors. *AIChE J.* **18**: 1079–1081 (1972).

28. C. T. Liou, H. C. Lim, and W. A. Weigand. Stability and uniqueness of a catalyst particle problem: Parameter optimization in Liapunov Functions. *AIChE J.* **19**: 321–327 (1973).

29. C. T. Liou, W. A. Weigand, and H. C. Lim. Sufficient conditions for uniqueness and local asymptotic stability for a class of distributed parameter systems: Nonadiabatic plug flow tubular reactors with recycle and feedback control. *Internatl. J. Control* **19**: 561–574 (1974).

30. C. T. Liou, H. C. Lim, and W. A. Weigand. Liapunov functional method for analysis of nonadiabatic tubular reactors with axial mixing and recycle. *Chem. Eng. Sci.* **29**: 705–711 (1974).

31. C. E. Huckaba. Biomedical engineering. *Chem. Eng.* **78**: 126 (1971).

32. R. L. Dedrick. Animal Scale-Up. In T. Teorell, R. L. Dedrick, and P. G. Condliffe (eds.), *Pharmacology And Pharmacokinetics*, Plenum Press, New York, 1972, pp. 117–145.

33. R. T. Williams. Interspecies Scaling. In T. Teorell, R. L. Dedrick, and P. G. Condliffe (eds.), *Pharmacology and Pharmacokinetics*, Plenum Press, New York, 1972, pp. 105–115.

34. V. F. Smolen, R. G. Barile, and D. Carr. Design and operation of a system for automatic feedback-controlled administration of drugs. *Med. Device Diagn. Ind.* **1**: 50–69 (1979).

35. G. R. Cooper and McGillem. *Probability Methods Of Signal And System Analysis*, Holt, Rinehart, and Winston, Chicago, 1971, p. 176.

36. P. Z. Marmarelis and V. Z. Marmarelis. *Analysis Of Physiological Systems: The White-Noise Approach*, Plenum Press, New York, 1978, pp. 131–180.

CHAPTER 3

Pharmacokinetic Analysis of Drug-Responding Systems: Drug Bioavailability Input–Response Relationship

DAVID CUTLER

The School of Pharmacy
University of London, Brunswick Square

Dr. Cutler's present address: Department of Pharmacy, University of Sydney, Sydney 2006, Australia.

CONTENTS

In mathematical modeling in pharmacokinetics two distinct objectives can be identified: (1) to facilitate investigations of the disposition of a drug and (2) to establish relationships between the drug input and the resulting response. Regarding the body as a drug-responding system, the distinction is between investigations into the structure of the system and into the behavior of the system.

Traditionally, pharmacokinetic modeling has relied on compartmental analysis. A compartment model is a proposed representation of the structure of the system in terms of the basic elements, the compartments, and relationships that describe their interconnection. For a particular drug input, solution of the equations describing the compartment model provides an expression for, say, the plasma concentration of the drug in terms of the model parameters and the mathematical description of the drug input. Thus a compartment model provides an input–response relationship (taking the plasma concentration as the system response) based on a proposed representation of the structure of the system.

The majority of applications employ linear compartment models on the supposition that the system which is modeled is a linear system. In this case a major simplification is possible in the development of input–response relationships. As shown in the following section, the required relationships can be developed on the basis of the linear property alone, without reference to any representation of the system structure. An obvious consequence of this result is that for a linear system, input–response relationships can be developed in complete ignorance of the structure of the system, apart from the property that all quantitatively important processes are linear. Another consequence is that the widespread success of compartment models in predicting responses such as drug plasma concentrations cannot be attributed to their most obvious feature, the proposed compartmentalized nature of the system, but is due solely to the linear property. The success of compartment models in this connection can be accepted as evidence that the modeled systems are linear (or approximately so) but not as evidence in favor of the proposed compartmentalized nature of the system.

The significant feature to emerge from these considerations is that for linear systems, investigations into the behavior of the system (the input–response relationships) can be regarded as being quite independent of investigations into the structure of the system. This property does not extend to nonlinear systems. For these systems, it appears to be necessary to take some account of the system structure to enable development of input–response relationships. Nonlinear systems are discussed in Chapter 4; in this chapter the analysis is confined to linear systems and to simple nonlinear systems that can be analyzed by related methods.

In general terms, an input–response relationship may be likened to a calibration curve. Once the relationship is established, it can be used to predict the drug response to a known input. The known input might be a new drug formulation or an "envisaged" formulation to be manufactured subsequently if the predicted response shows the desired features. Conversely, the input–response relationship may be used to deduce from an observed response the input that produced it. In contrast to a calibration curve, which relates individual values of the variables involved, the input–response relationships with which we are concerned relate functions of time. Consequently, their expression requires time-dependent operators rather than the single-valued functions that characterize a calibration curve. For linear systems, as shown in the following section, the time-dependent operator is a convolution integral.

The generalized input–response relationship to be derived is applied by taking particular interpretations of the terms "input" and "response." The *input* to the system is defined as the rate of delivery of the drug to the system; particular interpretations could be the rate of delivery of drug to the general circulation in an intravenous infusion or the release rate of drug from an orally administered formulation. Typical examples of a *response* would be the plasma concentration of the drug, a metabolite of the drug, or the intensity of the pharmacological effect of the drug. The choice of a suitable response may be determined by the objectives of the study or (in calculating an unknown input rate) by experimental or analytical convenience.

1. INPUT–RESPONSE RELATIONSHIP FOR A LINEAR SYSTEM

In this section the relationship between a general input and the resulting response for a linear system is derived (1). We denote by $\dot{A}(t)$ the rate of delivery of drug to the system at a particular point—say, P—at time t and by $Q(t)$ the resulting response at time t. If Q_1 is the response to the input $\dot{A}_1$ and Q_2 is the response to the input $\dot{A}_2$, the system is said to be *linear* if the response to the input $(\dot{A}_1 + \dot{A}_2)$ is $Q_1 + Q_2$. This property is often referred to as the *superposition principle*. In studying drug-responding systems it must be accepted that no system is strictly linear. At sufficiently high drug concentrations nonlinear effects will arise as a result of saturable metabolic or binding processes or ultimately as a result of solubility limitations. Implicit in the assumption of linearity is that the range of inputs considered is such that these nonlinear effects are not quantitatively significant.

We begin by considering a unit impulse input introduced at time zero at the point P and denote by $Q_\delta(t)$ the resulting response (called the *unit impulse response*) at time t. The requirements for an input that might be encountered in practice to be regarded as an impulse input is discussed subsequently; for the present, the unit impulse input may be taken to be a unit amount of drug introduced instantaneously. In general, the response $Q_\delta(t)$ may be expected to vary, depending on the time of application of the unit impulse input (say, on the time of day if a diurnal variation occurs in some factor influencing drug disposition). If this is so, the system is said to be a *time-variant system.* The analysis of such systems is discussed later; here we confine attention to *time-invariant* systems, which have the property that the unit impulse response is independent of the time of application of the unit impulse input.

If an amount of drug M is introduced at point P at time 0 as an impulse, the resulting response, by virtue of the linear property, is M times that for a unit impulse input, that is, the response is $MQ_\delta(t)$ at time t. Now consider a continuous input $\dot{A}(t)$ introduced at times $t \geqslant 0$ at point P. Over the short time interval $(T, T+dT)$ the continuous input delivers an amount $\dot{A}(T)dT$ to point P, and if the interval $(T, T+dT)$ is sufficiently short, this amount may be regarded as an impulse input. Again by virtue of the linear property, the resulting response is $\dot{A}(T)dT$ times the response to a unit impulse input. However, the input $\dot{A}(T)dT$ is introduced at time T, not time 0. The time elapsed between the introduction of this input and the observation of a response at time t is $t-T$ (for $t \geqslant T$; obviously, there is no response when $t<T$), so the quantity $\dot{A}(T)dT$ leads to a contribution $\dot{A}(T)dT\,Q_\delta(t-T)$ to the response measured at time t. Note that this result depends on the time-invariant property. For a time-variant system, the corresponding contribution to the response depends on the time T at which the amount $\dot{A}(T)dT$ is introduced as well as the elapsed time $t-T$.

The observed response $Q(t)$ due to the continuous input $\dot{A}(t)$ depends on the input over the time interval $(0, t)$. The superposition principle allows the response $Q(t)$ to be expressed (approximately) as the sum of the individual contributions over each time interval $(T, T+dT)$ for $0 \leqslant T \leqslant t$. Thus

$$Q(t) \approx \sum_{T=0}^{t} \dot{A}(T)Q_\delta(t-T)dT \tag{1}$$

As we pass to the limit $dT \to 0$, this approximate relationship becomes exact, with the sum replaced by an integral, to give

$$Q(t) = \int_0^t \dot{A}(T)Q_\delta(t-T)dT \tag{2}$$

The integral in equation 2 is called a *convolution integral.* It is often convenient to use the abbreviated notation $Q = \dot{A} * Q_\delta$, where the symbol $*$ stands for the convolution operation. An interpretation of convolution integrals in terms of areas is possible (as with ordinary integrals) (2) but is not very helpful in appreciating their physical significance. Equation 1 is perhaps most suitable for this purpose. This approximate equation shows the integral to be composed of a contribution from the input rate $\dot{A}(t)$, with the contribution of the rate at each time "weighted" according to the unit impulse response (which is a characteristic of the system) and the time $t-T$ that has elapsed since the component $\dot{A}(T)dT$ entered the system. If (as is often the case) $Q_\delta(t)$ is a decreasing function, the influence of a component $\dot{A}(T)dT$ decreases with time, more rapidly if $Q_\delta(t)$ is a rapidly decreasing function. If $Q_\delta(t)$ is a function that is initially zero and then increases to a maximum, the influence of a component $\dot{A}(T)dT$ is initially zero and then increases to a maximum. Another way of interpreting this equation is as an expression of the "aging" of the input $\dot{A}(t)$; the nature and rate of the aging process is described by $Q_\delta(t)$.

Within the limitations of the assumptions made, equation 2 summarizes concisely all the information necessary to relate the input and the response for a linear time-invariant system. In particular, all the relevant features of the system itself are expressed by the unit impulse response $Q_\delta(t)$. For example, if $Q_\delta(t)$ is known, the response $Q(t)$ for a given input $\dot{A}(t)$ can be predicted simply by evaluating the integral in equation 2 analytically or, if necessary, numerically. Less obvious is the fact that $\dot{A}(t)$ can be determined when $Q(t)$ and $Q_\delta(t)$ are known; this procedure, called *deconvolution*, is discussed in Section 6.2.

Before discussing applications of equation 2 we consider some extensions to this equation and some modifications to the derivation for more general applications. In the derivation of equation 2 the input $\dot{A}(t)$ is assumed to arise from a single source and be introduced at a single point P. In some cases it might be more reasonable to consider the input to be delivered to a specified region, rather than to a single point. Provided the unit impulse response is the same for any point within the region, equation 2 can be applied without change. This can be shown as follows.

Let $Q_\delta(r, t)$ denote the response to a unit amount of drug introduced into a volume element dr containing the point r in a region A [we do not assume $Q_\delta(r, t)$ to be measurable in practice]. Let the zero-time distribution of drug from a unit impulse input delivered to the region as a whole be such that $F(r)dr$ denotes the fraction of the unit amount of drug in the region that is present in the volume element dr containing point r. Any drug contained within this volume element at time 0 will give rise to a contribution $F(r)Q_\delta(r, t)dr$ to the total response $Q_{\delta,A}(t)$. Combination of all these contributions over the region A gives

$$Q_{\delta,A}(t) = \int_A F(r)Q_\delta(r, t)dr \tag{3}$$

where the integral is a volume integral over region A. In the event that $Q_\delta(r, t)$ is independent of r equal to $Q_\delta(t)$, we have from the last equation

$$Q_{\delta, A}(t) = Q_\delta(t) \tag{4}$$

since

$$\int_A F(r)dr = 1$$

If we now consider an input that delivers drug at the rate $\dot{A}(r, t)dr$ to the volume element dr in region A, we have

$$\int_0^t [\dot{A}(r, T)Q_\delta(r, t - T)dT]dr$$

as the contribution to the observed response $Q_A(t)$ to the input delivered to the entire region. The total response is given by the volume integral over the region A of these contributions; thus

$$Q_A(t) = \int_A \left[\int_0^t \dot{A}(r, T)Q_\delta(r, t - T)dT \right] dr \tag{5}$$

When $Q_\delta(r, t)$ is independent of r, equal to $Q_\delta(t)$, and if $\dot{A}(r, t)$ is a continuous function of r and t, the last equation becomes

$$\begin{aligned} Q_A(t) &= \int_0^t Q_\delta(t - T) \left[\int_A \dot{A}(r, T)dr \right] dT \\ &= \int_0^t \dot{A}_A(T)Q_{\delta, A}(t - T)dT \end{aligned} \tag{6}$$

where

$$\int_A \dot{A}(r, t)dr = \dot{A}_A(t)$$

is the total input to region A and $Q_{\delta, A}(t)$ is introduced from equation 4. Equation 6 has the same form as equation 2, showing that the same equation applies when the drug input is a point source or from a macroscopic region. The major assumption leading to equation 6 is that the unit impulse input $Q_\delta(r, t)$ is independent of position r in region A.

If $Q_\delta(r, t)$ is a function of position in region A, equation 6 follows with the assumption that the input $\dot{A}(r, t)$ can be written

$$\dot{A}(r, t) = \dot{A}_A(t)F(r) \tag{7}$$

where $F(r)$ is the function in equation 3 that describes the zero-time distribution of the unit impulse input. Equation 7 expresses the assumption that the zero-time distribution of the input $\dot{A}(r, t)$ is the same as that for the unit impulse input. The function $\dot{A}_A(t)$ could represent the dissolution of the drug from a solid, which is assumed to be independent of position. From equation 7

$$\int_A \dot{A}(r, t)dr = \int_A \dot{A}_A(t)F(r)dr$$
$$= \dot{A}_A(t)$$

since

$$\int_A F(r)dr = 1$$

Thus $\dot{A}_A(t)$ is the rate of delivery of drug to the region as a whole. Introduction of equation 7 into equation 5 results in

$$Q_A(t) = \int_A \left[\int_0^t \dot{A}_A(T)F(r)Q_\delta(r, t-T)dT \right] dr$$
$$= \int_0^t \dot{A}_A(T) \left[\int_A F(r)Q_\delta(r, t-T)dr \right] dT$$
$$= \int_0^t \dot{A}_A(T)Q_{\delta,A}(t-T)dT$$

by equation 3. This equation is the same as equation 6.

One situation in which the assumptions leading to equation 6 will be satisfied is when the input is delivered to a region that behaves as a compartment, as assumed when a compartment model is used.

In some cases it is convenient to consider point P or region A as the site of administration, but in other cases it is appropriate to consider the point or region to be remote from the site of administration. For example, after oral administration it is often of interest to consider the rate of delivery of drug to the general circulation. In this case a point P could be chosen in the vena cava while the site of administration is the gut. The rate $\dot{A}(t)$ in equation 2 is now the rate of delivery of the drug to the chosen point in the vena cava, following absorption of the drug from the gut and its passage through the liver. For this interpretation, it is necessary that the input delivered to point P be regarded as the sole source of drug to the system. This is because only a single source is included in the derivation of equation 2. However, with more than one source of drug, appropriate equations are readily derived with the aid of the superposition principle. Let $\dot{A}(t)$ be the input at point P, with $Q_\delta(t)$ denoting the unit impulse response, and let $\dot{A}'(t)$ be the input at a separate point P' with $Q'_\delta(t)$ denoting the response to a unit impulse input at this point. For each input, a contribution to the total response is obtained, each of the form indicated by equation 2. Addition of these contributions to give the total response $Q(t)$ yields

$$Q(t) = \int_0^t \dot{A}(T) Q_\delta(t-T)dT + \int_0^t A'(T) Q'_\delta(t-T)dT \quad (8)$$

When $Q(t)$ and $Q'_\delta(t)$ are known, this equation can be applied in the same way as equation 2. An application of this equation is discussed later in connection with the use of metabolite data in studies of oral absorption.

As noted in the derivation of this equation, equation 2 applies only for a time-invariant system. For a time-variant system, it is necessary to recognize that the unit impulse response depends on the time of application of the unit impulse. Accordingly, we write $Q_\delta(T, t-T)$ to denote the response at time t to a unit impulse input introduced at time T. The first argument, T, refers to the time of application of the unit impulse input; the second argument, $t-T$, refers to the time elapsed from the time of application of the unit impulse input to time t at which the response is noted. A continuous input $\dot{A}(t)$ delivers an amount $\dot{A}(T)dT$ over the time interval $(T, T+dT)$, which leads to the contribution to the response $Q(t)$ given by $\dot{A}(T)dT\, Q_\delta(T, t-T)$. Forming a sum analogous to that in equation 1 to represent the combined effect of all such contributions, and passing to the limit $dT \to 0$, we obtain the equation

$$Q(t) = \int_0^t \dot{A}(T) Q_\delta(T, t-T)dT \quad (9)$$

which is analogous to equation 2. The applications of equation 2 discussed in the following sections apply, with minor changes, to equation 9. The main difficulty in applying equation 9 is likely to be in specification of $Q_\delta(T, t-T)$, rather than in subsequent analysis.

2. INTEGRAL RELATIONSHIPS

In bioavailability studies it is sometimes useful to consider the total amount of drug, or the fraction of the administered dose, that enters the system. The required relationships are most easily developed by use of the relationship between the Laplace transforms of the functions in equation 2 that follows from that equation. The Laplace transform of a function $X(t)$ is given by

$$x(s) = \int_0^\infty e^{-st} X(t)dt$$

Since $e^{-st} \to 1$ as $s \to 0$, we have

$$\lim_{s \to 0} \{x(s)\} = \int_0^\infty X(t)dt \tag{10}$$

In particular, with $\dot{a}(s)$ denoting the Laplace transform of the input rate $\dot{A}(t)$, it follows that

$$\lim_{s \to 0} \{\dot{a}(s)\} = \int_0^\infty \dot{A}(t)dt$$

The integral in this equation is the total amount of drug that enters the system through the process described by the rate $\dot{A}(t)$. This is conveniently expressed in terms of the fraction F of the administered dose D that enters the system. Thus

$$\lim_{s \to 0} \{\dot{a}(s)\} = FD = \int_0^\infty \dot{A}(t)dt \tag{11}$$

The fraction F can be related to the response and the unit impulse response as follows. By a standard result of Laplace transform theory (3, 4), the convolution integral of equation 2 transforms to the product of the transforms of the functions in the integrand; thus

$$q(s) = \dot{a}(s)q_\delta(s)$$

with $q(s)$, $\dot{a}(s)$, and $q_\delta(s)$ denoting the Laplace transforms of $Q(t)$, $\dot{A}(t)$, and $Q_\delta(t)$, respectively. Applying the property expressed by equation 10, after taking $s \to 0$, we obtain

$$\lim_{s \to 0} \{q(s)\} = \lim_{s \to 0} \{\dot{a}(s)\} \lim_{s \to 0} \{q_\delta(s)\}$$

or

$$\int_0^\infty Q(t)dt = \int_0^\infty \dot{A}(t)dt \int_0^\infty Q_\delta(t)dt$$

Using equation 11, and rearranging, we have

$$F = \frac{\int_0^\infty Q(t)dt}{D \int_0^\infty Q_\delta(t)dt} \tag{12}$$

When responses $Q(t)$ and $Q_\delta(t)$ are interpreted as concentrations, equation 12 leads to the familiar area relationships for assessing the fraction of administered drug that is absorbed.

3. SEQUENTIAL PROCESSES

In absorption studies we are commonly concerned with the description of sequential processes, such as those involved in the absorption of a drug following the oral administration of a solid dosage form. In this case the release of the drug from the solid dosage form is followed by transport of the drug across the gut wall, in turn followed by passage of the drug through the liver. The overall process whereby drug presented in the solid dosage form is delivered to the general circulation is readily described in terms of the characteristics of the individual processes involved. Equations analogous to equation 2 arise.

Consider two processes, indicated by subscripts 1 and 2, arranged such that the response (or output) of process 1 serves as the input to process 2. Let $Q_{\delta,1}(t)$ be the unit impulse response of process 1 and $Q_{\delta,2}(t)$ be the unit impulse response of process 2. Following a unit impulse input to process 1, the input to process 2 is $Q_{\delta,1}(t)$; by equation 2 we have

$$Q_{\delta,12}(t)=\int_0^t Q_{\delta,1}(T)Q_{\delta,2}(t-T)dT$$

as the response of the composite system to a unit impulse input to process 1. It is convenient to use the symbol $*$ to denote the convolution operation and to write this equation as

$$Q_{\delta,12}(t)=Q_{\delta,1} * Q_{\delta,2}$$

If the output of process 2 serves as the input to a third process (subscript 3), we have

$$Q_{\delta,13}(t)=Q_{\delta,1} * Q_{\delta,2} * Q_{\delta,3}$$

as the response of the composite system of all three processes to a unit impulse input to process 1.

These relationships take a particularly simple form when expressed in terms of transfer functions (the Laplace transforms of the unit impulse responses). The last equation gives

$$q_{\delta,13}(s)=q_{\delta,1}(s)q_{\delta,2}(s)q_{\delta,3}(s)$$

where the lowercase letters denote the Laplace transforms of the corresponding terms of the previous equation. This relationship immediately extends to any number of sequential processes to give

$$q_{\delta,1n}(s)=q_{\delta,1}(s)q_{\delta,2}(s)\cdots q_{\delta,n}(s) \tag{13}$$

or

$$Q_{\delta,1n}(t)=Q_{\delta,1} * Q_{\delta,2} * \cdots * Q_{\delta,n} \tag{14}$$

The response $Q(t)$ to an input $\dot{A}(t)$ to process 1 is given by

$$Q(t) = \dot{A} * Q_{\delta,1n}$$

or

$$q(s) = \dot{a}(s) q_{\delta,1n}(s)$$

If one or more of the processes in a sequence is rapidly responding, the corresponding response—say, $Q_{\delta,k}$—approximates an impulse of magnitude F_k, where

$$F_k = \int_0^{\infty} Q_{\delta,k}(t)dt$$

is the fraction of drug not eliminated by process k. Equation 14 becomes

$$Q_{\delta,1n}(t) = F_k Q_{\delta,1} * Q_{\delta,2} * \cdots * Q_{\delta,k-1} * Q_{\delta,k+1} * \cdots * Q_{\delta,n}$$

The term $Q_{\delta,k}$ does not appear in this expression, and the overall process is dominated by the slower or rate-limiting steps. When a single step in a sequence is much slower than the others, the time dependence of the overall process will be dominated by this terms with the other terms each contributing a factor such as F_k defined above.

4. DETERMINATION OF UNIT IMPULSE RESPONSE

In the derivation of equation 2 the unit impulse input used to produce the response $Q_\delta(t)$ was defined as a unit amount of drug introduced "instantaneously." The unit impulse function may be defined more formally as a function $\delta(t)$ with the properties

$$\int_{t_1}^{t_2} \delta(t)dt = 1 \quad \text{for} \quad t_1 < t < t_2$$

and

$$\delta(t) = 0 \quad \text{for} \quad t \neq 0$$

These properties are, of course, not attainable with a real drug input. The practical requirements for an input to be regarded as an adequate approximation to an impulse input can be judged from equation 2. Consider an input $\dot{A}(t)$ that begins at time zero and decreases rapidly to zero, such that

$$\dot{A}(t) = 0 \quad \text{for} \quad t > t_0$$

for some suitably short time t_0. Equation 2 gives

$$Q(t)=\int_0^t \dot{A}(T)Q_\delta(t-T)dT$$

$$=\int_0^{t_0} \dot{A}(T)Q_\delta(t-T)dT$$

In this integral $0 \leqslant T \leqslant t_0$ and for sufficiently small t_0, we have

$$Q_\delta(t-T) \simeq Q_\delta(t) \quad \text{for} \quad t \gg t_0$$

That is, $Q_\delta(t)$ is approximately constant over the time interval $(t-t_0, t)$. When this is the case,

$$Q(t) \simeq Q_\delta(t) \int_0^{t_0} \dot{A}(T)dT$$

$$\simeq Q_\delta(t) \quad \text{for} \quad t \gg t_0$$

if the input delivers a unit amount of drug, since

$$\int_0^{t_0} \dot{A}(T)dT = 1$$

Consequently, a rapidly decreasing input produces a response that approximates a unit impulse response when the time interval $(0, t_0)$ over which the input takes nonzero values is sufficiently short that $Q_\delta(t)$ is approximately constant over a time interval of this duration. The values $Q_\delta(t)$ and t_0 should also be such that there is some time $t_1 \gg t_0$ for which the uncertainty in $Q_\delta(t)$ over the interval $(0, t_1)$ is not of practical importance, such as if t_1 were less than the first sample time judged to be suitable following a "genuine" impulse input. The value $Q_\delta(t)$ over $(0, t_1)$ might also be found by extrapolation by use of the measured $Q_\delta(t)$ for $t > t_1$.

An alternative approach to the calculation of $Q_\delta(t)$ is to determine the response $Q(t)$ following a known input $\dot{A}(t)$ and to evaluate $Q_\delta(t)$ by a deconvolution procedure. This procedure is the same as that required to evaluate $\dot{A}(t)$ when $Q_\delta(t)$ is known, which may be seen by writing equation 2 in the form

$$Q(t)=\int_0^t \dot{A}(t-\tau)Q_\delta(\tau)d\tau$$

which follows on the substitution $\tau = t - T$; the roles of $\dot{A}(t)$ and $Q_\delta(t)$ are now reversed. As a special case of the use of a known input, suppose that $\dot{A}(t)$ is constant, equal to R_0, over the period of the study. Then

$$Q(t)=R_0 \int_0^t Q_\delta(\tau)d\tau$$

or

$$Q_\delta(t) = \frac{dQ/dt}{R_0}$$

Thus $Q_\delta(t)$ can be obtained by differentiating with respect to time the response $Q(t)$ following the constant rate input R_0.

When equation 2 is used to determine an unknown input rate, two studies are necessary, one to determine $Q(t)$ and the other to determine $Q_\delta(t)$. The assumption that $Q_\delta(t)$ is time invariant is more likely to apply when both studies are conducted in the same subject, under the same test conditions. One approach that avoids the possibility that $Q_\delta(t)$ changes between studies is to conduct both studies simultaneously, with $Q_\delta(t)$ determined using an isotopically labeled dose of the drug.

5. APPLICATIONS

Various applications of the equations derived in the preceding sections follow when the generalized input and generalized response are given particular interpretations. These applications fall into one of two classes, either the prediction of the response for a known input or the calculation of the input rate from a measurement of the response following an input.

5.1 Prediction of the Response

The prediction of the response following a known input $\dot{A}(t)$ is achieved simply by evaluating, analytically or numerically, the integral in equation 2. This evaluation requires an analytical or numerical expression for the unit impulse response $Q_\delta(t)$. If the known input were an intravenous infusion, for example, the appropriate $Q_\delta(t)$ would be the response to a unit dose intravenous injection delivered as a bolus. If the input $\dot{A}(t)$ represented the in-vivo release rate of drug from a solid dosage form into the gut fluids, a unit dose oral solution (assumed to deliver the drug instantaneously to the gut fluids) would be the appropriate input to generate $Q_\delta(t)$. The choice of a suitable response is determined by the particular feature of the system that is of interest. Often $Q(t)$ and $Q_\delta(t)$ will be chosen as plasma concentrations of the drug. However, other choices will be appropriate in particular cases. For example, if the drug is used to treat a urinary tract infection, $Q(t)$ and $Q_\delta(t)$ could be chosen as the urinary concentration of the drug or of an active metabolite (or, say, a linear combination of the drug and metabolite concentrations to reflect their relative activities).

This type of prediction has been traditionally performed with the aid of a compartment model. To illustrate the connection between the present approach and that provided by a compartment model, we consider the case of a first-order absorption process, with

$$\dot{A}(t)=k_aFDe^{-k_at} \tag{15}$$

where k_a is the first-order rate constant and F is the fraction of the administered dose D that is absorbed. Following a unit dose rapid intravenous injection, a compartment model can be considered when the concentration $C_\delta(t)$ follows a polyexponential expression, say,

$$C_\delta(t)=\sum_{i=1}^{n} A_ie^{-m_it} \tag{16}$$

where the A_i and m_i are constants. The concentration $C(t)$ following the first-order input is obtained by evaluating the integral in equation 2, with $\dot{A}(t)$ given by equation 15 and $Q_\delta(t)=C_\delta(t)$ given by equation 16:

$$C(t)=k_aFD\left[\left(\sum_{i=1}^{n}\frac{A_i}{k_a-m_i}\right)e^{-m_it}+\left(\sum_{i=1}^{n}\frac{A_i}{m_i-k_a}\right)e^{-k_at}\right] \tag{17}$$

The use of this equation involves determination of the parameters A_i and m_i by fitting equation 16 to the concentration–time data after the bolus intravenous injection, followed by evaluation of equation 17 by use of the values of k_a, F, and D that characterize the known input. The corresponding approach with a compartment model is to derive from the parameters A_i and m_i, obtained by fitting equation 17 to the concentration–time data after the bolus intravenous injection, the parameters that characterize the compartment model. The differential equations describing the model, with the input given by equation 15, are then solved [e.g., by the method presented by Benet (5)] to give an expression for $C(t)$ of the same form as equation 17, with the parameters of the compartment model appearing instead of the parameters A_i and m_i. However, the compartment parameters appear in combinations that can be reduced to give the A_i and m_i from which they are originally derived. Thus the calculation of the model parameters is superfluous in the expression of the input–response relationship. The final expression is independent of these values, thus indicating that the compartment model is being used in this calculation as a mathematical device for handling the linear property. The direct calculation of equation 17 is much simpler.

The advantages of using equation 2 rather than the compartment approach are greater when nonexponential functions are involved. For an arbitrary input, the differential equations describing the compartment model might need to be solved numerically. Numerical evaluation of the integral of equation 2 is more straightforward. For a compartment model, the representation of $C_\delta(t)$ is restricted to a polyexponential expression of the form of equation 16. Alternatives that might appear more reasonable with a particular data set are precluded when the compartment approach is used, but any convenient function may be used in the numerical evaluation of equation 2.

Time-variant linear systems can be treated in the same way, with equation 9 providing the input–response relationship. When the time-varying unit impulse response $Q_\delta(T, t-T)$ is known, the response $Q(t)$ for a known input $\dot{A}(t)$ is obtained simply by evaluating (numerically if necessary) the integral in equation 9.

5.2 Calculation of In-Vivo Input Rates

When the unit impulse response $Q_\delta(t)$ is known, measurement of the response $Q(t)$ following an input $\dot{A}(t)$ allows calculation of $\dot{A}(t)$. This procedure, which is the "inverse" of the convolution operation, is called *deconvolution*. The following section is concerned with numerical procedures that can be used to perform the deconvolution operation. This section presents some applications of the general approach.

In bioavailability studies the absorption rate is usually interpreted to mean the rate of delivery of the drug to the general circulation following the administration of a dosage form. For this interpretation, we apply equation 2 with point P [the point at which the input $\dot{A}(t)$ is applied] as a point in the vena cava. The term $\dot{A}(t)$ then refers to the rate of delivery of drug to this point following, say, oral dosing with the formulation to be tested. The validity of equation 2 now requires that the unit impulse input used to produce the impulse response $Q_\delta(t)$ be applied to the same point P in the vena cava. In practice, a rapid intravenous bolus dose is administered in a peripheral vein; the validity of equation 2, for the present case, relies on the assumption that the dose administered in a peripheral vein is delivered, as a bolus, with negligible delay and negligible loss of drug, to the chosen point in the vena cava.

This interpretation of the input rate $\dot{A}(t)$ as the rate of delivery of drug to the general circulation arises as a consequence of the unit impulse input used to produce the impulse response $Q_\delta(t)$. With the same physical input (the drug formulation administered orally), a different interpretation of the input $\dot{A}(t)$ follows if the unit impulse input used to produce $Q_\delta(t)$ is a bolus input into the portal vein. The value $\dot{A}(t)$ is now the rate of delivery of drug into the portal vein after oral administration of the formulation.

Yet another interpretation of $\dot{A}(t)$ follows if $Q_\delta(t)$ is the response to a unit dose oral solution (equation 6, for a nonpoint source, would be appropriate here). In this case $\dot{A}(t)$ is the in-vivo release rate from the drug formulation. Thus, by appropriate choice of the unit impulse input, different aspects of the release or absorption of a formulation can be studied.

In applying equation 2 (or the related equations 6 and 9) to the prediction of the response, the response is determined by the aspect of the system that is of interest. In calculating an in-vivo input rate, the response on which this calculation is based can be chosen for computational or experimental convenience. The major requirement of a suitable response is that it be linearly related to the input to be determined.

The most common choice of a response is the plasma concentration of the administered drug. In equation 2, $Q_\delta(t)$ is the plasma concentration of the drug following the unit impulse input and $Q(t)$ is the plasma concentration of the drug following the input to be determined. Whole blood or free plasma concentrations could be used in the same way.

With the response interpreted as the plasma concentration of the drug, the integral relationship of equation 12 becomes

$$F = \frac{AUC}{D \cdot AUC_\delta}$$

where AUC_δ is the area under the plasma concentration–time curve after the unit impulse input and AUC is the area under the plasma concentration–time curve following the input to be determined. This is the familiar area ratio method of determining the extent of absorption.

The urinary excretion rate of the unchanged drug can also be used in applying equation 2, with $Q(t)$ the urinary excretion rate of unchanged drug following the input $\dot{A}(t)$ and $Q_\delta(t)$ the urinary excretion rate following the unit impulse input. Equation 2 could equally well be applied, with the same data, by using cumulative amounts of drug excreted unchanged in the urine. (If excretion rates are linearly related to the input, so are their integrals, the cumulative amounts excreted.) This approach has the advantage of not requiring calculation of the excretion rates from the raw data. Application of equation 12 gives

$$F = \frac{A_u(\infty)}{D \cdot A_{\delta,u}(\infty)}$$

where $A_{\delta,u}(\infty)$ is the total amount of drug excreted in the urine unchanged after the unit impulse dose and $A_u(\infty)$ is the total amount of drug excreted in the urine unchanged after the input $\dot{A}(t)$.

Measurement of drug concentrations in saliva provides another possible means of estimating input rates. Again, equation 2 provides the required relationship with $Q(t)$ and $Q_\delta(t)$ interpreted as the drug concentration in saliva. This use of salivary data does not require that a relationship be established between the drug concentration in plasma and saliva. As in other applications, the important property is the linear relationship between the measured quantity and the drug input.

Equation 2 can also be applied with the responses $Q(t)$ and $Q_\delta(t)$ interpreted as the concentration of a metabolite of the drug (say, in plasma or saliva) or the urinary excretion rate of the metabolite. In this application the assumption in the derivation of equation 2 that the input $\dot{A}(t)$ be the sole cause of the measured response may be of practical importance. Suppose that $\dot{A}(t)$ is interpreted as the rate of delivery of the unchanged drug to the general circulation, with $Q_\delta(t)$ the plasma concentration of a metabolite in the plasma following a unit dose intravenous bolus injection and $Q(t)$ the plasma concentration of the metabolite after the test dose. If the measured metabolite is formed in significant quantities in the gut, or during the first pass through the liver, the response $Q(t)$ must be regarded as the consequence of two separate inputs. One, due to the input $\dot{A}(t)$ arises as the parent drug that reaches the general circulation intact is converted subsequently to the measured metabolite; this contribution to the response is given by equation 2 as $\dot{A} * Q$. The second contribution arises as the metabolite that is formed in the gut, or on the first pass through the liver, itself enters the general circulation. No provision is made for this contribution in equation 2. Instead, we can use equation 8, with, in addition to $\dot{A}(t)$ and $Q(t)$ defined as above, $\dot{A}'(t)$ the rate of entry of metabolite into the general circulation and $Q'(t)$ the response (plasma concentration of metabolite) to a unit impulse input of the metabolite to the general circulation. In principle, equation 8 could be analyzed by the numerical deconvolution techniques discussed in the following section [say, by assuming particular expressions for $\dot{A}(t)$ and $\dot{A}'(t)$], but in practice some simplification is likely to be necessary. For example, suppose that the metabolite is formed on the first pass through the liver and that $\dot{A}'(t)$ can be attributed solely to this source. Further, suppose that the rate-limiting step in formation of the metabolite on the first pass is the rate of delivery of unchanged drug to the liver and that the approximation

$$\dot{A}'(t) = E_m \dot{A}(t)$$

can be made, with E_m denoting the fraction of the unchanged drug entering the liver that is converted to the measured metabolite. Equation 8 becomes

$$Q(t) = \int_0^t \dot{A}(T) Q_\delta(t-T)\,dT + \int_0^t E_m \dot{A}(T) Q'_\delta(t-T)\,dT$$

or

$$Q(t) = \int_0^t \dot{A}(T) Q_{\delta,\text{eff}}(t-T)\,dT \qquad (18)$$

where

$$Q_{\delta,\text{eff}}(t) = Q_\delta(t) + E_m Q'_\delta(t)$$

may be regarded as the "effective" unit impulse response. If E_m can be evaluated by other means, $Q_{\delta,\mathrm{eff}}(t)$ can be calculated from data on $Q_\delta(t)$ and $Q'_\delta(t)$, and the application of equation 18 is the same as that of equation 2.

If an oral solution dose is the unit impulse input used to generate $Q_\delta(t)$, with $\dot{A}(t)$ interpreted as the in-vivo release rate following an oral formulation, the need to consider more than one source of metabolite does not arise. Regardless of the subsequent fate of the released drug, $\dot{A}(t)$ can be regarded as the sole input. A process such as first-pass metabolism is accounted for by the unit impulse response $Q_\delta(t)$.

In many cases equation 2 can be applied to data arising from a nonspecific assay, such as one that fails to distinguish between the parent drug and its metabolites. The important property is that the response (here, a numerical value arising from the assay) be linearly related to the input. If the parent drug and the individual metabolites have this property, the same property will apply to a result from a nonspecific assay. However, if the assay also measures a metabolite that is formed in the gut, or during the first pass through the liver, the limitation discussed above, in connection with the use of metabolite data, will apply. This restriction does not apply when in-vivo release rates are determined with the aid of an oral solution reference dose.

Another application of equation 2 follows when the response is interpreted as the intensity of the pharmacological effect of the drug. When the intensity of the pharmacological effect is linearly related to the drug input, this application is the same as those already described, with $Q(t)$ and $Q_\delta(t)$ appropriately interpreted. However, with pharmacological data, nonlinear relationships are likely to occur. A procedure for treating data of this type has been developed by Smolen; this topic is discussed in Chapter 2.

6. NUMERICAL METHODS

For application of the methods discussed in the foregoing sections, numerical techniques are needed for evaluating convolution integrals and performing the deconvolution operation.

6.1 Evaluation of Convolution Integrals

Here we consider techniques for evaluating integrals of the form of equation 2 when the functions $\dot{A}(t)$ and $Q_\delta(t)$ are "known." Generally, $\dot{A}(t)$ will be given as an analytical function (but may be given numerically in some cases), whereas $Q_\delta(t)$ will generally be available from experimental data in the form of values $Q_\delta(t_i)$ at various times t_i.

One approach is to fit the $Q_\delta(t_i)$, t_i data to a function that allows the integral to be evaluated analytically for the particular function representing

$\dot{A}(t)$. An example of this approach is given by equation 17 with $Q_\delta(t)$ a polyexponential expression and $\dot{A}(t)$ representing a first-order input. Corresponding expressions could be derived for particular input functions with $Q_\delta(t)$ represented by polynomials or cubic splines.

A simple alternative approach is to use the analytical expressions for $\dot{A}(t)$ and $Q_\delta(t)$ to generate products $\dot{A}(T)Q_\delta(t-T)$ at preselected times $T=0, t_1, t_2, \cdots, t_n$, where $t_n = t$. With the use of these values the integral can then be evaluated by assuming the product $\dot{A}(T)Q_\delta(t-T)$ to vary linearly between the evaluated points, that is, by application of the trapezoid rule to the product $\dot{A}(T)Q_\delta(t-T)$. Provided the time intervals (t_i, t_{i+1}) are sufficiently short, there is no significant loss of accuracy in using this procedure (bearing in mind the level of accuracy required in pharmacokinetic calculations). The main advantage of this approach is simplicity of programming. Inclusion of different functions $\dot{A}(t)$ and $Q_\delta(t)$ requires simply routines to evaluate $\dot{A}(t_i)$ and $Q_\delta(t_n - t_i)$ at the required times t_i.

6.2 Numerical Deconvolution

Many methods for numerical deconvolution have been proposed. A comparative study of a number of methods has been conducted by Gamel et al. (6). Most of the methods they examined performed well on error-free data but were found to be very sensitive to data error. Problems due to data error are also referred to by Benet and Chiang (7), who applied a number of methods to pharmacokinetic data.

Most applications of numerical deconvolution to pharmacokinetic data have used methods of approximation that we refer to collectively here as *finite difference* methods (2, 7, 8). These methods involve rearrangement of equation 2,

$$Q(t_n) = \int_0^{t_n} \dot{A}(T)Q_\delta(t_n - T)dT$$

with $t = t_n$, to give

$$\int_{t_{n-1}}^{t_n} \dot{A}(T)Q_\delta(t_n - T)dT = Q(t_n) - \int_0^{t_{n-1}} \dot{A}(T)Q_\delta(t_n - T)dT$$

where $t_{n-1} < t_n$ is chosen so that a suitable approximation for $\dot{A}(t)$ can be employed over the time interval (t_{n-1}, t_n). As an example, suppose that $\dot{A}(t)$ is taken to be constant over the interval (t_{n-1}, t_n), equal to $\dot{A}_n$. The last equation gives

$$\dot{A}_n = \frac{Q(t_n) - \int_0^{t_{n-1}} \dot{A}(T)Q_\delta(t_n - T)dT}{\int_{t_{n-1}}^{t_n} Q_\delta(t_n - T)dT} \tag{19}$$

With $Q(t_n)$ known from experimental data (perhaps with the aid of an interpolation procedure) and a suitable representation for $Q_\delta(t)$ over the interval $(0, t_n)$, derived from the data following the impulse input, this equation expresses $\dot{A}_n$ in terms of the approximation for $\dot{A}(t)$ already derived over the interval $(0, t_{n-1})$. With

$$\dot{A}_1 = \frac{Q(t_1)}{\int_0^{t_1} Q_\delta(t_1 - T)dT} \tag{20}$$

we have a recurrence relationship for $\dot{A}_n$. Different variants of this method will arise when different methods are used to evaluate the integrals that appear in equations 19 and 20.

Alternative methods can be developed by use of different approximations for $\dot{A}(t)$ over the intervals (t_{n-1}, t_n). For example, in a method proposed by Chiou (9), $\dot{A}(t)$ is approximated by an impulse function over each time interval.

These methods have a common defect, namely, that the error in $\dot{A}(t)$ at any particular stage of the calculation accumulates as the calculation proceeds with estimates of $\dot{A}(t)$ for subsequent intervals. Furthermore, estimates of $\dot{A}(t)$ at each stage depend heavily on $Q_\delta(t)$ near $t=0$; in equation 19 the denominator is

$$\int_{t_{n-1}}^{t_n} Q_\delta(t_n - T)dT = \int_0^{t_n - t_{n-1}} Q_\delta(\tau)d\tau$$

The value of this integral depends on $Q_\delta(t)$ over the interval $(0, t_n - t_{n-1})$, perhaps represented by only a single data point.

More stable to data error are the least-squares methods (10, 11) that base the approximation for $\dot{A}(t)$ over the entire time range spanned by the data. The basis for the least-squares approach follows from a recognition of the fact that the only means of judging whether a particular approximation for $\dot{A}(t)$ is satisfactory is to compare the original response data $Q(t_n)$ with that predicted by the approximation for $\dot{A}(t)$. By the least-squares criterion, we choose the input function that minimizes the weighted sum of squares

$$S = \sum_{r=1}^{m} w_r[Q(t_r) - \hat{Q}(t_r)]^2 \tag{21}$$

where $Q(t_r)$ is the observed value of the response at time t_r $(r = 1, \ldots, m)$ and $\hat{Q}(t_r)$ is the predicted value of the response at time t_r; w_r determines the relative weight attached to a deviation at time t_r. If $\hat{\dot{A}}(t)$ denotes a particular approximation to the input function $\dot{A}(t)$, $\hat{Q}(t_r)$ is obtained by evaluating equation 2 at time t_r:

$$\hat{Q}(t_r) = \int_0^{t_r} \hat{\dot{A}}(T) Q_\delta(t_r - T)dT \tag{22}$$

Combination of equations 21 and 22 gives

$$S=\sum_{r=1}^{m} w_r\left[Q(t_r)-\int_0^{t_r}\hat{A}(T)Q_\delta(t_r-T)dT\right]^2 \tag{23}$$

The "best" approximation $\hat{A}(t)$ is chosen to be the one that minimizes S. The choice of the best approximation $\hat{A}(t)$ is made from a preselected class of functions. Suppose that $\hat{A}(t)$ can be expressed as an explicit function of time t and parameters θ_i, $i=1, \ldots, k$; say,

$$\hat{A}(t)=g(t, \theta_1, \ldots, \theta_k) \tag{24}$$

When this expression for $\hat{A}(t)$ is introduced into equation 23, an expression is obtained for S, after evaluating the integral, which is a function of the parameters θ_i, say,

$$S=U(\theta_1, \ldots, \theta_k) \tag{25}$$

Regarding S as a function of the parameters θ_i allows the use of a standard function minimization routine. The minimizing values of the parameters are introduced into equation 24 to give the required approximation $\hat{A}(t)$, which minimizes S.

In some cases equation 25 may represent an explicit expression for S in terms of the parameters θ_i. For example, if $Q_\delta(t)$ is expressed as a polyexponential function, as in equation 16, and with $\hat{A}(t)$ given by equation 15 (which specifies the class of functions as those representing a first-order input), the predicted response has the form given by equation 17. Equation 25 takes the form

$$S=\sum_{r=1}^{m} w_r\left[Q(t_r)-k_aFD\left\{\sum_{i=1}^{n}\frac{A_ie^{-m_it_r}}{k_a-m_i}+\left(\sum_{i=1}^{n}\frac{A_i}{m_i-k_a}\right)e^{-k_at_r}\right\}\right]^2$$

With A_i and m_i fixed, this equation expresses S as a function of the parameters k_a and F that are to be adjusted to find the minimum S. The minimizing values of k_a and F may then be used to construct the approximation $\hat{A}(t)$.

In other cases it might not be possible to obtain explicit expressions for S in terms of the parameters involved if the integral in equation 23 cannot be evaluated analytically. In these cases the integral can be evaluated numerically. In terms of a computer implementation, this method involves coding a routine for numerical integration to replace a routine that evaluates the explicit expression in conventional function minimization; otherwise the procedure is identical. Numerical examples are given by Cutler (10).

In studies using simulated data with added noise, with input functions following first-order kinetics and the cube-root dissolution law, the least-squares method has been shown to be stable to data error and to yield parameter estimates with an error of the same order of magnitude as the error in the data.

The use of this approach requires prior specification of the mathematical form of the input function. This specification might follow from theoretical considerations (perhaps a detailed model of the process of absorption, or release of drug from a dosage form) or from previous experience with similar cases. Alternatively, a mathematical form for the input function might be suggested by investigations with the same set of data by using another method. For example, the finite-difference methods might be used to indicate a suitable function. Another approach is to use the least-squares method with the input function approximated by a polynomial function of time. Polynomials are sufficiently flexible to give a reasonable approximation to a wide range of functions. Furthermore, it has been shown with simulated data that a polynomial may indicate the correct general form of the input function even if an adequate polynomial approximation is not possible. This has been shown for a rectangular input function, which cannot be adequately approximated by a polynomial of moderate degree (11).

In principle, a polynomial approximation can be developed by introducing in equation 24 the required polynomial expression, followed by minimization of equation 25 to determine the parameter values. As with curve fitting with polynomials, this procedure leads to a set of ill-conditioned equations (6). An alternative procedure, using orthogonal functions, has been developed by Cutler (11) that avoids the ill-conditioning problem. The procedure is related to the procedure of fitting orthogonal polynomials to experimental data (12).

The approximation $\hat{A}(t)$ is written in the form

$$\hat{A}_n(t) = \sum_{i=1}^{n} a_i g_i(t) \tag{26}$$

where the a_i are constants and the $g_i(t)$ are prescribed functions defined by the recurrence relationship

$$g_1(t) = 1$$

$$g_{i+1}(t) = t g_i(t) - \sum_{k=1}^{i} b_{i,k} g_k(t) \quad \text{for} \quad i = 1, 2, \ldots, n-1 \tag{27}$$

where the $b_{i,k}$ are constants. In equation 26 we write $\hat{A}_n(t)$ in place of $\hat{A}(t)$ to indicate that n terms are used to represent the input function, which, by the recurrence relationship in equation 27, leads to a polynomial of degree $n-1$.

If we write

$$Y_i(t) = \int_0^t g_i(T) Q_\delta(t-T) dT \tag{28}$$

and

$$V_i(t) = \int_0^t T g_i(T) Q_\delta(t-T)\,dT \tag{29}$$

the recurrence relation 27 gives, after multiplying by $Q_\delta(t-T)$ and integrating,

$$Y_1(t) = \int_0^t Q_\delta(T)\,dT$$

and

$$Y_{i+1}(t) = V_i(t) - \sum_{k=1}^{i} b_{i,k} Y_k(t) \quad \text{for} \quad i = 1, 2, \ldots, n-1 \tag{30}$$

We now select the constants $b_{i,k}$ such that the $Y_i(t)$ form an orthogonal set of functions for the given data set. The $Y_i(t)$ form an orthogonal set of functions if

$$\sum_{r=1}^{m} w_r Y_i(t_r) Y_j(t_r) = 0 \quad \text{for} \quad i \neq j$$

Evaluating equation 30 at times $t = t_r$; multiplying through by $w_r Y_s(t_r)$, with $s = 1, 2, \ldots, i$; and summing over the data, we obtain

$$\begin{aligned}\sum_{r=1}^{m} w_r Y_{i+1}(t_r) Y_s(t_r) &= \sum_{r=1}^{m} w_r V_i(t_r) Y_s(t_r) - \sum_{r=1}^{m} w_r Y_s(t_r) \sum_{k=1}^{i} b_{i,k} Y_k(t_r) \\ &= \sum_{r=1}^{m} w_r V_i(t_r) Y_s(t_r) - \sum_{k=1}^{i} b_{i,k} \sum_{r=1}^{m} w_r Y_k(t_r) Y_s(t_r)\end{aligned} \tag{31}$$

If the first i of the $Y_k(t)$ are orthogonal,

$$\sum_{r=1}^{m} w_r Y_k(t_r) Y_s(t_r) = 0 \quad \text{for} \quad k \neq s; \quad k, s = 1, \ldots, i$$

and equation 31 becomes

$$\sum_{r=1}^{m} w_r Y_{i+1}(t_r) Y_k(t_r) = \sum_{r=1}^{m} w_r V_i(t_r) Y_k(t_r) - b_{i,k} \sum_{r=1}^{m} w_r Y_k(t_r)^2 \quad \text{for} \quad k = 1, \ldots, i$$

Consequently, when

$$b_{i,k} = \frac{\sum_{r=1}^{m} w_r V_i(t_r) Y_k(t_r)}{\sum_{r=1}^{m} w_r Y_k(t_r)^2} \quad \text{for} \quad k = 1, \ldots, i \tag{32}$$

$Y_{i+1}(t)$ is orthogonal to $Y_1(t)$, $Y_2(t), \ldots,$ and $Y_i(t)$, provided the first i terms are orthogonal. For $i, k = 1$, equation 32 ensures that $Y_1(t)$ and $Y_2(t)$ are orthgonal.

Consequently, the entire set of functions $Y_i(t)$ are orthogonal with the constants $b_{i,k}$ given by equation 32. The same constants, through equation 27, generate the $g_i(t)$ that are used in equation 26 to represent the input function.

It remains to determine the constants a_i in equation 26, to minimize the weighted sum of squares in equation 23. Introducing equation 26 into equation 23, and using equation 28, we obtain

$$S=\sum_{r=1}^{m} w_r\left[Q(t_r)-\sum_{i=1}^{n} a_i Y_i(t_r)\right]^2 \tag{33}$$

Differentiation with respect to a_k and setting $\partial S/\partial a_k=0, k=1,\ldots,n$ gives

$$\sum_{r=1}^{m} w_r Q(t_r)Y_k(t_r)=\sum_{r=1}^{m} w_r \sum_{i=1}^{n} a_i Y_i(t_r)Y_k(t_r)=\sum_{i=1}^{n} a_i \sum_{r=1}^{m} w_r Y_i(t_r)Y_k(t_r) \tag{34}$$

At this point the benefit of generating the orthogonal functions $Y_i(t)$ becomes apparent. Since

$$\sum_{r=1}^{m} w_r Y_i(t_r)Y_k(t_r)=0 \quad \text{for} \quad i\neq k$$

by virtue of the orthogonality condition, the term on the right of equation 34 reduces to

$$a_k \sum_{r=1}^{m} w_r Y_k(t_r)^2$$

and a_k is given by the single division

$$a_k=\frac{\sum_{r=1}^{m} w_r Q(t_r)Y_k(t_r)}{\sum_{r=1}^{m} w_r Y_k(t_r)^2}$$

for $k=1,\ldots,n$. The values of these constants are introduced into equation 26 to give the desired approximation $\dot{A}_n(t)$.

In equation 26 the number of terms n is not generally known beforehand, and a suitable value for n must be determined as the calculation proceeds. This can be judged by calculating the residual mean square

$$\sigma_n^2=\frac{S_n}{m-n}$$

where S_n is the value of the weighted sum of squares S in equation 33 when n terms are used (when the polynomial has degree $n-1$) and m is the number of data points. In ideal cases, σ_n^2 decreases with increasing n until a plateau is reached and then increases. The first value of n on the plateau is a suitable choice. In "nonideal" cases, with data containing considerable noise, σ_n^2 decreases sharply after the plateau region. This final decrease is an artifact, due to the increased ability of higher degree polynomials to closely follow the error in the data. A suitable value of n is one on the plateau region, before the subsequent decline in σ_n^2. Numerical examples based on simulated data are given by Cutler (11).

Least-squares deconvolution methods can be applied to time-variant systems, with the sole modification being the procedure used to evaluate the integrals in equations 23 or 28 and 29. The time dependence of Q_δ must be recognized, as in equation 9. The main problem in using this approach is likely to be in specifying the time dependence of Q_δ rather than in subsequent evaluation.

7. INPUT–RESPONSE RELATIONSHIP BETWEEN STATISTICAL MOMENTS

Simple relationships can be derived for a linear system between the statistical moments of a drug input and the corresponding statistical moments of the resulting response. The statistical moments arise naturally as a means of describing the features of an input function, or the resulting response, when it is recognized that these processes are essentially stochastic in nature. For example, following the oral administration of a drug dose, we would not expect to be able to predict the behavior (say, time of absorption) of an individual molecule, whereas the ability to predict (or at least describe) the collective behavior of the population of molecules administered is a fundamental assumption of all studies of absorption.

To illustrate the connection between an input rate and the statistical characteristics of the same process, let $p(t)$ be the probability density function for the input process; $p(t)dt$ is the probability that a molecule that enters the system does so in the time interval $(t, t+dt)$. If the total number of molecules entering the system is n, the frequency interpretation of probability gives $np(t)dt$ as the number of molecules entering the system during the time interval $(t, t+dt)$. In terms of the drug input rate, this number is $\dot{A}(t)dt$. Thus

$$np(t)dt = \dot{A}(t)dt$$

or

$$np(t) = \dot{A}(t)$$

Since $p(t)$ is a probability density function,

$$\int_0^\infty p(t)dt = 1$$

and we have

$$n = \int_0^\infty \dot{A}(t)dt$$

Therefore

$$p(t) = \frac{\dot{A}(t)}{\int_0^\infty \dot{A}(t)dt} \tag{35}$$

The denominator on the right of equation 35 is the total amount of drug entering the system through the input $\dot{A}(t)$. Division by this term amounts to normalizing the input rate $\dot{A}(t)$ to give the probability density function.

We define the mean and variance of the input as (13, 14)

$$E(\dot{A}) = \frac{\int_0^\infty t\dot{A}(t)dt}{\int_0^\infty \dot{A}(t)dt} \tag{36}$$

and

$$V(\dot{A}) = \frac{\int_0^\infty [t - E(\dot{A})]^2 \dot{A}(t)dt}{\int_0^\infty \dot{A}(t)dt} \tag{37}$$

These definitions follow from the probability density function given by equation 35. Higher moments can also be defined, but their use is limited in practice by the errors involved in their calculation.

We are interested in the case in which the input $\dot{A}(t)$ produces a response $Q(t)$ according to equation 2. Corresponding to equations 36 and 37 we define the mean and variance of the response $Q(t)$ as

$$E(Q) = \frac{\int_0^\infty tQ(t)dt}{\int_0^\infty Q(t)dt} \tag{38}$$

and

$$V(Q) = \frac{\int_0^\infty [t - E(Q)]^2 Q(t)dt}{\int_0^\infty Q(t)dt} \tag{39}$$

Similarly, for the mean and variance of $Q_\delta(t)$,

$$E(Q_\delta) = \frac{\int_0^\infty tQ_\delta(t)dt}{\int_0^\infty Q_\delta(t)dt} \tag{40}$$

and

$$V(Q_\delta) = \frac{\int_0^\infty [t - E(Q_\delta)]^2 Q_\delta(t)dt}{\int_0^\infty Q_\delta(t)dt} \tag{41}$$

To establish a relationship between these quantities, we require the following results, which we present in terms of a general function $X(t)$, with $X = \dot{A}, Q$, or Q_δ in the following applications.

Writing $x(s)$ to denote the Laplace transform of $X(t)$, we obtain

$$x(s) = \int_0^\infty e^{-st} X(t)dt \tag{42}$$

As noted earlier (equation 10),

$$\lim_{s \to 0} \{x(s)\} = \int_0^\infty X(t)dt \tag{43}$$

On differentiating equation 42 with respect to s, we have

$$\frac{dx}{ds} = -\int_0^\infty te^{-st} X(t)dt \tag{44}$$

and thus

$$\lim_{s \to 0} \left\{\frac{dx}{ds}\right\} = -\int_0^\infty tX(t)dt \tag{45}$$

With the mean of $X(t)$ defined as

$$E(X) = \frac{\int_0^\infty tX(t)dt}{\int_0^\infty X(t)dt} \tag{46}$$

we have

$$E(X) = -\lim_{s \to 0} \left\{\frac{dx/ds}{x}\right\} \tag{47}$$

on using equations 43, 45, and 46.

Differentiation of equation 44 with respect to s gives

$$\frac{d^2x}{ds^2}=\int_0^\infty t^2e^{-st}X(t)dt$$

and hence

$$\lim_{s\to 0}\left\{\frac{d^2x}{ds^2}\right\}=\int_0^\infty t^2X(t)dt \tag{48}$$

The variance of $X(t)$ is defined as

$$V(X)=\frac{\int_0^\infty [t-E(X)]^2X(t)dt}{\int_0^\infty X(t)dt}$$

Expansion of the squared term in the integrand and use of equation 46 yields

$$V(X)=\frac{\int_0^\infty t^2X(t)dt}{\int_0^\infty X(t)dt}-E(X)^2 \tag{49}$$

If equations 48 and 43 are used, the last equation gives

$$V(X)=\lim_{s\to 0}\left\{\frac{d^2x/ds^2}{x}\right\}-E(X)^2 \tag{50}$$

We now use the results stated in equations 47 and 50 to relate the statistical moments of the input and the response for a time-invariant linear system. The input and response are related by equation 2; on taking Laplace transforms of equation 2, we obtain

$$q(s)=\dot{a}(s)q_\delta(s) \tag{51}$$

where $q(s)$, $\dot{a}(s)$, and $q_\delta(s)$ are the Laplace transforms of $Q(t)$, $\dot{A}(t)$, and $Q_\delta(t)$, respectively. Differentiation of equation 51 with respect to s yields

$$\frac{dq}{ds}=\dot{a}(s)\frac{dq_\delta}{ds}+q_\delta(s)\frac{d\dot{a}}{ds} \tag{52}$$

Division by equation 51 gives

$$\frac{dq/ds}{q(s)}=\frac{dq_\delta/ds}{q_\delta(s)}+\frac{d\dot{a}/ds}{\dot{a}(s)}$$

Applying the result stated in equation 47, we obtain

$$E(Q)=E(Q_\delta)+E(R) \tag{53}$$

with the terms in this equation defined by equations 36, 38, and 40.

Differentiation of equation 52 with respect to s gives

$$\frac{d^2q}{ds^2}=\dot{a}(s)\frac{d^2q_\delta}{ds}+2\left(\frac{d\dot{a}}{ds}\right)\left(\frac{dq_\delta}{ds}\right)+q_\delta(s)\left(\frac{d^2\dot{a}}{ds^2}\right)$$

Dividing by equation 51, we obtain

$$\frac{d^2q/ds^2}{q(s)}=\frac{d^2q_\delta/ds^2}{q_\delta(s)}+2\left(\frac{d\dot{a}/ds}{\dot{a}(s)}\right)\left(\frac{dq_\delta/ds}{q_\delta(s)}\right)+\frac{d^2\dot{a}/ds^2}{\dot{a}(s)}$$

Application of the result stated in equations 47 and 50 to this equation yields

$$V(Q)+E(Q)^2=V(Q_\delta)+E(Q_\delta)^2+2E(\dot{A})E(Q_\delta)+V(\dot{A})+E(\dot{A})^2$$

Using equation 53 for $E(Q)^2$, we obtain

$$V(Q)=V(Q_\delta)+V(\dot{A}) \tag{54}$$

Equations 53 and 54 demonstrate the additive property of the statistical moments, which is the basis of their usefulness in relating properties of the input to those of the response.

The mean and variance of an unknown input $\dot{A}(t)$ can be determined when data on $Q(t)$ and $Q_\delta(t)$ are available by calculating the moments of $Q(t)$ and $Q_\delta(t)$, according to equations 38–41 and applying equations 53 and 54 to give

$$E(\dot{A})=E(Q)-E(Q_\delta) \tag{55}$$

and

$$V(\dot{A})=V(Q)-V(Q_\delta) \tag{56}$$

Thus the moments of the input are readily determined from the response data. When the mathematical form of the input function is known (or one is assumed), it might be possible to obtain useful relationships between $E(\dot{A})$, $V(\dot{A})$, and the parameters describing the input. For example, for a first-order input, with

$$\dot{A}(t)=k_aFDe^{-k_at}$$

evaluation of equations 36 and 37 gives

$$E(\dot{A})=\frac{1}{k_a} \tag{57}$$

and

$$V(\dot{A})=\frac{1}{k_a^2}$$

Statistical moments also provide a convenient means of comparing two inputs. Let Q_1 be the response following the input $\dot{A}_1$ and Q_2 be the response following the input $\dot{A}_2$. Equations of the form of equations 55 and 56 apply for both inputs; assuming Q_δ to be the same for both inputs [so that $E(Q_\delta)$ and $V(Q_\delta)$ are the same], we have

$$E(\dot{A}_1) - E(\dot{A}_2) = E(Q_1) - E(Q_2)$$

and

$$V(\dot{A}_1) - V(\dot{A}_2) = V(Q_1) - V(Q_2)$$

allowing comparison of the mean and variance of the two inputs.

Statistical moments are particularly useful in interpreting an input that can be regarded as a sequence of linear processes. For the situation described by equations 13 or 14, the procedures leading to equations 53 and 54 give

$$E_{1n} = E_1 + E_2 + \cdots + E_n$$

where E_{1n} is the mean for the overall process and $E_1, E_2, \ldots, E_n$ are the means for the individual processes of the sequence. Similarly,

$$V_{1n} = V_1 + V_2 + \cdots + V_n$$

where V_{1n} is the variance for the overall process and $V_1, V_2, \ldots, V_n$ are the variances of the individual processes of the sequence. For a process such as absorption of drug following oral administration, the moments of the overall absorption process are the sum of the moments of the individual processes—say, of release from the dosage form, transport across the gut wall and transport through the liver.

It can be seen from the defining equations (e.g., equations 40 and 41) that a process with a unit impulse response that itself approximates an impulse function has mean and variance both zero, regardless of the magnitude of the response. Consequently, in interpreting the moments of a sequential process, very rapidly responding processes may be neglected as they make no contribution to the moments of the overall process.

8. ANALYSIS OF SIMPLE NONLINEAR SYSTEMS

In some cases it is possible to treat simple nonlinear systems by the methods of linear systems analysis. First, the derivation of equation 2 treats the input $\dot{A}(t)$ as a general function of time without reference to the process that gives rise to this input. Consequently, equation 2 applies equally well to linear or nonlinear input processes. By a "nonlinear" system is meant, in the present context, one characterized by saturable elimination or distribution processes. The simple systems discussed here are such that the nonlinearity can be incorporated into an "effective" input. This leads to a relationship between the actual input and an "effective" response.

As an example, suppose that the drug is bound to a readily saturated, low-capacity binding site, with other disposition processes being linear. When the amount of drug in the body is sufficiently large that these binding sites are saturated, the amount of drug bound to these sites will be constant and the remainder of the drug will follow linear disposition kinetics. Let B denote the amount of drug bound to the saturated sites and let $\dot{A}(t)$ be the drug input to the system. For an input containing sufficient drug to rapidly saturate the binding sites, we have an effective input

$$\dot{A}_{\text{eff}}(t) = \dot{A}(t) - B\delta(t) \tag{58}$$

which can be interpreted as the input to the system once the binding sites have been saturated, which is responsible for producing the resulting response $Q(t)$. This interpretation would be appropriate if the saturable binding process involved the plasma proteins or some other rapidly accessible site. The resulting response is

$$Q(t) = \dot{A}_{\text{eff}} * Q'_\delta \tag{59}$$

where Q'_δ is the response when $\dot{A}_{\text{eff}}$ is a unit impulse function, or when $\dot{A}(t)$ is an impulse input of magnitude $(1 + B)$. Combination of the last two equations results in

$$\begin{aligned} Q(t) &= \dot{A} * Q'_\delta - B\,\delta(t) * Q'_\delta \\ &= \dot{A} * Q'_\delta - BQ'_\delta \end{aligned}$$

or

$$(Q + BQ'_\delta) = \dot{A} * Q'_\delta \tag{60}$$

This equation expresses a relationship, of the same form as equation 2, between an "effective" response $Q + BQ'_\delta$ and the input $\dot{A}(t)$. The values of B and Q'_δ, required for the application of equation 60, may be determined by investigating the dose dependence of $Q(t)$ through equation 59. If the drug is administered as an impulse input of magnitude D (dose), with $\dot{A}(t) = D\delta(t)$, equation 58 gives

$$\dot{A}_{\text{eff}}(t) = (D - B)\delta(t)$$

Introduction of this expression into equation 59 gives

$$Q_{D\delta}(t) = (D - B)Q'_\delta(t)$$

where $Q_{D\delta}$ denotes the response to an input $D\delta(t)$. Evaluation of the last equation at sample times t_r results in

$$Q_{D\delta}(t_r) = DQ'_\delta(t_r) - BQ'_\delta(t_r) \tag{61}$$

If the approximations made in deriving equation 60 are valid, equation 61 shows that $Q_{D\delta}(t_r)$ is linearly related to D, with slope $Q'_\delta(t_r)$ and intercept $Q_{D\delta}(t_r) = -BQ'_\delta(t_r)$ at $D=0$. Thus the information required for the application of equation 60 can be obtained by examining the dose dependence of $Q_{D\delta}(t)$ at each sample time t_r.

As another example, suppose that an input $\dot{A}(t)$ is followed by a capacity-limited elimination process that is readily saturated, with zero-order elimination rate K_0 when the local drug concentration is sufficiently high. When this last condition is met, we can consider an effective input of the form

$$\dot{A}_{\text{eff}}(t) = \dot{A}(t) - K_0 \tag{62}$$

This interpretation would be appropriate when $\dot{A}(t)$ represents the release rate of drug from a formulation into the gut fluids, with K_0 representing a zero-order metabolic process occurring, say, in the gut wall. As in equation 59, we suppose that this effective input is linearly related to the observed response $Q(t)$ and write

$$Q(t) = \dot{A}_{\text{eff}} * Q'_\delta \tag{63}$$

where Q'_δ is the response when $\dot{A}_{\text{eff}}(t)$ is a unit impulse input [requiring an actual input $\dot{A}(t) = K_0 + \delta(t)$]. In physical terms, we assume that the metabolic process represented by K_0 is effectively saturated by the input, with the disposition of recirculating drug being governed by linear processes. The same approximation applies when the saturable process (whether saturated or not) is not quantitatively significant in regard to the overall disposition of the drug.

Combination of equations 62 and 63 gives

$$Q(t) = \dot{A} * Q'_\delta - K_0 \int_0^t Q'_\delta(T)\,dT$$

or

$$Q(t) + K_0 \int_0^t Q'_\delta(T)\,dT = \dot{A} * Q'_\delta \tag{64}$$

which relates the "effective" response

$$Q(t) + K_0 \int_0^t Q'_\delta(T)\,dT$$

to the input $\dot{A}(t)$ in the same way as $Q(t)$ and $\dot{A}(t)$ are related in equation 2. The information needed to construct the effective input can be obtained (as in the previous example) by examining the response to an impulse input of magnitude D. With $\dot{A}(t) = D\delta(t)$, equation 62 gives

$$\dot{A}_{\text{eff}}(t) = D\delta(t) - K_0$$

[Note that $\dot{A}_{\text{eff}}(t) = -K_0$ for $t > 0$; this merely implies that the processes that are combined to give this effective input result in a net loss of drug from the system for $t > 0$.] If $Q_{D\delta}(t)$ is written to denote the response to the input $D\delta(t)$, equation 63 gives

$$Q_{D\delta}(t_r) = DQ'_\delta(t_r) - K_0 \int_0^{t_r} Q'_\delta(T)dT$$

when evaluated at time t_r. If the assumptions made are valid, this equation predicts a linear relationship between $Q_{D\delta}(t_r)$ and dose D, with slope $Q'_\delta(t_r)$ and intercept

$$Q_{D\delta}(t_r) = -K_0 \int_0^{t_r} Q'_\delta(T)dT$$

at $D = 0$. Therefore, the dose dependence of $Q_{D\delta}(t_r)$ at each sample time t_r gives the information needed for the application of equation 64.

REFERENCES

1. D. Cutler. Linear systems analysis in pharmacokinetics. *J. Pharmacokin. Biopharm.* **6**: 265 (1978).
2. A. Rescigno and G. Segre. *Drug and Tracer Kinetics*, Blaisdell, Waltham, Mass., 1966, Chapter 4.
3. M. Spiegel. *Theory and Problems of Laplace Transforms*, Schaum's Outline Series, McGraw-Hill, 1965.
4. R. Churchill. *Operational Mathematics*, 2nd ed., International Student Edition, McGraw-Hill, Kogakusha, Japan, 1958, p. 37.
5. L. Benet. General treatment of linear mammillary models with elimination in any compartment as used in pharmacokinetics. *J. Pharm. Sci.* **61**: 536 (1972).
6. J. Gamel, W. Rousseau, C. Katholi, and E. Mesel. Pitfalls in digital computation of the impulse response of vascular beds from indicator–dilution curves. *Circ. Res.* **32**: 516 (1973).
7. L. Benet and C.-W. Chiang. The Use and Application of Deconvolution Methods in Pharmacokinetics. In *Abstracts of the 13th National Meeting of the A. Ph. A.*, Academy of Pharmaceutical Sciences, Chicago, 1972.
8. D. Vaughan and M. Dennis. Mathematical basis of point–area deconvolution method for determining in-vivo input functions. *J. Pharm. Sci.* **67**: 663 (1978).
9. W. Chiou. New compartment and model independent method for rapid calculation of drug absorption rates. *J. Pharm. Sci.* **69**: 57 (1980).
10. D. Cutler. Numerical deconvolution by least squares: Use of prescribed input functions. *J. Pharmacokin. Biopharm.* **6**: 227 (1978).
11. D. Cutler. Numerical deconvolution by least squares: Use of polynomials to represent the input function. *J. Pharmacokin. Biopharm.* **6**: 243 (1978).

12. G. Forsythe. Generation and use of orthogonal polynomials for data fitting with a digital computer. *J. Soc. Indust. Appl. Math.* **5**: 74 (1957).

13. D. Cutler. Theory of the mean absorption time, an adjunct to conventional bioavailability studies. *J. Pharm. Pharmacol.* **30**: 476 (1978).

14. K. Yamaoka, T. Nakagawa, and T. Uno. Statistical moments in pharmacokinetics. *J. Pharmacokin. Biopharm.* **6**: 547 (1978).

CHAPTER 4

Systems Analysis and Optimization of Drug Input Functions

D. P. VAUGHAN
P. G. WALTON

Sunderland Polytechnic
Tyne & Wear, United Kingdom

Dr. Vaughan is with the Department of Pharmacy; Dr. Walton is with the Department of Mathematics.

CONTENTS

Any theory should provide insight into the fundamentals and above all be directly applicable. Historically, pharmacokinetics has concentrated on defining a mammillary compartmental system to describe the drug concentration function in blood after intravenous administration. For no apparent reason the latter function has usually been assumed to be a monotonically decreasing function, analytically defined by a summation of exponentials. The application of the latter constrained hypothesis has tended to limit pharmacokinetic analysis to that of calculating intercompartmental rate constants and other semiempirical parameters.

In this chapter elementary systems analysis is applied to pharmacokinetics. In particular, hypothetical models are avoided where possible. To emphasize the redundancy of mammillary models, the limitations of modeling the body by matrix operators are expounded.

The application of linear systems analysis to the design of drug input functions is illustrated. The latter are essentially optimization problems. Since direct search and gradient optimization have been applied to pharmacokinetic problems, these algorithms and their principal limitations are discussed. A versatile and efficient nonlinear optimization has been applied to the design of drug input functions.

1. LINEAR SYSTEMS

An explanation of the meaning of the words "system" and "linear" is necessary. A system refers to any biological or physical unit that converts a quantitative input or "forcing function" $\dot{A}$ into a quantitative output or response Q. The input and the output are usually functions of the continuous variable time t and are thus generally represented by $\dot{A}(t)$ and $Q(t)$, respectively.

An essential requirement of a system is that the output $Q(t)$ should be determined completely by the input function, $\dot{A}(t)$ and the characteristics of the system. Symbolically, the relationship between $\dot{A}(t)$ and $Q(t)$ can be represented by

$$Q(t) = \Phi \dot{A}(t) \tag{1}$$

where the symbol Φ is an operator that represents the conversion of the input into the output. This operator is linear IF AND ONLY IF

$$\Phi[\dot{A}_1(t) + \dot{A}_2(t)] = \Phi \dot{A}_1(t) + \Phi \dot{A}_2(t) \tag{2}$$

for all admissible input functions $\dot{A}_1(t)$ and $\dot{A}_2(t)$. An obvious corollary is that if an operator is linear, then

$$\Phi[c\dot{A}(t)] = c\Phi \dot{A}(t) \tag{3}$$

where c is any constant.

A system is linear if its operator is linear (i.e.; if for any system the conversion of the input, through the system, to the output is governed by equations 1, 2, and 3, then the system is linear). Equations 1, 2, and 3 are frequently referred to as the *superposition principle* (addition principle), which in words is as follows. If $Q_1(t)$ and $Q_2(t)$ are the responses obtained from a system when inputs $\dot{A}_1(t)$ and $\dot{A}_2(t)$ are applied separately; the system is linear if and only if the input $\dot{A}_1(t)+\dot{A}_2(t)$ produces the response $Q_1(t)+Q_2(t)$ for all admissible input functions.

An important property of many linear systems is that of time-invariance, which means that the mapping of the input to the output is independent of any change of origin in time. Thus for a time-invariant linear system, if

$$Q(t)=\Phi\dot{A}(t)$$

then

$$Q(t-\tau)=\Phi\dot{A}(t-\tau) \tag{4}$$

for all τ and for all admissible inputs. The term "time invariance" implies that the output of the system only depends on past and not future events of the input. In other words, the system is *nonanticipatory*.

In pharmacokinetics the body is the system, and in the context of this chapter the quantitative output (response) produced by the absorption of drug into the blood (i.e., the input function) is the drug concentration–time function in the blood.

Although it is not necessary to impose restrictions at all on the input functions of linear time-invariant systems, we can logically restrict drug input functions to nonnegative functions of t defined for $t\geqslant 0$. Similarly, we can insist that the response $Q(t)$ is a nonnegative bounded function such that for $t\to\infty, Q(t)=0$. The response function should be nonnegative since negative drug concentrations have no physical meaning. For a finite amount of drug, infinite drug concentrations are not expected thus the response is bounded.

The restriction that $Q(t)=0$ for $t\to\infty$ is governed by the known behavior of the body toward exogenous compounds, namely, drug metabolism and drug elimination. Consequently, if the body is perturbed by some finite drug input, the lungs, liver, and kidney will eventually eliminate the drug and restore a zero drug concentration. Thus the effect produced by the perturbation of a finite drug input is only temporary. The latter consideration has immediately defined the body as a stable system, linear or otherwise.

A stable system is one in which perturbations are transient and the necessary and sufficient condition for stability is that for some finite input $\dot{A}(t)$, then $Q(t)=0$ for $t\to\infty$. An immediate consequence of the body being a stable system is that to obtain and maintain a particular drug concentration, the body must be driven by the drug input function.

Additionally, the existence of drug metabolism within and drug elimination from the body guarantees for a finite drug input that

$$\int_0^b Q(t)dt \text{ exists as } b \to \infty$$

or more formally, $Q(t)$ is a function that can be integrated on the interval $(0, \infty)$. The latter statement is independent of the linearity of the body to drug input.

The time-invariant operator Φ has a general structure that corresponds to the convolution of the input function $\dot{A}(t)$ with the characteristic response of the system $Q_\delta(t)$; where $Q_\delta(t)$ is the systems response to a unit impulse input $\delta 1$ occurring at $t=0$. Thus for any input function and characteristic response both defined for $t \geqslant 0$, the response of a time-invariant linear system is defined by

$$Q(t) = \int_0^t Q_\delta(\tau)\dot{A}(t-\tau)d\tau = \int_0^t Q_\delta(t-\tau)\dot{A}(\tau)d\tau \qquad (5)$$

$$t \geqslant 0$$

If the convolution of two time-dependent functions is represented symbolically by the symbol $*$, equation 5 can be written as

$$Q(t) = Q_\delta(t) * \dot{A}(t) = \dot{A}(t) * Q_\delta(t) \qquad (6)$$

Utilizing equations 4 and 6, we can represent the time-invariant linear operator Φ that converts the input of the system to the output $Q(t)$ by

$$\Phi = Q_\delta(t) * \qquad (7)$$

The latter is a quite remarkable and simple representation of a time-invariant linear system in that we need only to know the characteristic response of a system to analytically define the response to some particular input. Additionally, the convolution representation can be used to design drug input functions to give some desired response function. The response of a linear system to some input (i.e.; the convolution integral) can be derived as follows. Consider an input function $\dot{A}(t)$ defined for $t>0$; and from this function define a consecutive sequence of rectangular functions with areas $c_i = \dot{A}(\tau_i)\Delta\tau_i$ such that $\dot{A}(t)$ is approximated by this staircase function. Now the response of a linear system to a sequence of impulses of magnitude c_i that occur at time points τ_i is given by the superposition and time invariance rules as

$$Q(t) = \sum_{i=1} c_i H(t-\tau_i) Q_\delta(t-\tau_i) = \sum_{i=1} \dot{A}(\tau_i) H(t-\tau_i) Q_\delta(t-\tau_i)\Delta\tau_i$$

When the individual increments $\Delta\tau_i$ tend to zero, the summation becomes an integral and since $H(t-\tau_i)=0$ for $\tau_i > t$, the upper limit of integration is t;

letting $\Delta\tau_i \to 0$, then, the response is given by

$$Q(t) = \int_0^t \dot{A}(\tau) Q_\delta(t-\tau)\, d\tau$$

which is precisely the convolution integral of the input function $\dot{A}(t)$ and the characteristics response $Q_\delta(t)$.

Some immediate applications of the convolution integral in pharmacokinetics are described in Section 1.1.

1.1 Intravenous Infusions

Suppose that a unit bolus drug dose (i.e., impulse input) is injected into a vein and the blood drug concentration–time function, in some other vein, is observed and defined as the characteristic response of the body. It immediately follows from the convolution integral that the response to a constant rate infusion into the same vein as used for the impulse input; as given by

$$Q(t) = R_0 \int_0^t Q_\delta(t)\, dt$$

and that

$$Q(\infty) = R_0 \int_0^\infty Q_\delta(t)\, dt$$

where R_0 is the infusion rate (units of mass time^{-1}). Obviously, the time to achieve the final "steady-state" value $Q(\infty)$ is determined by the convergence rate of the integral $\int_0^t Q_\delta(t)dt$. For most drugs, this convergence rate is unacceptably slow and some other input is required to rapidly achieve steady-state concentrations. When the characteristic response is defined by

$$Q_\delta(t) = \sum_{i=1}^{N} A_i e^{-m_i t}$$

A_i and $m_i > 0$, the steady-state concentration $Q(\infty)$ can be immediately achieved and maintained for all time $t \geqslant 0$. Vaughan and Tucker (1), by direct application of linear systems analysis, have derived the drug input necessary to achieve this constant response. The required input consists of an impulse D, a constant rate infusion R_0, and $N-1$ exponential inputs $E_i(t)$, where

$$D = \frac{R_0 \sum_{i=1}^{N} A_i/m_i}{\sum_{i=1}^{N} A_i} \equiv \frac{Q(\infty)}{\sum_{i=1}^{N} A_i}$$

$$R_0 = \frac{Q(\infty)}{\sum_{i=1}^{N} A_i/m_i}$$

$$E_i = -Du_i e^{-c_i t} > 0$$

$$i = 1, 2, \ldots, N-1$$

The exponential coefficients $-c_i$ are the $N-1$ roots of the polynomial

$$\sum_{i=1}^{N} A_i \prod_{\substack{j=1 \\ j=i}}^{N} (S+m)_i$$

and the coefficients u_i are given by

$$\frac{\prod_{j=1}^{N} (m_j - c_i)}{c_i^2 \prod_{\substack{j=1 \\ j\neq 1}}^{N} (c_j - c_i)}$$

Exponential input functions require specially designed intravenous giving sets. Consequently, some practical approximation to exponential input functions is required. A staircase input function (i.e., stepped intravenous infusion rates) is a practical solution to the problem of inappropriate infusion equipment.

The exponential input functions $E_i(t)$ may be approximated by a staircase input function $\bar{S}(t)$ of the form

$$\bar{S}(t) = \sum_{i=1}^{n} R_{0_i}[H(t-\tau_{i-i}) - H(t-\tau_i)]$$

where $\tau_0 = 0$, $\tau_n = \infty$; $R_{0_n} = R_0$, and the step functions $H(t-\tau) = 1$ for $t \geqslant \tau$ and 0 for $t < \tau$. In this case the response of the system to the impulse input D and $\bar{S}(t)$ is

$$Q(t) = DQ_\delta(t) + \sum_{i=1}^{n} R_{0_i}\left[H(t-\tau_{i-1}) \int_0^{t-\tau_{i-1}} Q_\delta(t)dt - H(t-\tau_i) \int_0^{t-\tau_i} Q_\delta(t)dt\right] \tag{8}$$

Since $Q(t) \neq Q(\infty)$ for all $t \geqslant 0$, we are now faced with the problem of choosing a suitable integer n, suitable step heights R_{0_i}, $i = 2, \ldots, n-1$ (note that $R_{0_n} = R_0$) and suitable step lengths $(\tau_i - \tau_{i-1})$, $i = 1; 2, \ldots, n-1$, such that $Q(t)$ is as close as possible to $Q(\infty)$ for all $t \geqslant 0$. Clearly, this problem is an input optimization problem. Its solution is discussed in the last section of this chapter.

1.2 Multiple Dosing

Suppose that $Q(t)$ is known after some arbitrary but finite drug input into the body, for example, the blood drug concentration–time function after an oral drug formulation. In this case the response $\bar{Q}(t)$ to the repeated administration of the same drug input at regular time intervals $j\tau(j=0, 1, \ldots, n)$ is immediately defined by direct application of the superposition and time-invariance rules. Thus

$$\bar{Q}(t) = \sum_{j=0}^{n} H(t-\tau_j)Q(t-\tau_j)$$

and

$$\int_{n\tau}^{(n+1)\tau} \bar{Q}(t)dt = \sum_{j=0}^{n} \int_{j\tau}^{(j+1)\tau} Q(t)dt = \int_{0}^{(n+1)\tau} Q(t)dt$$

where $H(t-\tau_j)=1$ for $t \geqslant 0$ and 0 for $t < \tau_j$. Since for a finite input function the integral of $Q(t)$ on the interval $[0, \infty)$ exists, then for large n

$$\int_{n\tau}^{(n+1)\tau} \bar{Q}(t)dt \rightarrow \int_{0}^{\infty} Q(t)dt$$

Consequently, the multiple-dose response curve $\bar{Q}(t)$ is bounded and the area under the function in the interval $[n\tau, (n+1)\tau]$ converges to the definite integral of the single-dose response function $\int_0^\infty Q(t)dt$, and a periodic steady-state response $\bar{Q}_s(t)$ results where $\bar{Q}(t) = \bar{Q}(t-\tau)$.

The first moment m_s of the periodic steady-state response is given by

$$m_s = \frac{\int_{j\tau}^{(j+1)\tau} \bar{Q}_s(t)dt}{\tau} = \frac{\int_0^\infty Q(t)dt}{\tau}$$

The value of the first moment is frequently referred to as the mean steady-state response.

Given $Q(t)$ and some desired m_s value, the necessary dosage interval is obtainable by trivial calculation. However, an interesting problem is to fix the dosage interval τ at 12 hours and logically design the drug release from the formulation such that $\bar{Q}(t)$ is as close as possible to the desired response for all $t \geqslant 0$. For the latter problem, we write

$$Q(t) = \dot{A}(t) * Q_\delta(t)$$

where $Q_\delta(t)$ is the response obtained after an oral solution of a unit drug dose and $\dot{A}(t)$ is the in-vivo release of the drug from its formulation. For manufacturing reasons, we may be required to constrain $\dot{A}(t)$ to some relative simple or collection of relatively simple functions. For example,

$\dot{A}(t)$ may be constrained to a summation of exponential release rates; thus

$$\dot{A}(t) = \sum_{j=1}^{m} K_j D_j e^{-K_j t} \tag{9}$$

where $\sum_{j=1}^{m} D_j$ is the total amount of drug in the formulation and D_j is the amount of drug in the formulation that is released exponentially at a rate of K_j. Additionally, we may further suppose that for the first dose a scalar multiple $\bar{K} \cdot \dot{A}(t)$ of the subsequent doses is permitted. Thus

$$\bar{Q}(t) = \bar{K} \cdot \dot{A}(t) * Q_\delta(t) + \sum_{j=1}^{n} H(t-\tau)Q(t-\tau) \tag{10}$$

where

$$Q(t) = \dot{A}(t) * Q_\delta(t)$$

For some desired m_s value, we must investigate the dimension of m and calculate values for the variables $\bar{K}$; K_j, and D_j such that $\bar{Q}(t)$ is close to m_s for all $t \geqslant 0$. Again, the solution of this problem requires an efficient optimization algorithm: the solution is discussed subsequently.

1.3 Bioavailability

Consider a linear system whose $Q_\delta(t)$, defined for $t \geqslant 0$, is nonnegative such that the integral on $[0; \infty)$ exists. For a nonnegative input, $\dot{A}(t)$ defined for $t \geqslant 0$; into such a system

$$Q(t) = \dot{A}(t) * Q_\delta(t)$$

Provided the input is finite [i.e., the integral of $\dot{A}(t)$ on $[0; \infty)$] exists, then

$$\int_0^\infty Q(t)dt = \int_0^\infty \dot{A}(t)dt \cdot \int_0^\infty Q_\delta(t)dt$$

When considering drug inputs into the body the integral of $\dot{A}(t)$ on $[0; \infty)$ is the total amount of drug that enters the system. Consequently, we can state that for a finite drug input into the body, the total area under the observed response function is directly proportional to the drug dose. This is Dost's law of corresponding areas. In making this statement we have tacitly assumed that the input function and the unit impulse input are both applied at the same point. If input occurs at the same point distinct from the impulse input point used to characterize the system, then $\dot{A}(t)$ is the apparent input function at the impulse point. This distinction becomes important when $Q_\delta(t)$ is defined as the blood drug concentration–time function after a unit intravenous bolus drug dose and then $Q(t)$ is defined as the response to an oral drug dose D_0. In this case the total oral drug dose may not be absorbed and some of the dose may be metabolized by the intestinal wall or the liver during the process of transporting the drug to the impulse input point. Consequently, $\int_0^\infty \dot{A}(t)dt$ will be less than the total oral drug dose D_0. The ratio r given by

$$r = \frac{100 \int_0^\infty \dot{A}(t)dt}{D_0} = 100 \frac{\int_0^\infty Q(t)dt}{D_0 \int_0^\infty Q_\delta(t)dt}$$

is the percentage of the oral drug dose that reaches the impulse input point (i.e., r is the bioavailability of an oral drug dose).

Derivation of the latter relationships, which have been variously rediscovered by other workers, has been presented previously (2).

1.4 Determination of In-Vivo Drug Input Functions

Given the response of a linear system to some arbitrary input function and the characteristic response of the system, the deconvolution of $Q(t)$ and $Q_\delta(t)$ will define the input function. Unfortunately, this is an ill-conditioned problem since $Q(t)$ is not known analytically. However, it is always possible to derive a staircase input function which approximates the true input function (3). Recently the Loo–Riegelman method for the determination of in-vivo drug absorption has been generalized and shown to be a particular example of linear systems analysis (4).

Another approach to deconvolution is to define the input function as a polynomial and optimize this defined function such that its convolution with the characteristic response generates a function that is close to the observed response (5).

2. COMPARTMENTAL MODELS AND MATRIX OPERATORS

The analytical structure of a systems characteristic response depends on the systems variables and their interrelationships. In a general sense, the totality of the characteristic responses cannot be defined. Nevertheless, all time-invariant operators can always be expressed as a fraction in its lowest terms of linear homogenous differential equations (6).

Provided certain general assumptions can be made about a system, a linear time-invariant operator can be represented as a matrix operator where the matrix has constant coefficients. A powerful motivation for traversing such a route is that the analysis of matrix operators is fully solved in a mathematical sense and the resulting representation embraces the majority of mathematical models that have been applied to pharmacokinetic problems.

Consider a system whose state at any time is assumed to be completely described by means of N functions $x_1(t), x_2(t), \ldots, x_N(t)$. Assume further that the rate of change of all these functions at any time t depends only on the values of these functions at this time. The analytic transliteration of these statements is a set of differential equations of the form

$$\frac{dx_i}{dt}=f(x_1, x_2, \ldots, x_N) \qquad i=1, 2, \ldots, N$$

with an associated set of initial conditions

$$x_i(0)=c_i \qquad i=1, 2, \ldots, N$$

Since by assumption the relationships between the variables and their derivatives do not involve functions of time the differential equations can be expressed in matrix form by

$$\dot{\mathbf{x}}=\mathbf{A}_1\mathbf{x}+\mathbf{A}_2\mathbf{x}^2+\cdots$$

where the dots signify terms involving higher powers of the variable vector **x** and the matrices **A** are constant coefficient matrices. If the higher-order terms are ignored, the behavior of the system is determined by a linear system with constant coefficients

$$\dot{\mathbf{x}}=\mathbf{A}\mathbf{x} \qquad x_i(0)=c_i \qquad i=1, 2, \ldots, N \tag{11}$$

where

$$\mathbf{A}=\mathbf{A}_1$$

The solution of equation 11 for any particular $x_i(t)$ is readily determined by taking Laplace transforms and applying Cramer's rule. Thus for $i=1, 2, \ldots, N$,

$$x_i(t)=\mathcal{L}^{-1}\frac{|\mathbf{B}|}{|s\mathbf{I}-\mathbf{A}|}=\mathcal{L}^{-1}\frac{P(s)}{F(s)}$$

where **I** is the identity matrix and s is the Laplace variable. Matrix **B** is derived from the matrix $s\mathbf{I}-\mathbf{A}$ by replacing the ith column by the vector of initial conditions. The determinant $|s\mathbf{I}-\mathbf{A}|$ is a polynomial in s of degree N, which can be resolved into linear factors:

$$|s\mathbf{I}-\mathbf{A}|=(s-\lambda_1)^{k_1}(s-\lambda_2)^{k_2}\cdots(s-\lambda_m)^{k_m}=F(s)$$

where $N=k_1+k_2+\cdots+k_m$ and $\lambda_j (j=1, 2, \ldots, m)$ are the roots of the polynomial $F(s)$. Since matrix **A** has real coefficients, the polynomial $F(s)$ has real coefficients. Consequently, complex roots must occur in complex conjugate pairs. We may suppose that $\lambda_1, \lambda_2, \ldots, \lambda_q$ are real, whereas λ_{q+1}, λ_{q+2}, and all subsequent pairs of successive roots are a complex conjugate pair so that $k_{q+1} = k_{q+2}$ and so on.

We can resolve $P(s)/F(s)$ into partial fractions of the form

$$\sum_{i=1}^{m} \left(\sum_{j=1}^{k_i} \frac{A_{ij}}{(s-\lambda_i)^{(k_i+1-j)}} \right)$$

the inverse of which determines $x_i(t)$, $i = 1, 2, \ldots, N$. On inverse transformation the real roots will contribute the terms

$$\sum_{i=1}^{q} \left(\sum_{j=1}^{k_i} \frac{A_{ij} e^{\lambda_i t} \cdot t^{(k_i-j)}}{(k_i-j)!} \right)$$

while the complex conjugate pairs of root will contribute

$$\sum_{i=q+r}^{m-1} \left(\sum_{j=1}^{k_i} \frac{(A^*_{ij} \cos \beta_i t - \hat{A}_{ij} \sin \beta_i t) t^{(k_i-j)} e^{\alpha_i t}}{(k_i-j)!} \right)$$

$$r = 1, 3, 5, \ldots$$

where

$$\lambda_{q+r} = \alpha_{q+r} + i\beta_{q+r} \qquad \lambda_{q+r+1} = \alpha_{q+r} - i\beta_{q+r}$$

and

$$A_{q+r,j} = A^*_{q+r,j} + i\hat{A}_{q+r,j} \qquad A_{q+r+1,j} = A^*_{q+r,j} - i\hat{A}_{q+r,j}$$

From this complete solution of $\mathcal{L}^{-1} P(s)/F(s)$ we can immediately note that if any root of $F(s)$ has a zero or positive real part, then $x_i(t)$ cannot have a zero limit as $t \to \infty$. Consequently, if $x_i(t) = 0$ for $t \to \infty$, it is necessary and sufficient that all the roots of $F(s)$ have negative real parts. As a corollary, it is necessary but not sufficient that $|\mathbf{A}| \neq 0$ and that all the coefficients of $F(s)$ are greater than zero. The latter follows from the fact that

$$F(s) = |s\mathbf{I} - \mathbf{A}| = s^N + a_1^{N-1} + a_2^{N-2} + \cdots + a_{N-1}s + (-1)^N |\mathbf{A}|$$

where $a_m (m = 1, 2, \ldots, N-1)$ is $(-1)^m$ times the sum of all the m square principle minors of $\mathbf{A}$. Since matrix $\mathbf{A}$ has real elements, all the coefficients of $F(s)$ are real. Obviously, if $|\mathbf{A}| = 0$, then zero is a root of $F(s)$ and if any $a_m = 0$, then all the roots cannot have negative real parts. If $F(s)$ has all roots with negative real parts, we can express $F(s)$ in terms of its factors; thus

$$F(s) = \pi(s + \lambda_i) \cdot \pi[(s + \alpha_i)^2 + \beta_i^2]$$

where $-\lambda$ are real roots and $-\alpha_i \pm i\beta_i$ are the complex roots. Noting that $F(s)$ consists of factors that all have only positive signs, it follows that all a_m and $-1^N|A|$ must be positive.

If the initial condition vector has zero elements except for one element; say $x_q(0)$, and this element is one [i.e., $x_q(0)=1$], then the $x_i(t)$, $i=1, 2, \ldots, N$ are the characteristic responses of the system to a unit impulse input occurring at point q. Let these characteristic responses be denoted by $G_i(t)$. For a system initially at rest [i.e., $x_i(0)=0$ for all i], the response of the system to some input function occurring at point q is given by

$$\dot{\mathbf{x}}=\mathbf{A}\mathbf{x}+\mathbf{f}$$

with $x_i(0)$ as a null vector and

$$\mathbf{f}=\begin{bmatrix} f_1(t) \\ f_2(t) \\ \vdots \\ f_N(t) \end{bmatrix}$$

where $f_i(t)=0$ for $i \neq q$ and $f_q(t)$ is a nonnegative function defined for $t \geqslant 0$.

Again, the solution for $x_i(t)$ is readily obtained by the application of Laplace transforms and Cramer's rule. For any particular $x_i(t)$, then,

$$x_i(t)=\mathscr{L}^{-1}\frac{|\hat{\mathbf{B}}|}{|s\mathbf{I}-\mathbf{A}|}=\mathscr{L}^{-1}[G_i(s)\cdot f_q(s)]$$

where the matrix $\hat{\mathbf{B}}$ is obtained from the matrix $s\mathbf{I}-\mathbf{A}$ by replacing column i by vector $\mathbf{f}$. Since

$$\mathscr{L}^{-1}[G_i(s)\cdot f_q(s)]=\int_0^t G_i(\tau)\cdot f_q(t-\tau)dt \equiv G_i(t) * f_q(t)$$

any particular response of the system is given by the convolution of the characteristic response of the system to a unit impulse input at point q and the input function applied at point q.

We may consider $f_q(t)$ to be a summation of functions, say $f_q(t)=\hat{f}_1(t)+\hat{f}_2(t)\ldots$, in which case

$$x_i(t)=\mathscr{L}^{-1}G_i(s)\cdot f_q(s)=G_i(t)*\hat{f}_1(t)+G_i(t)*\hat{f}_2(t)+\cdots$$

Thus the matrix operator is a linear operator. Alternatively, $f_q(t)$ could be a time-translated function $H(t-p)\hat{f}(t-p)$, where $H(t-p)$ is zero for $t \leqslant p$ and one for $t>p$. In this case

$$\begin{aligned} x_i(t)&=\mathscr{L}^{-1}G_i(s)e^{-sp}\hat{f}(s) \\ &=H(t-p)\int_0^{t-p} G(\tau)\hat{f}(t-p-\tau)dt \end{aligned}$$

In other words, the response to a shifted input is merely the time-translated response of the system to an unshifted input.

We have thus established that a system represented by equation 11 is a linear time-invariant system, or equivalently that the constant coefficient matrix in equation 11 is a linear operator. Such a linear operator can obviously be used to simulate the responses of a time-invariant linear system.

As we have seen, if $G_i(t)=0$ for $t\to\infty$, some of the properties of matrix **A** are rigorously defined. But no general statement about all the individual elements of **A** can be made. However, if we also insist that all $G_i(t)$ are non-negative functions, it turns out that all the diagonal elements of **A** must be negative and all the off-diagonal elements must be nonnegative (7, 8). To exemplify this, let the **A** matrix in equation 11 be one of the following matrices:

$$\begin{pmatrix} -4 & 3 \\ 2 & -3 \end{pmatrix} \quad \text{or} \quad \begin{pmatrix} -4 & 2 \\ 3 & -3 \end{pmatrix}$$

Both these matrices have identical polynomials $|\mathbf{I}s-\mathbf{A}|$ where $F(s)=s^2+7s+6$, which has two distinct real negative roots. Letting the unit impulse point q be 1, we see that both matrices give identical characteristic responses $G_1(t)$ but different characteristic responses $G_2(t)$. For both matrices, $G_1(t)$ and $G_2(t)$ are nonnegative bounded stable functions. Consequently, it is impossible to precisely determine the structure of **A** from a knowledge of $G_1(t)$ alone.

In general, we are thus forced to accept that there is an equivalent set of matrices, with identical eigenvalues, which will serve to map the input functions into the responses. All these equivalent matrices can be transformed by a change of variable into the Jordan, or classical normal, canonical form that displays the eigenvalues of **A** along the diagonal. The eigenvalues of a matrix are equivalent to the roots of $|\mathbf{A}-\mathbf{I}s|$ and the two terms are interchangeable. The Jordan canonical form is fundamental in state-space analysis of linear systems and in control engineering.

Clearly, if we are interested in the mutual mapping of input and output functions, any of the equivalent matrices can be arbitrarily chosen as the operator.

All we have illustrated is a dual approach to the analysis of linear systems. The first approach is the straightforward application of the convolution equation, and the second approach involves the additional step of defining a constant coefficient matrix operator to simulate the system. The matrix operator has the advantage of illustrating the analytical structure of the characteristic responses, provided we accept the simplifying assumptions.

It is important to realize that the matrix operator is, in general, only a simulator of the system. Direct physical interpretation of the elements of **A** or of the eigenvalues of **A** must be viewed with suspicion in most cases.

The latter is aptly illustrated by reference to current pharmacokinetic practice. Suppose that following a unit drug impulse input into some vein we observe the blood drug concentrations in another vein and we insist, for no obvious reason, that the characteristic response is given by

$$y(t) = \sum_{i=i}^{N} A_i e^{-m_i t} \tag{12}$$

where A_i and m_i are real and greater than zero and $m_i < m_{i+1}$. Since $y(0) > 0$, any matrix simulator of this function requires $x_i(0) = 1$ where $x_i(t)$, say, $x_1(t)$, is related to $y(t)$ by $x_1(t) = (\sum A_i) \cdot y(t)$. The Laplace transform of (12) is given by

$$\mathcal{L}\, y(t) = \frac{P(s)}{F(s)} = \frac{\sum_{i=1}^{N} \left[A_i \prod_{\substack{j=1 \\ j \neq i}}^{N} (s + m_j) \right]}{\prod_{i=1}^{N} (s + m_i)} \equiv \frac{\sum_{i=1}^{N} A_i \cdot \prod_{j=1}^{N-1} (s + \gamma_j)}{\prod_{i=1}^{N} (s + m_i)}$$

The polynomial $P(s)$ is negative when $s = m_j$ for odd subscript values and positive for even subscript values. Consequently, $P(s)$ has real distinct negative roots that strictly separate the distinct real numbers $-m_i$. Any matrix with all real and distinct negative eigenvalues and whose first principal minor has eigenvalues that strictly separate the eigenvalues of the original matrix could be suitable as a simulator of $y(t)$.

Two classical matrices that satisfy the latter conditions are a bordered diagonal matrix $\mathbf{A}_1$, and a tridiagonal matrix $\hat{\mathbf{A}}_1$, where

$$\mathbf{A}_1 = \begin{bmatrix} a_{11} & a_{12} & a_{13} & \cdots & a_{1N} \\ a_{21} & & & & \\ a_{31} & & \text{diagonal } (a_{ii}) & & \\ \vdots & & & & \\ a_{N1} & & & & \end{bmatrix} \quad \text{and } \hat{\mathbf{A}}_1 = \begin{bmatrix} a_{11} & a_{12} & 0 & & & \\ a_{21} & a_{22} & a_{23} & 0 & 0 & \\ 0 & a_{32} & a_{33} & a_{34} & 0 & \\ \vdots & \vdots & \vdots & \vdots & \vdots & \\ & 0 & x & x & x & 0 \\ 0 & 0 & 0 & x & x & x \\ & 0 & 0 & 0 & x & a_{nn} \end{bmatrix}$$

In $\mathbf{A}_1$ let $a_{ii} = -\gamma_{i-1}$ and $a_{1i} = -a_{ii}$ for $i = 2, 3, \ldots, N$. Also let

$$a_{11} = -\left(\sum_{j=1}^{N} m_j - \sum_{j=1}^{N-1} \gamma_j \right)$$

and

$$a_{j1} = -\left[\frac{\prod_{i=1}^{N} (m_i - \gamma_{j-1})}{\gamma_{j-1} \prod_{\substack{i=1 \\ i \neq j-1}}^{N-1} (\gamma_i - \gamma_{j-1})} \right]$$

$j = 2, 3, \ldots, N$

With these latter values $\mathbf{A}_1$ has all diagonal elements <0; all off-diagonal elements a_{ij} and $a_{ji}(j=2,3,\ldots,N)>0$, eigenvalues of $-m_i$, and $|a_{11}|>\sum_{j=2}^{N} a_{j1}$

For initial conditions of $x_1(0)=1$ and $x_j(0)=0$ for $j=2,3,\ldots,N$, the solution for $x_1(t)$ is given by

$$x_1(t)=\mathscr{L}^{-1}\left(\frac{\prod_{i=1}^{N-1}(s+\gamma_i)}{\prod_{i=1}^{N}(s+m_i)}\right)$$

Consequently, a bordered diagonal matrix can always be constructed to simulate the observed variable $y(t)$. The appropriate $\mathbf{A}_1$ matrix can be transformed by a similarity transform into a matrix of the form $\hat{\mathbf{A}}_1$ where the similarity transform preserves the sign of the off-diagonal and diagonal elements and the column sum relationships of $\mathbf{A}_1$. Thus a tridiagonal matrix can also be constructed as a simulator of $y(t)$. The appropriate matrices $\mathbf{A}_1$ and $\hat{\mathbf{A}}_1$ correspond exactly to the matrices associated with the mammillary and catenary compartmental models depicted in Figure 1.

For a mammillary model, with $N=3$, we interpret $x_2(t)$ and $x_3(t)$ as the mass of drug in two different tissue types. For the catenary case, we could

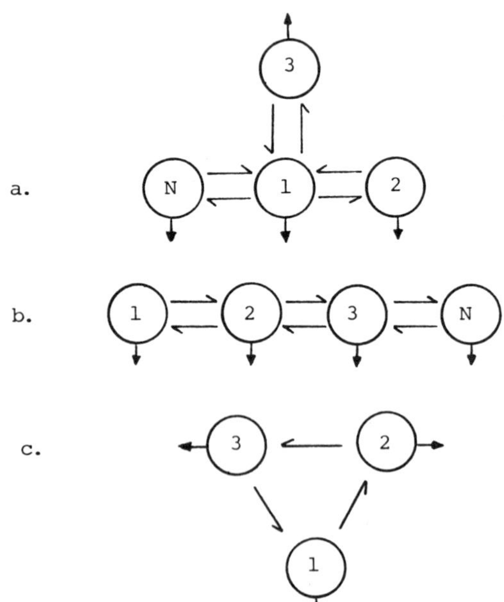

Figure 1. Compartmental models: (*a*) mammillary model; (*b*) catenary model; (*c*) cyclic model.

interpret $x_2(t)$ and $x_3(t)$ as the mass of free and bound drug within the cells, respectively. The latter are quite different explanations as to the physical phenomena that generate the observed response $y(t)$.

The use of mammillary models is so entrenched in pharmacokinetics that the analytical structure of the characteristic response associated with a constant coefficient matrix has been totally ignored. As a consequence, it is frequently believed that if the blood drug concentration–time function after an intravenous bolus dose is not a strictly monotonically decreasing function, the system is nonlinear (9). The latter view is invalid. Consider the constant coefficient matrix **C** associated with a cyclic compartmental structure (see Figure 1)

$$\mathbf{C}=\begin{pmatrix} -a_{11} & 0 & a_{31} \\ a_{12} & -a_{22} & 0 \\ 0 & a_{23} & -a_{33} \end{pmatrix}$$

where $\sum_{i=1}^{3} a_{ji} \geqslant 0$ for $j=1, 2, 3$. Matrix **C** has eigenvalues that are either (1) all real and distinct, (2) one real eigenvalue of multiplicity 1 and a distinct real eigenvalue of multiplicity 2, or (3) one real eigenvalue and a pair of complex conjugate eigenvalues. All the eigenvalues of **C** have negative real parts.

For initial conditions $x_1(0)=1$, $x_2(0)=0$, and $x_3(0)=0$, the solution $x(t)$ of $\dot{\mathbf{x}}=\mathbf{C}\mathbf{x}$ for all real and distinct eigenvalues is given by either

$$x_1(t)=\bar{A}_1 e^{-m_1 t}-\bar{A}_2 e^{-m_2 t}+\bar{A}_3 e^{-m_3 t}$$

or

$$x_1(t)=\bar{A}_1 e^{-m_1 t}+\bar{A}_2 e^{-m_2 t}-\bar{A}_3 e^{-m_3 t}$$

where

$$m_1<m_2<m_3; \qquad \bar{A}_1, \bar{A}_2, \bar{A}_3>0; \qquad \text{and } \sum_{j=1}^{3} \bar{A}_j=1$$

Obviously, regardless of the eigenvalues of **C**, the response function $x_1(t)$ is not a strictly decreasing function of t.

When considering the design of drug input functions or the response of a linear system to some particular input, it is immaterial how the system operates on the input. Once the characteristic response, $Q_\delta(t)$ has been defined, it is an unnecessary diversion to define a matrix operator that cannot be unique and to calculate intercompartmental rate constants. Consequently, the use of compartmental models for such calculations should be abandoned in favour of the simple and direct approach specified by linear systems analysis. This approach is adopted in the next section on the optimization of drug input functions.

3. OPTIMIZATION

3.1 Formulation of the Problem

3.1.1 *Curve Fitting*

Suppose that the response $Q(t_i)$ of a system is known at a set of time points $t_i(i=1, 2, \ldots, m)$; call these values the *observed values*, and let $Q(t_i) \equiv f_i^{\text{obs}}$ for $i=1, 2, \ldots, m$. Further suppose that some generating mathematical expression, with n adjustable parameters (say, $x_1, x_2, \ldots, x_n$), is known for $Q(t)$. For any particular set of x_i values; a set of values $Q(t_i)$ can be calculated by means of the generating expression; call these calculated values f_i^{cal} $(i=1, 2, \ldots, m)$. Provided f_i^{obs} is a perfect set of data and provided the generating function is exact; a set of x_i values can always be chosen such that $f_i^{\text{obs}} - f_i^{\text{cal}} = 0$ for all i.

The process of finding the appropriate set of x_i values is that of optimization. However, for most problems the observed data, f_i^{obs} is subject to random error and it is impossible to find a set of x_i values such that all the observed and calculated values coincide; consequently, a set of x_i values must be chosen such that f_i^{cal} and f_i^{obs} are close to each other for all i. Usually, closeness is defined by the least-squares criterion. In such case a best set of x_i values is obtained when the objective function $F(\mathbf{x})$ is at a minimum, where

$$F(\mathbf{x}) = \sum_{i=1}^{m} (f_i^{\text{obs}} - f_i^{\text{cal}})^2 \equiv \sum_{i=1}^{m} [f_i(\mathbf{x})]^2$$

The surface of $F(\mathbf{x})$ may exhibit multiple minima in the parameter space $\mathbf{x}$, and each $\mathbf{x}$ vector at these minima represent a best set of x_i values. However, it is assumed that there is a global minimum where the value of $F(\mathbf{x})$ is less than the corresponding values of $F(\mathbf{x})$ at any other minimum. Consequently, the problem of optimization is to minimize $F(\mathbf{x})$ by seeking the global minimum.

3.1.2 *Optimization of Drug Input Parameters*

Suppose that the desired response $Q(t)$ of a system to drug input has been specified at a set of m time points, and let $Q(t_i) \equiv f_i^{\text{obs}}$ $(i=1, 2, \ldots, m)$. Further suppose that the characteristic response $Q_\delta(t)$ of the system is known and that for a particular type of input function $F(t)$; it is necessary to adjust the input function variables $(x_1, x_2, \ldots, x_n)$ such that the response of the system $Q(t_i)$ is close to the desired response f_i^{obs}. For a particular set of x_i values $i=1, 2, \ldots, n$, the response of the system $Q(t)$ is defined by the convolution of the input function and the characteristic response. Consequently, a set of values $Q(t_i)$ for a set of x_i values can be calculated by means of the convolution integral; call these values the calculated values and define $Q(t_i)$ as f_i^{cal}.

The desired response of the system f_i^{obs} is specified and is thus exact. However, there is no guarantee, for a particular input function, that the system is capable of being driven to the desired values. Consequently, the problem is to find best values of the input function parameters—x_i values—such that the response of the system is close to the desired response. Again, this involves the minimization of the least-squares objective function $F(\mathbf{x})$.

3.2 Optimization Algorithms

The methods for minimizing a function of several variables

$$F(\mathbf{x}) = F(x_1, x_2, \ldots, x_n)$$

may be divided into two main classes:

1. Direct search methods that do not involve calculation of the derivative of $F(\mathbf{x})$. For example, the method due to Powell (10), using conjugate directions, and the simplex method proposed by Nelder and Mead (11) are derivative-free methods.
2. Gradient methods that require the first derivatives of $F(\mathbf{x})$ or the first and second derivatives of $F(\mathbf{x})$. Newton's method requires the first and second derivatives, whereas the Gauss–Newton and variable metric algorithms require only the first derivatives.

A particularly vexing problem in nonlinear optimization problems is the distinct possibility that the algorithm converges to a local as opposed to the global solution. This problem is prevalent in curve fitting of multiple exponential functions to experimental data.

The majority of algorithms for obtaining global solutions are either impossible to implement or require an unacceptable amount of computation. Perhaps the simplest solution to the problem of false convergence is to step away from the point of apparent convergence, restart the algorithm, and compare the two solutions, repeating as necessary until agreement is obtained. Obviously, the utilization of such an approach depends on the convergence rate of the particular algorithm. With a slow algorithm the computational time will rapidly become unacceptable.

At the current stage of development it cannot be expected that an algorithm will pick out the global solution if the problem has more than one minimum. Nor is it realistic to ask that a particular algorithm solve all possible problems. Rather, the criterion of usefulness should be that the algorithm solves most of the problems posed (i.e., is the algorithm robust).

Himmelblau (12) has compared 15 different unconstrained nonlinear algorithms on 15 different minimization problems. The variable metric algorithms (e.g., Fletcher's) and two nongradient methods (Powell's and Nelder and Mead's) are particularly robust.

The Nelder–Mead simplex algorithm is conceptually simple and easy to program. Consequently, it has become extremely popular, especially with engineers, and its use has been recently advocated for pharmacokinetic problems (13). The enthusiasm for the algorithm is at times irrational. The Nelder–Mead algorithm, like all others, can falsely converge to a point other than the minimum. This difficulty is prevalent when the surface has a long curved valley with steep sides (11). Additionally and most significantly, the algorithm is painfully slow, especially in the neighborhood of a minimum. Interestingly enough, the gradient-free method due to Powell (10) is just as robust but is significantly faster in execution.

Given a group of equally robust optimization algorithms the most important criterion is the execution time. This property becomes paramount if an optimization algorithm is to be executed on a microcomputer, where the electronic operational time is considerably slower than that of a mainframe computer.

A comparison of the execution times of several optimization algorithms is given in Table 1. The immediate and obvious conclusion from these data is that variable metric algorithms are faster than the nongradient methods. In particular, the very robust variable metric method, based on Fletcher's algorithm; is the quickest when compared with the other methods (12). Some applications for the latter algorithm are given subsequently. The structure and limitations of some optimization algorithms are as follows.

3.2.1 *Nelder–Mead Method*

To minimize a function $F(\mathbf{x})$ of several variables [e.g., $F(\mathbf{x})=\sum_{i=1}^{m}(f_i^{\text{obs}}-f_i^{\text{cal}})^2$], the Nelder–Mead method defines an initial simplex in the n-dimensional variable space. The simplex is defined by $n+1$ points, the vertices $V_i(i=0,1,2,\ldots,n)$ that have coordinates $\mathbf{x}_i$. The variable space is searched for the location of a minimum by alterations in the size and shape of the simplex. At each iteration the value of $F(\mathbf{x})$ at each of the $n+1$ vertices is evaluated. Let these values be F_i and let $F_h=\max_i F_i$, with corresponding coordinates x_h and $F_1=\min_i F_i$, with corresponding coordinates x_1. The coordinates $\mathbf{x}_h$ corresponding to F_h are the worst set of variable values for the current simplex. Essentially, at each iteration, the algorithm replaces the worst set of values $\mathbf{x}_h$ by a better set and thus converges to a minimum. Movement of the simplex is controlled by reflection, expansion, and contraction. The algorithm is as follows:

1. Define an initial simplex and calculate $F(\mathbf{x})$ at each vertex.
2. Reflect $\mathbf{x}_h$ and calculate a new set of coordinates $\mathbf{x}_r$. Reflection is defined by

$$\mathbf{x}_r = (1+\alpha)\bar{\mathbf{x}} - \alpha x_h$$

where α is a preset reflection coefficient ($\alpha > 0$) and

$$\bar{\mathbf{x}} = \frac{1}{n} \sum_{\substack{i=0 \\ i \neq h}}^{n} \mathbf{x}_i$$

which is the centroid of all the current $\mathbf{x}_i$ excluding $\mathbf{x}_h$.

3. Calculate the value of F_r, and if:

   a. Reflection has improved the worst point (i.e., $F_1 < F_r < F_i < F_h$ for at least one i), replace x_h by x_r. Redefine the simplex and return to step 2, thus completing the iteration.

   b. Reflection has produced a new best point (i.e., $F_r < F_1$), the simplex is expanded in that direction by calculating a new set of coordinates $\mathbf{x}_e$. Expansion is defined by $\mathbf{x}_e = \gamma \mathbf{x}_r + (1-\gamma)\bar{\mathbf{x}}$ where γ is a preset expansion coefficient ($\gamma > 1$). Calculate the value of F_e, and if expansion has produced another best point (i.e., $F_e < F_r < F_1$), replace $\mathbf{x}_h$ by $\mathbf{x}_e$; otherwise replace $\mathbf{x}_h$ by $\mathbf{x}_r$. Redefine the simplex and return to step 2, thus completing the iteration.

   c. Reflection has produced a new worst point (i.e., $F_h \leqslant F_r$ or $F_r < F_h$), the simplex is contracted by calculating $\mathbf{x}_c = \beta \mathbf{x}_h + (1-\beta)\bar{\mathbf{x}}$, where β is a preset contraction coefficient ($0 < \beta < 1$). Calculate the value F_c and if $F_c \leqslant \min(F_h, F_r)$, replace $\mathbf{x}_h$ by $\mathbf{x}_c$; otherwise the contraction of the simplex is increased by halving the distances from the best point [i.e., replace all $\mathbf{x}_i$ by $(\mathbf{x}_i + \mathbf{x}_1)/2$]. Redefine the simplex and return the step 2, thus completing the iteration.

The termination criterion is that the search is concluded when the standard deviation θ falls below a preassigned value, where

$$\theta = \left[\frac{\sum_{i=0}^{n} (F_i - \bar{F})}{n} \right]^{1/2}$$

where $\bar{F}$ is the mean of the function values.

The algorithm requires a large number of functional evaluations and is very slow in comparison with other methods (see Table 1). The number of functional evaluations is not significantly affected by the shape of the initial

Table 1. Comparison of Relative Execution Times of Optimization Algorithms Based on 15 Test Problems Adapted from Himmelblau (12)

Algorithm	Relative Execution Time
Fletcher (21), VM[a]	1.0
Davidon; Fletcher, and Powell (22), VM	2.6
Broydon (23), VM	2.6
Goldstein–Price (24), VM	3.1
Powell (10), conjugate direction—NG[b]	3.4
Hook–Jeeves (25), pattern search—NG	5.3
Nelder–Mead (11), simplex—NG	5.6
Fletcher–Reeves (26), conjugate gradient—NG	5.6

[a]VM, variable metric.
[b]NG, Nongradient.

simplex. However, the scale and orientation of the initial simplex have a dramatic effect on the number of functional evaluations. This sensitivity to orientation makes a very accurate prediction desirable. Unfortunately, there is no satisfactory way of obtaining the initial orientation (14).

The strategy of (α; β; γ) affects the number of function evaluations. Nelder and Mead recommended the strategy (1, 0.5, 2), but the strategy (2, 0.25, 0.25) is superior (14).

A version of the Nelder–Mead algorithm is used in FUNFIT (13).

3.2.2 *Newton Method*

The Newton method is based on the assumption that near a minimum $F(\mathbf{x})$ is a quadratic in n variables. For this method, assemble the variables x_i into a vector $\mathbf{x}$, $\mathbf{x}=(x_1, x_2, \ldots, x_n)^T$ and define

1. $\mathbf{x}^{(k)}$ as the vector of variables after the kth iteration in the algorithm. With this definition, $\mathbf{x}^{(0)}$ is the vector of initial estimates of the x_i values [i.e., $\mathbf{x}^{(0)}$ is the vector of starting values]
2. $\mathbf{g}^{(k)}$, the vector of first-order partial derivatives of $F(\mathbf{x})$ with respect to the x_1 values; as

$$\mathbf{g}^{(k)} = \left(\frac{\partial F(\mathbf{x})}{\partial x_i}, \frac{\partial F(\mathbf{x})}{\partial x_2}, \ldots, \frac{\partial F(\mathbf{x})}{\partial x_n} \right)^T_{\mathbf{x}=\mathbf{x}^{(k)}}$$

where the subscript indicates that the vector is evaluated for values of $\mathbf{x}$ specified by $\mathbf{x}^{(k)}$

3. $\mathbf{G}^{(k)}$, the Hessian matrix of second order partial derivatives of $F(\mathbf{x})$, as

$$\mathbf{G}^{(k)} = \begin{bmatrix} \frac{\partial^2 F(\mathbf{x})}{\partial x_1 \partial x_1} & \frac{\partial^2 F(\mathbf{x})}{\partial x_1 \partial x_2} & \cdots & \frac{\partial^2 F(\mathbf{x})}{\partial x_1 \partial x_n} \\ \frac{\partial^2 F(\mathbf{x})}{\partial x_2 \partial x_1} & \frac{\partial^2 F(\mathbf{x})}{\partial x_2 \partial x_2} & \cdots & \frac{\partial^2 F(\mathbf{x})}{\partial x_2 \partial x_n} \\ \vdots & & & \\ \frac{\partial^2 F(\mathbf{x})}{\partial x_n \partial x_1} & \frac{\partial^2 F(\mathbf{x})}{\partial x_n \partial x_2} & \cdots & \frac{\partial^2 F(\mathbf{x})}{\partial x_n \partial x_n} \end{bmatrix}_{\mathbf{x}=\mathbf{x}^{(k)}}$$

With these definitions $\mathbf{x}^{(k)}$, $k=0, 1, 2, \ldots$, is given by the Newton algorithm as

$$\mathbf{x}^{(k+1)} = \mathbf{x}^{(k)} + \lambda^{(k)} \mathbf{s}^{(k)}$$

where

$$\mathbf{s}^{(k)} = -(\mathbf{G}^{(k)})^{-1} \cdot \mathbf{g}^{(k)}$$

The step length $\lambda^{(k)}$ may be chosen as unity.

To operate the algorithm, the following steps are used:

1. Specify $\mathbf{x}^{(0)}$ and calculate $F[\mathbf{x}^{(0)}]$.
2. Set $k=0$.
3. Calculate the new variable vector by

$$\mathbf{x}^{(k+1)} = \mathbf{x}^{(k)} + \lambda^{(k)} \mathbf{s}^{(k)}$$

4. Evaluate $F[\mathbf{x}^{(k+1)}]$, increment k by one and return to step 3. The process is terminated when $F(\mathbf{x})$ has reached a minimum.

The algorithm is iterative in that a sequence of new vectors $\mathbf{x}^{(1)}, \mathbf{x}^{(2)}, \ldots$ is calculated that should rapidly converge to the optimal vector $\mathbf{x}$ that minimizes $F(\mathbf{x})$. The method may fail if $F(\mathbf{x})$ is not a quadratic in n variables near a minimum. However, this is a reasonable approximation for most nonlinear functions, and if the initial estimates are very close to the optimum the algorithm rapidly converges. Obviously this requires some knowledge of the location of the minimum and as a consequence precludes Newton's method from general use.

Another disadvantage of Newton's method is that the second derivatives, as well as the first derivatives of $F(\mathbf{x})$; are required. It is also necessary to invert the Hessian matrix at each iteration. If the Hessian $\mathbf{G}^{(k)}$ of $F(\mathbf{x}^k)$ is singular for any $\mathbf{x}^{(k)}$, the method fails at this point.

These disadvantages have led to the development of a number of quasi-

Newton methods that attempt to retain, as far as possible, the rapid convergence properties of Newton's method but that are more robust. In these methods the Hessian matrix is replaced by some approximation that does not involve the calculation of the second derivatives of $F(\mathbf{x})$ (e.g., Gauss–Newton and variable metric methods), and in some methods the process of inverting matrices is also avoided (e.g., variable metric methods).

3.2.3 *Gauss–Newton Method*

In the Gauss–Newton method we again consider the minimization of

$$F(\mathbf{x}) = \sum_{i=1}^{m} (f_i^{\text{obs}} - f_i^{\text{cal}})^2 = \sum_{i=1}^{m} (f_i)^2$$

To avoid the difficulties of calculating the Hessian matrix of second-order partial derivatives $\mathbf{G}$ and its inverse $\mathbf{G}^{-1}$, we replace f_i by a linear approximation such that

$$\mathbf{G} \approx 2\mathbf{J}^T\mathbf{J}$$

where $\mathbf{J}$ is the Jacobian matrix of first-order partial derivatives and is given by

$$\mathbf{J} = \begin{bmatrix} \dfrac{\partial f_1}{\partial x_1} & \dfrac{\partial f_1}{\partial x_2} & \cdots & \dfrac{\partial f_1}{\partial x_n} \\ \dfrac{\partial f_2}{\partial x_1} & \dfrac{\partial f_2}{\partial x_2} & \cdots & \dfrac{\partial f_2}{\partial x_n} \\ \vdots & & & \\ \dfrac{\partial f_m}{\partial x_1} & \dfrac{\partial f_m}{\partial x_2} & \cdots & \dfrac{\partial f_m}{\partial x_n} \end{bmatrix}$$

This approximation ensures that $\mathbf{G}$ is at least positive semidefinite. Consequently, the inverse $(2\mathbf{J}^T\mathbf{J})^{-1} \approx \mathbf{G}^{-1}$ is relatively simple to evaluate and failures due to the singularity of $\mathbf{G}$ are avoided. With this approximation of $\mathbf{G}$ the algorithm for minimization is exactly as described in the Newton method.

The Gauss–Newton method is applicable only to least-squares problems, and the success of the method clearly depends on the exactness of the linear approximation.

The classical Gauss–Newton method uses a step length $\lambda^{(k)}$ at each iteration of unity. A modified algorithm chooses an optimal step length at each iteration by considering the function of one variable

$$\phi(\lambda) = F(\mathbf{x}^{(k)} + \lambda\mathbf{s}^{(k)})$$

Ideally, $\lambda^{(k)}$ should minimize $\phi(\lambda)$ with $\lambda \geqslant 0$. However; it may be impossible to calculate $\lambda^{(k)}$ precisely and in practice large errors are tolerated. A version of the Gauss–Newton algorithm is used in the program NONLIN (15).

3.2.4 *Variable-Metric (Fletcher) Method*

Davidson (16) suggested that the inverse Hessian matrix of second-order derivatives of a function could be calculated iteratively in the solution of a minimization problem. Consequently, the need to calculate second derivatives and the need for matrix inversion could be completely avoided as well as the problem associated with linear approximation encountered in the Gauss–Newton method. This provides the basis of many optimization algorithms; in which the inverse Hessian is calculated iteratively, which are collectively known as *variable-metric algorithms*. This class of quasi-Newton methods is generally applicable to a wide class of optimization problems and is more efficient than nongradient methods.

Considering as before a function of n variables $F(\mathbf{x})$ that is expressed as a least-squares problem,

$$F(\mathbf{x}) = \sum_{i=1}^{m} (f_i^{\text{obs}} - f_i^{\text{cal}})^2$$

the structure of the variable metric algorithms is as follows:

1. Assemble the n variables in a vector $\mathbf{x}$; specify $\mathbf{x}^{(0)}$; calculate $F(\mathbf{x}^{(0)})$; and set $k=0$.
2. Calculate the new variable vector $\mathbf{x}^{(1)}$ by the steepest descent method; that is,

$$\mathbf{x}^{(1)} = \mathbf{x}^0 - \lambda^{(k)}\mathbf{g}^{(0)}$$

   where the step length $\lambda^{(k)} \geqslant 0$ is unity unless $F(\mathbf{x}^{(0)}) < F(\mathbf{x}^{(1)})$.
3. Increment k by one and calculate the vector $\mathbf{x}^{(k+1)}$ by

$$\mathbf{x}^{(k+1)} = \mathbf{x}^{(k)} - \lambda^{(k)}\mathbf{H}^{(k)}\mathbf{g} = \mathbf{x}^{(k)} + \lambda^{(k)}\mathbf{s}^{(k)}$$

   where the metric matrix $\mathbf{H}^{(k)}$, the approximation to the inverse Hessian of second-order derivatives, is calculated iteratively by

$$\mathbf{H}^k = \mathbf{H}^{(k-1)} + \mathbf{A}^{(k)}$$

   The metric $\mathbf{A}^{(k)}$ depends on the variable-metric method used. In the Fletcher method (17),

$$\mathbf{A}^{(k)} = -\frac{\boldsymbol{\delta}^{(k-1)}\boldsymbol{\gamma}^{(k-1)T}\mathbf{H}^{(k-1)}}{\boldsymbol{\delta}^{(k-1)T}\boldsymbol{\gamma}^{(k-1)}} - \frac{\mathbf{H}^{(k-1)}\boldsymbol{\gamma}^{(k-1)}\boldsymbol{\delta}^{(k-1)T}}{\boldsymbol{\delta}^{(k-1)T}\boldsymbol{\gamma}^{(k-1)}} + \left(1 + \frac{\boldsymbol{\gamma}^{(k-1)T}\mathbf{H}^{(k-1)}\boldsymbol{\gamma}^{(k-1)}}{\boldsymbol{\delta}^{(k-1)T}\boldsymbol{\gamma}^{(k-1)}}\right)\frac{\boldsymbol{\delta}^{(k-1)}\boldsymbol{\delta}^{(k-1)T}}{\boldsymbol{\delta}^{(k-1)T}\boldsymbol{\delta}^{(k-1)}}$$

where $\boldsymbol{\delta}^{(k-1)} = \mathbf{x}^{(k)} - \mathbf{x}^{(k-1)}$ and $\boldsymbol{\gamma}^{(k-1)} = \mathbf{g}^{(k)} - \mathbf{g}^{(k-1)}$. The step length is unity unless $F^{(k+1)} > F^{(k)}$, in which case $\lambda^{(k)}$ is reduced in size and the metric $H^{(0)} = I$, the identity matrix.

4. Calculate $F^{(k)}$ and return to step 3 if sufficient accuracy has not been achieved.

In Fletcher's method the step length is unimportant and optimization of its value is not required: this is not the case with some other variable-metric methods.

4. FUNCTIONAL OPTIMIZATION AND DRUG INPUT OPTIMIZATION – APPLICATIONS OF FLETCHER'S VARIABLE-METRIC ALGORITHM

4.1 Exponential Curve Fitting

The mathematical solutions of classical pharmacokinetic models are given by sums of exponential terms. The generalized equation may be written as

$$f^{\text{cal}} = \sum_{i=1}^{n} A_i e^{-m_i t}$$

where f^{cal} is the drug concentration at time t, n is the number of exponential terms, and A_i and m_i are the parameters to be determined. The least-squares function to be minimized is

$$F = \sum_{i=1}^{n} w_i (f_i^{\text{cal}} - f_i^{\text{obs}})^2$$

where f_i^{obs} are the observed drug concentrations at n time values t_i and w_i is a weight function that is often taken as unity.

Unfortunately, the hypersurface F for the latter function usually exhibits many local minima. It is important to realize that no optimization algorithm can guarantee a global minimum. It might be, for a particular problem, that one algorithm is superior to other algorithms yet inferior on other problems of a similar form. Consequently, it is important to have more than one optimization algorithm for tackling this type of problem. When different algorithms achieve similar optimal results, it is possible to place more confidence on the results.

To illustrate the latter, the results of three different optimization algorithms (variable metric as per Fletcher's algorithm, Gauss–Newton as per NONLIN and Nelder–Mead as per FUNFIT), are compared in Table 2. The minimization problem was to optimize a summation of two and then three exponential

Table 2. Least-Squares Fits to Pancuronium Plasma Concentrations after Intravenous Injection[a]

Exponential Parameters	Algorithm		
	Fletcher's VM	NONLIN	FUNFIT
(a) A_1	2.372	1.983	10.66
m_1	−0.200	−0.237	−0.400
A_2	0.568	0.659	0.620
m_2	−0.00619	−0.00745	−0.00686
$F_{\text{least squares}}$	3.193×10^{-2}	5.102×10^{-2}	2.199×10^{-2}
(b) A_1	2.372	1.452	4.924
m_1	−0.199	−0.287	−0.303
A_2	0.395	0.455	0.0408
m_2	−0.00687	−0.0302	−0.169
A_3	0.176	0.399	0.601
m_3	−0.00502	−0.00417	−0.00663
$F_{\text{least squares}}$	3.191×10^{-2}	7.131×10^{-2}	2.410×10^{-2}
(c) A_1	0.9464	0.9464	0.9464
m_1	−0.03716	−0.0376	−0.03761
A_2	0.2373	0.2373	0.2374
m_2	−0.00293	−0.002093	−0.002095
$F_{\text{least squares}}$	0.008194	0.008194	0.008194

[a] Parts a and b list bi- and triexponential fit to experimental data from subject I.A., respectively. Part c lists biexponential fit to experimental data from subject. NONLIN and FUNFIT parameters are taken from reference 13 and the experimental data, from reference 18.

functions to the same observed blood concentrations of pancuronium after an intravenous bolus (18).

All three algorithms give different results for the four-variable problem (two exponential function), which indicates that none of the algorithms have converged to the global minima. This is confirmed by the least-squares fits for the six-variable problem (three-exponential function). In the latter problem there are two additional variables and the least-squares fit should either improve over the four-variable problem or the results essentially reduce to a four-variable case. However, both FUNFIT and NONLIN give worse least-squares values for an increased number of variables. This is not the case with the variable-metric algorithm, and the solution tends to collapse to a four-variable case with $m_3 \rightarrow m_2$. These data clearly illustrate that neither algorithm has found a global minimum.

The least-squares values quoted (see Table 2) cannot be used to directly compare the different algorithms since the methods have different stopping criteria, and it is possible to improve on the least-squares values quoted for the variable-metric algorithm by implementing a "step-out search" method at the minimum that we have incorporated into the algorithm. The example used in Table 2 was deliberately chosen to illustrate the need to apply a number of algorithms when minimizing exponential functions.

For a different set of pancuronium data; all three algorithms gave similar results (see Table 2), and in this case some confidence can be placed on the results.

4.2 Optimization of Intravenous "Staircase" Infusions

A good approximation to a constant plasma drug concentration can be achieved by the intravenous administration of an initial bolus loading dose and stepped constant rate intravenous infusion (1).

With this type of input function, the response of the system $Q(t)$ is given by equation 8 and the optimization problem is to minimize the least-squares function

$$F=\sum_{i=1}^{n}\left[Q(\infty)-Q(t_i)\right]^2$$

where $Q(\infty)$ is the desired constant plasma concentration and $Q(t_i)$ are the calculated concentrations at n time values t_i as defined by equation 8.

As an example of this type of problem, the intravenous input function for lignocaine that will give drug concentrations close to a desired constant concentration $Q(\infty)$ of 1.47 μg/ml is optimized. The characteristic response $Q_\delta(t)$ to a 1-mg intravenous impulse of lignocaine is

$$Q_2(t)=0.276e^{-0.123t}+0.0084e^{-0.00673t}$$

A four-step staircase input function (i.e., $n=4$ in equation 8) is optimized, and this function is depicted in Figure 2.

The magnitude of the last step in the staircase input function, (R_{04}), is not a variable since its exact value is given by $Q(\infty)/\int_0^\infty Q_\delta(t)dt$. Similarly, the magnitude of the impulse loading dose D is not a variable and its value is given by $Q(\infty)/Q_\delta(+0)$. With the latter two parameters defined, there are six variables in the problem, $(R_{0_1}, R_{0_2}, R_{0_3}, \tau_1, \tau_2$, and $\tau_3)$. These variables have been optimized by the variable-metric method (Fletcher's algorithm), where the least-squares fit was over forty equally spaced time points in the time period 0–4 hours. The calculated and optimized parameters are given in the Table 3.

Vaughan and Tucker (1) have previously considered this problem and estimated the R_{0_i} and τ_i values by a graphical method (see Table 3). However,

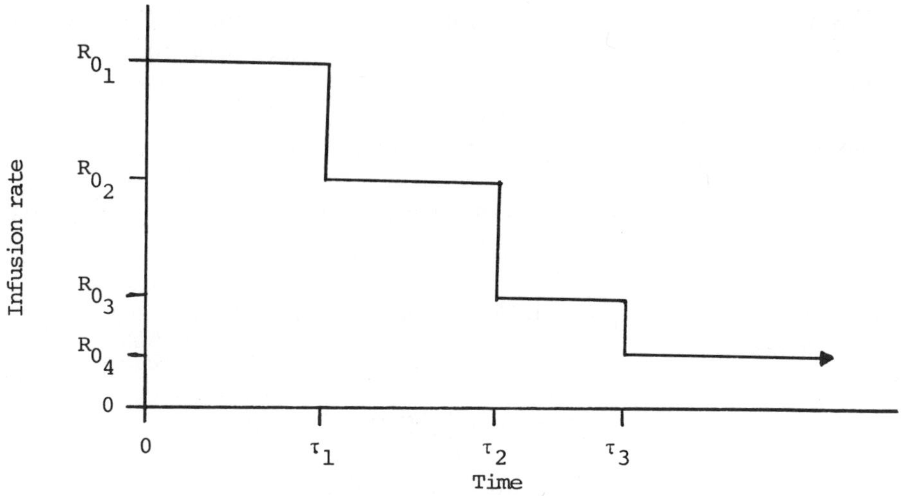

Figure 2. "Staircase" input function.

Table 3. Comparison of Graphical and Optimal Staircase Inputs for Lignocaine

Bolus Drug Dose	Optimal Values, 40.9 mg[a]	Graphical Estimates,[b] 40.9 mg[a]
Infusion Rates		
R_{0_1}	7.31 mg/minute	4.4 mg/minute
R_{0_2}	3.77 mg/minute	2.25 mg/minute
R_{0_3}	1.65 mg/minute	1.55 mg/minute
R_{04}	1.00^+ mg/minute	1.00^+ mg/minute
Duration of infusions		
τ_1	1.6 minutes	15 minutes
τ_2	27.5 minutes	39 minutes
τ_3	70.4 minutes	87 minutes
Least-squares fit	0.0356	0.08
Deviation from ideal	−3% to +5%	−8.6 to +5%

[a]Calculated values.
[b]Data adapted from reference 1.

the optimized results give a substantial reduction in the deviation from the ideal constant response.

4.3 Design of Sustained-Release Formulations

By the use of sustained-release formulations it is possible to reduce the frequency of drug administration to a 12-hour or even a 24-hour interval.

However, if a single drug release rate is used, the time required to achieve the desired steady-state concentration may be prolonged. Consequently, it is desirable to design formulations with multiple drug release rates and to use an initial loading dose. To illustrate the use of optimization (Fletcher's algorithm) in the initial design of sustained-release formulations, consider the following problem.

Given the characteristic response of a system $Q_\delta(t)$; simultaneously optimize:

1. The parameters ($D_1, D_2, D_3, K_1, K_2, K_3$) of a multiple exponential input function $\dot{A}(t)$,

$$\dot{A}(t) = \sum_{j=1}^{3} K_j D_j e^{-K_j t}$$

where D_j is the amount of drug in a formulation that is released exponentially at a rate K_j and $D_1 + D_2 + D_3$ is the total amount of drug in the formulation

2. The magnitude $\bar{K}$ of an initial loading dose such that the response $\bar{Q}(t)$ of the system to a loading dose and repeated administration of the formulation every 12 hours is close to a desired constant response m_s

For this type of repeated administration, the total response of the system $\bar{Q}(t)$ is defined by equation 10 where $m = 3$ in equation 9.

The optimization problem is to minimize the function of seven variables $\dot{A}$,

$$\dot{A} = \sum_{i=1}^{n} [m_s - \bar{Q}(t_i)]^2$$

where the $\bar{Q}(i)$ are the values of $\bar{Q}(t)$ at n time points t_i. Let $Q_2(t)$ be the characteristic response of the system (e.g.; blood–plasma drug concentrations or urinary excretion rates of drug) to a unit oral solution drug dose, and let

$$Q_\delta(t) = \frac{1}{15}(-38.05e^{-0.462t} + 29.29e^{-0.1386t} + 8.76e^{-1.54t})$$

The repeated oral administration of 15 mg of drug as a solution drug dose every 6 hours will, in about 36 hours, achieve a mean steady-state response of 22.3. Let the latter value be the desired constant response, and minimize $\dot{A}$ with respect to the seven input variables where the dosage interval is 12 hours.

Since the $Q_\delta(t)$ is an oral solution dose that will have a term involving drug absorption (possibly a first-order input of $1.54e^{-1.54t}$), the range of K_i is restricted to < 1.5. Also, since it seems undesirable to have drug release from the formulation that is less than the smallest exponential parameter in $Q_\delta(t)$; the K_i values are restricted by $0.15 > K_i$. These restrictions on the K_i values are achieved by including a penalty function into the optimization (19).

The optimized parameters for the seven variable problem are given in Table 4. It turns out that all seven variables are unnecessary and reduce to five variables (i.e., two of the K_i values are equal). Consequently, only two exponential release rates of the drug from the formulation are required.

When the release of drug from the formulation is further restricted to a single exponential function (i.e., a three-variable problem) and $\dot{A}$ optimized, the least-squares fit (see Table 4) is only marginally inferior to that obtained with five variables. Consequently, for this particular case a single release rate and a loading dose is sufficient to achieve the desired result (see Figure 3). This is not the case if the loading dose requirement is omitted.

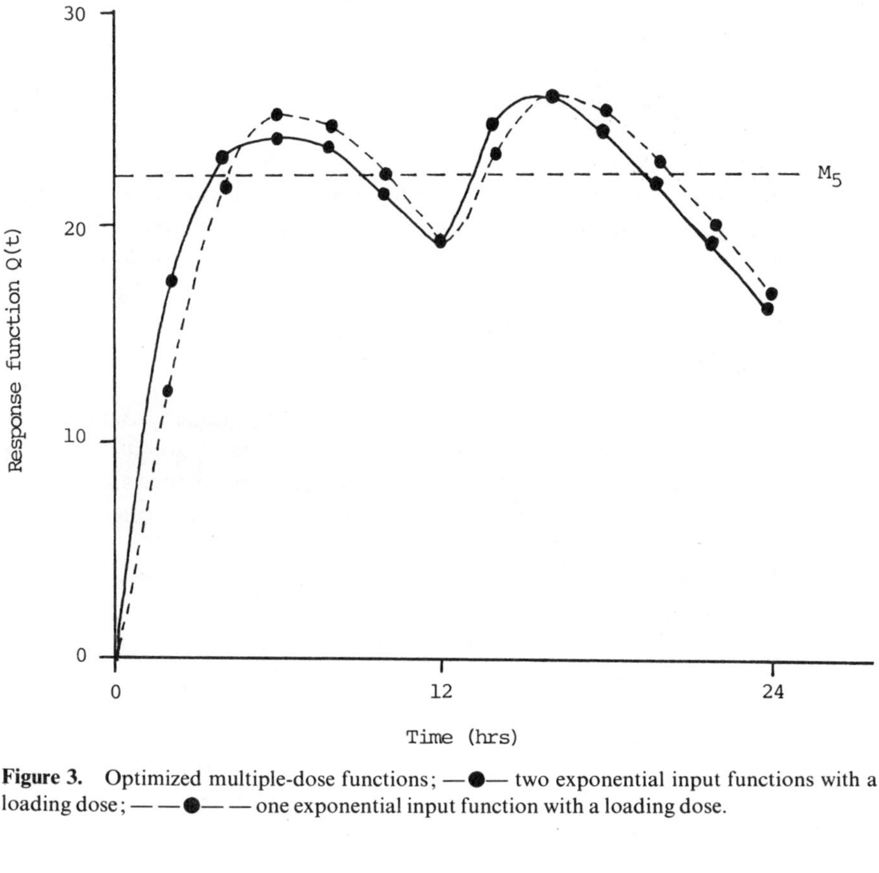

Figure 3. Optimized multiple-dose functions; —●— two exponential input functions with a loading dose; — —●— — one exponential input function with a loading dose.

Table 4. Optimized Input Parameters for a Multiple-Exponential Sustained-Release Preparation and the Optimized Initial Loading Dose

Drug dose D_j	Exponential release rate
Seven-Variable Problem	
$D_1 = 11.2$	$K_1 = 0.15$
$D_2 = 17.2$	$K_2 = 0.15$
$D_3 = 6.9$	$K_3 = 1.5$
Initial loading dose $\bar{K} = 1.912$	
Least-squares value $F = 122.8$	
Three-Variable Problem	
$D_1 = 36.04$	$K_1 = 0.205$
Initial loading dose $\bar{K} = 1.751$	
Least-squares value $F = 182.4$	

4.4 Optimization of Drug Input Parameters for Nonlinear Systems

Some drugs, for example, phenytoin, exhibit a nonlinear relationship between the dose and the plasma concentrations. Nonlinear differential equations (e.g., Michaelis–Menten type) are required to explain this phenomenon. These differential equations describing such systems do not have analytical solutions, and numerical solutions must be sought. The fitting of parameters in such equations to experimental data requires a nonlinear optimization routine. To illustrate the type of approach required, a worked example follows.

After oral administration of a micronized suspension of phenytoin (600 mg of phenytoin in 20 ml), the plasma drug concentrations are as given in Figure 4, and after oral administration of the same drug dose in a tablet formulation (six 100-mg Enkefal® tablets), the plasma drug concentration are as given in Figure 5.

To describe plasma concentrations $C(t)$ after an oral suspension, the following nonlinear model was adopted:

$$\frac{dC}{dt} = \frac{DK_a e^{-K_a t}}{V} - \frac{K_m C}{K_e + C} \qquad C(0) = 0 \tag{13}$$

This model is a simple nonlinear system with first-order drug input. The parameters V, the volume of the system, and K_m and K_e, the metabolic and elimination rates, are system dependent whereas the administered dose D

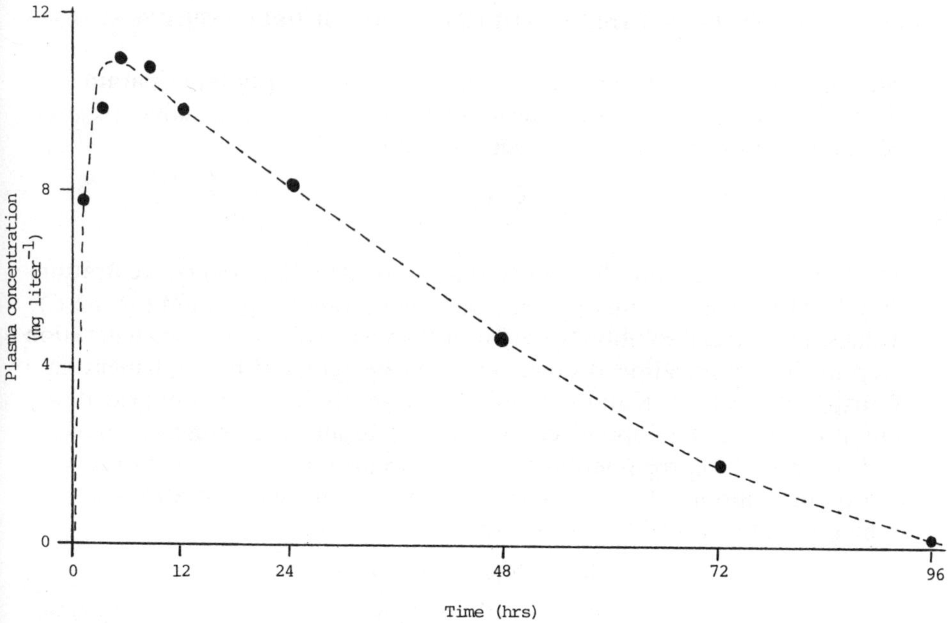

Figure 4. Calculated plasma concentrations of phenytoin (dashed line) and observed concentrations (●) after a micronized suspension.

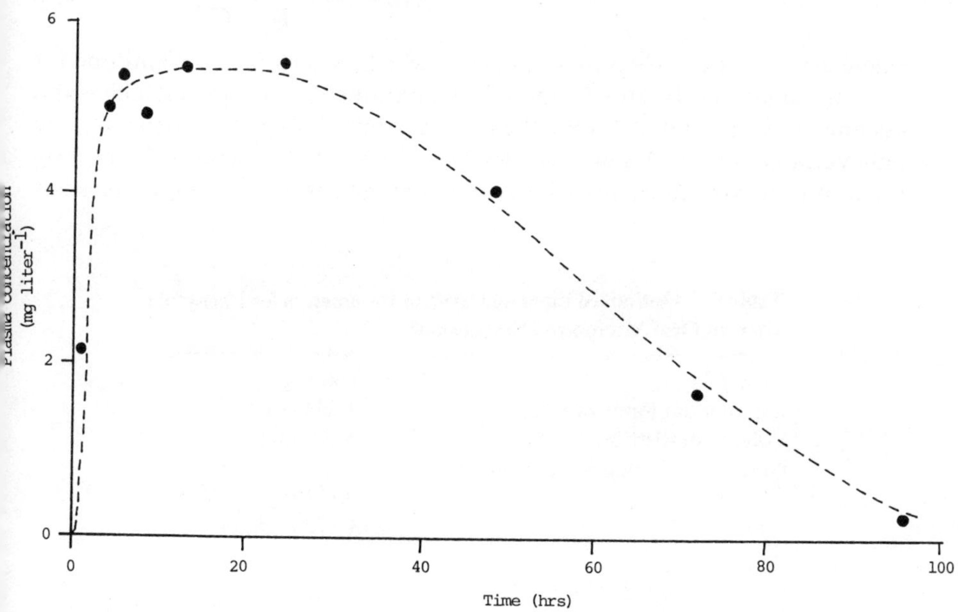

Figure 5. Calculated plasma concentrations of phenytoin (dashed line) and observed concentrations (●) after Enkefal tablets..

and the release rate K_a are the system-independent drug input parameters. To fit the experimental data to the latter equation, the four variables (K_a, K_m, K_e, and V) must be chosen. As usual, we minimize

$$\dot{A} = \sum_{i=1}^{n} [C_i^{\text{obs}} - C_i^{\text{cal}}]^2$$

where the C_i values are the observed and calculated plasma concentrations (mg/liter) at n time points t_i. Since there is no exact expression for the C_i^{cal} values, a numerical solution to equation 10 must be obtained at each iteration step in the optimization routine. This can be achieved by implementing a fourth-order Runge–Kutta method for the solution of the nonlinear differential equation. The optimized system and input parameters are given in Table 5, and the corresponding plasma concentrations are given in Figure 4.

For description of the behavior of the plasma concentrations after a tablet dose, two possible models are

$$\frac{dC}{dt} = \frac{DK_a e^{-K_a t}}{V} - \frac{K_m C}{K_e + C} \tag{14}$$

and

$$\frac{dC}{dt} = \frac{DK_a e^{-K_a t}}{V} - \frac{K_0}{V}[1 - H(t-\tau)] - \frac{K_m C}{K_e + C} \tag{15}$$

where $H(t-\tau)$ is the Heaviside function, which is zero for $t<\tau$ and one for $t \geqslant \tau$. In equations 14 and 15 the system parameters are not variables and assume the values obtained for the oral suspension data. Consequently, the only variables are the input variables. In equation 15 it is assumed that drug input into the system occurs by way of a first- and zero-order input function

Table 5. Optimized Input and System Parameters for Phenytoin after an Oral Micronized Suspension[a]

Dose D[b]	600 mg
Exponential input rate K_a	1.234 hours^{-1}
Volume of distribution V	51.99 liters
Nonlinear elimination parameters	
(K_m)	0.162 mg/(liter/hour)
(K_e)	1.172 mg/liter
Least-squares value $F = 0.93$	

[a] Experimental data for phenytoin obtained from reference 20.
[b] The dose is a nonvariable.

Table 6. Optimized Input Parameters for Phenytoin after Oral Administration of a Tablet Formulation[a]

First-Order Absorption	
Dose D	345 mg
Exponential input rate K_a	0.036 hours^{-1}
Zero-Order Absorption	
Zero-order input rate K_0	101.9 mg/hours
Duration of input (τ)	2 hours
Least-squares value $F = 0.602$	

[a]The system parameters VK_m and K_e are nonvariables and are as given in Table 5. Plasma concentrations of phenytoin were obtained from reference 20.

(variables D, K_a, K_0, and τ). In this case the total drug input into the system is $D + K_0\tau$.

When equation 14 is used to describe the drug concentrations after a tablet dose, the optimized fit to the observed data is poor. However, when equation 15 is used to fit the observed data, reasonable agreement is obtained. The optimized input parameters for equation 15 are given in Table 6, and the corresponding plasma concentrations are given in Figure 5.

From the data on the optimized input parameters for the tablet formulation, the following observations can be made:

1. A substantial part of the administered dose is released into solution by a zero-order process, and the first-order release is slow in comparison to the micronized suspension. This is consistent with the tablet containing large phenytoin particles. If this is correct, rigorous controls on the raw drug and the dissolution of the formulation are necessary to avoid variations in plasma concentrations resulting from the manufacturing process.
2. The bioavailability of the tablet formulation relative to the micronized suspension is 91%. The relative bioavailability as determined from the areas under the two functions is only 68%. However, in nonlinear systems the area under the observed plasma concentrations is not directly related to the total drug input and relative areas do not correspond to the true bioavailability.

This and the preceding examples illustrate the wide variety of pharmacokinetic and pharmaceutical problems in which nonlinear optimization routines are applicable.

REFERENCES

1. D. P. Vaughan and G. T. Tucker. General derivation of the ideal intravenous drug input required to achieve and maintain a constant plasma drug concentration. Theoretical application to lignocaine therapy. *Eur. J. Clin. Pharmacol.* **10**: 433–440 (1976).
2. D. P. Vaughan. A model independent proof of Dost's Law of corresponding areas. *J. Pharmacokin. Biopharm.* **5**: 271–276 (1977).
3. D. P. Vaughan and M. Dennis. Mathematical basis of the "point-area" deconvolution method for determining in vivo input functions. *J. Pharm. Sci.* **67**: 663–667 (1978).
4. D. P. Vaughan and M. Dennis. Mathematical basis and generalization of the Loo–Riegelman method for the determination of in vivo drug absorption. *J. Pharmacokin. Biopharm.* **8**: 83–98 (1980).
5. D. Cutler. Numerical deconvolution by least squares—use of polynomials to represent the input function. *J. Pharmacokin. Biopharm.* **6**: 243–263 (1978).
6. B. M. Brown. *The Mathematical Theory of Linear Systems*, Chapman and Hall, London, 1961, Chapter 14.
7. J. Z. Hearon. Theorems on linear systems. *Ann N.Y. Acad. Sci.* **97**: 37–67 (1963).
8. Theorems of S. Karlin and O. Taussky. Cited by R. Bellman in *Introduction to Matrix Analysis*, McGraw-Hill, New York, 1960, pp. 159–182.
9. J. M. van Rossum, C. A. M. van Ginneken, P. Th. Henderson, H. C. J. Ketelaars, and T. B. Vree. Pharmacokinetics of Biotransformation. In J. M. van Rossum (ed.), *Kinetics of Drug Action*, Vol. 47 of *Handbook of Experimental Pharmacology*, Springer-Verlag, New York, 1977.
10. M. J. D. Powell. An efficient method for finding the minimum of a function of several variables without calculating derivatives. *Comput. J.* **7**: 155–162 (1964).
11. J. A. Nelder and R. Mead. A simplex method for function minimization. *Comput. J.* **7**: 308–313 (1965).
12. D. M. Himmelblau. A Uniform Evaluation of Unconstrained Optimization Techniques. In F. A. Lootsma (ed.), *Numerical Methods for Non-linear Optimization*. Academic Press, New York, 1972.
13. P. V. Pederson. Curve fitting and modeling of pharmocokinetics and some practical experiences with NONLIN and a new program FUNFIT. *J. Pharmacokin. Biopharm* **5**: 513–531 (1977).
14. J. M. Parkinson and D. Hutchinson. An investigation into the efficiency of variants on the simplex methods. In F. A. Lootsma (ed.), *Numerical Methods for Non-linear Optimization*. Academic Press, New York, 1972.
15. C. M. Metzler. *A user's Manual for NONLIN, The Upjohn Co., Technical Report 7292/69/7292/005*, Kalamazoo, Mich., 1969.
16. W. C. Davidson. Variable metric method for minimization. *A.E.C. Research and Development Report, ANL—5990*, 1959.

17. R. Fletcher. A Survey of Algorithms for Unconstrained Optimization. In W. Murray (ed.), *Numerical Methods of Unconstrained Optimization*. Academic Press, New York, 1972.

18. P. V. Pederson. Curve fitting and modeling in pharmacokinetics: Reply from the author. *J. Pharmacokin Biopharm* **6**: 447–449 (1978).

19. A. V. Fiacco and G. P. McCormick. The sequential unconstrained minimization technique for nonlinear programming. *Manage. Sci.* **10**: 601–606 (1964).

20. P. J. Pentikäinen, P. J. Neuvonen, and S. M. Elfving. Bioavailability of four brands of phenytoin tablets. *Eurp. J. clin. Pharmacol.* **9**: 213–218 (1975).

21. R. Fletcher. A new approach to variable metric algorithms. *Comput. J.* **13**: 317–322 (1970).

22. R. Fletcher and M. J. D. Powell. A rapidly convergent descent method for minimization. *Comput. J.* **6**: 163–168 (1963).

23. C. G. Broydon. A class of methods for solving non-linear equations. *Math. Comput.* **19**: 577–584 (1965).

24. A. A. Goldstein and J. F. Price. An effective algorithm for minimization. *Num. Math.* **10**: 184–189 (1967).

25. R. Hooke and T. A. Jeeves. Direct search solution of numerical and statistical problems. *J. Assoc. Comput. Mach.* **8**: 212–221 (1961).

26. R. Fletcher and C. M. Reeves. Function minimization by conjugate gradients. *Comput. J.* **7**: 149–154 (1964).

CHAPTER 5

Pharmacokinetic-Model-Based Optimization of Drug Inputs Exemplified by an Administration Strategy of Insulin

T. DEUTSCH

Laboratory of Chemical Cybernetics
Eötvös Loránd University of Sciences
Budapest, Hungary

M. SCHULZ

Biomedical Research Division
The Hospital for Sick Children
Toronto, Ontario, Canada

G. TAMÁS, Jr.

1st Department of Internal Medicine
Semmelweis Medical University
Budapest, Hungary

CONTENTS

The primary aim in therapy is to determine the optimal dosage of drugs for an individual patient or group of patients. To reach this goal, three therapeutic strategies are used as illustrated in Figure 1. Although the optimization of treatment is sought in each case, the ways to achieve it are different.

The optimal a priori drug input represents the best treatment for a hypothetical average patient of a given population. It can be calculated with the mathematical modeling and statistical evaluation of the observed reactions of a representative group of patients to a given drug treatment (1).

The optimal individualized therapy strives to adapt treatment to the physiological characteristics of a given patient. In the open-loop control of drug response, optimization of therapy is based on calculations made by use of the pretreatment clinical parameters of the individual patient (2, 3). In this case therapeutic strategy is not influenced by the patient's individual reactions to the predetermined drug therapy.

In the closed-loop control of drug effect the observed characteristics and intensity of drug response are used to modify drug input according to the individual need of the patient during therapy (4–6).

In the following only the individualized open-loop drug input optimization is discussed. In optimal drug therapy a given drug is administered with maximal therapeutic efficacy. The efficacy and adverse effects are primarily functions of the mode of administration of the drug. The time course of the therapeutic and toxic effects can be controlled by an appropriate administration strategy.

The intensity and time patterns of the drug-elicited response are determined by the individual characteristics of the drug input–pharmacological response output relationship of the patient. Providing a basis for drug input optimization, the mathematical models that describe this relationship can help to guide clinical therapy in a more rational way.

This chapter contains a brief discussion of the mathematical formulation of the drug input–pharmacological response output relationship and of the drug input optimization problem. A general mathematical method—the mixed-integer linear programming—is presented for the solution of several types of open-loop drug input optimization problem. The application of physiologically based and black-box-type drug input–pharmacological response output models and the elaborated algorithm are demonstrated for an open-loop insulin therapy in diabetics.

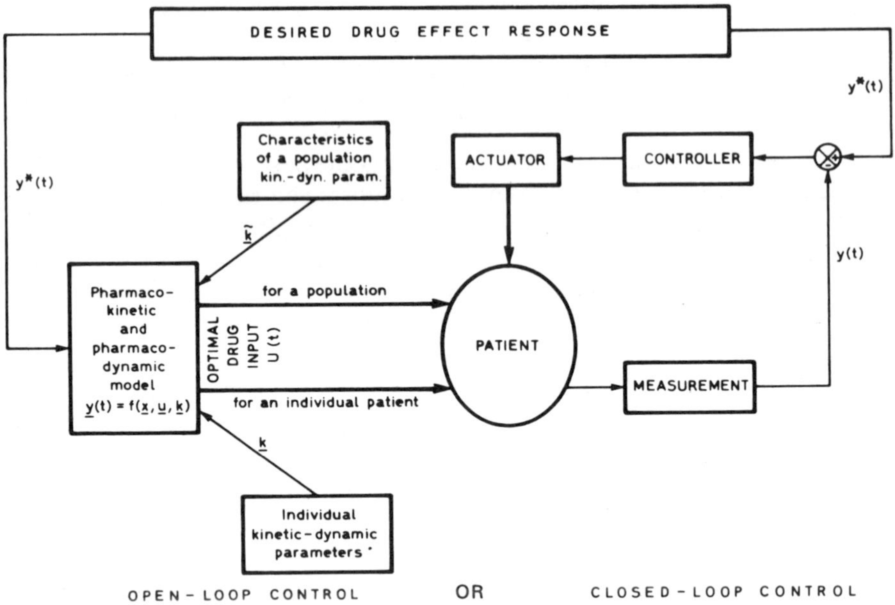

Figure 1. Different therapeutic strategies in drug treatment.

1. MATHEMATICAL MODELS AND METHODS IN DRUG INPUT OPTIMIZATION

General concepts and methods are briefly discussed that have been applied to optimize insulin therapy in diabetics.

1.1 Mathematical Modeling of the Drug Input–Pharmacological Response Output Relationship

For modeling this relationship, we consider the body as a drug-responding system (5). Drug effect is the consequence of the presence of the parent drug and/or its metabolites at their sites of action. The relationship between drug input and drug-elicited response output is depicted schematically in Figure 2.

In the case of one drug input and pharmacological response, the relationship can be formulated as follows:

$$\dot{\mathbf{x}}(t)=\mathbf{A}(t)\cdot\mathbf{x}(t)+\mathbf{B}(t)\cdot u(t)+\mathbf{C}(t)\cdot l(t)\quad \mathbf{x}(0)=\mathbf{x}_0 \tag{1}$$

and

$$y(t)=\mathbf{D}(t)\cdot\mathbf{x}(t) \tag{2}$$

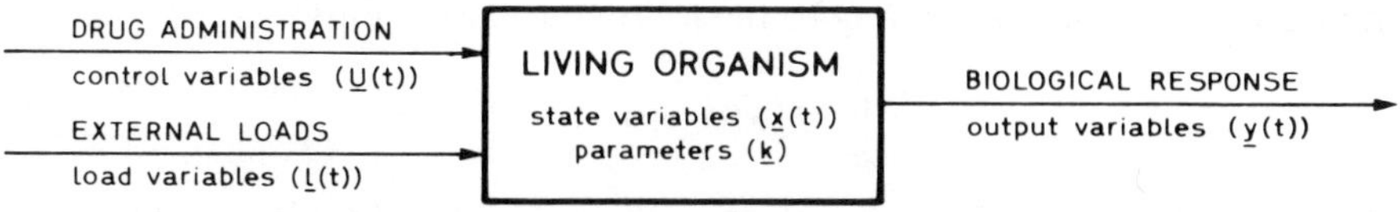

Figure 2. Input–output relationships in drug therapy.

where $\mathbf{x}(t)$ = state vector of dimension N characterizing the internal state of the system at time t

$y(t)$ = observed pharmacological response at time t

$u(t)$ = drug input at time t

$l(t)$ = external load or disturbance at time t

$\mathbf{A}(t)$ = matrix of dimensions $N \times N$ characterizing the system dynamics at time t

$\mathbf{B}(t)$, $\mathbf{C}(t)$, $\mathbf{D}(t)$ = vectors of dimension N characterizing the effect of drug input and external load on the time profile of state variables and the transformation between state and observed variables at time t, respectively

Equations 1 and 2 are termed *state* and *observation equations*, respectively. Throughout this chapter linear system dynamics is supposed.

The state of the system is determined by its initial state and the inputs during time t. The rationale for distinguishing two kinds of input at the formulation of insulin therapy is discussed in Section 3. The observed variable $y(t)$ can be any quantifiable patient response, such as blood level, urinary recovery, and pharmacological response. The matrix **A** and the vectors **B**, **C**, and **D** contain the pharmacokinetic and pharmacodynamic model parameters (**k**, vector of dimension P) characterizing the individual patient. They may be constant but can depend on time. The estimation of these parameters is an essential preliminary step of the individualization of drug therapy.

1.2 Mathematical Formulation of Drug Input Optimization

Drug input optimization consists of determining the strategy for the administration of a given drug to achieve maximal therapeutic efficacy. The administration strategy is defined by the route, dose, and time schedule of drug input.

To be able to evaluate the efficacy of a given drug input strategy, a characteristic measure must be defined. This is termed *clinical cost function*. The optimal treatment is defined by the minimal value of the clinical cost function.

The clinical cost function is determined by the trajectories of state, control, and output variables according to the following expression:

$$J=\int_0^T f[\mathbf{x}(t), y(t), u(t), t]dt \tag{3}$$

where T denotes the duration of drug therapy. The clinical cost function may be the measure of the administered amount of drug, the anticipated risk of the given administration strategy, or the deviation of the actual response from some desired level. The optimal drug input is defined by the following expression:

$$J_{\text{opt}}=\min_{u(t)} J[\mathbf{x}_0, y_0, u(t)]=J[\mathbf{x}_0, y_0, u_{\text{opt}}(t)] \tag{4}$$

In the subsequent problems we suppose that the administration rate of drug can be modified only in discrete times during the therapy. The duration of drug treatment is divided into K time periods with a length of $h=T/K$. Drug input is supposed to be constant or instantaneous (bolus type) during or at the beginning of each time interval and is denoted by $u(t_k)$ in the kth period. The state and output variables have a value of $\mathbf{x}(t_k)$ and $y(t_k)$ at the end of the kth time interval.

The discrete solution of the time-variant linear differential equation system (equation 1) is given by the following formula:

$$\mathbf{x}(t_k)=\mathbf{H}(t_k, 0)\cdot\mathbf{x}_0+\sum_{j=1}^{k}\int_{(j-1)h}^{jh}\mathbf{H}(t_k, \tau)\cdot[b(\tau)\cdot u(t_j)+c(\tau)\cdot 1(\tau)]d\tau \tag{5}$$

where $\mathbf{H}(t, 0)$ is the state transition matrix of the system that transforms the initial state $\mathbf{x}_0$ of the system into its actual state $\mathbf{x}(t)$. The numerical calculation of $\mathbf{H}$ may be found elsewhere (7).

It can be noted that in time-invariant cases the elements of $\mathbf{H}$ are constant during treatment and are only functions of time differences $(t_k-\tau)$. In time-variant cases, however, the actual matrix must be recalculated for each interval. It is evident from equation 5 that it provides a linear relation for calculation of the state of the system from its initial state and from the inputs up to time t

In the design of drug optimization strategies several limiting factors must be taken into consideration in most cases. Generally the constraints relating to the control, state, and output variables can be formulated in the following way:

$$U_{\min}\leqslant u_k\leqslant U_{\max} \qquad k=1, 2, \ldots, K \tag{6}$$

$$\mathbf{X}_{k,\min}\leqslant\mathbf{x}_k\leqslant\mathbf{X}_{k,\max} \qquad k=1, 2, \ldots, K \tag{7}$$

$$Y_{k,\min}\leqslant y_k\leqslant Y_{k,\max} \qquad k=1, 2, \ldots, K \tag{8}$$

where $U_{\min}$ and $U_{\max}$ represent the minimal and maximal drug input rates, respectively, and $\mathbf{X}_{k,\min}$, $Y_{k,\min}$ and $\mathbf{X}_{k,\max}$, $Y_{k,\max}$ denote the allowable minimal and maximal values of state variables and response intensities, respectively. The latter bounds may depend on the time elapsed from the start of treatment. Generally these lower and upper limits indicate the desired range of drug action or represent the therapeutic and toxic threshold levels, respectively. The conditions to be satisfied by any permissible drug input profile are then formulated by equality and inequality constraints (equations 6–8).

In the case of discrete time intervals, the continuous definition of clinical cost function given by equation 3 is transformed into the following relationship:

$$J = \sum_{k=1}^{K} f[\mathbf{x}(t_k), y(t_k), u(t_k), t_k] \tag{9}$$

2. SOLUTION OF OPEN-LOOP DRUG INPUT OPTIMIZATION PROBLEMS BY MIXED-INTEGER LINEAR PROGRAMMING

During the last decade several general methods have been developed for the optimization of drug inputs. The general impulse control problem was treated by Bellman (8), Buell et al. (9) and Pierce and Schumitzky (10), using dynamic programming (8, 9) and a new algorithm suitable to solve semiinfinite dimensional problems (10). Wheeler and Sheiner (11) have given a general formulation of the individualized open-loop therapy. The quadratic programming was applied for the solution of the problem. Smolen et al. (12) used a functional analytic method to treat time-optimal drug administration.

The general applicability of mixed-integer linear programming is illustrated here for open-loop drug input optimization.

A general linear programming problem can be formulated as follows (13):

$$\mathbf{L} \cdot \mathbf{Z} \leqslant \mathbf{b} \tag{10}$$

$$\mathbf{c}^T \cdot \mathbf{Z} \rightarrow \min \tag{11}$$

where $\mathbf{L}$ = matrix of the problem
$\mathbf{Z}$ = column vector of unknowns
$\mathbf{c}^T$ = transpose of the cost-coefficient vector
$\mathbf{b}$ = constant vector [usually termed as right-hand side (RHS)]

A linear programming problem consists of determining the minimal value of a linear expression of several variables subject to linear equality and/or inequality constraints. If the unknown vector $\mathbf{Z}$ contains some element(s) restricted to have only integer values, the problem is termed a *mixed-integer linear programming problem.* Different algorithms have been developed for solving this kind of problem (13).

In many drug therapies the control variables (doses and administration times) have only discrete values. These constraints are quite general in case of oral administration. Moreover, auxiliary integer variables must be introduced into the definition of drug input optimization to transform non-linear relations into linear expressions, as we see later.

The vector of unknowns of the linear programming problem is composed of the state, control, and output variables. In most cases, however, several auxiliary variables and equations are needed to define the clinical cost function. In the following, three open-loop drug administration problems are presented.

Only the definition of cost function is demonstrated in detail; the equations describing the system dynamics and the constraints relating to state, control, and/or output variables are not discussed separately because their formulation directly follows from the state equations and the characteristics of the problem to be solved. Their mathematical form is supposed to be identical to those given by equations 5 through 8.

2.1 "Tracking" Problem in Drug Input Optimization

The therapeutic goal is to determine the drug administration strategy ensuring a time course of drug effect as close as possible to the one prescribed.

The clinical cost function is defined by the sum of the absolute values of deviations between the prescribed and elicited responses:

$$J = \sum_{k=1}^{K} |y_k - y'_k| \rightarrow \min \tag{12}$$

where y'_k denotes the prescribed drug-induced response intensity at the end of the kth time period.

The clinical cost function must be transformed into a linear form suited for linear programming. This can be accomplished by introducing the artificial variables d_k, $k = 1, 2, \ldots, K$ and the following auxiliary inequality relationships:

$$\begin{aligned} &(y_k - y'_k) \leq d_k \\ \text{and} \quad &(y'_k - y_k) \leq d_k \end{aligned} \qquad k = 1, 2, \ldots, K \tag{13}$$

With the use of the auxiliary vector **d** the transformed linear form of the clinical cost function is given as follows:

$$J = \sum_{k=1}^{K} d_k \rightarrow \min \tag{14}$$

The linear programming problem is composed of equations 5 through 8, 13, and 14. Its solution provides the optimal drug administration strategy $u_k, k=1, 2, \ldots, K$ and simultaneously the predicted pharmacological response profile $y_k, k=1, 2, \ldots, K$ during treatment.

2.2 Time-Optimal Control Problem in Drug Input Optimization

The therapeutic aim is to determine the drug administration strategy, ensuring that the physiological response achieves its desired intensity in a minimal time.

Since the only explicit variables are the state, observed, and control variables, time cannot enter explicitly into the clinical cost function. The only way to minimize time is to construct an objective function that imposes a penalty when response intensity has not reached its desired value. The severity of penalty increases with time. For this reason, the following power function is used to formulate the clinical cost function (14):

$$J = \sum_{k=1}^{K} 10^{(k-K/2)}(y' - y_k) \rightarrow \min \tag{15}$$

where y' denotes the desired level of pharmacological response. The term $K/2$ is used in the exponent for symmetrical reasons only. The linear programming problem is composed of equations 5 and 15. Its solution yields the time-optimal drug input and the expected evolution of the controlled physiological response variable.

It is important to note that the proposed solution is not the mathematically exact solution of the time-optimal control problem. However, the facility to take into account time-dependent constraints regarding the state and/or control variables is the great advantage of this method. A comparative study demonstrated the good practical utility of this approximate method (14).

2.3 Drug Input Optimization with a Minimum Number of Different Drug Input Rates

The ease and convenience of drug therapy requires a minimal number of medical interventions. The convenient time of interventions is also determined by practical considerations. The therapeutic goal is to determine the rates and durations of consecutive infusions so that the number of necessary changes in the infusion rates will be minimal and the elicited effect will develop in a preselected therapeutic range. Duration of different infusions may only be a multiple of a predetermined time interval.

At first the logical relationships concerning the possible changes in administration rates must be formulated by linear expressions. For this reason, logical variables w_k, $k=1, 2, \ldots, K-1$ are introduced that may have only two distinct values, zero or one. The relation between successive control variables (input rates) can be given as follows:

$$w_k \cdot (u_{k+1} - u_k) = 0 \qquad k=1, 2, \ldots, K-1 \tag{16}$$

If $w_k=1$, the successive drug input rates are identical (i.e., $u_{k+1}=u_k$). Whenever $w_k=0$, the necessary modification in administration rates can be performed. From equation 16 it is evident that the number of w_k values having a value of one gives the number of intervals where drug input remains unaltered. To minimize the number of interventions, the sum of w_k values must be maximized. The clinical cost function can be formulated by the following expression:

$$J = \sum_{k=1}^{K-1} w_k \rightarrow \max \tag{17}$$

Introducing the artificial variables d_k, $k=1, 2, \ldots, K-1$ representing the products defined by equation 16 and a constant M that is greater than the possible maximal value of the differences $(u_{k+1} - u_k)$, we can replace the nonlinear relationship (equation 16) by the following three linear constraints:

$$d_k \leqslant u_{k+1} - u_k + (1 - w_k) \cdot M \tag{18}$$

$$d_k \geqslant u_{k+1} - u_k - (1 - w_k) \cdot M \qquad k=1, 2, \ldots, K-1 \tag{19}$$

$$d_k = 0 \tag{20}$$

The linear programming problem is composed of equations 5 through 8 and 17 through 20. Its solution yields the rates and durations of consecutive infusions and the model-predicted evolution of the controlled response variable. The application of the method for open-loop insulin administration is presented in Section 4.

The illustrated problems show only a few possible applications of mixed-integer linear programming. A wide variety of drug input optimization problems with apparently nonlinear therapeutic goals can be treated by this mathematical tool by use of appropriate transformations. The nonlinearity of the system can often be overcome by stepwise linearization about the expected trajectory of the system. Finally, a great advantage of linear programming is that it always provides global optimums.

3. MODELING OF INSULIN INPUT–GLYCEMIA OUTPUT RELATIONSHIP IN DIABETICS FOLLOWING CARBOHYDRATE INTAKE

The leading symptom of diabetes mellitus is an elevation of the blood glucose level. The origin of this disease has not yet been determined; however, all diabetics—regardless of the severity of their state—have relative or absolute insulin deficiency. Insulin is involved in most metabolic processes influencing carbohydrate, protein, and fat metabolism. In the complex fuel homeostatic system, beside insulin, several other hormones play significant role; however, their effects are neglected in this work. This simplification is justified by the fact that in the glycemias investigated in the frame of this study, insulin effect was dominant.

Before the elaborated mathematical models are discussed, the physiological background of blood glucose regulation and carbohydrate absorption is reviewed.

3.1 Blood Glucose Regulation

The blood glucose control system is one of the most complex homeostatic systems of the body. It serves to maintain a relatively constant extracellular glucose level when faced with different disturbances. A greatly simplified diagram of the control system is shown in Figure 3. The diagram indicates also the cases where externally administered insulin is used for normoglycemic control. The presented feedback control system is composed of the following components (15):

1.	Controlled variable	extracellular glucose level
2.	Sensor	beta-cells
3.	Control variable	insulin level
4.	Load variable	carbohydrate ingested
5.	Set point	basal glucose level
6.	Error signal	deviation between basal and actual glucose level
7.	Actuator variables	glucose uptake and glucose production

The dynamics of secretion and disposition is the determinant factor in insulin effectiveness. The chain of events that leads to the release of insulin on stimulation of the pancreatic beta cells by glucose was modeled by Grodsky (16), Bergman and Urquhart (17), and Cerasi et al. (18). Bergman and Urquhart (17) pointed out that the release patterns of insulin to different glucose stimuli could be modeled formally with two parallel elements: one responsive to the absolute concentration of glucose perfusing the gland (proportional element) and the other, to the rate of increase of glucose level (positive derivative element). As we show later, the algorithm of artificial pancreas is based on this approach.

Insulin disposition was modeled by linear compartmental models (6, 18–20). In the range of 5–400 mU/liter plasma insulin levels, no significant pattern indicating nonlinearity was observed. The mean total distribution

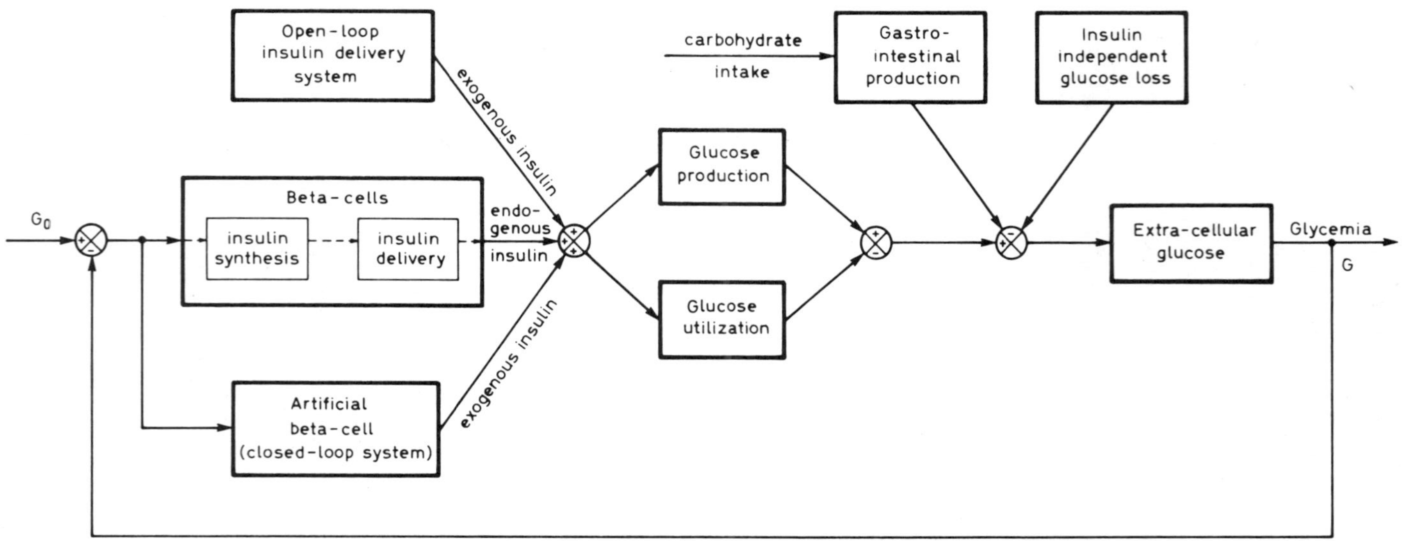

Figure 3. Closed-loop (feedback) and open-loop (feedforward) control of blood glucose.

volume of insulin is, for healthy subjects, 157 ml/kg body weight, suggesting an interstitial distribution for insulin. The total plasma clearance is equal to 0.78 liter/minute (19).

Glucose distributes rapidly in extracellular space, as described by linear compartmental models (6, 18, 20, 21). The glucose entering systemic circulation is produced mainly by the liver. It is derived from two sources: (1) breakdown of glycogen (glycogenolysis) and (2) formation of new glucose (gluconeogenesis) (22). In the fasted state, glucose production by the liver is approximately 0.14–0.18 g/minute (21)

Two types of glucose utilization may be distinguished: (1) insulin independent loss, mainly in the brain, red blood cells, and renal medulla; and (2) loss depending on the insulin level. In diabetics with glucose levels higher than 2 g/liter, urinary glucose excretion may be considerable (glucosuria).

The concentration of circulating insulin serves to coordinate fuel storage and fuel mobilization into and out of various depots. The most important effect of insulin is its ability to increase the rate of glucose transport through the membranes of most cells with a particular efficacy in skeletal muscle and adipose tissues (22). The other control action of insulin takes place in the liver, influencing the breakdown and synthesis of glycogen. Several models concerning hepatic insulin action on glucose metabolism have been reported (23, 24); however, fundamental controversies remained to be solved. A common feature of both types of insulin effect is their delayed appearance. Several hysteretic patterns in hepatic insulin action have been observed (21, 22).

3.2 Digestion and Absorption of Carbohydrates

The experimental results demonstrated by Borgström et al. (25) and Dahlquist and Borgström (26) concerning digestion of starches and lactose and absorption of glucose and galactose are briefly reviewed. These processes determine the absorption patterns of test meals given in our studies.

During the first phase of carbohydrate digestion—in the mouth and in the stomach—only the starches are partially hydrolyzed to maltose and isomaltose by amylase emzyme of the saliva. The disaccharides remain practically intact. The absorption of monosaccharides is also very poor in the lack of hydrolysis of disaccharides.

As the pancreatic secretion contains large quantities of amylase, the unhydrolyzed starch content of the food entering the duodenum is almost totally converted into maltose and isomaltose before passing the jejunum. Maltose is not absorbed in the duodenum; its absorption takes place from the jejunum and from the proximal part of the ileum. The absorption of lactose begins at a higher level of the small intestine (in the duodenum) and is practically complete before the lower part of the jejunum.

The sites of glucose and galactose absorption are approximately the same as those of lactose. The absorption begins in the distal part of the duodenum and is complete in the first 50 cm of the jejunum. The absorption rates of the two monosaccharides are approximately the same (27).

The absorption of disaccharides is the result of enzymatic hydrolysis in the epithelial cells, splitting them into their constituent monosaccharides. The digested products are then immediately absorbed into the portal blood.

3.3 Mathematical Models of Insulin Input–Glycemia Output Relationship in Insulin-Dependent Diabetics Following Carbohydrate Intake

Insulin-dependent diabetics are deficient in endogenous insulin secretion; exogenously administered insulin substitutes to elicit responses manifesting as changes in blood glucose levels. According to the discussion in Section 1.1, this dynamic behavior of the drug (insulin) responding system can be described by state and observation equations that characterize the pharmacokinetics of insulin and its action on glycemia (pharmacodynamics), respectively.

During a meal the blood glucose control system has two inputs: exogenous insulin and glucose entering systemic circulation. Consequently, the mathematical model must define two relationships: insulin effect on glucose uptake from extracellular space and effect of carbohydrate intake on systemic glucose input and on the rise of glycemia.

Two models have been elaborated by using different approaches. The first model (model 1) gives a simple linear compartmental description for the insulin input–glycemia output relationship. On the other hand, it attempts to characterize carbohydrate digestion and absorption by physiological terms to render it applicable for meals with different carbohydrate content.

The second model (model 2) uses the superposition principle of linear systems (28) and black-box analysis of control engineering (4) to define the insulin input–glycemia output and carbohydrate input–glycemia output relationships. It operates with experimentally determined transfer functions, not seeking their physiological interpretation.

3.3.1 Model 1

The mathematical model is given as follows:

$$\begin{bmatrix} \dot{x}_1 \\ \dot{x}_2 \\ \dot{x}_3 \\ \dot{x}_4 \\ \dot{x}_5 \end{bmatrix} = \begin{bmatrix} -(k_1+k_{12}) & k_{21} & k_2 & 0 & -1 \\ k_{12} & -k_{21} & 0 & 0 & 0 \\ 0 & 0 & -k_2 & 0 & 0 \\ 0 & 0 & 0 & -k_3 & 0 \\ 0 & 0 & 0 & k_4 & -k_5 \end{bmatrix} \cdot \begin{bmatrix} x_1 \\ x_2 \\ x_3 \\ x_4 \\ x_5 \end{bmatrix} + \begin{bmatrix} l_1 \\ 0 \\ l_3 \\ 0 \\ 0 \end{bmatrix} + \begin{bmatrix} 0 \\ 0 \\ 0 \\ u_i \\ 0 \end{bmatrix} \qquad (21)$$

and

$$y = G = \frac{x_1}{V_B} \tag{22}$$

Equation 21 represents the state equation and equation 22, the observation equation. In equations 21 and 22 the following notations were used:

x_1	glucose mass in the blood
x_2	glucose mass in the interstitial fluid
x_3	galactose mass
x_4	insulin mass
x_5	variable characterizing insulin effect on glycemia fall
G	glycemia
V_B	volume of blood
k_1	first-order rate constant of glucose uptake from bloodstream into intracellular water (independent of insulin level)
k_{12}, k_{21}	first-order rate constants of glucose distribution
k_2	first-order rate constant of galactose–glucose conversion
k_3	first-order elimination rate constant of insulin
k_4	constant characterizing the insulin sensitivity of the patient
k_5	constant characterizing the time delay of insulin action
l_1	systemic glucose input from carbohydrate absorption
l_3	systemic galactose input from carbohydrate absorption
u_i	rate of insulin infusion

As is shown in equation 21, one distribution space was supposed for insulin and galactose. The kinetics of glucose distribution was formulated in the model. Glucose utilization was described by two parallel processes depending on glucose and insulin concentrations, respectively. The x_5 variable reflects the overall insulin effect on glycemia that is a result of parallel transport and metabolic processes; x_5 is the function of insulin mass in the body with a first-order time lag. It must also be noted that several parameters in model 1 (especially k_4) follow diurnal variations (circadian rhythm); therefore, they refer only to the time of their determination (29).

To complete model 1, the mathematical form of l_1 and l_3 must be defined. The calculation of systemic glucose and galactose input following carbohydrate intake was based on the following hypotheses: (see Section 3.2):

1. The mouth and stomach act as pure time delay elements in the absorption process of monosaccharides; time delay is denoted by t_d.
2. Emptying of the stomach is continuous with a duration of t_e.

3. Passage of the "food plug" in the intestinal tract has a constant linear velocity v.
4. The beginning of maltose absorption is displaced by a distance X_d in comparison to lactose.
5. Absorption of monosaccharides has an apparent first-order kinetics.
6. The rate-limiting step in digestive and absorptive processes is the hydrolysis of disaccharides into their constituent monosaccharides.

The digestive and absorption processes are illustrated in Figure 4. The mathematical form of systemic monosaccharide inputs l_1 and l_3 can be deduced as follows.

The amount of unhydrolyzed maltose and lactose at distance X in an intestinal element of length dX is given below (the quantities of polysaccharides and disaccharides are expressed as monosaccharide equivalents):

$$dq(X, t) = q(0, t-t') \cdot \exp\left[\frac{-k_a \cdot (X - X')}{v}\right] dX \tag{23}$$

where $q(0, t-t') = \begin{cases} \dfrac{D}{vt_e} & \text{if } t' \leqslant t \leqslant (t' + t_e) \\ 0 & \text{otherwise} \end{cases}$

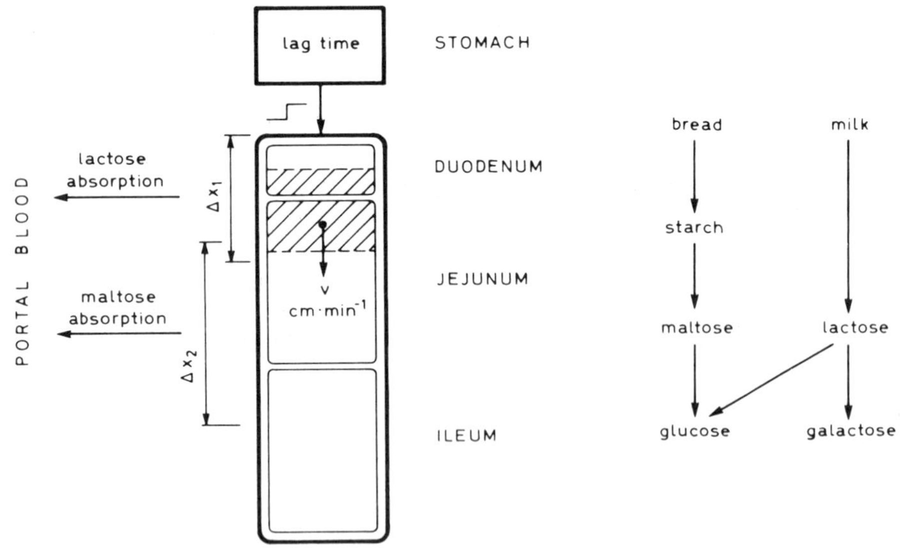

Figure 4. Schematic diagram of digestion and absorption of carbohydrates: ΔX_1 and ΔX_2 represent intestinal sections of lactose and maltose absorption, respectively (26).

$q(0, t-t')$ = maltose and lactose content of food entering the duodenum at time $(t-t')$ in an intestinal element of unit length.
k_a = first-order apparent rate constant of absorption
D = corresponding carbohydrate dose.

The total amount of absorbable disaccharides present in the intestinal tract at time t can be calculated by integrating equation 23 between appropriate limits that are the actual lower and upper locations of the food plug:

$$Q(t) = \int_{X_1}^{X_2} dq(X, t) \tag{24}$$

where
$$X_1 = \begin{cases} X' & \text{if} \quad t \leqslant t' + t_e \\ X' + v(t - t' - t_e) & \text{if} \quad t \geqslant t' + t_e \end{cases}$$

and
$$X_2 = \begin{cases} X' & \text{if} \quad t < t' \\ X' + v(t - t') & \text{if} \quad t' < t \leqslant t' + t_e \\ X_1 + v \cdot t_e & \text{if} \quad t > t' + t_e \end{cases}$$

In equation 23, X' and t' have the following values:

$$X' = 0, \quad t' = t_d \qquad \text{for lactose}$$

$$X' = X_d, \; t' = t_d + X_d/v \qquad \text{for maltose}$$

Finally, the systemic input rates are given as follows:

$$I_1(t) = k_{a,M} \cdot Q_M(t) + \frac{k_{a,L}}{2} \cdot Q_L(t) \tag{25}$$

$$I_3(t) = \frac{k_{a,L}}{2} \cdot Q_L(t) \tag{26}$$

The subscripts M and L refer to maltose and lactose, respectively. Thus model 1 is composed of equations 21 through 26. Application of model 1 is illustrated in Section 4.

3.3.2 *Model 2*

For describing the insulin and carbohydrate input–glycemia output relationships, the black-box-type models of control engineering are used. This approach was originally proposed for pharmacodynamic modeling by Smolen (4).

From aspects of control engineering, insulin therapy in diabetics after carbohydrate intake is illustrated in Figure 5. In the lack of endogenous insulin secretion the block diagram represents an open-loop control system.

The meal (carbohydrate intake) can be considered as a load input variable,

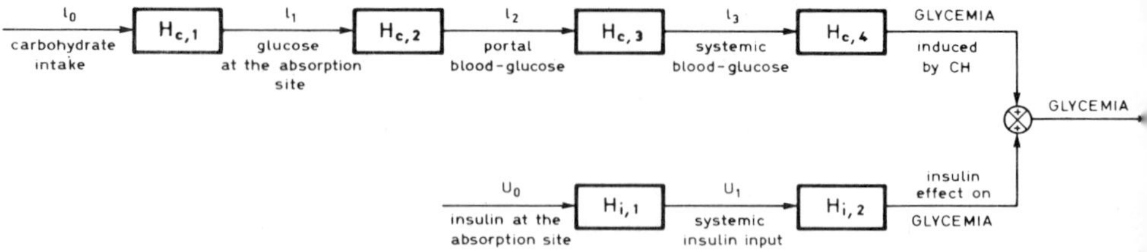

Figure 5. Black-box model of effects of insulin administration and carbohydrate intake on glycemia.

whereas insulin input represents the control variable. The effects of these variables on glycemia are characterized by the transfer functions $H_c(s)$ and $H_i(s)$ (s refers to Laplace transform). In case of linear systems the system output is the sum of the effects of control and load input variables.

The $H_c(s)$ transfer function can be decomposed into the following four parts corresponding to the consecutive processes leading to the rise of glycemia:

1. The carbohydrate input is transformed by the gastrointestinal system into monosaccharides at their sites of absorption ($H_{c,1}$).
2. Monosaccharides pass the gut wall, producing a portal glucose and galactose input ($H_{c,2}$).
3. The portally absorbed monosaccharides are transformed by the liver into systemic glucose inputs ($H_{c,3}$).
4. Finally, this systemic glucose input elicits a glycemic response ($H_{c,4}$).

The overall transfer function is defined by the multiple of elementary transfer functions as follows:

$$H_c(s) = \prod_{j=1}^{4} H_{c,j}(s) \tag{27}$$

Although this decomposition is very useful for diagnostic purposes, for insulin input optimization it is sufficient to determine the overall transfer function given by equation 27.

If insulin is administered subcutaneously, intramuscularly, or intraperitoneally, an absorption transfer function $H_{i,1}$ must be used. For intravenous insulin administration,

$$H_i(s) = H_{i,2}(s) \tag{28}$$

The glycemic response can be computed as follows:

$$G(s) = H_c(s) \cdot l_0(s) + H_i(s) \cdot u_i(s) \tag{29}$$

Smolen (5) demonstrated that if an impulse input is used for system identification, not even the mathematical form of the appropriate transfer function must be determined. After normalization by the administered insulin dose, the directly registered blood glucose profile following an intravenous insulin bolus defines H_i in time domain. The meal can also be considered as an impulse; however, the direct action of carbohydrate intake on glycemia is not visible because of insulin administration. The insulin effect can be subtracted from the registered glycemia–time profile by using convolution between the previously determined transfer function H_i and insulin input function u_i during the meal period. This method of determining the effect of carbohydrate intake on glycemia is demonstrated in Section 4.

If models 1 and 2 are compared, it can be noted that model 1 makes it possible to identify the insulin and carbohydrate absorption effects from a single experiment. Model 2 requires a preliminary insulin impulse test to determine the effect of carbohydrate intake on blood glucose level. For model 2, the computed absorption profile is distorted by diurnal variations of insulin sensitivity k_4. Furthermore, model 2 provides an absorption profile only for the meal actually tested. Absorption profiles produced by meals with different carbohydrate contents can be predicted by using model 1. The use of model 2 for a given meal is more advantageous because of its simplicity for open-loop control design.

4. OPTIMIZATION OF OPEN-LOOP INSULIN ADMINISTRATION STRATEGY IN DIABETICS FOLLOWING CARBOHYDRATE INTAKE

Diabetes mellitus is generally treated by subcutaneous insulin injections given once or twice daily. With the increasing life-span of diabetics, the frequency and severity of complications (retinopathy and nephropathy) also show a rising tendency. According to our present knowledge, insulin-controlled normoglycemia prevents, or at least retards, the development of these specific complications.

As with the classical insulin therapy, this goal can only be reached with difficulty, and not in all patients. Several other methods have been tried to control glycemia: pancreas transplantation, implantation of beta cells, or implantable capillary units for pancreatic islets. These attempts are intended to ensure a correct pattern (appropriate timing and dosage) of insulin input in diabetics.

Mechanical devices providing normoglycemic control by insulin infusion have been developed in the last years. The artificial beta cells constitute the first human imitation of a gland of internal secretion. A commercial version of artificial pancreas has been elaborated by Clemens et al. (30) (BIOSTATOR ®), which is a modular system designed to simulate the function of the normal beta cell. This closed-loop control system monitors continuously the blood glucose level of the patient and administers appropriate amounts of insulin calculated by control algorithms (31–34). These devices are too large; therefore, smaller portable and possibly implantable systems have been developed. As an appropriate biocompatible glucose sensor has not yet been constructed, the recently used portable systems are open-loop devices dosing insulin without glycemia measurement. The open-loop systems are composed of drug reservoir, peristaltic pump, flow rate controller, and a battery; insulin can be administered intravenously (35, 41), subcutaneously (40, 43), or portally (36, 37).

Several attempts have been made to elaborate appropriate open-loop insulin administration programs for short- and long-term regulation for animals (37) and humans (38, 40–42). The insulin administration strategy has been determined by trial–error methods and by using closed-loop control systems to determine insulin requirement during the test period (36, 39, 41).

4.1 Experimental Protocol

Investigations were performed in five juvenile diabetics. The study was approved by the Research Committee of Semmelweis Medical University, and the patients were informed of the purpose of the study before giving consent to participate. All were male subjects aged between 19 and 33 years, and they were within 15% of their desirable body weight. Their diabetes was of several years' standing; they had no detectable C-peptide rest-secretion and insulin-binding antibodies influencing the insulin therapy and the tests performed.

As a research tool, BIOSTATOR ® GCIIS (30) (Glucose Controlled Insulin Infusion System, Miles Laboratories, Elkhardt, Indiana) was used, consisting of:

1. A glucose sensor unit for continuous polarographical measurement of blood glucose, making use of a membrane coated by immobilized glucose oxidase enzyme
2. A microcomputer process controller, which permits constant-rate insulin–dextrose infusion, glucose-controlled dextrose infusion, and glucose-controlled insulin infusion
3. An infusion system

4. A printer–plotter unit recording a 1-minute average of glycemia and insulin and dextrose infusions given by BIOSTATOR® at 1-minute intervals

Intravenous catheters were inserted for infusions and for the withdrawal of venous blood. The closed-loop artificial beta cell is shown in Figure 6.

Patients have usually been connected to the BIOSTATOR® for 3 days. In all cases Actrapid MC insulin (Novo Industry A/S, Coppenhagen, Denmark) was administered. Two tests and a calculated open-loop insulin treatment were performed in each patient.

4.1.1 *Insulin Impulse Test (IIT, IITC)*

Depending on the state of the patient's insulin–glucose system, two types of insulin impulse test were applied for measuring insulin effect on glycemia.

During the insulin impulse test with conditioning (IITC), simultaneous insulin and dextrose infusions ($u_{i,c}, u_{d,c}$) were given to simulate the average condition of a meal period. The rate of insulin infusion was calculated from the amount of insulin administered by the artificial pancreas to normalize blood glucose during a test meal as follows:

$$u_{i,c} = \frac{\sum_{j=1}^{180} u_{i,a}(j)}{180} \cdot 0.8$$

where $u_{i,a}$ is the insulin infusion rate in the jth minute during FCA test and $u_{i,c}$ is the insulin infusion rate for conditioning.

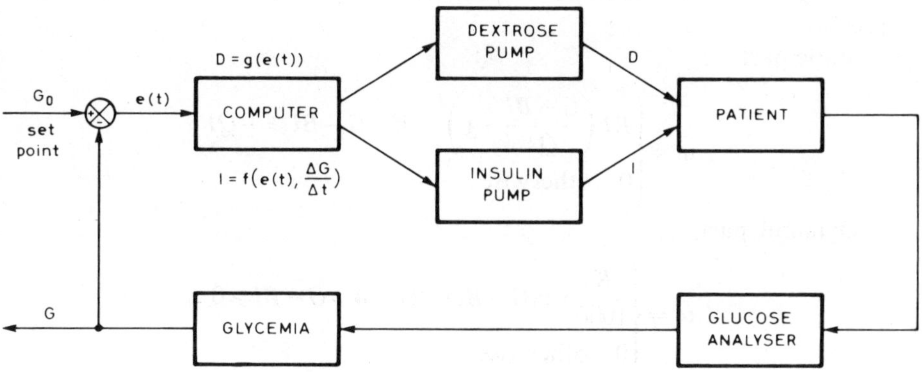

Figure 6. Glucose-controlled insulin and dextrose infusion system (BIOSTATOR®).

Glycemia was maintained at a preselected level (1.1 g/liter) using feedback dextrose control simultaneously with the constant insulin infusion ($u_{i,c}$). After quasistabilization of blood glucose concentration, the controller was adjusted to deliver dextrose at the mean rate of the previous period ($u_{d,c}$). When steady state was established, a maximum-rate insulin impulse (FI) was given for 3 minutes. Infusions $u_{i,c}$ and $u_{d,c}$ were continued for 50 minutes after insulin impulse.

In the Insulin Impulse Test (IIT) without conditioning, the BIOSTATOR ® was adjusted to maintain blood glucose level at 1.3 g/liter by feedback insulin control. Insulin infusion was used to counterregulate only endogenous glucose production. After steady state had been established, the controller was reprogrammed from feedback control to constant rate insulin administration and an insulin bolus of 2 units was injected intravenously. The blood glucose profile was recorded during 50 minutes.

4.1.2 *Feedback Controlled Absorption (FCA) Test*

Patients received one of the two different test meals at normal (0.7–0.9 g/liter) blood glucose levels. The two test meals had the following composition:

Test meal 1 — 1 roll, 200 ml of milk, 10 g of butter, and 1 egg (30 g of starch and 12 g of lactose),

Test meal 2 — 1/2 roll, 300 ml of milk, 10 g of butter, and 20 g of ham (15 g of starch and 15 g of lactose).

Insulin infusion rates were calculated by the dynamic +static insulin feedback control algorithm of the BIOSTATOR ®. This operation mode makes the insulin infusion dependent on the static value and the rate of blood glucose level changes, respectively, according to the following expression:

Static part

$$u_i^s = \begin{cases} RI\left(\dfrac{G-BI}{QI}+1\right)^2 & \text{if} \quad G-BI \geqslant -QI \\ 0 \quad \text{otherwise} \end{cases}$$

Dynamic part

$$u_i^d = \begin{cases} \dfrac{K}{1000}\cdot m(G-BI)\cdot RI & \text{if} \quad G-BI \geqslant 0 \\ 0 \quad \text{otherwise} \end{cases}$$

where $K = KR$ for raising glucose level and KF for falling glucose level.

The total insulin infusion can be expressed as:

$$u_i = \begin{cases} u_i^s + u_i^d & \text{if } \; 0 \leqslant u_i^s + u_i^d \leqslant FI \\ FI & \text{if } \; u_i^s + u_i^d > FI \\ 0 & \text{otherwise} \end{cases}$$

where $G = 1$ minute average of glycemia
BI = prescribed basal glucose level
RI = basal insulin infusion rate
QI = the inverse of static gain
m = slope of glucose level change estimated by the last five measurements

For all subjects, the control parameters found earlier to be optimal for juvenile diabetics were used: $KR=150$, $KF=50$, $BI=80$ mg/100 ml, $QI=$ 15 mg/100 ml, $RI=0.2$ mU/(minute/kg body weight), and $FI=300$ mU/minute.

A glucose–controlled dextrose infusion was used in this test only to counterregulate possible hypoglycemia under 0.6 g/liter. The maximum infusion rates of insulin and dextrose are limited to FI and FD, respectively, and are determined by the size of pump tubing and concentration of the solution used. In case the control algorithm computes higher values than the maximum rates, the system will deliver insulin and dextrose at FI and FD. The effect of carbohydrate intake on glycemia was detectable for 3–4 hours, depending on the composition of the test meals.

4.1.3 Open-Loop Control of Glycemia Following Carbohydrate Intake(OCCI)

The OCCI study was performed 1 or 2 days later at the same time of day as the FCA. The patients received the same meal as in the FCA test. During OCCI the patients were treated by an open-loop insulin delivery system simulated on BIOSTATOR ®, using its constant-rate insulin infusion program. The consecutive insulin infusions defining the optimal insulin administration strategy were calculated from the results of IITC/IIT and FCA tests, respectively (see Section 4.3).

4.2 Data Analysis

The optimization of open-loop insulin administration is based on the individual characteristics of the patients. Therefore, before optimizing insulin treatment, postprandial individual model parameters must be determined. Corresponding to the models discussed above, two identification methods were used. The calculations were made on an ICL 1903 computer.

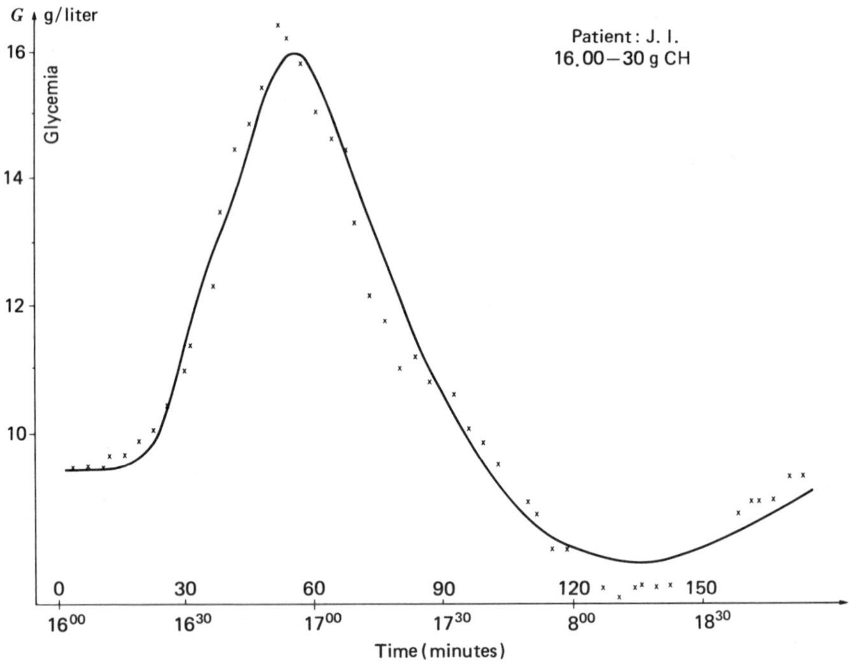

Figure 7. Time variation of glycemia following ingestion of test meal 1 using BIOSTATOR® control: ×, observed values; ——, calculated by use of model 1 with the following parameters: $k_1=0$; $k_5=0.053$ minute^{-1}; $t_e=15$ minutes; $k_2=0.040$ minute^{-1}; $k_{12}=0.2$ minute^{-1}; $X_d=20$ cm; $k_3=0.09$ minute^{-1}; $k_{21}=0.18$ minute^{-1}; $k_{a,L}=0.052$ minute^{-1}; $k_4=1.42\times10^{-5}$ (g/minute)/mU; $t_1=17$ minutes; $k_{a,M}=0.029$ minute^{-1}; $v=1$ cm/minute (45). The observed data were fitted by the NONLIN program (44) with a sum of squares of deviation of 2.1×10^{-3}.

In the following sections the investigations are presented for patient D. L. consuming test meal 1 and measuring insulin sensitivity by IITC and for patient J. I. consuming test meal 2 and performing IIT. In Figures 7 and 8 two time scales are presented: relative time of measurements in minutes (upper scale) and the actual time of the day (lower scale).

4.2.1 *Parameter Estimation of Model 1*

In Model 1 the subjects were characterized by their absorption and insulin sensitivity parameters included in equations 21–26. Figures 7 and 8 show the results of identification procedures for two patients. The figures present the measured and the fitted glycemia during FCA test. The estimated model parameters are given in the legends of the figures.

The glucose distribution rate constants (k_{12} and k_{21}) were calculated

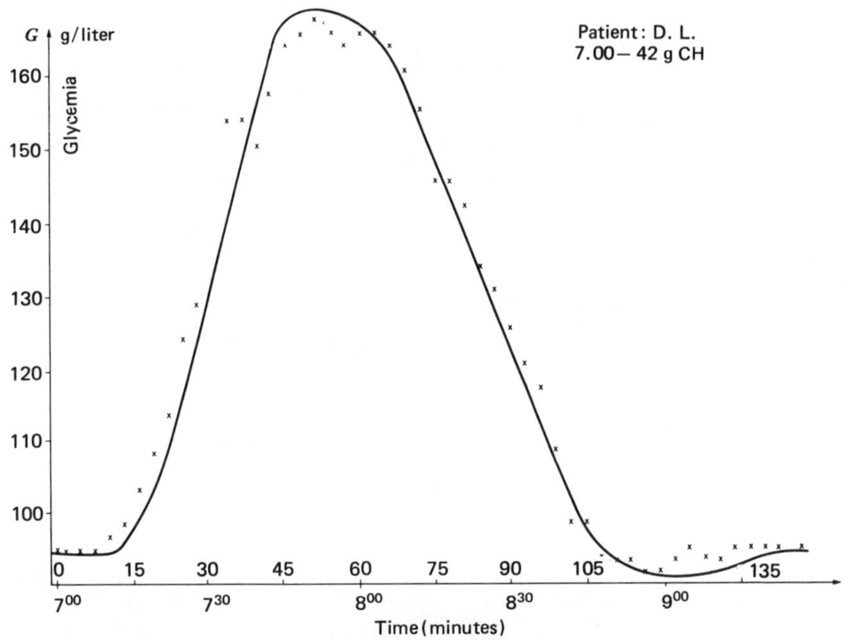

Figure 8. Time variation of glycemia following ingestion of test meal 2 using BIOSTATOR® control: × ; observed values; ——, calculated by use of model 1 with the following parameters: $k_1=0$; $k_5=0.050$ minute^{-1}; $t_e=15$ minutes; $k_2=0.036$ minute^{-1}; $k_{12}=0.2$ minute^{-1}; $X_a=20$ cm; $k_3=0.08$ minute^{-1}; $k_{21}=0.18$ minute^{-1}; $k_{a,L}=0.068$ minute^{-1}; $k_4=1.06\times10^{-5}$ (g/minute)/mU; $t_1=10$ minutes; $k_{a,M}$ 0.014 minute^{-1}; $v=1$ cm/minute (45). The observed data were fitted by the NONLIN program (44) with a sum of squares of deviation of 2.5×10^{-3}.

from experiments performed in patient K. I. using an intravenous dextrose infusion, as illustrated in Figure 9. It must be emphasized that the model parameters (especially k_4) are characteristic of the time interval of the study. Their application for other periods of the day must be made with caution.

The estimated absorption rate constants for lactose and maltose are in good agreement with the experimental observations (25, 26). The parameter estimations of models were performed by using the NONLIN program (44).

4.2.2 Linear System Analysis of Data

In case of model 2 the patients' characteristics were formulated by experimentally measured transfer functions; their mathematical description was not sought. The determination of system transfer functions was performed in two steps:

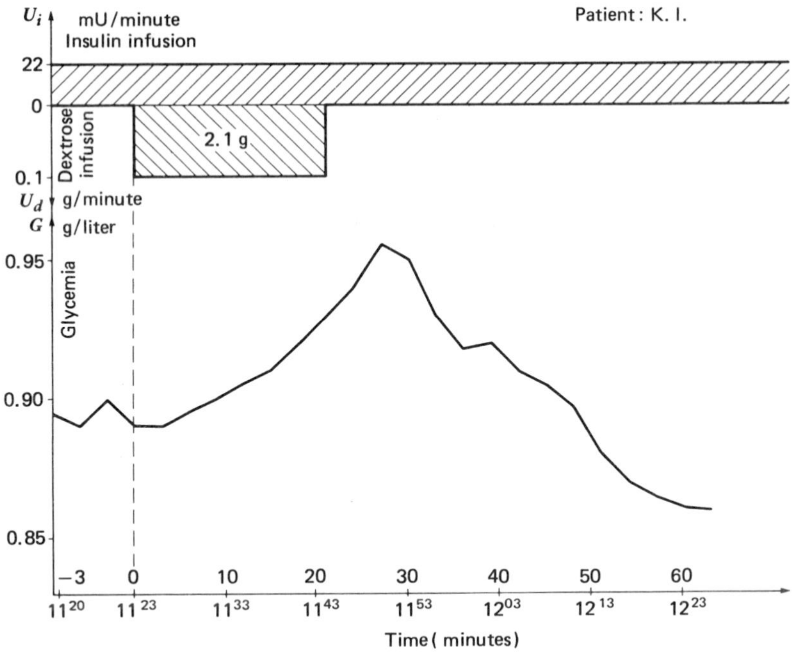

Figure 9. Temporal variation of glycemia during and after intravenous dextrose infusion.

1. Determination of the intravenous insulin input–glycemia output (H_i) transfer function using kinetic data of IITC/IIT
2. Calculation of the carbohydrate intake–glycemia transfer function (H_c) using H_i function and data of FCA test

Theoretically, H_i can be determined by recording the fall in blood sugar after an insulin impulse as in IIT. Figure 10 shows glycemia registered during IIT in patient J. I. The transfer function was obtained from the glycemia–time series normalized by the insulin dose. This curve obviously contains noises; therefore, a preliminary filtering by spline approximation was performed before using it for subsequent calculations.

The H_i function, however, depends on the state of the system (the patient), taking into consideration the hysteretic action of insulin mainly on the liver. In other words, the observed glycemia following an insulin bolus will be determined partly by the previous history of the system and especially by the previous insulin treatment. Therefore, the linearity hypothesis is an approximation only, and it is important to define the insulin transfer function in a state characterizing the planned investigation for which it will be used

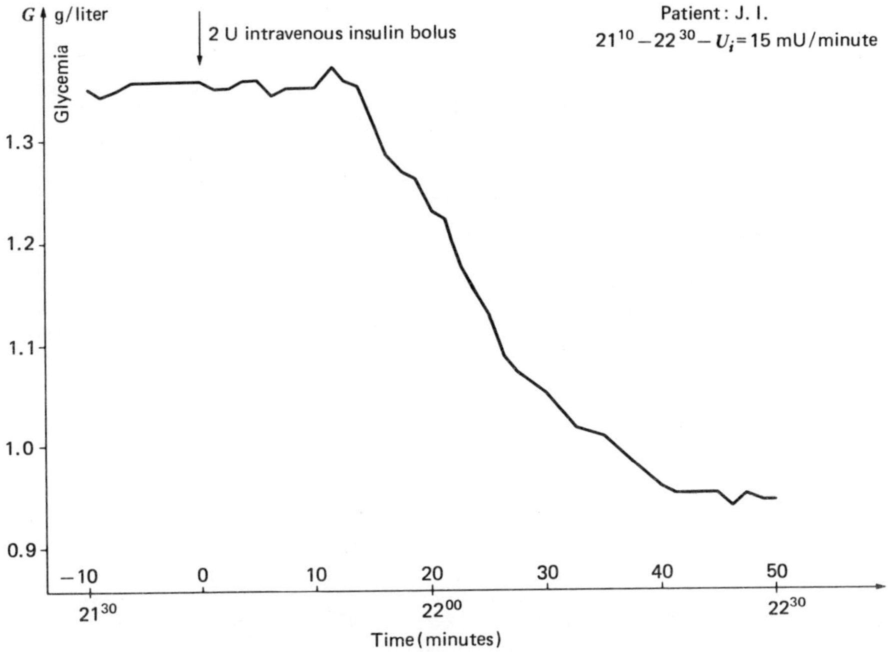

Figure 10. Insulin impulse test without conditioning (**IIT**).

(i.e., a meal period). As a consequence of this, IITC was performed in three patients.

A typical set of data—glycemia response and the rates of dextrose and insulin infusions—are shown in Figure 11. The measured glycemia response, normalized by the insulin dose and smoothed, gave the transfer function H_i characterizing the overall insulin effect on blood glucose. (Insulin impulse was assumed to be a Dirac delta.)

On the basis of both types of insulin impulse test, it could be established that in this glycemic range of juvenile diabetes there was no direct blood glucose control of glucose utilization as was shown in healthy subjects (21).

The transfer function between carbohydrate input and glycemia output could not be measured directly. Test meals would have produced too high blood glucose concentration (3–4 g/liter) without insulin control. Therefore, H_c transfer function was computed on the basis of equation 29:

$$H_c(s) = \frac{G_c(s)}{l_0(s)} = \frac{G(s) - H_i(s) \cdot u_i(s)}{l_0(s)} \tag{30}$$

where l_0 represents the carbohydrate input function.

This function may be considered as an impulse because its duration can

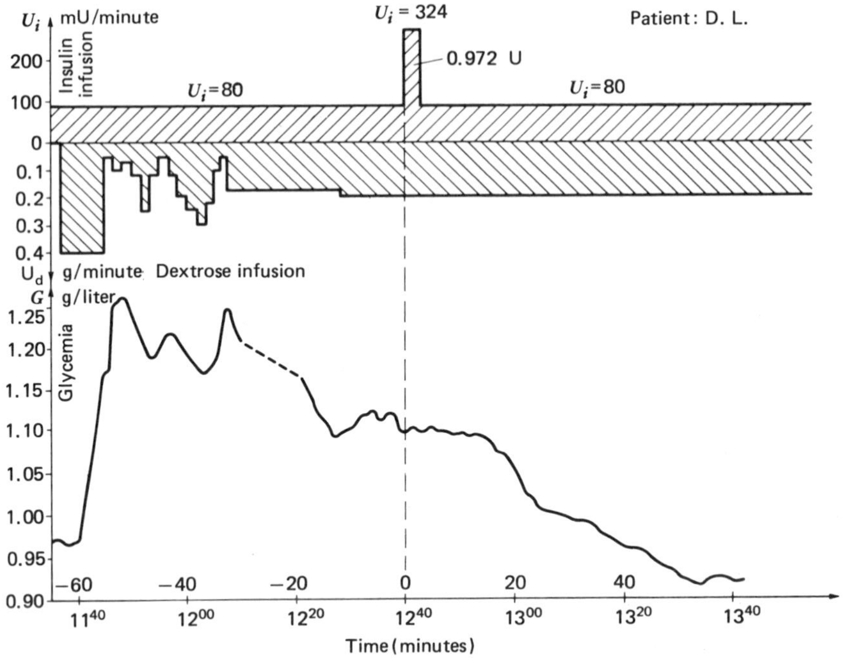

Figure 11. Insulin impulse test with conditioning (**IITC**).

be neglected in relation to the whole absorption period. Considering that time is discrete and H_i is independent of glycemia, the carbohydrate-induced glycemia in the jth minute can be calculated from equation 30 by transforming it in time domain:

$$G_c(j)=G(j)-\sum_{k=1}^{j} u_{i,a}(k)\cdot H(j-k+1) \tag{31}$$

where $G(j)$ = measured glycemia in FCA test in jth minute
$u_{i,a}(t)$ = insulin input in FCA test in kth minute
$G_c(j)$ = blood glucose level that would have been observed without insulin administration in jth minute
$H(j-k+1)$ = effect of insulin administered in kth minute on glycemia in jth minute

Figures 12 and 13 show illustrations of absorption tests used for calculation.

The computed G_c and G_i functions for both test meals are presented in Figures 14 and 15. The term G_c presents the expected glycemia profile that would have been measured without insulin administration; G_i, however, is only hypothetical as a result of the counterregulatory mechanisms being activated in the hypoglycemic state.

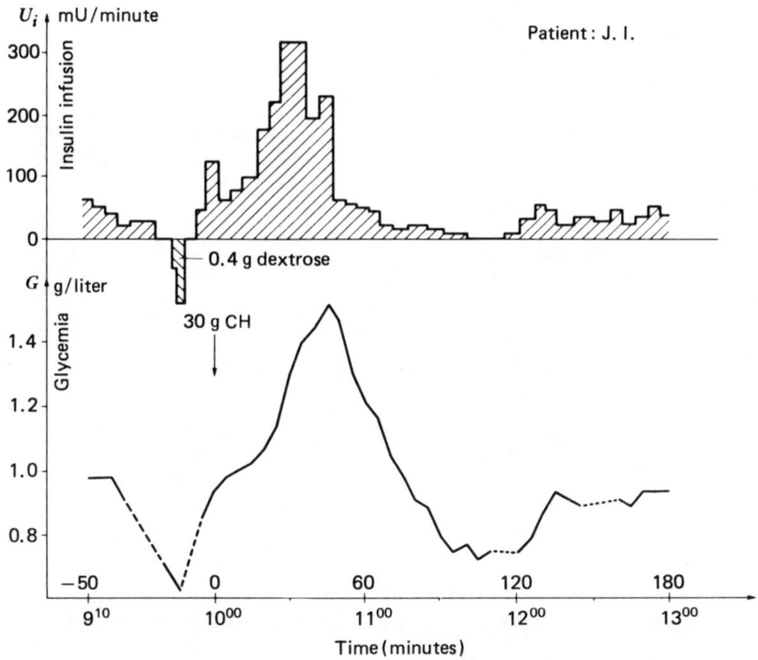

Figure 12. Feedback-controlled absorption test (**FCA**) with test meal 1.

The interpretation of G_c curves must be made with caution. They not only contain the effect of carbohydrate absorption, but are influenced by diurnal variations of insulin sensitivity and liver glucose production. This fact follows from the different time periods of IICT–IIT and FCA tests. To estimate this latter effect, the saturation value of G_c profile can be used, which is expected to be equal to D/V_G, where D represents the ingested carbohydrate mass and V_G is the distribution volume of glucose, respectively. The value of V_G can be estimated as 20% of each kilogram of body weight. Comparison of expected and measured saturation values of G_c profiles shows the contribution of diurnal variations to the apparent glucose absorption effect to be approximately 30%.

The systemic glucose input profile can be determined as the time derivative of the cumulative G_c curve. The systemic glucose input rate for the two test meals is shown in Figures 16 and 17. In spite of disturbing effects of diurnal variations (discussed previously), these curves clearly indicate the different absorption sites of lactose (peak 1) and maltose (peak 2). The temporary stagnation in blood glucose fall after the second absorption peak may be due to the galactose–glucose transformation in the liver increasing glucose input into systemic circulation.

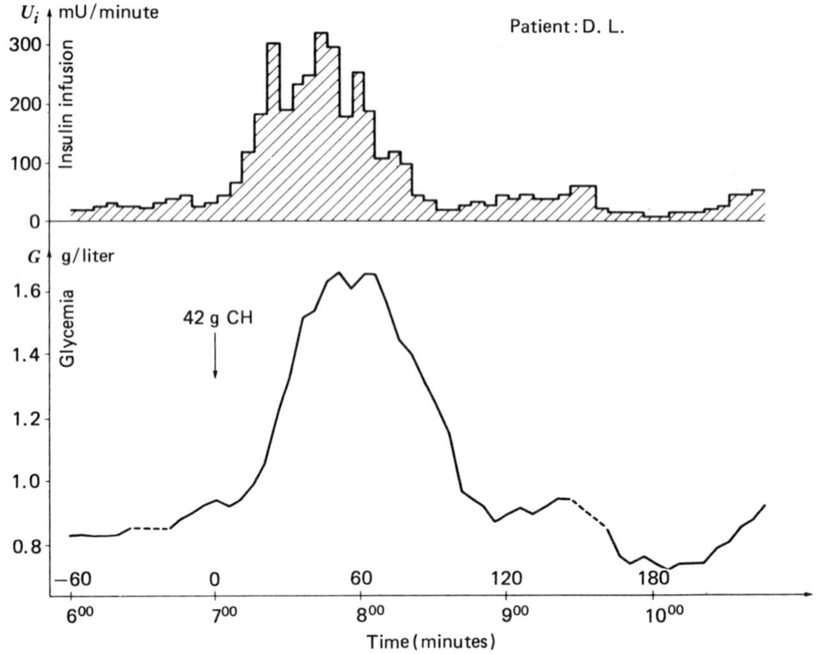

Figure 13. Feedback-controlled absorption test (**FCA**) with test meal 2.

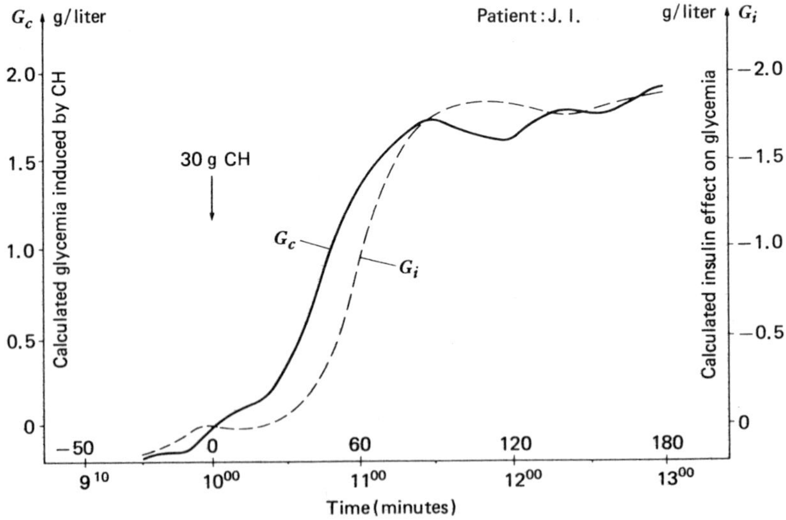

Figure 14. Calculated glycemia rise $\mathbf{G}_c$ and glycemia fall $\mathbf{G}_i$ following ingestion of test meal 1: $\mathbf{G}_i$ characterizing insulin effect on glycemia was determined by convolution of transfer function $\mathbf{H}_i$ (Figure 10) normalized by insulin dose and insulin input profile during FCA test (Figure 12), respectively; $\mathbf{G}_c$ characterizing the effect of carbohydrate absorption on glycemia was calculated from equation 31.

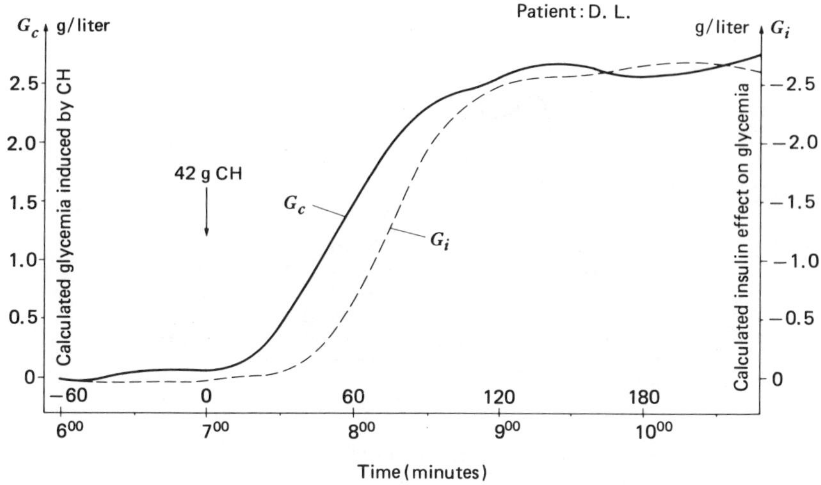

Figure 15. Calculated glycemia rise $\mathbf{G}_c$ and glycemia fall $\mathbf{G}_i$ following ingestion of test meal 2: $\mathbf{G}_i$ characterizing insulin effect on glycemia was determined by convolution of transfer function $\mathbf{H}_i$ (Figure 11) normalized by insulin dose and insulin input profile during FCA test (Figure 13), respectively; $\mathbf{G}_c$ characterizing the effect of carbohydrate absorption on glycemia was calculated from equation 31.

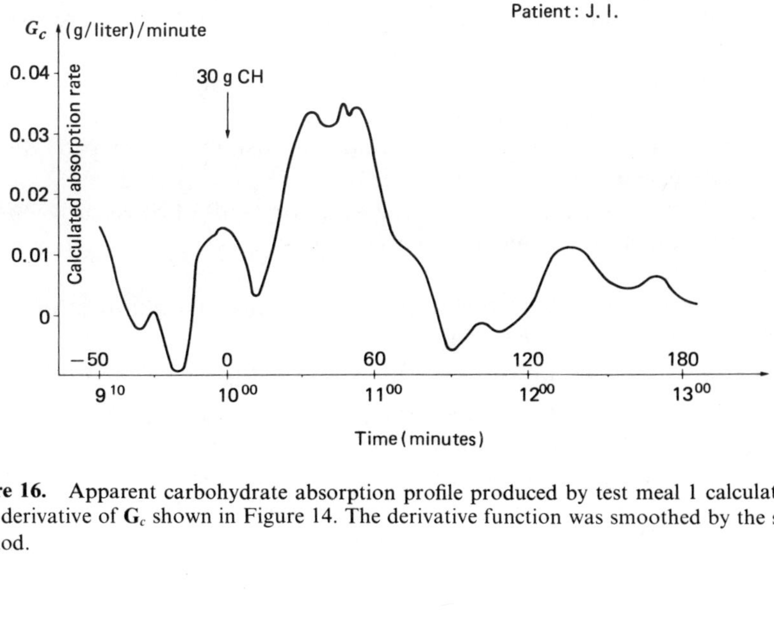

Figure 16. Apparent carbohydrate absorption profile produced by test meal 1 calculated as time derivative of $\mathbf{G}_c$ shown in Figure 14. The derivative function was smoothed by the spline method.

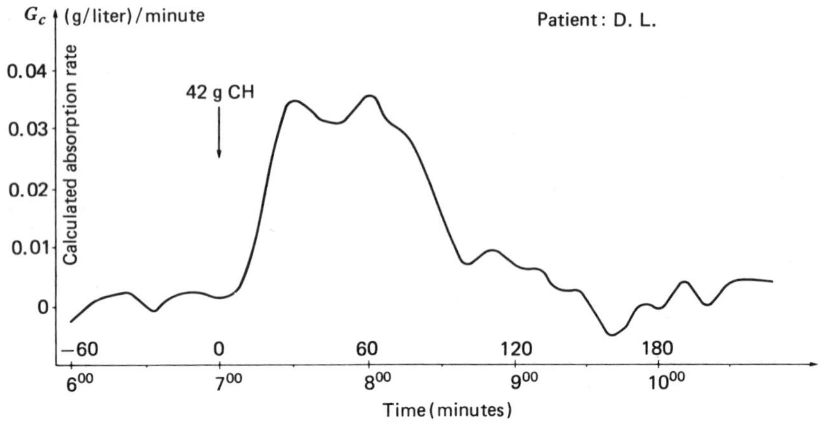

Figure 17. Apparent carbohydrate absorption profile produced by test meal 2 calculated as time derivative of $\mathbf{G}_c$ shown in Fig. 15. The derivative function was smoothed by the spline method.

4.3 Calculation of Optimal Square-Wave Insulin Treatment for a Meal Period

The lack of endogenous feedback blood glucose control in insulin-dependent diabetics can be partly compensated by open-loop insulin therapy having feedforward control characteristics. This means that insulin can be administered in anticipation of the subsequent carbohydrate intake before rising of glycemia.

For determining the optimal insulin treatment using intravenous square-wave insulin administration (open-loop control), the previously described models were used. Our aim was to compute an insulin therapy providing an appropriate blood glucose–time profile during a meal period.

The problem is to determine the rates and durations of consecutive insulin infusions for different test meals in a way that:

1. Changes in infusion rate should be performed at multiples of a pre-chosen time interval ($h = 15$ minutes),
2. The rate of insulin infusion should be limited ($u_{i,\max} = 300$ mU/minute),
3. The glycemia profile should be in a predetermined range during therapy defined on the basis of blood glucose reponse in the FCA test (50–75 minutes after carbohydrate intake blood glucose should reach its maximum, which should not be higher than that produced by BIOSTATOR ® control; at 110–130 minutes glycemia should decrease below 1.0 g/liter

and, to prevent hypoglycemia, the postabsorptive blood glucose level should not be significantly lower than its pretreatment value).

4. The number of necessary changes in the infusion rates should be minimal.

This problem is identical to that discussed in Section 2.3. Its mathematical definition and solution by mixed-integer programming are presented in Section 2.3 as well. In Figures 18 and 19 the glycemia profiles and insulin infusions are illustrated for both patients during the FCA test and OCCI absorption studies.

As it is shown in Figure 19, the optimized open-loop therapy based on the insulin impulse test with preceding conditioning gave excellent results. All constraints were satisfied and only two different insulin administration rates were necessary to achieve this goal. In case of the insulin test without conditioning, the calculated optimal therapy led to a relatively different shape of the glycemia curve compared to the corresponding FCA profile (Figure 18). This deviation may be due to the inaccuracy of the determination of insulin effect on glycemia.

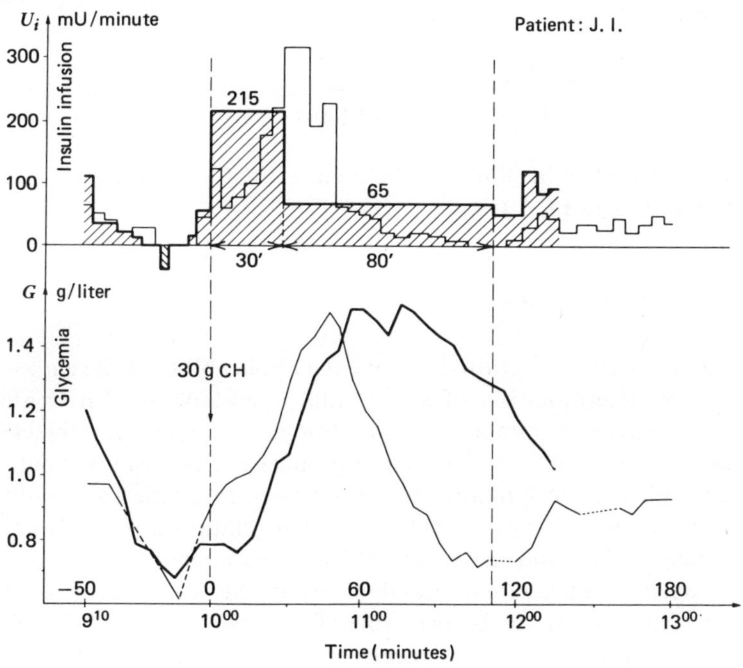

Figure 18. Comparison of closed-loop controlled **FCA** test and open-loop controlled **OCCI** study using test meal 1 : ——, **FCA** test; ——, **OCCI** study.

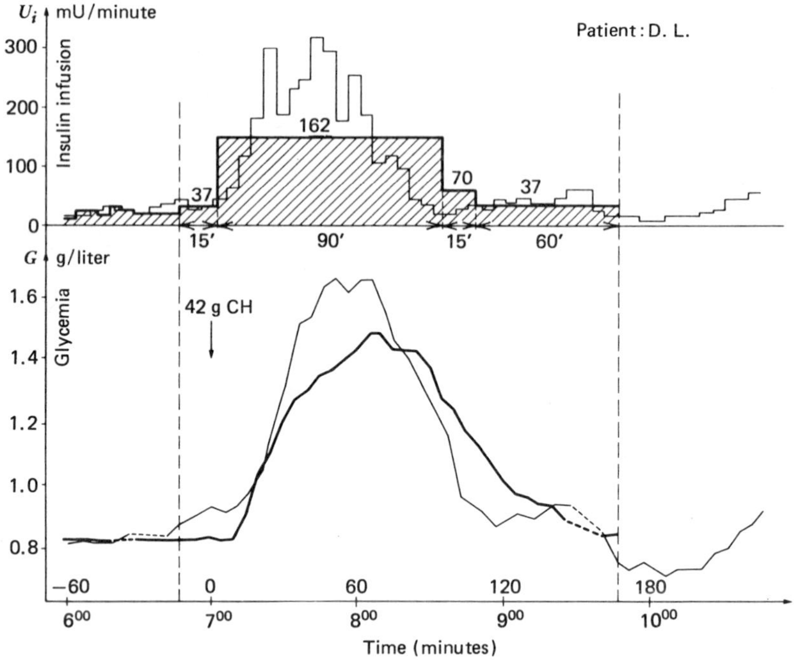

Figure 19. Comparison of closed-loop controlled **FCA** test and open-loop controlled **OCCI** study using test meal 2: ——, **FCA** test; ——, OCCI study.

The total amount of insulin administered in OCCI studies was approximately the same as in FCA tests.

5. CONCLUSIONS

The results presented in Section 4.3 prove the applicability of the elaborated method in the determination of an optimal open-loop insulin treatment following carbohydrate intake. The physiologically based and black-box models can be effectively used for the optimization of insulin input. The results also indicate the fundamental importance to define the conditions under which the insulin input–glycemia output relationship is determined. Simultaneous insulin and dextrose infusions can simulate the average conditions during a meal; therefore, their use in the calculations of insulin effect on glycemia seems to be desirable. The general applicability of the elaborated absorption model for meals of different carbohydrate content remains to be demonstrated.

The results indicate that open-loop insulin administration strategies, because of their feedforward control character, may produce a glycemic profile similar to that obtained by feedback control. Our method evidently requires a preliminary individualization of the treatment by means of insulin sensitivity and carbohydrate absorption tests.

It appears from our experimental results obtained in five patients that, in general, two different infusion rates suffice to ensure a physiological blood glucose profile. It can be noted that the method discussed in this chapter is suitable, with minor modifications, for determination of the optimal insulin administration strategy also in cases where it is given by other than the intravenous route. The commercially available portable open-loop systems that administer insulin only at discrete rates and durations could also be optimized with the described method.

Two important problems must be solved in the future. The first consists of simplifying the method for routine clinical use. The second problem is to elaborate an algorithm for long-term normoglycemic control by open-loop devices. For solving this problem, the circadian variations must be incorporated into our approach.

ACKNOWLEDGMENTS

We would like to express our thanks to Professor V. F. Smolen for his helpful advice. Not only have we learned much from him, but also his original problem solving continues to be a constant source of inspiration to us. We wish to thank Mr. Z. Gabányi and Mr. S. Fritsch for their programming assistance, Miss I. Badics for her drawings, Mrs. Á. Horváth for her help in translation, and Mrs. A. Molnár for typing the manuscript. This work was supported, in part, by the Research Council of Ministry of Health, Hungary (1-22-0302-01-2/M).

REFERENCES

1. J. Gaillot, J. L. Steimer, A. J. Mallet, J. J. Thebault, and A. Bieder. *J. Pharmacokin. Biopharm.* **7**: 579 (1979).
2. L. B. Sheiner, B. Rosenberg, and K. L. Melmon. *Comput. Biomed. Res.* **5**: 441 (1972).
3. G. E. Mawer. *Clin. Pharmacokin.* **1**: 67 (1976).
4. V. F. Smolen. Pharmacokinetic Engineering Approach to Drug Delivery System Design and the Optimization of Drug Effects, *IEEE Proc. Internatl. Conf. Cybern. Soc.*, November 1–3, Washington, D. C., 1976, p. 340.
5. V. F. Smolen, Practical Pharmacodynamic Engineering in the Design, Development and Evaluation of Optimal Drug Products. In A. H. Beckett and H. S. Bean (eds.), *Recent Advances in Pharmaceutical Sciences*, Vol. 5, Academic Press, New York, 1980.

6. M. Inoue, F. Kajiya, H. Inada, A. Kitabatake, M. Hori, S. Fukui, and H. Abe, *Comput. Biomed. Res.* **9**: 217 (1976).

7. D. M. Wiberg. *Theory and Problems of State Space and Linear Systems*, McGraw-Hill, New York, 1971.

8. R. Bellman. *Math. Biosci.* **12**: 1 (1971).

9. J. Buell, R. Jeliffe, R. Kalaba, and R. Sridhar. *Math. Biosci.* **6**: **67** (1972).

10. J. G. Pierce and A. Schumitzky. *J. Optimiz. Theory Appl.* **18**: 537 (1976).

11. L. A. Wheeler and L. B. Sheiner. *J. Pharmacokin. Biopharm.* **4**: 487 (1976).

12. V. F. Smolen, B. D. Turrie, and W. A. Weigand. *J. Pharm. Sci.* **61**: 1941 (1972).

13. G. Zoutendijk. *Mathematical Programming Methods*, North Holland, Amsterdam, 1976, pp. 211–263.

14. K. A. Fegley, S. Blum, J. A. Bergholm, A. J. Calise, J. E. Marowitz, et al. *IEEE Transact. Automat. Contr.* **16**: 759 (1971).

15. M. Tixier, J. L. Beneytout, M. Bridier, D. Fredon, J. P. Michel, and R. Menier. *System Theory Application for Study of Blood Sugar Level Regulation*, 11th FEBS Meeting, Copenhagen, August 1977, Abstract A1-10-105.

16. G. M. Grodsky. *J. Clin. Invest.* **51**: 2047 (1972).

17. R. N. Bergman and J. Urquhart. *Rec. Progr. Hormone Res.* **27**: 583 (1971).

18. E. Cerasi, G. Fick, and M. Rudeno. *Eur. J. Clin. Invest.* **4**: 267 (1974).

19. R. S. Sherwin, K. J. Kramer, J. D. Tobin, E. A. Insel, J. E. Liljenquist, M. Berman, and R. Andres. *J. Clin. Invest.* **53**: 1481 (1974).

20. L. C. Gatewood, E. Ackermann, J. Rosevar, G. D. Molnar, and T. W. Burns. *Comput. Biomed. Res.* **2**: 1 (1968).

21. P. A. Insel, J. E. Liljenquist, J. D. Tobin, R. S. Sherwin, P. Watkins, R. Andres, and M. Berman. *J. Clin. Invest.* **55**: 1057 (1975).

22. A. C. Guyton. *Textbook of Medical Physiology*, 5th ed., Saunders, Philadelphia, 1976, pp. 1038–1050.

23. R. N. Bergman. *Fed. Proc.* **36**: 265 (1977).

24. E. R. Carson and D. G. Cramp. *Internatl. J. Biomed. Comput.* **7**: 21 (1976).

25. B. Borgström, A. Dahlquist, G. Lundh, and J. Sjövall. *J. Clin. Invest.* **36**: 1521 (1957).

26. A. Dahlquist and B. Borgström. *Biochem. J.* **81**: 411 (1961).

27. A. C. Guyton, *Textbook of Medical Physiology*, 5th ed., Saunders, Philadelphia, 1976, pp. 881–889.

28. D. L. Cutler. *J. Pharmacokin. Biopharm.* **6**: 265 (1978).

29. D. T. Krieger, ed. *Endocrine Rhythms*, Raven Press, New York, 1979.

30. A. H. Clemens, P. H. Chang, and R. W. Myers. *Horm. Metab. Res.* (Suppl.) **7**: 23 (1977).

31. A. M. Albisser, B. S. Leibel, T. G. Ewart, Z. Davidovac, C. K. Botz, and W. Zingg. *Diabetes* **23**: 389 (1974a).

32. A. H. Clemens, P. H. Chang, and R. W. Myers. *Horm. Metab. Res.* (Suppl.) **23**: 397 (1974a).

33. W. Kerner, Ch. Thum, Gy. Tamás, Jr., W. Beischer, A. H. Clemens, and E. F. Pfeiffer. *Horm. Metab. Res.* **8**: 256 (1976).

34. E. F. Pfeiffer, Ch. Thum, and A. H. Clemens. *Horm. Metab. Res.* **6**: 339 (1974).

35. K. D. Hepp, R. Renner, H. J. Funcke, H. Mehnert, R. Haerten, and H. Kresse. *Horm. Metab. Res.* (Suppl.) **7**: 72 (1977).

36. A. M. Albisser, W. S. Jackman, R. Ferguson, A. Bahoric, and Y. Gorya. *Med. Progr. Technol.* **5**: 187 (1978).

37. A. M. Albisser, C. K. Botz, and B. S. Leibel. *Diabetologia* **16**: 129 (1979).

38. J. Bojsen, T. Deckert, K. Kolendorf, and B. Lorup. *Diabetes* **28**: 974 (1979).

39. C. K. Botz, E. B. Marliss, and A. M. Albisser. *Diabetologia* **17**: 45 (1979).

40. J. C. Pickup, H. Keen, J. A. Parsons, and K. G. M. M. Alberti, *Lancet* ii: 870 (1979).

41. K. Irsigler and H. Kritz. *Diabetes* **28**: 196 (1979).

42. J. V. Santiago, A. H. Clemens, W. L. Clarke, and D. M. Kipinis. *Diabetes* **28**: 71 (1979).

43. W. V. Tamborlane, R. S. Sherwin, M. Genel, and P. Felig. *New Engl. J. Med.* **300**: 573 (1979).

44. C. M. Metzler, G. L. Elfring, and A. J. McEwen. *Biometrics* **30**: 562 (1974).

45. A. C. Guyton, *Textbook of Medical Physiology*, 5th ed., Saunders, Philadelphia, 1976, p. 862.

CHAPTER 6

Kinetic Hysteresis as a Tool for Analysis of Pharmacokinetic Data

JOSEPH V. BONDI

Merck Sharp and Dohme Research Laboratories
West Point, Pennsylvania

ROBERT D. TANNER

Chemical Engineering Department
Vanderbilt University
Nashville, Tennessee

When a pharmacological response is closely related in time to the presence of the drug in plasma or tissues, it suggests, but does not prove, that the compound itself is the active agent. If, however, the response is clearly unrelated to plasma or tissue levels, the possibility must be considered that a metabolic product mediates the action of the drug [*Brodie* (1)].

CONTENTS

A highly desirable goal in understanding drug action in the body is the correlation of drug plasma levels with a reliable pharmacological measure of the body's response to that drug. As is often the case, practical constraints preclude such correlations since pharmacological end points are often diffuse or at best difficult to quantitate. In fact, few instances can be found in the literature where correlations of pharmacological activity with drug plasma level have been achieved. Several of these are discussed as part of this chapter. The introductory quotation above would suggest at least three specific types of situation that may arise: (1) correlation of drug plasma or tissue levels with a pharmacological effect; (2) identification of a metabolic product as the actual pharmacophore; or (3) correlation of drug plasma or tissue levels with a pharmacological effect that does not show a one-to-one relationship. It is easy to see that case 2 may also result in a time-dependent relationship. For the sake of this discussion, a time-dependent relationship is defined to mean those instances when the peak pharmacological response does not occur concurrent with the peak drug plasma or tissue levels. In actuality, there are probably more situations where some degree of time dependency exists than for those of a non-time-dependent nature. However, it is necessary at the onset of this discussion to set this general phenomenon of drug levels and pharmacological response measurement into perspective. This being done, we may now classify in a very broad way, two types of problem:

1. The administered agent enters the general circulation and functions as the active pharmacophore, eliciting a pharmacological response that can be quantitated.
2. The administered agent undergoes metabolism, either prior or subsequent to its entry into the general circulation. One or more of these metabolic products in turn are responsible for the measured pharmacological response.

This categorization then parallels that defined by Brodie. It encompasses not only those situations when the pharmacological effect occurs while drug (or metabolite) plasma levels are within measurable levels, but also those that arise when the effect occurs subsequent to detectable levels of drug or metabolite in the body. The need for this modified definition becomes clearer as this chapter develops. Thus this discussion treats examples from each of these main classifications and, through the use of a technique known as *kinetic hysteresis analysis*, shows how models can be developed that will provide clues on the mechanism of action of a drug. At the very least, this tool will provide new insights into kinetic pathways responsible for the observed pharmacological effect(s). It is not, however, the intent of this discussion to review traditional approaches to a pharmacokinetic analysis of the effect of drug plasma levels. For this, the reader is referred to previous references (2, 3) and other chapters in this text. Instead, we attempt to show, by way of examples, by using (1) chlorothiazide, a drug that does not undergo metabolism, and (2) chlordiazepoxide, a drug undergoing extensive metabolism, how the concept of kinetic hysteresis analysis can provide valuable information toward establishing a relationship between the drug plasma level and its corresponding pharmacological effect.

1. WHAT IS KINETIC HYSTERESIS?

In attempting to understand and model the behavior of a drug in vivo, one usually begins by obtaining plasma-level profiles of the drug following both an intravenous dose and an oral dose (provided the compound is absorbed orally). These data provide insights regarding the metabolic fate of the compound. For example, a decrease in the renal clearance between an intravenous and oral dose may suggest a decrease in the filtration rate due to saturation of plasma protein binding following an intravenous dose, especially if the ratio of the amount absorbed orally to the intravenous dose is low. Until a complete drug metabolism study is conducted, one may experience difficulty in selecting the most appropriate pharmacokinetic model, that is, the model that is best able to predict the behavior of drug in experiments not yet conducted, and also model the relationship existing between drug plasma levels and pharmacological effect.

What is attempted here is to demonstrate that a technique called *kinetic hysteresis* can be a useful tool in identifying metabolic pathways and in selecting a model to describe a particular set of conditions. In a recent review, Tanner states (4):

> Hysteresis is defined in physics as "the failure of a property that has been changed by an external agent to return to its original value when the cause of the change is removed." The word comes from the Greek husteresis, a shortcoming. In magnets it is often exhibited as "the failure of the magnetization in that body to return to its original value when the external field is reduced."
>
> In practice, hysteresis has been generalized to refer to deviations from, not just an original or starting point, but from any point along a hysteresis trajectory. When the trajectory of ascent differs from the trajectory of descent of a process (even though the starting and finishing points are the same), that phenomenon also is referred to as hysteresis.

Several nonpharmacokinetic examples are briefly discussed to illustrate the use of kinetic hysteresis to discriminate among models. Again quoting from that earlier review (4):

> To make this description more concrete, we examine the counterclockwise curve of malachite green formation, *d(P)/dt*, as a function of the product of horseradish peroxidase enzyme–hydrogen peroxide complex (*ES*), and leucomalachite green (S_2), in Figure 1. The data used for this cross plot are those taken by B. Chance (5) in an early stopped-flow study of the peroxidase system. This cross plot, connecting the implicit common time points that originally appeared in reference 6. illustrates that the early time points (initial transient trajectory) lie below the later time points (stationary-state trajectory). This example of a kinetic enyme hysteresis curve demonstrates what type of information can be inferred from the trajectory's direction and shape.
>
> The primary effect, easily discernible and not readily confounded by experimental error (because of the many experimental points involved), is that of direction. The direction of the curve in Figure 1 is counterclockwise. At first glance, it would seem that whatever would cause a change in direction would be due to some nonlinear effect, since the curve is not linear. Invoking nonlinearity, in fact, was shown to be unnecessary (6) from a simulation of the linear kinetic network

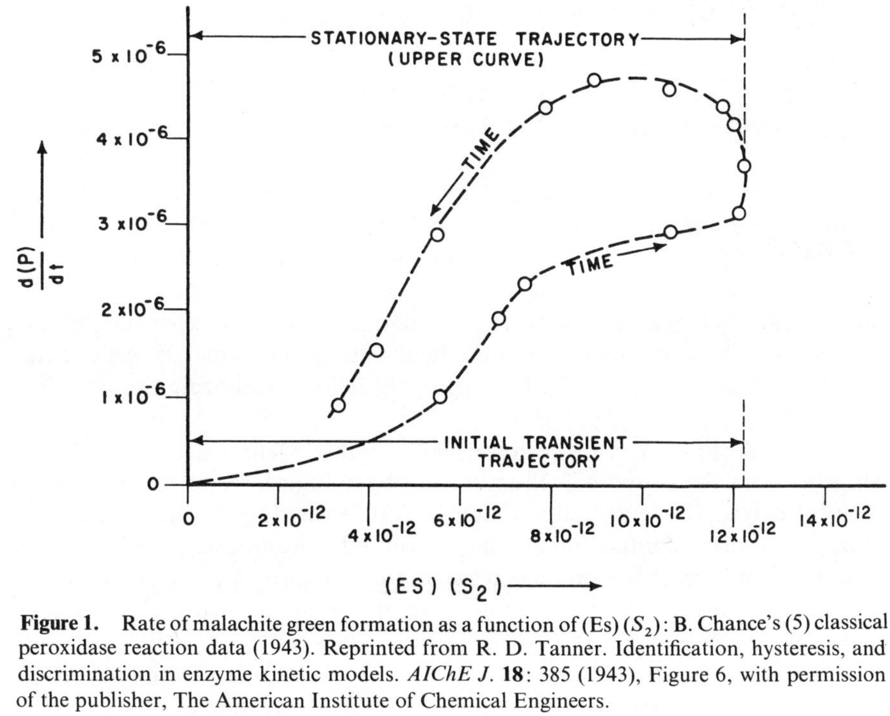

Figure 1. Rate of malachite green formation as a function of (Es) (S_2): B. Chance's (5) classical peroxidase reaction data (1943). Reprinted from R. D. Tanner. Identification, hysteresis, and discrimination in enzyme kinetic models. *AIChE J.* **18**: 385 (1943), Figure 6, with permission of the publisher, The American Institute of Chemical Engineers.

of: $A \rightarrow B \rightarrow C \rightarrow D$ that led to a counterclockwise hysteresis curve when $d(D)/dt$ was plotted as a function of (B). Here parentheses indicate concentrations, and t, time.

As expected from the law of mass action and the assumption of elementary kinetic reactions, a cross plot of $d(D)/dt$ against (C) leads to a linear curve, with a slope equal to the rate constant of the step C to D.

It is seen from the above simple analysis that a tool is available to discriminate between two models: one, $A \rightarrow B \rightarrow D$ and the other, $A \rightarrow B \rightarrow C \rightarrow D$, when $d(D)/dt$ is plotted against (B). If that plot is linear, (C) is in negligible concentration if it exists at all, but if nonlinear, (C) is significant to the system. Return to the peroxidase example shown in Figure 1. The original model proposed by Chance in 1943 postulated that only one intermediate state, ES, was present. The graphical consequence of the presence of only one intermediate in the proposed model is that a cross plot of the data would be linear. In Figure 1, $(ES)(S_2)$ is plotted on the abscissa rather than (ES) alone, in order to take into consideration the two substrate, nonlinear system. Since the curve in Figure 1 is distinctly a counterclockwise hysteresis function, however, analysis implied that more than one intermediate enzyme–substrate complex must exist. This implication was verified independently of the hysteresis analysis when Chance later postulated and subsequently measured, in 1952, two enzyme–substrate complexes along with a free-radical intermediate state (16).

2. CORRELATION OF DRUG PLASMA OR TISSUE LEVELS WITH A PHARMACOLOGICAL EFFECT

Drug plasma levels can be generally assumed to be indicative of drug levels in the tissues and bear some proportionality to each other based on mathematical models. The correctness of any model can be assessed only through its continued use to predict the outcome of new experiments. Refinement of model parameters and/or pathways by comparison with experimental data is a process familiar to anyone in the field of pharmacokinetics. An example of one such attempt from the literature will help to elaborate the principles involved.

Levy et al. (8) used a two-compartment model to demonstrate the relationship between the observed reduction in physiological performance and the dose of D-lysergic acid diethylamide (LSD). Assuming elimination of drug from the central compartment, they observed a hysteresis-type loop when measured subject performance was plotted against the model predicted fraction of dose in the tissue compartment. Figure 2 from their original article is reproduced here.

Theorizing that the site of action of LSD was isolated from the general body tissue, a compartment they termed a "slowly accessible" compartment, the original model was revised as shown in the following diagram:

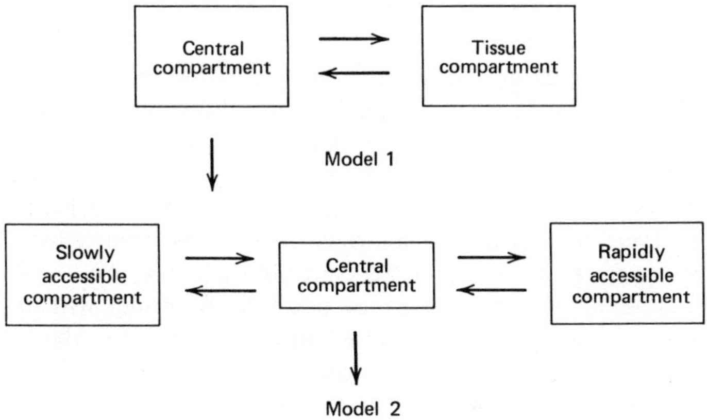

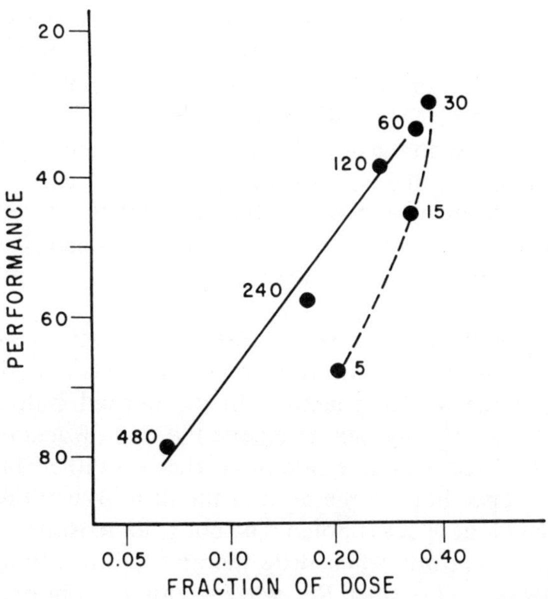

Figure 2. Relationship between the fractional amount of LSD in the tissue compartment of model 1 and the intensity of the pharmacological effect. The number next to each symbol represents the time in minutes when the measurements were made. Reprinted from G. Levy, M. Gibaldi, and W. J. Jusko. Multicompartment pharmacokinetic models and pharmacologic effects. J. Pharm. Sci. **58**(4): 422–424 (1969), Figure 2, with permission of the publisher, The American Pharmaceutical Association.

Again, a plot of performance versus fraction of dose in this slowly accessible compartment was made, this time resulting in a linear relationship. In this fashion, the authors made use of the hysteresis curve to develop a three-compartment "linear" model.

The authors were careful to emphasize that a model is an attempt to simplify the real biologic system. The fact that the second model, selected on the basis of a comparison of a pharmacological response and fraction of dose in the selected compartment as estimated from drug plasma levels, provides the expected linear relationship hypothesized as evidence that a close approximation to the real biologic system has been achieved. This latter point cannot be overemphasized since in each situation the goal is to achieve as close an approximation as possible. A model will always be incomplete, but if well posed will offer an explanation for the "missing" data needed to clarify a more complex question.

As noted at the onset, some pharmacological responses exhibit a time-dependent phenomena. A very elegant treatment of one such example was presented by Nagashima et al. (9), who described the kinetics of the pharmacological effect following the administration of warfarin in humans. The following discussion is based on the administration of a racemic mixture of warfarin. More recently Levy et al. (28) reported that there were no pronounced pharmacokinetic or pharmacodynamic interactions between single large doses of (*R*)-(+)- and (*S*)-(−)-warfarin in humans. Further, they showed that the predictions based on the model to be discussed have still held when a correction was made for the relative contribution of each enantiomer. However, recognition must be made of the fact that the net effect of this during chronic drug administration has yet to be determined. Therefore, one is cautioned to keep this in mind as the evolution of the warfarin model is discussed.

Peak hypoprothrombopenic activity occurs 2–4 days after a single dose of warfarin anticoagulant. It is known that warfarin inhibits only the synthesis of vitamin K-dependent clotting factors. In the normal state, the rate of synthesis R_{syn} of these clotting factors equals the rate of degradation R_{deg}. On administration of the drug, the rate of synthesis is either diminished or ceases completely depending on the dose of the drug. When the maximum amount of anticoagulant effect is noted (i.e., body homeostasis occurs), R_{syn} again equals R_{deg}. Therefore, when drug therapy is discontinued, the disproportionality again occurs since R_{syn} will increase until normal levels are restored. Since it is not possible to measure these rates, Nagashima et al. (9) developed their equations using prothrombin times as a measure of pharmacological activity of warfarin. The derivation of the equation is not discussed here, but the final form in terms of prothrombin activity P is

$$P = P^{\circ} - a[1 - e^{-k_d t}] + bt \tag{1}$$

where

$$a=\frac{m}{k_d}\log\left(\frac{C_p^\circ}{C_{p_{\min}}}\right)+\frac{mk_e}{2.3k_d^2}$$

$$b=\frac{mk_e}{2.3k_d}$$

This equation applies only in the drug concentration range where there is a linear relationship between log C_p (plasma level of warfarin) and the prothrombin time P. Thus C_p must exceed the minimum concentration $C_{p_{\min}}$ necessary to cause a hypoprothrombopenic response and be less than $C_{p_{\max}}$, the amount above which no further pharmacological effect takes place. The constant C_p° is the plasma concentration at zero time (obtained by back extrapolation of the linear portion of a log C_p–time plot). The two constants k_d and k_e represent first-order rate constants for the degradation of the clotting cofactors and the drug elimination rate, respectively; m is the slope of the line obtained from a plot of the ratio of the observed to the normal prothrombin time versus the plasma level of the drug.

The actual method of calculation is somewhat involved but could be carried out simply with the aid of a digital computer. Nagashima et al. showed that the prothrombin complex activity at a given time is a function of the plasma warfarin concentration and that the apparent delay in the warfarin effect is a consequence of the prothrombin activity being a function of both the rate of synthesis and rate of degradation of vitamin K-dependent clotting factors. A value for k_d of 1.21 day^{-1} was found for all 30 subjects. The utility of their method of analysis lies in the fact that since k_d is an apparent constant, the level of prothrombin synthesis can be calculated from equation (2) once the level of prothrombin activity desired has been determined:

$$R_{\text{syn}}=k_dP \tag{2}$$

A standard curve of R_{syn} versus C_p is constructed initially for each subject, and thereby the level of C_p required to maintain a specific level of prothrombin activity is quickly calculated. It is noted that a kinetic hysteresis curve "cusp" can also be used to infer the equality of synthesis and degradation rates in enzymatically controlled reactions (10).

The body exhibits many processes which exhibit a lag between the drug plasma profile curve and the pharmacologic effect with time. Many of these are linked to homeostatic mechanisms within the body. Renal excretion of electrolytes is yet another example of such a process. In simple terms, the elimination of sodium, potassium and chloride depend on body intake of these electrolytes. During times of profuse sweating, the body attempts to conserve these elements and the renal excretion component decreases. Even during the administration of diuretic agents, the body attempts to prevent a change in the electrolyte balance and a process of electrolyte conservation is initiated (13).

The action of the diuretic chlorothiazide illustrates both the body's electrolyte conserving mechanism and how kinetic hysteresis aided in the qualitative development of a model describing the interaction between drug, electrolyte excretion and electrolyte conservation. This example is taken from a paper originally presented in 1973 by Loo et al. (11). The following information will serve as further introduction to this example. Sodium ions are filtered by the glomeruli and are actively reabsorbed mainly in the proximal tubule and to a lesser extent in the distal tubule. Reabsorption of sodium in the tubules (both proximal and distal portions) has been shown to be an active process; that is, it requires the expenditure of energy. The exact nature of this process is poorly understood (12). Proximal reabsorption operates on a large quantity of Na^+ and increases roughly in proportion to the filtered load. No evidence of being limited by a maximum rate within physiological ranges of filtered load have been demonstrated. In conditions in which salt intake is decreased, the body shows an ability to increase the reabsorption of Na^+ so that sodium depletion does not occur. It is believed that altered tubular permeability to sodium ions is responsible for this conservation effect.

For the purpose of this discussion, the assumption is made that "enhanced" reabsorption of sodium proceeds by a mechanism different from the one that controls sodium reabsorption under normal conditions. This auxiliary process is mediated by physiological control. Whether a specific receptor is involved in this latter process is not known; however, it is believed that the hormone aldosterone is capable of causing enhanced sodium reabsorption. Release of the hormone is thought to be mediated by renin released in the glomeruli, possibly as a result of increases in the rate at which sodium is eliminated by the body (13).

Thiazide diuretics cause sodium to be excreted in greater than normal amounts. It is believed that the presence of the drug in the plasma filtrate as it passes through the tubule inhibits the reabsorption of sodium, giving rise to the saluretic effect (14–16).

With the foregoing facts and assumptions in mind, we now show how a model can be constructed for the relationship for the saluretic effect following the administration of a thiazide diuretic and the levels of the diuretic in plasma and urine. The data were obtained from a three-way crossover study involving six human volunteers (17) utilizing an intravenous injection, an oral solution, and a commercial tablet formulation of chlorothiazide. Plasma and urinary drug levels as well as the excretion of sodium in the urine were measured at regular intervals following dosing.

The following information was obtained from that study:

1. Following the intravenous dose, the drug was eliminated rapidly (90% in 2 hours) and almost exclusively by the kidney.
2. On oral administration, approximately 25% of the dose was absorbed from solution and 20% from tablets. The rates of absorption were comparable, although the onset of absorption was slower following tablet than solution administration.
3. Orally administered chlorothiazide was excreted by the kidneys as the unchanged molecule. Excretion was rapid and virtually complete within 24 hours.
4. Based on renal clearance measurements, tubular secretion as well as glomerular filtration were involved in excretion of chlorothiazide. Beyer and Baer (16) report that the predominant route of elimination is by tubular secretion. Breckenridge and Rosen (18) and Hucker et al. (19) have reported that the drug is extensively bound to plasma proteins. At high plasma concentrations, as would be encountered following the intravenous dose, a smaller percentage of the total drug would be bound to plasma proteins. Since only unbound drug is filterable, all else being equal, one would expect higher renal clearances of drug for the intravenous dose. Such is indeed observed.
5. The total amount of sodium excreted over a 24-hour period was comparable for all three doses.

Values for k_e, k_1, and k_2 were obtained from a two-compartment open model fit for the intravenous data in each volunteer. Plots of the rate of sodium excretion versus the observed drug plasma were constructed for each subject. A representative plot of these data is shown in Figure 3.

A model can now be proposed to describe the relationship between drug plasma level and rate of sodium excretion following administration of a thiazide diuretic. The following symbols are used throughout this discussion:

R°	initial amount of sodium receptors in body
C_p	concentration of drug in plasma
D	drug in biophase (i.e., at site of action)
R	amount of free receptor
DR	drug receptor complex
D_u	amount of drug eliminated in urine
V	rate of sodium excretion

Drug in the plasma partitions reversibly into the biophase, where it will

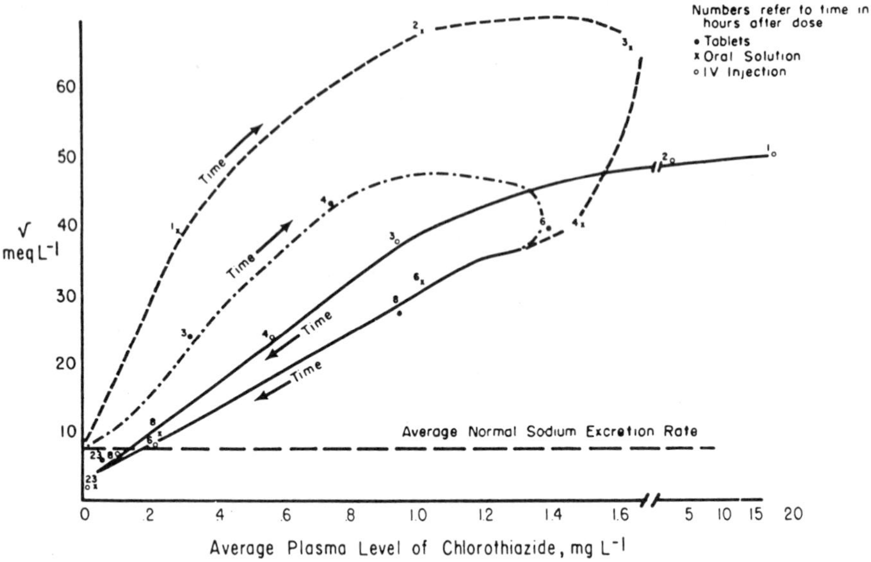

Figure 3. Sodium excretion rate as a function of average chlorothiazide plasma level.

complex with the receptor. This can be represented simply as

$$\text{Dosage form} \xrightarrow{k_a} C_p \underset{k_2}{\overset{k_1}{\rightleftharpoons}} D$$
$$C_p \xrightarrow{k_e}$$

$$D + R \underset{k_4}{\overset{k_3}{\rightleftharpoons}} DR$$

Scheme 1

Where k_a and k_e are the first-order absorption and elimination rate constants, respectively. A differential equation relating C_p and DR can be written from the model in Scheme I.

If one defines the rate of sodium excretion as

$$V = k_5 DR \tag{3}$$

then following rearrangement and substitution, one obtains

$$V = \frac{k_5}{k_4}\left[\frac{k_3}{k_2}(R)\frac{d(C_p)}{dt} + \frac{k_3 k_1}{k_2}(R)C_p - \frac{d(DR)}{dt}\right] \tag{4}$$

which relates the rate of sodium excretion in terms of drug plasma level that can be measured.

Computer simulations were then prepared for the oral dose with different drug absorption profiles: (1) one in which the dose would be absorbed by a slow first-order process that would be essentially complete in 5 hours and (2) a zero-order rate constant of 22 mg/hour, a value similar to that estimated from the actual data obtained. Values for k_3 and k_4 were varied over a considerable range, and R° was set at two widely separated values. Several selected examples are shown in Figures 4 and 5. It is obvious from these two figures that the magnitude of the various parameters can alter the area within the hysteresis loops. Also evident is the fact that regardless of the range chosen for these rate constants, direction of the pathways cannot be altered. Both these factors give additional insights into the model and the relative contribution of each rate constant to the shape of the hysteresis loop. The lack of conformity of the direction obtained from the model and that obtained from the data are sufficient justification to seek an alternate model for the relationship. Therefore, a modification in the proposed model was made as follows:

1. When excess body sodium is lost, compensatory sodium reabsorption occurs in the renal tubules. Thus, when a negative sodium balance occurs, the rate of excretion will be a function of both the compensatory reabsorption process and the drug–receptor complex. Therefore, one may

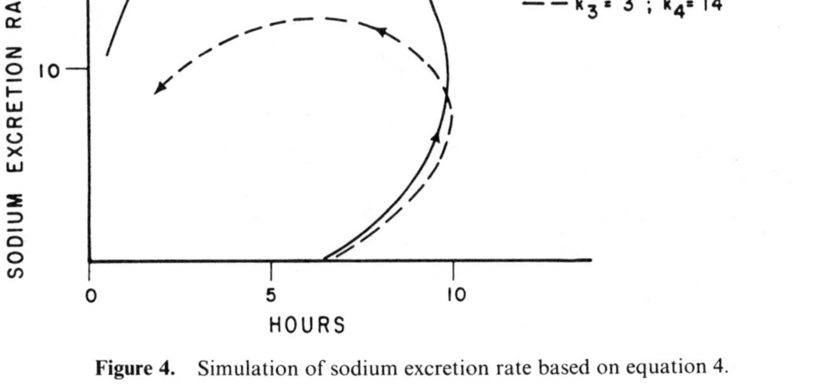

Figure 4. Simulation of sodium excretion rate based on equation 4.

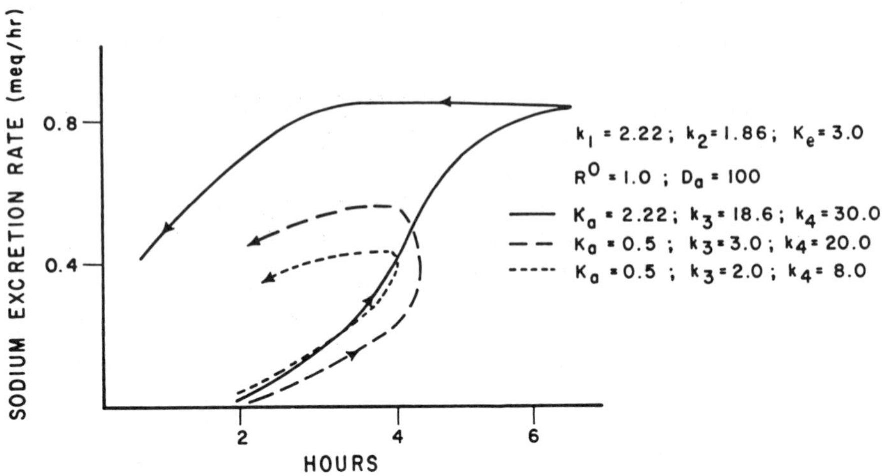

Figure 5. Simulation of sodium excretion rate based on equation 4.

propose that compensation is proportional to the difference between the sodium pool and that being excreted. In other words, let

$$\mathrm{Na}^+_{\mathrm{in}} - \mathrm{Na}^+_{\mathrm{out}} = \alpha$$

so that

$$\text{compensation} = 0 \quad \text{when} \quad \alpha \geqslant 0$$

and

$$\text{compensation} = f(\alpha) \quad \text{when} \quad \alpha < 0$$

Accordingly, equation 3 would be modified to include the compensation term as

$$V = k_5 DR + f(\alpha) \tag{5}$$

Thus, if $f(\alpha)$ becomes sufficiently negative at any time in the experiment, its contribution could change a counterclockwise curve into a clockwise one.

2. The sodium receptor is located in the kidney; therefore, drug present in the urine becomes the rate-determining factor. The fact that this does not alter the observed clockwise hysteresis effect is shown in Figure 6, where the sodium excretion rate is plotted against D_u, drug present in the urine. Therefore, D_u can be qualitatively interchanged with C_p for purposes of hystersis curve analysis.

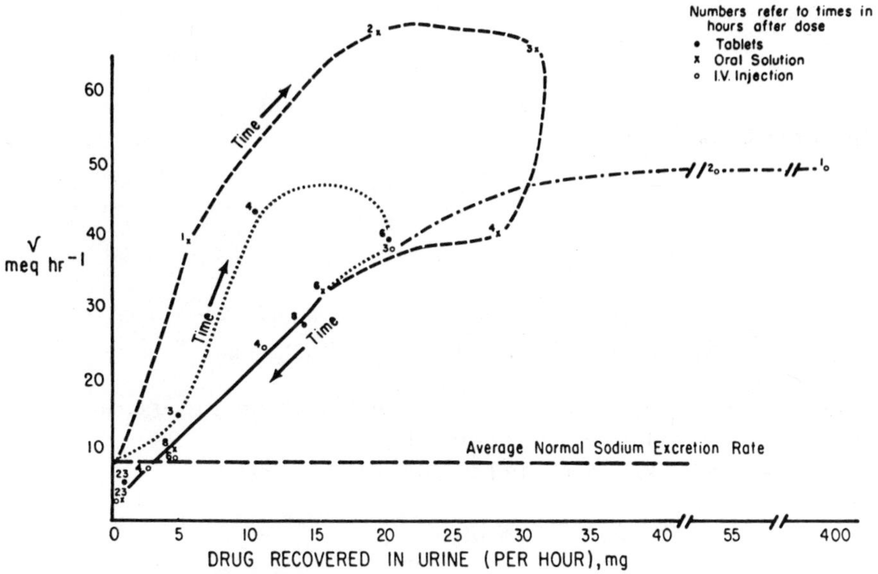

Figure 6. Sodium excretion rates as a function of chlorothiazide in urine.

3. The receptor is able to bind Na^+ as well as drug so that the total receptor in the kidney at any time is

$$R^\circ = R + NaR + D_uR \tag{6}$$

Note is made of the likelihood that formation of D_uR is favored over NaR.

Therefore,

$$D_u + R \frac{k_6}{k_7} = D_uR \tag{7}$$

and

$$dD_uR = k_6(D_u)(R) - k_7 D_uR \tag{8}$$

But $R = R^\circ - NaR - D_uR$; therefore,

$$\frac{dD_uR}{dt} = k_6(D_u)[R^\circ - NaR - D_uR] - k_7 D_uR \tag{9}$$

and

$$\frac{dD_uR}{dt} = k_6(D_u)R^\circ - k_6(D_u)(NaR) - k_6(D_u)(D_uR) - k_7 D_uR \tag{10}$$

Solving for D_uR:

$$D_uR = \frac{1}{k_6D_u + k_7}\left[k_6(D_u)R^\circ - k_6(D_u)NaR - \frac{dD_uR}{dt}\right] \tag{11}$$

and since $V = k_5D_uR + f(\alpha)$,

$$D_uR = \frac{V - f(\alpha)}{k_5}$$

and

$$V = \frac{k_5k_6(D_u)R^\circ}{k_6(D_u) + k_7} - \frac{k_5k_6(D_u)[NaR]}{k_6(D_u) + k_7} - \frac{k_5d[D_uR]}{k_6(D_u) + k_7dt} + f(\alpha) \tag{12}$$

Therefore, at low D_u a slight depression of V compared to the rate in the absence of drug will occur (see Figure 7).

As D_u increases, $k_6D_u \gg k_7$, and equation 12 reduces to

$$V = k_5R^\circ - k_5NaR - \frac{k_5}{k_6(D_u)} \cdot \frac{dD_uR}{dt} + f(\alpha) \tag{13}$$

As the receptor becomes saturated, dD_uR/dt approaches zero; NaR is very small and, in the absence of compensation, a maximum rate of $V/(V_{\max})$ is predicted.

What is the effect as D_u decreases? The term dD_uR/dt will become negative; therefore, the third term in equation 12 becomes positive. One would therefore expect the relationship shown in Figure 8—that is, the upper branch of a counterclockwise hysteresis loop. The term dD_uR/dt will affect the shape and

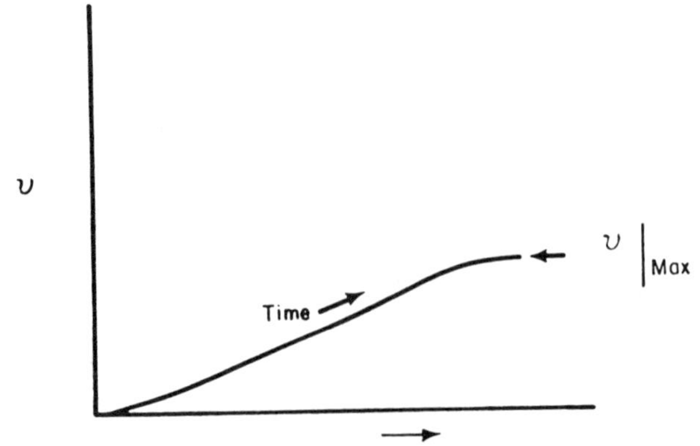

Figure 7. Relationship between sodium excretion rates and amount of drug; effect of increasing values of D_v.

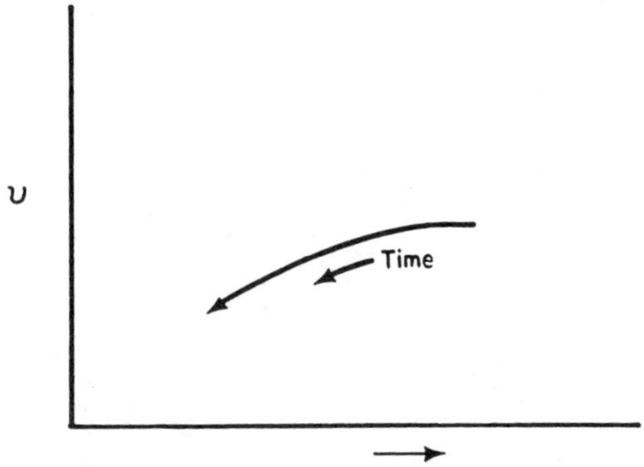

Figure 8. Relationship between sodium excretion rates and amount of drug; effect of decreasing values of D_v.

magnitude of the area within the loop. When urine levels are high, V_{max} may be attained rapidly, whereas if drug levels are low, V_{max} may never be reached and the initial slope will not be the same for all cases.

Initially, little compensation is likely to occur unless massive amounts of sodium are lost within a short period of time. Since compensation causes a decrease in the amount (rate) of sodium excreted in terms of the time course shown in Figure 5, one would expect to see rates less than those in the absence of any compensation. Therefore, the relationship would be as shown in Figure 9*a* or 9*b* for late times.

It is interesting to note that attainment of V_{max} is not a necessary condition for compensation. Clockwise hysteresis can be observed as D_u decreases provided

$$f(\alpha) > \frac{k_5}{k_1 D + k_2} \frac{dD_u R}{t}$$

If the two are equal for all times, a straight line might be observed.

To summarize for the third case, then, we can see from the kinetic hysteresis analysis that the model proposed is a reasonable one. It is able to predict qualitatively the direction of the hysteresis loop and also the existence of a maximum rate of sodium excretion. The model is not dependent on any specific route of administration of the drug and is capable of describing both intravenous and oral sodium excretion rates as a function of drug levels.

It is also apparent that excretion rates less than normal may be observed even after all drug has been cleared from the body if the sodium balance has not been restored. Such is indeed observed in Figures 5 and 6 for very late times.

The model describes the excretion of sodium in normal individuals.

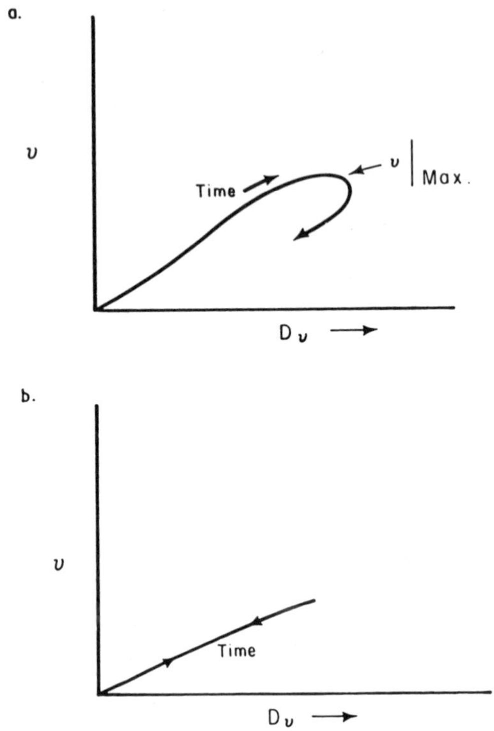

Figure 9. Effect of compensatory sodium reabsorption on relationship between sodium excretion rates and drug: (*a*) $f(\alpha) >$ equation 13; (*b*) $f(\alpha) \simeq$ equation 13.

Extension of this model to edematous individuals has not been attempted because of lack of adequate data, although the procedure described here would be followed.

3. IDENTIFICATION OF METABOLIC PATHWAYS

Development of models capable of prediction often require refinement beyond the scope of classical pharmacokinetic analysis. A case in point was the description of the behavior of chlordiazepoxide in dogs as reported by Kaplan et al. (20). Using both two- and six-compartment models, they could predict drug dosages for individual animals, but a single model was not generally applicable to all dogs or without varying the parameters on a case-by-case basis. One reason for this lack of generality was the considerable variability in the model parameters from animal to animal.

Tanner and Wilhelm (21, 22) used an enzyme kinetic model to describe the steps in the chlordiazepoxide degradation sequence in the dog to describe the process by which the body catabolized the chemical moiety. This is discussed in some detail in Section 4.

4. HYSTERESIS AND A POSSIBLE SHUNTING PATHWAY IN THE DEGRADATION SEQUENCE OF CHLORDIAZEPOXIDE HCL IN THE DOG

This section is a summary of references 21 and 22 and shows how hysteresis can be used as a qualitative tool for predicting possible new reaction routes. The primary degradation sequence for chlordiazepoxide (Librium®) in a dog's blood plasma can be depicted as

$$C \rightarrow N \rightarrow L \rightarrow P \tag{14}$$

where C = chlordiazepoxide
N = N-demethyl chlordiazepoxide (desmethyl chlordiazepoxide)
L = lactam (demoxypam)
P = products (demoxypam metabolites and elimination from the body)

To overcome the problem associated with classical multicompartment (linear) pharmacokinetic models, it was proposed that the variation in parameters describing a given dog (in a study comparing two dogs) was due to catabolic enzyme differences. Perhaps the actual drug-degrading enzymes for chlordiazepoxide are in the hepatic microsomal metabolizing system.

Conjecturing (for modeling purposes) that enzymes are responsible for chlordiazepoxide degradation, the drug degradation can be pictured by the scheme

$$C \xrightarrow{E_1} N \xrightarrow{E_2} L \xrightarrow{E_3} P \tag{15}$$

where $E_n (n = 1, 2, 3)$ is the denoted enzyme for the indicated reaction. The hope of such a model is that, when other effects are taken into consideration such as absorption in the tissue phase, the only varying parameters will be E_1, E_2, and E_3. If this is valid, the appropriate dose of drug required to meet bioavailability requirements could be sharpened when compared to the less specific body weight basis.

Unfortunately, as is true in too many cases, extraction of the many parameters, including the enzyme levels for the above nonlinear model (when expressed in mathematical form) from the collected data, turned out to be a problem of nonuniqueness: too many parameters for too few data points. Therefore, even though the enzyme postulate seemed attractive, its benefit in the model compared to the more traditional linear model still needs to be established. The study did seem to indicate, however, that enzyme levels between the two dogs in the study could differ by a factor of 2 or 3. On the other hand, the more qualitative technique of kinetic hysteresis could still be applied meaningfully. In this case it was utilized to confirm whether there was one primary degradation pathway as stated in the literature.

A plot of the lactam rate data projected into the first quadrant [by adding a "mean" first-order degradation term $k(L)$ describing the degradation of L to P] as a function of the N-demethyl moiety in Kaplan et al.'s dog 2 is pictured in Figure 10. This is a clockwise hysteresis curve. A similar clockwise hysteresis curve was also obtained for the data from the other dog. To better understand the meaning of the direction of this curve, the linear network

$$A \longrightarrow B \longrightarrow C \longrightarrow D \longrightarrow E \xrightarrow{k} P \quad (B \xrightarrow{k_{\text{shunt}}} E) \tag{16}$$

was studied, and the following three generalizations (22) could be made for a plot of $[d(E)/dt + k(E)]$ versus (C):

1. When k_{shunt} is 0, counterclockwise hysteresis (with no shunting) results.

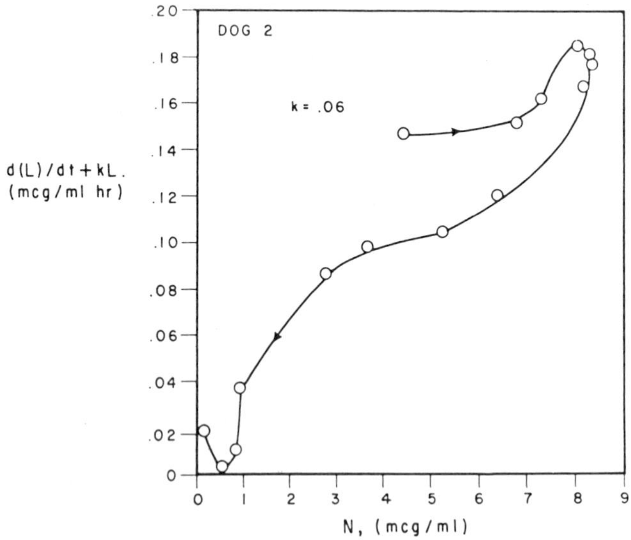

Figure 10. Demoxypam formation rate as a function of N-demethyl chlordiazepoxide concentration. Reprinted from S. A. Kaplan, M. Lewis, M. A. Schwartz, E. Postma, S. Cotler, C. W. Alruzzo, T. L. Lee, and R. E. Weinfeld, Pharmacokinetic model for chlordiazepoxide HCl in the dog. *J. Pharm. Sci.* 59:1569–1574 (1970), Figure 10, by permission of the publishers, The American Institute of Chemical Engineers.

2. When k_{shunt} is large, clockwise hysteresis (with significant shunting) results.
3. When k_{shunt} takes on intermediate values, both clockwise and counter-clockwise hysteresis in a "figure-8-shaped" curve (with moderate shunting) results.

Even when the tissue phase effects are taken into account, the above generalizations hold as shown in Figure 11, where k_{10} in the ordinate corresponds to the degradation constant k above.

Previous work indicates that without marked changes in the enzyme level (e.g., by induction or repression), the hysteresis behavior is primarily a function of the reaction sequence, so that the nonlinearities would be insignificant in determining the hysteresis direction. To relate the network (e.g., by second-order reactions) model above with the chlordiazepoxide model, A would correspond with chlordiazepoxide, C with N-demethyl chlordiazepoxide, and E with the lactam; P would be the same for both models. The intermediates B and D would then represent enzyme–substrate complexes.

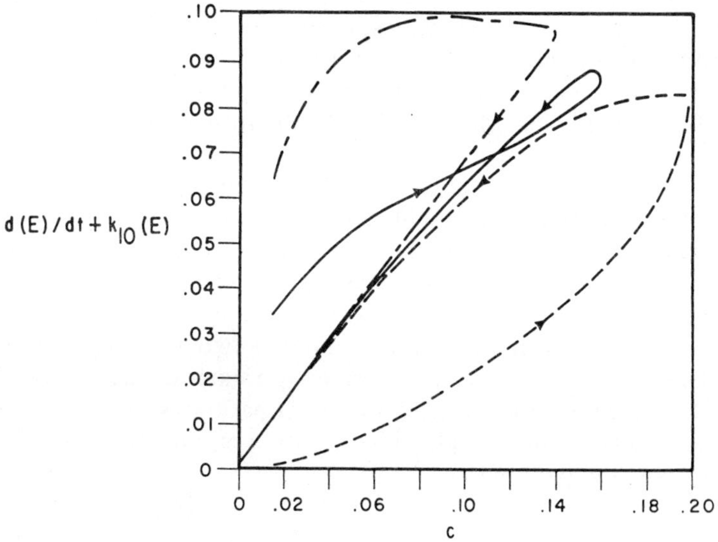

Figure 11. Simulation of the linearized chlordiazepoxide model demonstrating that the tissue phase compartments do not alter the hysteresis curve directions. Significant shunting, therefore, leads to a clockwise hysteresis curve and its absence, to a counterclockwise curve. Reprinted from S. A. Kaplan, M. Lewis, M. A. Schwartz, E. Postma, S. Cotler, C. W. Alruzzo, T. L. Lee, and R. E. Weinfeld, Pharmacokinetic model for chlordiazepoxide HCl in the dog. *J. Pharm. Sci.* 59: 1569–1574 (1970), Figure 7, by permission of the publishers, The American Institute of Chemical Engineers.

The presence of clockwise hysteresis for the in-vivo data taken for both the dogs in the study (shown in Figure 10 for one) would seem, therefore, indicative of a parallel, minor pathway, heretofore not realized. No new data were required for this interpretation, but confirmation of such a new route would require the measurement of intermediates along the suggested pathway.

Recent work has shown that "mixing" effects or partitioning effects due to specific tissue affinity for drug in plasma can result in clockwise hysteresis. This explanation may be more feasible since no clinical evidence has been found to support a chemical basis for the reversal in direction.

Drug-induced enzyme production in the body is a well-established fact. These enzymes may affect the metabolism of that drug per se or another drug that is coadministered. Drugs that stimulate their own metabolism are termed *autoinductive*, whereas those that stimulate the metabolism of other drugs coadministered are termed *heteroinductive* (24). In these situations one is dealing with a direct effect on the time course of the drug in the body. One example of a pharmacokinetic treatment of the auto- or heteroinductive enzyme effects of carbamazipine was recently presented by Levy et al. (25). Another example in which enzymes play a major role in the metabolism of drugs is the chemical restructuring of salicylates. Prior to their renal elimination, the conjugation of salicylates is mediated by enzymes. Levy and Tsuchiya (26) proposed a model to describe the elimination of salicylic acid from the body. The model incorporates the classical enzyme model, a Michaelis–Menten expression to describe the formation of salicyluric acid from the drug precursor.

As the vigor of drug metabolism studies becomes more prevalent, it is likely that pharmacokinetic models will require the incorporation of enzymatic pathways to more completely characterize drug disposition. The potential for such models to more accurately characterize the "average" patient is high. The concept of slow and fast acetylators (27) has been helpful in describing the disposition of procainamide in two distinct patient populations. Conceivably, the kinetic hysteresis approach described for chlordiazepoxide will be helpful in elucidating such pathways for other drugs and unify the models to apply to all patients with a minimal number of characterizing (changing) parameters.

5. CONCLUSIONS

One basic problem associated with modeling of kinetic phenomena is the difficulty in discriminating between candidate models. Although parameter estimation will aid in this selection, choice of initial values is often difficult and tedious. The ability to evaluate a model in a qualitative fashion offers the investigator another dimension in which to scrutinize a process. It is in this area that kinetic hysteresis finds utility. As shown in the foregoing, if directional trends observed do not follow those suggested by the proposed model, a modification of that model is in order. Furthermore, selection among models by the method of kinetic hysteresis analysis may provide clues to steps within a process that would go unnoticed with the use of conventional methods. Used cautiously, and in keeping with the limitations of the data, hysteresis curve analysis appears to aid in pharmacokinetic experimental designs by reducing the number of experiments needed for the elucidation of reaction mechanisms and pathways.

REFERENCES

1. B. B. Brodie. In T. B. Binns (ed.), *Absorption and Distribution of Drugs*. Williams and Wilkins, Baltimore, 1964, p. 212.
2. M. Gibaldi and D. Perrier. *Pharmacokinetics*. Marcel Dekker, New York, 1975.
3. J. G. Wagner. *Biopharmaceutics and Relevant Pharmacokinetics*. Drug Intelligence Publications, Indiana, 1971.
4. R. D. Tanner. Kinetic hysteresis in enzyme and fermentation systems. *Ann. Rep. Fermant. Processes* **2**: 73 (1978).
5. B. Chance. The kinetics of the enzyme–substrate compound of peroxidase. *J. Biol. Chem.* **151**: 553–577 (1943).
6. R. D. Tanner. Identification, hysteresis, and discrimination in enzyme kinetic models. *AIChEJ*. **18**: 385 (1972).
7. B. Chance. The kinetics and stoichiometry of the transition from the primary to the secondary peroxidase peroxide complexes. *Arch. Biochem. Biophys.* **41**: 416 (1952).
8. G. Levy, M. Gibaldi, and W. J. Jusko. Multicompartment pharmacokinetic models and pharmacologic effects. *J. Pharm. Sci.* **58** (4): 422–424 (1969).
9. R. Nagashima, R. A. O'Reilly, and G. Levy. Kinetics of pharmacologic effects in man: The anticoagulant action of warfarin. *Clin. Pharm. Therap.* **10**: 22–35 (1969).
10. R. D. Tanner. The role of perturbations, shunts, cusps and convexity reversals in elucidating enzyme kinetic mechanisms and hysteresis pathways. *Chem. Eng. Sci.* **29**: 169–179 (1974).
11. J. C. K. Loo, R. D. Tanner, and J. V. Bondi. The role of hysteresis in selecting a model to describe the elimination of body sodium by a diuretic. Presented at the *AIChE* Meeting, Detroit, June 1973.
12. V. B. Mouhtcastle (ed.). *Medical Physiology*, Vol. 1, Mosby, St. Louis, 1968, pp. 329–331.
13. I. H. Mills. Renal regulation of sodium excretion. *Ann. Rev. Med.* **21**: 75–98 (1970).
14. K. H. Beyer and J. E. Baer. Effects of drugs on active transport. *Ciba Foundation Symposium on Enzymes and Drug Action*, 1962, pp. 60–82.
15. J. E. Baer et al. The physiological disposition of chlorothiazide in the dog. *J. Pharm. Exp. Ther.* **125**: 295–302 (1959).
16. K. H. Beyer and J. E. Baer. Physiological basis for the action of newer diuretic agents. *Pharmacol. Rev.* **13**: 517–562 (1961).

17. E. L. Foltz. Unpublished data, Merck, Sharp & Dohme Research Laboratories, 1970.

18. A. Breckenridge and A. Rosen. The binding of chlorothiazide to plasma proteins. *Biochimica et Biophysica Acta* **21**: 75–98 (1970).

19. H. B. Hucker, et al. Effects of halofenate on binding of various drugs to human plasma proteins and on plasma half-life of antipyrine in monkeys. *J. Pharm. Sci.* **61**: 1490–1492 (1972).

20. S. A. Kaplan, M. Lewis, M. A. Schwartz, E. Postma, S. Cotler, C. W. Alruzzo, T. L. Lee, and R. E. Weinfeld. Pharmacokinetic model for chlordiazepoxide HCl in the dog. *J. Pharm. Sci.* **59**: 1569–1574 (1970).

21. R. D. Tanner and D. E. Wilhelm. An enzyme pharmacokinetic model for chlordiazepoxide HCl in the dog—Part 1. Lactam catabolism. *AIChE Symp. Ser.* No. 172, **74**: 53 (1978).

22. R. D. Tanner and D. E. Wilhelm. An enzyme pharmacokinetic model for chlordiazepoxide HCl in the dog—Part II. Hysteresis and a possible shunting pathway. *AIChE Symp. Ser.*, No. 172, **74**: 64 (1978).

23. R. D. Tanner and L. H. DeAngelis. Sigmoidal and growth rate kinetic hysteresis in biochemical systems. *Chem. Eng. J.* **8**: 113 (1974).

24. A. H. Conney. Pharmacological implications of microsomal enzyme induction. *Pharmacol. Rev.* **19**: 317 (1967).

25. R. H. Levy, A. A. Loi, and M. S. Dumain. Time-dependent kinetics IV: Pharmacokinetic theory of enzyme induction. *J. Pharm. Sci.* **68**(3): 398 (1979).

26. G. Levy and T. Tsuchiya. Salicylate accumulation kinetics in man. *New Engl. J. Med.* **287**(9): 430 (1972).

27. M. M. Reidenberg et al. Polymorphic acetylation procainamide in Man. *Clin. Pharmacol. Ther.* **17**: 722 (1975).

28. G. Levy, R. A. O'Reilly, and L. B. Wingard, Jr. Comparative pharmacokinetics of coumarin anticoagulants XXXV: Examination of possible pharmacokinetic interaction between (*R*)-(+)- and (*S*)-(−)-warfarin in humans. *J. Pharm. Sci.* **67**(6): 867–868 (1978).

CHAPTER 7

Mathematical Modeling of Diffusion Processes in Drug Delivery Polymeric Systems

NIKOLAOS A. PEPPAS
School of Chemical Engineering
Purdue University
West Lafayette, Indiana

CONTENTS

In the continuous research effort for the development of improved pharmaceutical formulations, polymeric materials provide a means of precise, reproducible, and safe release of drugs in biological systems (1–9). Controlled-release polymeric formulations for pharmaceutical applications have been developed in recent years and have been applied with considerable success in ocular therapy (3, 6), contraception (4), treatment of narcotic addiction (1, 10), immunization (11), treatment of diabetes (12), treatment of nausea (9, 13), and other biological and biomedical uses.

Chapter 7 in Volume 3 and other excellent reviews (1–3, 7, 9) discuss some of the important considerations in the polymer preparation, drug–polymer formulation, mode of drug release, in-vitro and in-vivo experiments, and overall design and evaluation of controlled-release systems. As pointed out in the recent review by Langer (1), polymeric systems for release of drugs by use of diffusive, swelling, chemical and magnetic control mechanisms are presently either commercially available or in the stage of final testing (1, 14).

Mechanistic aspects of the diffusion phenomena observed in drug delivery systems are by necessity related to an accurate mathematical model and to the structural characteristics of the polymeric material under consideration. However, very few reviews address these two aspects of controlled-release systems (15–17).

The objective of this chapter is to review and critically evaluate existing mathematical models for drug release from polymeric systems and to point out specific areas of modeling where more work is needed. Modeling of these systems is an area that has received relatively little attention, especially in view of the recent developments of "unconventional" types of drug release system (1), such as swelling and magnetically controlled systems. The few existing models have been used to analyze experimental data of a variety of formulations. Unfortunately, lack of a systematic analysis and classification is responsible for the use of inappropriate models, not necessarily describing the experimental conditions of the work of many investigators.

Mathematical modeling of diffusion processes in these systems may serve two purposes: (1) drug release rates and diffusion behavior may be predicted by solution of an appropriate model, thereby reducing the number of experiments needed; and (2) a proposed mathematical model with proper parameter fitting may lead to elucidation of the physics of a particular drug transport phenomenon.

In this review we first examine the fundamentals of solute diffusion through polymers as related to Fickian and non-Fickian diffusion. These equations with appropriate boundary conditions constitute the initial models that can be applied to various drug release polymer systems. The classification proposed by Langer (1) is used here, to analyze systems with diffusive, swelling, and chemical control of drug release.

1. MATHEMATICAL MODELING OF DIFFUSION PROCESSES

The process of drug release from a polymer, when the controlled release system is placed in contact with a fluid, can be described in most cases by Fickian diffusion. Some exceptions to this mechanism include the recently reported swellable release systems, which are discussed later. In modeling reservoir or matrix-type systems, the equations describing Fickian diffusion are solved with appropriate initial and boundary conditions to provide the following information:

1. Determination of the release rate dM_t/dt and the normalized quantity of drug M_t/M_∞ released in the surrounding medium (penetrant).
2. Analysis of drug concentration profiles in the polymer during release. Usually these profiles are reported in terms of normalized concentration of drug $c_i/c_{i,0}$ as a function of dimensionless depth or position x/δ for various dimensionless times $\mathscr{D}_{im}t/\delta^2$.
3. Determination of the concentration profile of a countercurrently diffusing penetrant. This information is important in the expression of the drug diffusion coefficient $\mathscr{D}_{im}$ as a function of structural changes in the polymer, as expressed by the change of concentration of penetrant in the system and its possible effect on polymer state transitions.

1.1 Fick's Law

Mathematical modeling of controlled-release systems is based on Fick's law of diffusion, which is expressed by equation 1 for three-dimensional diffusion in a binary system, by use of standard notation reported in Bird et al. (18):

$$\mathbf{J}_i^* = -c\mathscr{D}_{im}\nabla x_i \tag{1}$$

where $\mathbf{J}_i^*$ is the molar flux of diffusing component i (solute) with respect to the molar-average velocity $\mathbf{v}^*$, x_i is the mole fraction of the solute, and $\mathscr{D}_{im}$ is the solute diffusion coefficient in the polymer (in units $L^2 \cdot T^{-1}$). Although Fick's law is written for concentration-independent diffusion coefficients in the form present above, this is not always true. The molar flux $\mathbf{J}_i^*$ is defined according to equation 2, where c_i is the concentration and $\mathbf{v}_i$ the velocity of component i:

$$\mathbf{J}_i^* = c_i(\mathbf{v}_i - \mathbf{v}^*) \tag{2}$$

Equation 1 is only one of many convenient forms of Fick's law, some of which are tabulated in Table 1.

Table 1. Form of Fick's Law of Diffusion (Adapted from Reference 18)[a]

Equation	Parameters	
$\mathbf{J}_i^* = -c\mathscr{D}_{im}\nabla x_i$	$\mathbf{J}_i^* = c_i(\mathbf{v}_i - \mathbf{v}^*)$	$x_i = c_i/c$
$\mathbf{j}_i = -\rho\mathscr{D}_{im}\nabla\omega_i$	$\mathbf{j}_i = \rho_i(\mathbf{v}_i - \mathbf{v})$	$\omega_i = \rho_i/\rho$
$\mathbf{n}_i - \omega_i(\mathbf{n}_i + \mathbf{n}_m) = -\rho\mathscr{D}_{im}\nabla\omega_i$	$\mathbf{n}_i = \rho_i\mathbf{v}_i$	$\omega_i = \rho_i/\rho$
$\mathbf{N}_i - x_i(\mathbf{N}_i + \mathbf{N}_m) = -c\mathscr{D}_{im}\nabla x_i$	$\mathbf{N}_i = c_i\mathbf{v}_i$	$x_i = c_i/c$

[a]For definitions of symbols, see the notation list at the end of this chapter.

A useful expression of Fick's law can be obtained by rewriting the continuity equation

$$\frac{\partial c_i}{\partial t} + (\nabla \cdot \mathbf{N}_i) = R_i \tag{3}$$

in the absence of molar rate of production of species i (i.e., $R_i = 0$), using Fick's law as stated in equation 1 to give

$$\frac{\partial c_i}{\partial t} + (\mathbf{v} \cdot \nabla c_i) = \mathscr{D}_{im}\nabla^2 c_i \tag{4}$$

For stationary liquid phases or solids, $\mathbf{v} = 0$, and equation 4 gives the so-called second law of Fickian diffusion:

$$\frac{\partial c_i}{\partial t} = \mathscr{D}_{im}\nabla^2 c_i \tag{5}$$

In most cases of controlled-release systems, Fickian diffusion occurs through thin films or membranes where diffusion can be considered one-dimensional (along the axis x) as in Figure 1. Therefore, under the assumptions of ideal thermodynamic systems, concentration-independent diffusion coefficients, and one-dimensional diffusion, we can write

$$J_i^* = -\mathscr{D}_{im}\frac{dc_i}{dx} \tag{6}$$

where $c_i = x_i c$.

Integration of this equation between the interfacial concentrations c'_{i1} and c'_{i2} of a membrane or polymer film of thickness δ, under the assumption of constant flux, gives

$$J_i^* = \mathscr{D}_{im}\frac{(c'_{i1} - c'_{i2})}{\delta} \tag{7}$$

Since experimental determination of the interfacial concentrations of drug i

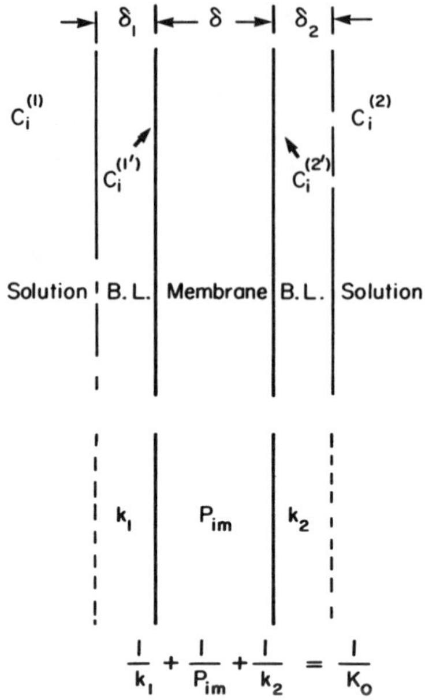

Figure 1. Fickian diffusion of component i through thin polymer film of thickness δ.

is rather cumbersome, the concentration in the bulk solution can be used, if expressed by means of a thermodynamic partition coefficient K. This coefficient K is defined as in equation 8 and is usually determined by simple drug absorption experiments on membranes (e.g., see reference 19).

$$K = \frac{c'_{i1}}{c_{i1}} = \frac{c'_{i2}}{c_{i2}} = \frac{\text{concentration of drug at interface}}{\text{concentration of drug in bulk}} \tag{8}$$

Then equation 7 can be written in the familiar form

$$J_i^* = \frac{\mathcal{D}_{im} K}{\delta} (c_{i2} - c_{i1}) \tag{9}$$

where the term $\mathcal{D}_{im}K/\delta$ represents the drug permeability coefficient P_{im} (in units $L \cdot T^{-1}$). Many investigators prefer an alternative definition of permeability $P'_{im} = \mathcal{D}_{im} \cdot K$ (in units $L^2 \cdot T^{-1}$), which is used especially when the thickness of the sample is unknown.

Finally, equation 5 under the same assumptions can be written in the familiar form

$$\frac{\partial c_i}{\partial t} = \mathcal{D}_{im} \frac{\partial^2 c_i}{\partial x^2} \tag{10}$$

1.2 Solution of Diffusion Equation

Solutions of the diffusion equations (equations 6 and 10) for drug diffusion in polymer samples of various geometric shapes are available in standard monographs (20, 21). Crank (20) presents solutions for various initial and boundary conditions in infinite and semiinfinite media and for plane sheets, cylinders, and spheres.

A variety of mathematical techniques can be used for the solution of equation 10. Three techniques—separation of variables, Laplace transformations, and the method of reflection and superposition—can provide solutions for most of the diffusion problems of interest to researchers working with drug diffusion in polymers.

For example, a solution of equation 10 can be obtained with the use of separation of variables, by assuming

$$c_i(x, t) = X(x)T(t) \tag{11}$$

and solving the two resulting ordinary differential equations to obtain a general solution of the form

$$c_i(x, t) = \sum_{n=1}^{\infty} (A_n \sin \lambda_n x + B_n \cos \lambda_n x)\exp(-\lambda_n^2 \mathscr{D}_{im} t) \tag{12}$$

The parameters A_n, B_n, and λ_n can be determined from the initial and boundary conditions of the specific problem.

Solutions such as the one of equation 12 are typical of the concentration profiles that are obtained for drug diffusion in polymers. The flux of drug through a polymer–dissolution medium interface dM_t/dt, can be calculated by evaluating the term $\mathscr{D}_{im}(\partial c/\partial x)$ at appropriate values of x. Finally, the total amount of drug diffusing at time t, M_t, can be calculated by integrating the flux dM_t/dt from $t = 0$ to the specified time t.

1.3 Effect of Polymer Structure on Drug Diffusion Modeling

1.3.1 Concentration-Dependent $\mathscr{D}_{im}$

Three important coefficients were introduced in the previous analysis. The diffusion coefficient $\mathscr{D}_{im}$ and the permeability coefficient P_{im} express diffusive characteristics of the drug–polymer system, whereas the partition coefficient K takes into consideration thermodynamic interactions of the drug–polymer system. Typical values of the diffusion coefficients of drugs in polymers range from 10^{-6} to 10^{-7} cm^2/second for diffusion in rubbery polymers and from 10^{-10} to 10^{-12} cm^2/second for diffusion in glassy polymers. Values of $\mathscr{D}_{im}$ for specific solute–polymer systems can be found in the *Polymer Handbook* (22) and other more specialized references (1, 21, 23).

In the previous analysis, the diffusion coefficient was assumed constant at constant temperature, that is, independent of solute concentration. When this assumption cannot be made (although by necessity in most drug controlled-release systems analysis, researchers assume that $\mathscr{D}_{im}$ is independent of concentration), equation 10 can be rewritten as

$$\frac{\partial c_i}{\partial t} = \frac{\partial}{\partial x}\left[D(c_i)\frac{\partial c_i}{\partial x}\right] \tag{13}$$

Analytical and numerical methods of solution of equation 13 for different functions of $D(c_i)$ are included in Crank (20). Of particular interest is an exponential dependence of the diffusion coefficient on concentration according to equation 14

$$D(c_i) = D_{s'} \exp[\beta(c_i - c_{s'})] \tag{14}$$

which was proposed by Fujita (24). Here $D_{s'}$ and $c_{s'}$ are surface diffusion coefficient and concentration, respectively, and β is a constant of the system. Other free-volume-based expressions of $D(c_i)$ can be found in Crank (20).

1.3.2 Thermodynamic Considerations

An important consideration in the development of Fick's law, which leads to the concentration dependence of the diffusion coefficient, is the assumption of thermodynamically ideal systems. The gradient responsible for the flux J_i^* in equation 6 is a concentration gradient. However, for systems departing from thermodynamic ideality, Fick's law is expressed in terms of the chemical potential gradient $\partial\mu_i/\partial x$. As shown by Lightfoot (23), a more general expression of equation 6 is then:

$$J_i^* = -c\mathrm{D}_{im}\frac{x_i}{RT}\frac{\partial \mu_i}{\partial x} \tag{15}$$

The chemical potential μ_i can be expressed in terms of the activity α_i as

$$\mu_i = RT \ln \alpha_i + \mu_i^0 \tag{16}$$

leading to

$$J_i^* = -c\mathrm{D}_{im}x_i\frac{\partial \ln \alpha_i}{\partial x} \tag{17}$$

Since the activity α_i can be written in terms of the activity coefficient γ_i,

$$x_i\frac{\partial \ln \alpha_i}{\partial x} = \frac{\partial x_i}{\partial x} + x_i\frac{\partial \ln \gamma_i}{\partial x} \tag{18}$$

we can finally write

$$J_i^* = -c\mathrm{D}_{im}\left(1 + \frac{\partial \ln \gamma_i}{\partial \ln x_i}\right)\frac{dx_i}{dx} \tag{19}$$

By comparison of equations 6 and 19, one can define an effective $\mathscr{D}_{im}$ as

$$\mathscr{D}_{im} = \mathrm{D}_{im}\left(1 + \frac{\partial \ln \gamma_i}{\partial \ln x_i}\right) \tag{20}$$

Since the functional dependence of the activity coefficient γ_i on drug concentration c_i is rather difficult to obtain for most drug release systems already reported in the literature, this term has usually been omitted. Obviously, for ideal systems, the term $(\partial \ln \gamma_i / \partial \ln x_i)$ is zero. In this analysis D_{im} is an activity-based diffusion coefficient that is much less dependent on concentration than $\mathscr{D}_{im}$.

1.3.3 *Polymer Morphology Effects*

Drug diffusion through polymers is also affected by morphological and structural characteristics of the polymer. These include degree of crystallinity and size of crystallites, degree of swelling (for swollen matrices and membranes), size of the "mesh" of cross-linked polymer networks, porous structure and tortuosity for porous materials, and transitional and relaxational phenomena observed in swellable polymeric systems.

As stated earlier, for rubbery polymers (i.e., polymers above their glass transition temperature T_g), Fickian diffusion is observed. The diffusion coefficient is dependent on the volume fraction of the solvent in the polymer, the cross-linking density, and the size of the solute as shown by theories developed by Yasuda et al. (25, 26) and Peppas et al. (27, 28). The general dependence of $\mathscr{D}_{im}$ on these parameters is expressed by equation 21:

$$\frac{\mathscr{D}_{im}}{\mathscr{D}_{iw}} = f\left(\frac{k_1}{\tau^2} \cdot \frac{\bar{M}_c - \bar{M}_c^*}{\bar{M}_n - \bar{M}_c^*}\right)\exp\left(-\frac{k_2 r_i^2}{Q_m - 1}\right) \tag{21}$$

where $\mathscr{D}_{im}$ and $\mathscr{D}_{iw}$ are the diffusivities of solute in the membrane and in water, respectively, under isothermal conditions; $\bar{M}_c$ and $\bar{M}_n$ are the number-average molecular weights between cross-links (for the network membrane) and before cross-linking (for the original polymer chains), respectively; $\bar{M}_c^*$ is the value of $\bar{M}_c$ below which no diffusion of the drug can occur, τ is the tortuosity of a nonporous membrane describing the tortuous path between cross-links and entanglements rather than through pores r_i is a characteristic radius for the solute, Q_m is the degree of swelling expressed as υ_2^{-1}, where υ_2 is the polymer volume fraction in the completely swollen membrane, and k_1 and k_2 are constants characteristic of the system. It is evident from this analysis that the cross-linked structure of polymer membranes shows a "screening effect" on the diffusion of solutes through membranes. For un-cross-linked polymers, the screening effect is provided by the mesh formed by entangled chains (29, 30), whereas in semicrystalline polymers the crystallites act as physical cross-links (31). The main mechanism of diffusion is through the water (solvent) regions of the membrane, as shown experimentally with a variety of polymers (26, 27, 32). Increase in size of the solute leads to significant decrease of $\mathscr{D}_{im}$.

Similar behavior with appropriate theoretical models has been reported by Vrentas and Duda (33). In their analysis, the controlling structural parameter is the ratio of the critical molar volume of the penetrant to the critical molar volume of a polymeric "jumping" unit ξ.

In semicrystalline polymers, drug diffusion is slowed down as a result of the presence of crystallites. The volume fraction of crystallites and their size affect the diffusion coefficient. Simple semiempirical equations have been used to describe this behavior (31). Finally, in porous polymeric films the drug diffusion coefficient $\mathscr{D}_{\mathrm{eff}}$ can be expressed in terms of the void fraction ε, the tortuosity τ, and the drug diffusion coefficient through the water-filled pores $\mathscr{D}_{iw}$ as

$$\mathscr{D}_{\mathrm{eff}} = \mathscr{D}_{iw} \frac{\varepsilon}{\tau} \tag{22}$$

Additional details on the effect of the polymer structure on drug diffusion can be found in recent reviews (16, 17).

1.4 Other Aspects of Modeling

1.4.1 Generalized Fickian Diffusion

Earlier (Section 1.3.2) it was recognized that a more accurate description of drug diffusion through polymers with the use of Fick's law should include the chemical potential gradient ($\partial \mu_i / \partial x$) rather than the concentration gradient. However, certain cases of specialty-type controlled-release polymer formulations, especially reservoir systems with charged membranes or polar drugs, must be modeled by a generalized Fickian diffusion equation.

Lightfoot (23) points out that in the presence of an electrostatic potential gradient $\partial \phi / \partial x$ and/or a pressure gradient $\partial P / \partial x$, equation 15 must be generalized to include these terms:

$$J_i^* = -c\mathrm{D}_{im} \cdot \frac{x_i}{RT} \left[\frac{\partial \mu_i}{\partial x} + \bar{V}_i \frac{\partial P}{\partial x} + \nu_i F \frac{\partial \phi}{\partial x} \right] \tag{23}$$

where $\bar{V}_i$ is the specific volume of the solute, ν_i is the ionic charge, and F is the Faraday constant. The system is electrically neutral and the membrane phase m is constrained to zero velocity.

1.4.2 Multicomponent Drug Diffusion

In the previous analysis, the diffusion coefficient D_{im} was preferred to $\mathscr{D}_{im}$. It was pointed out the D_{im} is less concentration-dependent and that it is used when chemical potential rather than concentration gradients are used. Actually, the generalized Fickian equation (equation 23) is a simplified form of equation 24 that describes multicomponent diffusion through polymers. Modeling of multicomponent diffusion in drug delivery system is still far from developed, although there are many cases where this theory can be applied. For example, in pharmaceutical formulations consisting of a polymer, various additives (e.g., plasticizers or stabilizers) and a drug, the drug release rate will be affected by the concurrent diffusion of other components from or through the polymer phase. In this case $(n-1)$ coupled equations of diffusion can be written for a system of n components, where the membrane or polymer phase m is considered as one of the phases with velocity $v_m=0$. These equations are known as the *Stefan–Maxwell equations* and can be written as

$$\mathbf{d}_i=\sum_{j=1}^{n}\frac{x_i x_j}{D_{ij}}(\mathbf{v}_j-\mathbf{v}) \tag{24}$$

with three sets of restraints,

$$D_{ij}=D_{ji} \tag{25}$$

$$\sum_{i=1}^{n}\frac{x_i}{D_{ij}}=0 \tag{26}$$

and

$$\sum_{i=1}^{n}\mathbf{d}_i=0 \tag{27}$$

In these equations, D_{ij} are the multicomponent diffusion coefficients for a pair of components. Since the Stefan–Maxwell equations are derived from the nonequilibrium thermodynamic theories of Onsager, equation 25 expresses the Onsager reciprocity and equation 27 is a result of the Gibbs–Duhem equation.

In this analysis the term $\mathbf{d}_i$ expresses the driving force for multicomponent diffusion; it is given by equation 28 for one-dimensional problems:

$$cRTd_i=c_i\frac{\partial\mu_i}{\partial x}+(c_i\bar{V}_i-\omega_i)\frac{\partial P}{\partial x}+c_i v_i F\frac{\partial\phi}{\partial x} \tag{28}$$

Solutions of the Stefan–Maxwell equations for simplified cases of diffusion of solutes in membranes can be found elsewhere (18, 23, 34). General considerations of the dependence of flux on the chemical potential gradient are described in standard references (e.g., 20) and in Meares (35).

1.4.3 Non-Fickian Diffusion

Although drug diffusion through most types of commercially available release polymeric system is described by Fickian diffusion, recently there has been considerable interest in the development of "swelling-controlled" delivery systems (1). Hopfenberg and Hsu (36), for example, have described release systems of Sudan Red IV from glassy polymers to *n*-hexane. Most of these systems are cast from polymer solutions in an organic phase and thus are not applicable for drug delivery. However, efforts have been made to use also hydrophilic dry glassy polymers that, on swelling in water, release the drug with a controlled rate (27, 37, 38). In these cases anomalous diffusion is observed as a result of relaxation of the macromolecular chains. Relaxational effects are the result of polymer transition from the glassy to the rubbery state due to water (or solvent) swelling. The mode of transport of the solvent is described usually by case-II transport as in equation 29:

$$\frac{\partial c_s}{\partial t} = \frac{\partial}{\partial x}\left[D(c_s)\frac{\partial c_s}{\partial x} - v'c_s\right] \tag{29}$$

where v' is the velocity of the moving front separating the glassy from the rubbery state. As a result of this transition, the diffusion coefficient of the drug $\mathscr{D}_{im}$ may increase by three or four orders of magnitude as diffusion proceeds from the glassy to the rubbery state.

The mechanisms of swelling-controlled release systems and their mathematical modeling have been reviewed recently by Korsmeyer and Peppas (39). They have defined mathematical and physical conditions under which zero-order release of drugs can be observed by defining the "swelling interface number" *Sw*. This is a dimensionless number expressed as the ratio of the velocity of the penetration front of the dissolution medium divided by the drug diffusion coefficient. For values of $Sw \leqslant 1$, zero-order release of the drug is observed, and macromolecular relaxations at the moving front between the glassy core and the gel-like phase control the mechanism of release. For values of $Sw \geqslant 1$, Fickian diffusion of the drug is observed. This analysis has been used for the design of zero-order release systems (38). In addition, anomalous transport mechanisms have been observed experimentally by many investigators, especially when modeling diffusion from swellable tablets (40). However, in most cases, the Fickian diffusion analysis has been used, despite some disagreement between theory and experiments.

1.5 Boundary-Layer Effects

Modeling of diffusion processes is based on Fickian or non-Fickian equations, which describe the dependence of concentration (or activity) on position and time. As noted before, integration of these equations provides information on the solute (drug) concentration in the polymer. However, in many experimental situations it is more practical to determine the concentration of a solute in the bulk rather than at the polymer–penetrant interface. In cases of in-vitro experiments with stagnant or poorly agitated solutions around the polymer, boundary layers are formed. Consequently, determination of the diffusivity of a solute through a polymer should take in consideration diffusion resistances due to the boundary layers. Boundary-layer effects have been considered for drug diffusion from polymer matrices by Baker and Lonsdale (15), and for solute diffusion through polymer films by many researchers, including Colton et al. (19).

Specifically, in drug diffusion through membranes, equation 30 applies, where k_1 and k_2 are the mass-transfer coefficients of the two sides of the membrane (Figure 1), K_0 is the overall mass-transfer coefficient, and $\mathscr{D}_{im}$ refers to the solute diffusion coefficient in the membrane:

$$\frac{1}{K_0}=\frac{1}{k_1}+\frac{\delta}{\mathscr{D}_{im}}+\frac{1}{k_2} \tag{30}$$

Estimation of k_1 and k_2 for certain experimental conditions of agitation in diffusion cells has been discussed by Colton (41).

For drug release through a single polymer–solvent interface (as observed in matrix systems), equation 30 is again applicable with $1/k_2=0$. Frequently the parameters k_1 and k_2 are expressed in terms of appropriate fluxes and the corresponding thickness of the boundary layers δ_1 and δ_2, using again an integrated version of Fick's law such as equation 7. With adequate agitation the mass-transfer coefficients become sufficiently large, so that the main resistance to diffusion is contributed by the polymer (41).

2. MODELING OF CONTROLLED-RELEASE DEVICES

Having established the basis for the analysis of diffusion in polymers, we turn now to specific applications in modeling problems of controlled drug delivery polymeric systems. Using Langer's classification of these systems (1), we discuss diffusion, swelling, and chemically controlled systems.

2.1 Diffusion-Controlled Systems

2.1.1 Reservoir (Membrane) Systems

In reservoir or membrane release systems, the drug or biologically active agent is enclosed in relatively large quantities in a permeable synthetic membrane and is placed in contact with a fluid (usually water) at constant temperature. The drug may be incorporated in pure form or in solution. After an initial period of transient diffusion, steady state is established and diffusive release rates can be easily determined.

Two interesting cases of mathematical modeling are distinguished. According to Baker and Lonsdale's classification (15), they are devices with (1) constant activity and (2) nonconstant drug activity sources.

Constant-Activity Sources. Constant-activity reservoir-type devices include systems where the drug activity is maintained constant throughout prolonged use. Modeling of these devices is done by applying Fick's law in the integrated form of equation 9. Expressing the flux J_i^* in terms of the actual release rate dM_t/dt, we can write

$$\frac{dM_t}{dt}=\frac{\mathscr{D}_{im}KA}{\delta}(c_{i2}-c_{i1}) \tag{31}$$

where A is the effective membrane area for diffusion of the drug. This equation is applicable to thin film geometry with thickness δ (see Figure 2). The total amount of drug released as a function of time can be determined by simple integration of equation 31:

$$M_t=\frac{\mathscr{D}_{im}KA(c_{i2}-c_{i1})}{\delta}t=K_1 t \tag{32}$$

For cylindrical devices with internal and external radii r_i and r_e respectively, equation 33 can be derived

$$\frac{dM_t}{dt}=\frac{\mathscr{D}_{im}KA}{\ln(r_e/r_i)}(c_{i2}-c_{i1}) \tag{33}$$

by integrating equation 34, an alternative form of equation 10 in cylindrical coordinates, at steady state, that is, with $\partial c_i/\partial t=0$ (20, Chapter 5).

$$\frac{\partial c_i}{\partial t}=\frac{1}{r}\frac{\partial}{\partial r}\left(r\mathscr{D}_{im}\frac{\partial c_i}{\partial r}\right) \tag{34}$$

Again the total amount of drug released, M_t, can be determined by integration of equation 33:

$$M_t=\frac{\mathscr{D}_{im}KA(c_{i2}-c_{i1})}{\ln(r_e/r_i)}t=K_2 t \tag{35}$$

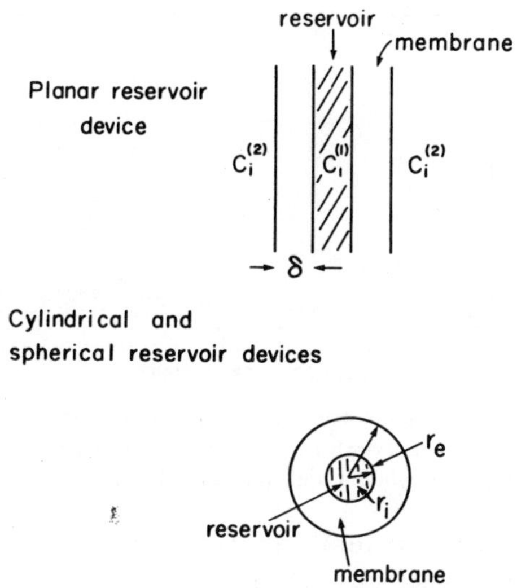

Figure 2. Modeling of planar, cylindrical, and spherical reservoir systems.

In equations 33 and 35 the area A is equal to $2\pi l$, where l is the length of the cylinder. In both derivations for slab (equation 32) and cylinder (equation 35) geometries, edge effects are considered negligible. Conditions allowing this assumption are discussed in Crank (reference 20, Chapter 4.4).

For spherical reservoir devices, an alternative form of equation 10 using spherical coordinates can be solved at steady state (reference 20, Chapter 6):

$$\frac{\partial c_i}{\partial t} = \mathscr{D}_{im}\left(\frac{\partial^2 c_i}{\partial r^2} + \frac{2}{r}\frac{\partial c_i}{\partial r}\right) \tag{36}$$

to give

$$\frac{dM_t}{dt} = \frac{4\pi\mathscr{D}_{im}K}{(r_e - r_i)/r_e r_i}(c_{i2} - c_{i1}) \tag{37}$$

The total amount of released drug is expressed by equation 38:

$$Mt = \frac{4\pi\mathscr{D}_{im}K(c_{i2} - c_{i1})}{(r_e - r_i)/r_e r_i}t = K_3 t \tag{38}$$

It is interesting to note that in all three cases the amount of drug released M_t is proportional to the release time t. This type of behavior is frequently called "zero-order release behavior" and is highly desirable in many pharmaceutical applications, since the device can provide drug for long periods of time at constant release rates.

Obviously the release rate depends on the geometry of the system, the drug solubility in the polymer membrane (as expressed by the partition

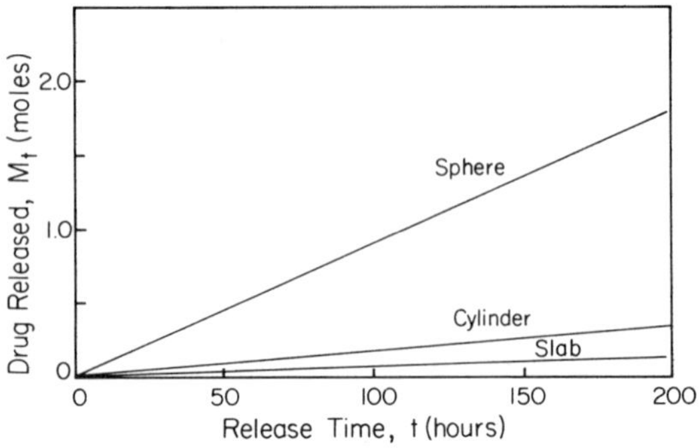

Figure 3. Comparison of quantities of drug released M_t from planar, cylindrical, and spherical reservoir systems of same thickness $\delta = 0.1$ cm. Diffusion coefficient $\mathscr{D}_{im} = 10^{-6}$ cm^2/second, $K = 1$, $\Delta c_i = 10^{-2}$ mole/cm^3. For cylinder and sphere $r_e = 0.5$ cm, $r_i = 0.4$ cm.

coefficient K), and the structural characteristics of the polymer (which affect the drug diffusion coefficient $\mathscr{D}_{im}$).

The models and equations derived in this section are applicable only at steady state, and they are subjected to all the assumptions involved in the derivation of equation 9. For concentration-dependent diffusion, Crank (20) shows that the mean value of the diffusion coefficient may be expressed as in equation 39 for all geometrical shapes discussed here.

$$\bar{\mathscr{D}}_{im} = \frac{\int_{c_{i1}}^{c_{i2}} \mathscr{D}_{im} dc}{c_{i2} - c_{i1}} \tag{39}$$

Figure 3 shows some theoretical predictions of amount of released drug for three comparable reservoir devices with constant drug activity source.

Non-Constant-Activity Sources. Modeling of non-constant-activity reservoir systems is important for devices where the drug is available in solution, below the solubility limit. Some of these models may also be applied to the late release stage of a constant-activity reservoir system, where most of the drug has been depleted, and the drug activity cannot be kept constant. For these systems, Baker and Lonsdale (15) have formulated the mathematical solution (see also Figure 4).

Again using Fickian diffusion as in equation 9 and expressing the concentration in terms of amounts of released and remaining drug M_{t2} and M_{t1}, respectively, and volumes of reservoir and surrounding fluid V_1 and V_2, we can write

$$\frac{dM_t}{dt} = \frac{\mathscr{D}_{im} K A}{\delta}(c_{i2} - c_{i1}) = \frac{\mathscr{D}_{im} K A}{\delta}\left(\frac{M_{t2}}{V_2} - \frac{M_{t1}}{V_1}\right) \tag{40}$$

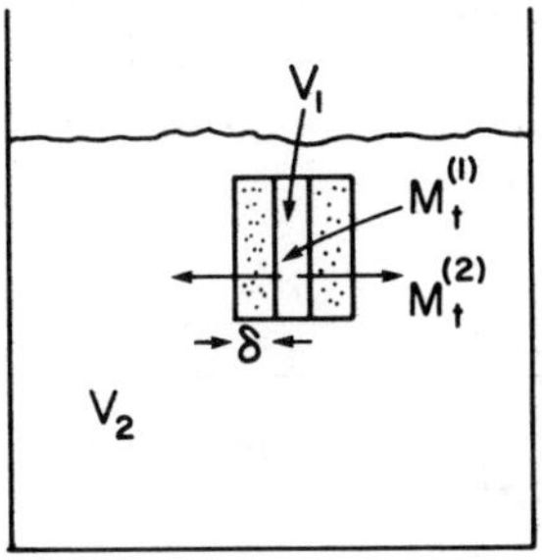

Figure 4. Diffusion of drug from a non-constant-activity reservoir system.

Since the total amount of drug M_∞ can be expressed as

$$M_\infty = M_{t2} + M_{t1} \tag{41}$$

and at the initiation of the drug release ($t=0$) all the drug is in the device, that is, $M_{t1} = M_\infty$, equation 40 can give

$$\frac{dM_{t1}}{dt} = -\frac{M_\infty \mathscr{D}_{im} KA}{V_1 \delta} \exp\left[\frac{-\mathscr{D}_{im} KAt}{\delta}\left(\frac{1}{V_1} + \frac{1}{V_2}\right)\right] \tag{42}$$

Consequently, drug release behavior for non-constant-activity devices is first order. Equation 42 is only a partial solution of the general problem of solute diffusion through a membrane in a diffusion cell. It was proposed by Colton (19, 41) and has been used for the determination of the solute diffusion coefficient $\mathscr{D}_{im}$ using the Kaufmann–Leonard diffusion cell (27, 28, 42).

Effect of System History. The previous analysis concentrated mostly on the steady-state behavior of reservoir devices. However, in many cases experimental data are in disagreement with predicted release behavior (such as the release lines depicted in Figure 3) as far as the initial part of the release curve is concerned. This phenomenon can be easily explained by considering the history of the device.

If the reservoir device is used shortly after manufacture (as the case would be with novel devices tested in the laboratory), an initial induction period, known as *time-lag effect*, is observed before drug release at a constant rate is achieved. Similarly, reservoir devices that are used after relatively long periods of storage (as the case might be with commercially available devices) show a fast increasing time-dependent drug release rate at the initial stage of the release behavior as a result of a phenomenon known as the *burst effect*.

Mathematical analysis of the time-lag and burst effects is straightforward, and it has been presented by Baker and Lonsdale (15), based on solutions of the Fickian diffusion equation obtained in Crank (reference 20, Chapter 4.3.3).

In this case drug diffusion through a thin membrane with constant interfacial concentration of c_{i1} at $x=0$ and c_{i2} at $x=\delta$ is considered. The membrane is assumed to have an initial drug concentration $c_{i,0}$. Then equation 10 can be solved by using separation of variables to yield the concentration profile in the membrane:

$$\frac{c_i-c_{i1}}{c_{i2}-c_{i1}}=\frac{x}{\delta}+\frac{2}{\pi(c_{i2}-c_{i1})}\sum_{n=1}^{\infty}\frac{c_{i2}\cos n\pi-c_{i1}}{n^2}\sin\frac{n\pi x}{\delta}\exp\left[-\frac{\mathscr{D}_{im}n^2\pi^2 t}{\delta^2}\right] \tag{43}$$
$$+\frac{4c_{i,0}}{\pi(c_{i2}-c_{i1})}\sum_{m=0}^{\infty}\frac{1}{(2m+1)}\sin\frac{(2m+1)\pi x}{\delta}\exp\left[-\frac{\mathscr{D}_{im}(2m+1)^2\pi^2 t}{\delta^2}\right]$$

As stated earlier (Section 1), to determine M_t, equation 43 is differentiated to obtain the flux $\mathscr{D}_{im}(\partial c_i/\partial x)_{x=\delta}$ at $x=\delta$ and then integrated with respect to time t to obtain equation 44:

$$M_t=\frac{\mathscr{D}_{im}(c_{i1}-c_{i2})}{\delta}+\frac{2\delta}{\pi^2}\sum_{n=1}^{\infty}\frac{c_{i1}\cos n\pi-c_{i2}}{n^2}\left\{1-\exp\left[-\frac{\mathscr{D}_{im}n^2\pi^2 t}{\delta^2}\right]\right\}$$
$$+\frac{4c_{i,0}\delta}{\pi^2}\sum_{m=0}^{\infty}\frac{1}{(2m+1)^2}\left\{1-\exp\left[-\frac{\mathscr{D}_{im}(2m+1)^2\pi^2 t}{\delta^2}\right]\right\} \tag{44}$$

For devices exhibiting time-lag effect (with use shortly after manufacture), $c_{i,0}$ and c_{i2} are zero and c_{i1} is finite. Therefore, equation 44 is simplified to give

$$M_t=\frac{\mathscr{D}_{im}c_{i1}t}{\delta}-\frac{c_{i1}\delta}{6}-\frac{2c_{i1}\delta}{\pi^2}\sum_{n=1}^{\infty}\frac{(-1)^n}{n^2}\exp\left[-\frac{\mathscr{D}_{im}n^2\pi^2 t}{\delta^2}\right] \tag{45}$$

which at long times approaches the line

$$M_t=\frac{\mathscr{D}_{im}c_{i1}}{\delta}\left(t-\frac{\delta^2}{6\mathscr{D}_{im}}\right) \tag{46}$$

For devices exhibiting burst effect (use after long periods of storage), c_{i2} is again zero, but $c_{i,0}$ and c_{i1} are finite and equal. Then equation 44 gives an expression similar to equation 45, which at long times approaches the line

$$M_t=\frac{\mathscr{D}_{im}c_{i1}}{\delta}\left(t+\frac{\delta^2}{3\mathscr{D}_{im}}\right) \tag{47}$$

Plots of M_t versus time for the time-lag and burst effects are shown in Figure 5. As seen in equations 46 and 47, the intercepts of the steady-state portion of these graphs are two characteristic times, θ_l and θ_b, known as the time-lag and burst time, respectively:

$$\theta_l=\frac{\delta^2}{6\mathscr{D}_{im}} \quad \text{and} \quad \theta_b=-\frac{\delta^2}{3\mathscr{D}_{im}} \tag{48}$$

Determination of θ_l and θ_b for various devices is important for the pre-

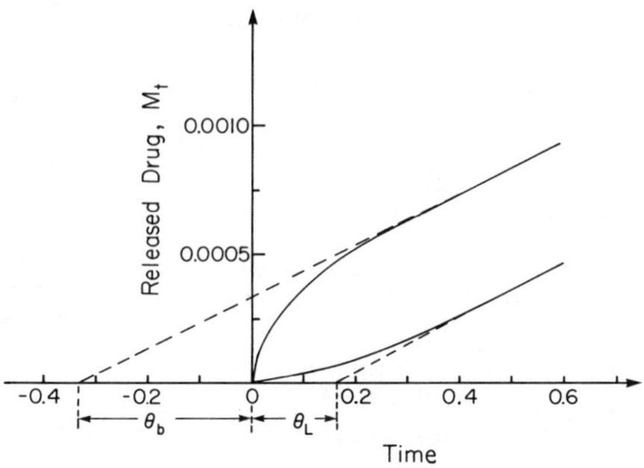

Figure 5. Released drug for reservoirs exhibiting burst and time-lag effects: $\mathscr{D}_{im}=10^{-6}$ cm^2/second, $\delta=10^{-3}$ cm, $c_{i,0}=1$ mole/cm^3.

diction of drug release in reservoir systems at short times. Time-lag experiments have found a very useful application in the determination of the diffusion coefficient $\mathscr{D}_{im}$ of a drug in a membrane by use of rather simple drug release experiments. Again the previous analysis is applicable as long as the assumptions of Fickian diffusion are satisfied.

In conclusion, reservoir systems are rather easily modeled. The equations derived earlier have been used for the description of the release behavior of ocular, contraceptive, and transdermal drug release systems (1).

2.1.2 *Matrix (Monolithic) Systems*

Matrix (monolithic) devices are available in many geometric shapes. Usually the drug or bioactive agent is incorporated either as a solution or as a dispersion in the polymer phase.

Systems with Dissolved Drug. In many matrix systems the drug is dissolved in the polymer below its solubility limit, either by preparing a drug–polymer solution, casting it in a desirable geometrical form and partially or totally evaporating the solvent, or by soaking the polymer in a drug solution.

For plane sheets of thickness δ, with initial drug concentration $c_{i,0}$, surfaces kept at c_i, and negligible edge effects, equation 10 can be solved and integrated to give (reference 20, Chapter 4.3.2)

$$\frac{M_t}{M_\infty}=1-\sum_{n=0}^{\infty}\frac{8}{(2n+1)^2\pi^2}\exp\left[\frac{-\mathscr{D}_{im}(2n+1)^2\pi^2 t}{\delta^2}\right] \tag{49}$$

At long times, the first term of the summation of this expression is dominant

$(n=0)$, and this equation can be simplified as follows:

$$\frac{M_t}{M_\infty}=1-\frac{8}{\pi^2}\exp\left[-\frac{\mathscr{D}_{im}\pi^2 t}{\delta^2}\right] \quad \text{for} \quad \frac{M_t}{M_\infty}>0.6 \tag{50}$$

An alternative solution of equation 10 under the same boundary conditions but for small times is

$$\frac{M_t}{M_\infty}=4\left(\frac{\mathscr{D}_{im}t}{\delta^2}\right)^{1/2}\left\{\pi^{-1/2}+2\sum_{n=1}^{\infty}(-1)^n\, i\text{erfc}\,\frac{n\delta}{\sqrt{\mathscr{D}_{im}t}}\right\} \tag{51}$$

where

$$i\text{erfc}\, x=\int_x^\infty \text{erfc}\,\xi\, d\xi=\pi^{-1/2}e^{-x^2}-x\,\text{erfc}\, x$$

and erfc is the complimentary error function.* This equation can be further simplified to give

$$\frac{M_t}{M_\infty}=4\left(\frac{\mathscr{D}_{im}t}{\pi\delta^2}\right)^{1/2} \quad \text{for} \quad \frac{M_t}{M_\infty}<0.6 \tag{52}$$

Equations 50 and 52 are considered by many investigators as convenient forms for the analysis of drug release from polymer matrices. However, they can introduce considerable error (15) and they should be avoided if possible. Instead, the exact solution of equation 49 must be used, always recalling the special boundary conditions under which this expression was developed. For small times, the amount of drug released is a function of the square root of time. Finally, expressions of the release rate dM_t/dt can be readily obtained by integrating equation 49 or the simplified equations 50 and 52.

The previous analysis neglects external mass-transfer resistance effects during drug release from a matrix. Paul and McSpadden (43) considered this case and presented appropriate solutions for semiinfinite slabs.

Similar modeling can be applied for the prediction of dissolved drug release from cylindrical matrix systems. Crank (reference 20, Section 5.3.1) provides the solution of equation 34 for a solid cylinder of radius r, initially loaded with dissolved drug at a concentration $c_{i,0}$. The surface is kept at concentration c_i, and edge effects are negligible. The amount of released drug is calculated according to equation 53:

$$\frac{M_t}{M_\infty}=1-\sum_{n=1}^{\infty}\frac{4}{r^2\alpha_n^2}\exp(-\mathscr{D}_{im}\alpha_n^2 t) \tag{53}$$

where α_n are the positive roots of the Bessel function of the first kind of order zero. These roots are tabulated in standard references (20).

*Values of error functions and related functions are tabulated in Crank (20).

A useful approximation at small times is

$$\frac{M_t}{M_\infty}=4\left(\frac{\mathscr{D}_{im}t}{\pi r^2}\right)^{1/2}-\frac{\mathscr{D}_{im}t}{r^2}-\frac{1}{3}\left(\frac{\mathscr{D}_{im}t}{\pi r^2}\right)^{3/2} \quad \text{at} \quad \frac{M_t}{M_\infty}<0.4 \tag{54}$$

For long times, only the first term of the summation of equation 53 is kept. Again the release rates dM_t/dt are obtained by differentiating equation 54 with respect to time.

For spherical matrices under the same boundary conditions, the total quantity of released drug is calculated (reference 20, Section 6.3.1) as

$$\frac{M_t}{M_\infty}=1-\frac{6}{\pi^2}\sum_{n=1}^{\infty}\frac{1}{n^2}\exp\left[-\frac{\mathscr{D}_{im}n^2\pi^2 t}{r^2}\right] \tag{55}$$

A simplified solution for small times is

$$\frac{M_t}{M_\infty}=6\left(\frac{\mathscr{D}_{im}t}{r^2}\right)^{1/2}\left\{\pi^{-1/2}+2\sum_{n=1}^{\infty}\text{ierfc}\frac{nr}{\sqrt{\mathscr{D}_{im}t}}\right\}-3\frac{\mathscr{D}_{im}t}{r^2} \tag{56}$$

A useful approximation for $M_t/M_\infty<0.4$ is

$$\frac{M_t}{M_\infty}=6\left(\frac{\mathscr{D}_{im}t}{\pi r^2}\right)^{1/2}-3\frac{\mathscr{D}_{im}t}{r^2} \tag{57}$$

For long times, the first term of the summation of equation 55 is the dominant one, and we can write

$$\frac{M_t}{M_\infty}=1-\frac{6}{\pi^2}\exp\left[-\frac{\mathscr{D}_{im}\pi^2 t}{r^2}\right] \tag{58}$$

Release rates dM_t/dt can be calculated by simply differentiating equations 55, 57, and 58.

Recently Fu et al. (44) developed a unified mathematical model for drug release from polymer matrix systems. The model is applied to flat disks or cylindrical rods, and edge effects are considered. The general approximate solution is

$$\frac{M_t}{M_\infty}=1-\frac{8}{r^2 l^2}\sum_{m=1}^{10}\frac{\exp(-\mathscr{D}_{im}\alpha_m^2 t)}{\alpha_m^2}\cdot\sum_{n=0}^{10}\frac{\exp(-\mathscr{D}_{im}\beta_n^2 t)}{\beta_n^2} \tag{59}$$

where r and l are the radius and length of these devices, respectively, α_m are the roots of a zero-order Bessel function, and $\beta_n=(2n+1)\pi/2l$. The model has been applied with considerable success to a variety of pharmaceutical formulations.

Systems with Dispersed Drug. When the matrix system consists of a drug dispersed in the polymer at a concentration $c_{i,0}$ that is greater than the drug solubility in the polymer $c_{i,s}$, the previously developed models do not apply.

In this case most researchers prefer to use the well known pseudo-steady-state approximation model developed by Higuchi (45). This model assumes that the drug is uniformly dispersed in the matrix, that the particle size is much smaller in comparison to the polymer film thickness, that the concentration at the interface c_i is always zero, that there is no polymer volume change, and that boundary effects are negligible. Only Fick's first law is used in the form of equation 6. This equation is integrated over the polymer film layer of thickness x^*, which contains only dissolved drug:

$$\frac{dM_t}{dt}=\mathscr{D}_{im}A\,\frac{(c_{i,s}-0)}{x^*} \tag{6}$$

A mass balance over the dispersed drug area can also be written as

$$dM_t=\left(c_{i,0}-\frac{c_{i,s}}{2}\right)dx^* \tag{61}$$

By solving equations 60 and 61, the value of x^* is obtained, which is substituted into equation 61. The final equation is integrated over time to yield

$$M_t=A[\mathscr{D}_{im}c_{i,s}(2c_{i,0}-c_{i,s})t]^{1/2} \tag{62}$$

The release rate is expressed by

$$\frac{dM_t}{dt}=\frac{A}{2}\,[\mathscr{D}_{im}c_{i,s}(2c_{i,0}-c_{i,s})]^{1/2}\cdot t^{-1/2} \tag{63}$$

The Higuchi model predicts a square root of time dependence for the drug released in a well-stirred infinite medium. It has been used to model the release behavior of numerous pharmaceutical formulations, but it has also been misused by being applied to dissolved drug systems, although derived only for dispersed systems.

Paul and McSpadden (43) have extended this model to drug release from matrix systems with finite external mass-transfer resistance as expressed by the following surface boundary condition:

$$\frac{dM_t}{dt}=k_1c_{i,0} \tag{64}$$

By pseudo-steady-state approximation, equation 65 is obtained.

$$M_t=A\left(c_{i,0}-\frac{c_{i,s}}{2}\right)\left\{\left[\left(\frac{\mathscr{D}_{im}}{k_1}\right)^2+\frac{2\mathscr{D}_{im}c_{i,s}t}{\left(c_{i,0}-\dfrac{c_{i,s}}{2}\right)}\right]^{1/2}-\frac{\mathscr{D}_{im}}{k_1}\right\}$$
$$+\frac{Ac_{i,s}}{2}\left\{\frac{(\mathscr{D}_{im}/k_1)^2}{\left[(\mathscr{D}_{im}/k_1)^2+2\mathscr{D}_{im}c_{i,s}t\Big/\left(c_{i,0}-\dfrac{c_{i,s}}{2}\right)\right]^{1/2}}-\frac{\mathscr{D}_{im}}{k_1}\right\} \tag{65}$$

This equation reduces to the Higuchi model of equation 62 for $k_1 = \infty$.

Recognizing the need for a complete solution of this modeling problem, Paul and McSpadden (43) gave the exact solution of drug diffusion from dispersed matrix systems by solving equation 10 with the following boundary conditions:

$$c_i = 0 \quad \text{at} \quad x = 0, \qquad c_i = c_{i,s} \quad \text{at} \quad x = x^* \qquad (66)$$
$$(c_{i,0} - c_{i,s}) \frac{dx^*}{dt} = \mathscr{D}_{im} \frac{\partial c_i}{\partial x}$$

The exact solution is

$$c_i = c_{i,s} \frac{\operatorname{erf} \xi}{\operatorname{erf} \xi^*} \qquad (67)$$

with

$$\xi = \frac{x}{2(\mathscr{D}_{im} t)^{1/2}} \quad \text{and} \quad \xi^* = \frac{x^*}{2(\mathscr{D}_{im} t)^{1/2}} \qquad (68)$$
$$\sqrt{\pi} \xi^* \exp(\xi^{*2}) \operatorname{erf} \xi^* = \frac{c_{i,s}}{c_{i,0} - c_{i,s}}$$

The total amount of released drug can be readily calculated as

$$M_t = \frac{2 c_{i,s} A}{\operatorname{erf} \xi^*} \left(\frac{\mathscr{D}_{im} t}{\pi} \right)^{1/2} \qquad (69)$$

Equation 69 should be used instead of equation 62 when more accurate description of experimental values is desirable. An approximate solution for transient diffusion with finite mass transfer (as expressed by equation 64), can be obtained as

$$M_t = \frac{2 A c_{i,s}}{\operatorname{erf} \xi^*} \left(\frac{\mathscr{D}_{im} t}{\pi} \right)^{1/2} - \frac{\mathscr{D}_{im} A c_{i,0}}{k_1} \qquad (70)$$

Obviously for $k_1 = \infty$, equation 70 reduces to equation 69.

The original Higuchi model has been extended to cylindrical matrices by Roseman and Higuchi (46, 47) and to spherical matrices by Baker and Lonsdale (15).

For cylindrical matrices with $c_{i,0} \gg c_{i,s}$, the fractional drug release is expressed as in equation 71:

$$\frac{M_t}{M_\infty} + \left[1 - \frac{M_t}{M_\infty} \right] \left[\ln \left(1 - \frac{M_t}{M_\infty} \right) \right] = \frac{4 \mathscr{D}_{im}}{r^2} \cdot \frac{c_{i,s}}{c_{i,0}} t \qquad (71)$$

For spherical matrices, the corresponding expression for $c_{i,0} \gg c_{i,s}$ is

$$\frac{M_t}{M_\infty} - \frac{3}{2} \left[1 - \left(1 - \frac{M_t}{M_\infty} \right)^{2/3} \right] = - \frac{3 \mathscr{D}_{im}}{r^2} \cdot \frac{c_{i,s}}{c_{i,9}} t \qquad (72)$$

Release rates dM_t/dt can also be determined from these equations.

In the previous analysis it was noted that "zero-order release" cannot be obtained with matrix systems in the form of slabs, cylinders, or spheres. Recently, however, Rhine et al. (48) described the development and modeling of an inwardly releasing hemisphere matrix system that can provide essentially zero-order release rate. A pseudo-steady-state approximation was used, and the amount of released drug was calculated as

$$M_t = M_\infty - \frac{2}{3}\pi c_{i,0}(r_e^3 - r_{x^*}^3) \int_{r_i}^{r_{x^*}} 2\pi r^2 c_i(r)dr \tag{73}$$

where r_e and r_i are the external and internal radii of the hemisphere, respectively, and r_{x^*} is the radial position of the interface between dissolved and dispersed drug in the matrix. Rhine et al. (48) show that the release rate from this type of matrix system is almost constant for long periods of time.

Approximate analytical solutions for planar and spherical geometries have been recently developed by Lee (49) in an effort to avoid the discrepancies of the pseudo-steady-state approximation. Moving boundary problems involving drug diffusion were solved by use of the integral heat balance method. Cases of release into an infinite or constant finite volume were considered, and the complete solutions can be found in that work. As is evident from the previous analyses, prediction of release rates dM_t/dt, and total amounts of released drug M_t for monolithic devices of various shapes is mathematically rather cumbersome. Therefore, numerical solutions have been developed by Cobby (50) and other investigators to predict release rates from matrix systems.

2.1.3 *Diffusion in Porous Systems*

Although considerable experimental work has been reported on the release of drugs through porous polymeric materials (1), mathematical modeling is still at a rather primitive stage. For diffusion of drug through a porous polymer with initial concentration $c_{i,0}$ above the drug's solubility $c_{i,s}$, Higuchi (51) developed a widely accepted model that incorporates the void fraction ε and tortuosity τ of the polymeric system in the diffusion coefficient $\mathscr{D}_{\mathrm{eff}}$. The model is based on a pseudo-steady-state approximation, and the total amounts of released drug can be calculated as

$$M_t = A[\mathscr{D}_{\mathrm{eff}} c_{i,s}(2c_{i,0} - \varepsilon c_{i,s})t]^{1/2} \tag{74}$$

where

$$\mathscr{D}_{\mathrm{eff}} = \mathscr{D}_{iw}\frac{\varepsilon}{\tau} \tag{75}$$

Here $\mathscr{D}_{iw}$ is the solute diffusion coefficient in water.

Similar models for other geometries and experimental situations have been discussed by Roseman and Higuchi (46), (47), Higuchi and Fessi et al. (52). Drug binding phenomena on the polymer have been treated by Desai et al. (53), who proposed an alternative form of equation 74:

$$M_t = A(\mathscr{D}_{\text{eff}} c_{i,s}\{2c_{i,0} - c_{i,s}[\varepsilon + K(1-\varepsilon)]\} t)^{1/2} \tag{76}$$

where K is the partition coefficient of the drug defined as in equation 8.

These models fail to predict the unique release behavior observed in controlled-release monolithic devices developed by Langer and his co-workers for the sustained release of macromolecules (1). It has been shown that in these systems solute diffusion occurs almost exclusively through large interconnecting channels at almost zero-order release rates (54). Two preferred modeling methods have emerged in the last year. The first one, developed by Swan and Peppas (55), treats the release of drugs from porous systems as a dissolution- and diffusion-controlled phenomenon. Dissolution is described by the third term of equation 77, where k is the dissolution constant:

$$\frac{\partial c_i}{\partial t} = \mathscr{D}_{\text{eff}} \frac{\partial^2 c_i}{\partial x^2} + k(c_{i,s} - c_i) \tag{77}$$

Solution of this equation for semiinfinite and finite systems predicts constant drug release rates over a long period of times (56). The second approach is based on the principles of percolation theory as applied to porous systems and is presently under investigation.

2.1.4 *Systems with Rate-Controlling Barriers*

Limited modeling studies of drug diffusion through monolithic devices with rate-controlling barriers are available. Lee et al. (57) have reported the preparation of PHEMA-based multilayered systems with rate-controlling properties (57). For a cylindrical double-layered monolithic device, equation 78 is applicable:

$$\frac{dM_t}{dt} = \frac{A r_0 c_{i,s} \mathscr{D}_{ib}}{c_{i,m}\delta} \left[\frac{\mathscr{D}_{im} c_{i,s} \delta}{\mathscr{D}_{im}\delta - \dfrac{\mathscr{D}_{ib} c_{i,b} r_0}{2c_{i,m}} \ln\left(\dfrac{r^2}{r_0^2}\right)} \right] \tag{78}$$

where $\mathscr{D}_{ib}$ and $\mathscr{D}_{im}$ are the drug diffusivities in the barrier layer and matrix, respectively; $c_{i,b}$ and $c_{i,m}$ are the corresponding drug solubilities; δ is the thickness of the barrier layer; r_0 is the radius of the matrix cylinder; and r is the radial position of the receding drug boundary.

2.2 Swelling-Controlled Systems

Numerous pharmaceutical formulations are prepared by incorporating a drug in a polymer matrix in a dissolved or dispersed phase and evaporating the solvent. In most of these formulations the polymer is in the glassy state and drug diffusion is extremely slow as a result of the low diffusion coefficient. However, when the polymer is placed in contact with a thermodynamically compatible liquid (water for hydrophilic polymers or organic solvents for other polymers), considerable swelling and volume expansion are observed and drug diffusion occurs through the relaxing gel-like polymer phase (see also Section 1.4.3).

Preliminary modeling of drug release from swellable hydrophilic matrices was reported by Lapidus and Lordi (58). Using a pseudo-steady-state approximation, they used equation 74 for drugs with limited water solubility and equation 79 for completely dissolved drugs when the matrix is hydrated:

$$\frac{M_t}{M_\infty} = 2\left(\frac{\mathscr{D}_{im}}{\pi\delta^2}\right)^{1/2} \tag{79}$$

Good (37) modeled a similar problem by considering fast water absorption and expressing the time-dependent diffusion coefficient of the drug as

$$\mathscr{D}_{im}(t) = D_s \cdot \frac{M_{ts}}{M_{\infty s}} \tag{80}$$

where M_{ts}, $M_{\infty s}$, and D_s refer to the solvent penetrating the polyer. Equation 81 presents an expression for the total amount of released drug M_t:

$$\frac{M_t}{M_\infty} = 1 - \frac{8}{\pi^2} \sum_{n=0}^{\infty} \frac{1}{(2n+1)^2} \exp\left[-\frac{(2n+1)^2\pi^2 T}{\delta^2}\right] \tag{81}$$

This expression is similar to equation 49 with the exception that T is an auxiliary variable given by

$$T = \int_0^t \mathscr{D}_{im}(t)dt \tag{82}$$

Good (37) presents various techniques of calculation of this variable.

Semiempirical expressions for prediction of the release rate of swellable drug delivery systems were also reported by Bamba et al. (59, 60). All these models assume fast swelling of the polymer matrix and negligible volume change.

Since considerable swelling of polymer matrices is observed during in-vitro experiments with polymeric formulations, Peppas et al. (40) have considered the modeling of swellable matrix systems with volume change. Diffusion equations for these systems have been solved to yield concentration profiles that successfully predict drug diffusion through hydrophilic systems. A complete analysis of mathematical modeling of swelling-controlled systems is presented in two recent reviews by Peppas and Korsmeyer (39, 61).

2.3 Chemically Controlled Systems

Chemically controlled systems include bioerodible and pendant-group polymer matrices. These drug delivery systems are becoming very popular because of their special characteristics, such as complete biodegradation of the polymer and release rates controlled by the geometric shape of the device (62).

Here we consider models proposed for polymer dissolution and bioerodible systems.

2.3.1 Polymer Dissolution and Bioerodible Systems

Modeling of polymer dissolution processes has been reported for a variety of geometric shapes and materials. Since surface kinetics is important, knowledge of the expected functional expression of the dissolution rate is important.

Cooney (63, 64) developed simple expressions for polymer dissolution of cylindrical, spherical, and other devices. Hopfenberg (65) derived expressions for the release of drug from erodible slabs, cylinders, and spheres. For a sphere or a cylinder, the erosion rate dM_t/dt is described in terms of an erosion constant k_e and the continuously changing available area for biodegradation A_e:

$$\frac{dM_t}{dt}=k_e A_e \tag{83}$$

Solution of this equation for various geometries gives

$$\frac{M_t}{M_\infty}=1-\left(1-\frac{k_e t}{c_{i,0} l}\right)^n \tag{84}$$

Here $n=1$ for a plane sheet of thickness $\delta=2l$, $n=2$ for a cylinder of radius $r=l$, and $n=3$ for a sphere of radius $r=l$.

This model has been successfully applied to the description of bioerodible systems exhibiting uniformity and complete biodegradation in the absence of diffusive contributions.

When diffusion from the surface is also important, the Fickian diffusion (equation 10) is solved with appropriate boundary conditions and in conjunction with equation 85, which defines the position of the eroding front:

$$x(t)=\delta-k_e t \tag{85}$$

Lee (49) reported solutions of this problem for drug release from a planar geometry under perfect sink conditions. For drugs dispersed in the matrix at a concentration $c_{i,0}$ greater than the solubility limit $c_{i,s}$, the released amount of drug can be calculated as

$$\frac{M_t}{M_\infty} = \xi' + \frac{k_e \delta \psi}{\mathscr{D}_{im}} - \frac{\xi' c_{i,s}(3 + \psi')}{6 c_{i,0}} \tag{86}$$

where

$$\xi' = \frac{x(t) - \delta}{\delta}$$

$$\psi = \frac{1}{12\psi''}\left[6\left(\frac{c_{i,0}}{c_{i,s}}\right) - 4 - \psi'\right]\left[\xi - \frac{1}{2\psi''}\ln(1 + 2\xi'\psi'')\right]$$

$$\psi' = \frac{c_{i,0}}{c_{i,s}} + \xi'\psi'' - \left[\left(\frac{c_{i,0}}{c_{i,s}} + \xi'\psi''\right)^2 - (1 + 2\xi'\psi'')\right]^{1/2}$$

and

$$\psi'' = \frac{1}{2}\left(1 - \frac{c_{i,0}}{c_{i,s}}\right)\left(\frac{k_e \delta}{\mathscr{D}_{im}}\right)$$

For dissolved drug systems, the solution is of the form

$$\frac{M_t}{M_\infty} = \left(\frac{4\psi}{3}\right)^{1/2} + \left(\frac{k_e \delta}{\mathscr{D}_{im}}\right) \tag{87}$$

2.3.2 *Pendant-Chain Systems*

Modeling of pendant-chain delivery systems is not based on diffusion equations, but rather on the kinetics of the reaction that leads to the removal of the pendant chains. Kinetic models have been proposed for specific systems, and the reader is directed to the research work of Harris et al. (66) and Ringsdorf (67) for further analysis.

3. CONCLUSIONS

Modeling of drug release from or through controlled delivery polymeric systems has been achieved with a variety of simple and sophisticated mathematical models, based predominantly on the steady-state and transient description of drug diffusion by use of Fick's law as in equations 6 and 10. Modeling of drug release from reservoir (membrane) and matrix (monolithic) devices is straightforward, and equations for the prediction of release rates and the total amount of released drug are available for slabs, cylinders, spheres, and (in some cases) even more complicated geometric shapes.

Areas where more accurate mathematical description is presently needed include drug release from swellable and porous materials. Consideration of countercurrent solvent diffusion, polymer state transitions, and porous structure will render present models applicable to a variety of novel pharmaceutical formulations that are presently modeled by empirical equations or through parametric fitting.

With the advent of codelivery polymeric systems, new models will need to be developed for interacting and noninteracting multicomponent diffusion through polymers.

Finally, models for chemically controlled delivery systems seem to adequately predict experimental data.

ACKNOWLEDGMENTS

The author wishes to acknowledge the valuable assistance of R. Korsmeyer in the preparation and thorough review of the manuscript. Professor R. Langer (Massachusetts Institute of Technology), Dr. V. Smolen (Pharma-Control Corporation), and my research collaborators Professor E. Doelker and Dr. R. Gurny (University of Geneva) are also thanked for simulating discussions on problems of mathematical modeling of drug delivery polymeric systems.

NOTATION

Roman Letters

A	area for diffusion of drug
A_e	erosion area
A_n	Parameter (equation 12) determined by initial and boundary conditions
B_n	parameter determined by initial and boundary conditions
c	total concentration
c_i	drug concentration
$c_{i,0}$	initial drug concentration
$c_{i,s}$	drug solubility in polymer matrix
c_s	solvent concentration

$c_{s'}$	surface concentration of drug
d_i	diffusion driving force
$\mathscr{D}_{\mathrm{eff}}$	effective diffusivity of drug
$\mathscr{D}_{im}$	diffusion coefficient of drug i in membrane or matrix m
$\bar{\mathscr{D}}_{im}$	mean diffusion coefficient
$\mathscr{D}_{iw}$	diffusion coefficient at drug i in water
$\mathbf{D}_{ij}$	multicomponent diffusion coefficient for pair of diffusants
$\mathbf{D}_{im}$	activity-based diffusion coefficient of drug in membrane
$D(c_i)$	drug concentration dependent diffusion coefficient
$D_{s'}$	surface diffusion coefficient
F	Faraday constant
j_i	mass flux of diffusant i relative to the molar-average velocity v^*
J_i^*	molar flux of diffusant i relative to the molar-average velocity v^*
k	dissolution constant
k_1, k_2, k_3	constants
k_1, k_2	mass-transfer coefficients (where related to mass transfer)
k_e	erosion kinetic constant
K	partition coefficient (equation 8)
K_1, K_2, K_3	constants
K_0	overall mass-transfer coefficient
l	length of device (cylinder)
$\bar{M}_c$	number-average molecular weight between cross-links for polymer network
$\bar{M}_c^*$	$\bar{M}_c$ below which no diffusion of a drug can occur
$\bar{M}_n$	number-average molecular weight of un-cross-linked polymer
M_t	quantity of drug released at time t
M_{ts}	quantity of solvent penetrating matrix at time t
M_∞	quantity of drug released at time $t=\infty$ (initial loading)
$M_{\infty s}$	quantity of solvent penetrating matrix at time $t=\infty$ (maximum swelling)
n	exponent (equation 83)
n_i	mass average flux relative to stationary coordinates
N_i	molar average flux relative to stationary coordinates
P_{im}, P'_{im}	permeability coefficient of drug i in membrane m
Q_m	membrane degree of swelling
r	radius

r_e, r_i	external and internal radii
r_i	drug (solute) radius equation 21)
R	gas constant
T	temperature
T_g	glass transition temperature of polymer
T	auxiliary variable for swollen polymers (equation 81)
t	time of release
v_i	velocity of diffusant i
v_m	velocity of membrane (=0)
v	mass-average velocity $=\sum_i \rho_i v_i / \sum_i \rho_i$
v'	moving front velocity due to polymer state transition
v^*	molar-average velocity $=\sum_i c_i v_i / \sum_i c_i$
V_1, V_2	volume of device and release medium
$\bar{V}_i$	specific volume of drug
x	position in polymer film
x^*	thickness of matrix layer containing only dissolved drug
x_i	mole fraction of drug i

Greek Letters

α_i	drug activity
α_n	roots of Bessel function of first kind of order zero
β_n	parameter in equation 59
β	constant of concentration dependent diffusion equation (equation 14)
γ_i	drug activity coefficient
δ	thickness of polymer film, membrane or planar matrix
δ_1, δ_2	thickness of boundary layers
$\delta(t)$	time-dependent thickness
ε	void fraction (porosity) of porous membrane or matrix
θ_b, θ_l	characteristic burst and time-lag effect times
μ_i	chemical potential of drug
μ_i^0	chemical potential at reference state
ν_i	ionic charge of diffusant i
ξ, ξ^*	dimensionless parameters (equation 68)
ξ'	dimensionless position (equation 85)

ρ_i	mass concentration of diffusant i
ρ	total mass concentration
τ	membrane or matrix tortuosity
υ_2	polymer volume fraction in swollen membrane
ϕ	electrostatic potential
ψ, ψ', ψ'''	parameters of Lee models (equation 85)
ω_i	mass fraction of diffusant i

Subscripts

i	diffusant (drug)
im	component i diffusing through membrane or matrix
j	other diffusants
m	membrane, matrix
s	solvent (release medium)
s'	surface conditions
1, 2	values of properties in liquid phases around membrane or matrix

Superscripts

interfaces between polymer and liquid

Overline

$\bar{}$	mean value

REFERENCES

1. R. Langer. Polymeric delivery systems for controlled drug release. *Chem. Eng. Commun.* **6**: 1 (1980).
2. R. W. Baker and H. K. Lonsdale. Controlled delivery—an emerging use for membranes. *Chem. Technol.* **5**: 669 (1975).
3. A. S. Michaels. Therapeutic Systems for Controlled Administration of Drugs: A New Application of Membrane Science. In H. B. Hopfenberg (ed.), *Permeability of Plastic Films and Coatings to Gases, Vapors and Liquids*, Plenum Press, New York, 1974, p. 409.
4. A. Zaffaroni. Controlled-delivery therapy is here. *Chem. Technol.* **6**: 756 (1976).
5. G. G. Allan, J. F. Friedhoff, W. J. McConnell, and J. C. Powell. The controlled release of bioactive compounds from polymeric systems. *J. Macromol. Sci., Chem.* **10**: 223 (1976).

6. S. K. Chandrasekaran, R. Capozza, and P. S. L. Wong. Therapeutic systems and controlled drug delivery. *J. Membr. Sci.* **3**: 271 (1978).

7. N. B. Graham. Polymeric inserts and implants for the controlled release of drugs. *Br. Polym. J.* **10**: 260 (1978).

8. D. R. Paul. Polymers in Controlled Release Technology. In D. R. Paul and F. W. Harris (eds.), *Controlled Release Polymeric Formulations*, ACS Symposium Series, Vol. 33, American Chemical Society, Washington, D. C., 1976, p. 1.

9. A. S. Michaels. Synthetic polymeric membranes: Practical applications. *Pure Appl. Chem.* **46**: 193 (1980).

10. R. A. Abrahams and S. M. Ronel. Biocompatible implants for the sustained zero-order release of narcotic antagonists. *J. Biomed. Mater. Res.* **9**: 355 (1975).

11. I. Preis and R. Langer. A single step immunization by sustained antigen release. *J. Immunol. Methods* **28**: 593 (1979).

12. H. M. Creque, R. Langer, and J. Folkman. One month sustained release of insulin from a polymer implant. *Diabetes* **29**: 37 (1980).

13. A. Michaels, S. Chandrasekaran, and J. Shaw. Drug permeation through human skin: Theory and in-vitro experimental measurement. *AIChE J.* **21**: 985 (1975).

14. A. R. Casola. Status of Delivery Systems for Drugs and Food Additives as Viewed by FDA. In R. J. Kostelnik (ed.), *Polymeric Delivery Systems*, Gordon and Breach, New York, 1976, p. 293.

15. R. W. Baker and H. K. Lonsdale. Controlled Release: Mechanisms and Rates. In A. C. Tanquarry and R. E. Lacey (eds.), *Controlled Release of Biologically Active Agents*, Plenum Press, New York, 1974, p. 15.

16. G. L. Flynn. Influence of Physico-chemical Properties of Drug and System on Release of Drugs from Inert Matrices. In A. C. Tanquary and R. E. Lacey (eds.), *Controlled Release of Biologically Active Agents*, Plenum Press, New York, 1974, p. 73.

17. C. E. Rogers. Structural Factors Governing Controlled Release. In D. R. Paul and F. W. Harris (eds.), *Controlled Release Polymeric Formulations*, ACS Symposium Series, Vol. 33, American Chemical Society, Washington, D. C., 1976, p. 15.

18. R. B. Bird, W. E. Stewart, and E. N. Lightfoot. *Transport Phenomena*, Wiley, New York, 1960.

19. C. K. Colton, K. A. Smith, E. W. Merrill, and P. C. Farrell. Permeability studies with cellulosic membranes. *J. Biomed. Mater. Res.* **5**: 459 (1971).

20. J. Crank. *The Mathematics of Diffusion*, Clarendon Press, Oxford, 1975.

21. J. Crank and G. S. Park. *Diffusion in Polymers*, Academic Press, London, 1968.

22. J. Brandrup and E. H. Immergut (eds.), *Polymer Handbook*, Wiley, New York, 1975.

23. E. N. Lightfoot. *Transport Phenomena and Living Systems*, Wiley, New York, 1974.

24. H. Fujita. Diffusion in polymer-diluent systems. *Fortschr. Hochpolym.-Forsch.* **3**: 1 (1961).

25. H. Yasuda, A. Peterlin, C. K. Colton, K. A. Smith, and E. W. Merrill. Permeability of solutes through hydrated polymer membranes, Part III. *Makromol. Chem.* **126**: 177 (1969).

26. H. Yasuda and C. E. Lamaze. Permeability of solutes in homogeneous water-swollen polymer membranes. *J. Macromol. Sci. Phys.* **B5**: 111 (1971).

27. C. T. Reinhart, R. W. Korsmeyer, and N. A. Peppas. Macromolecular network structure and its effects on drug and protein diffusion. *Internatl. J. Pharm. Technol*, **2**: 9 (1981).

28. N. A. Peppas, C. T. Reinhard, and H. J. Moynihan. Diffusive Characteristics of Polymer

Membranes for Protein Separation: Polymer Physical Considerations. Presented at Summer National AIChE Meeting, Detroit, Michn., August 1981.

29. R. J. Pace and A. Datyner. Statistical mechanical model of diffusion of simple penetrants in polymers, Part I. *J. Polym. Sci., Polym. Phys.* **17**: 437 (1979).

30. R. J. Pace and A. Datyner. Statistical mechanical model of diffusion of simple penetrants in polymers, Part III. *J. Polym. Sci. Polym. Phys.* **17**: 465 (1979).

31. V. T. Stannett, W. J. Koros, D. R. Paul, H. K. Lonsdale, and R. W. Baker. Recent advances in membrane science and technology. *Adv. Polym. Sci.* **32**: 69 (1979).

32. D. R. Paul, M. Garcin, and W. E. Garmon. Solute diffusion through swollen polymer membranes. *J. Appl. Polym. Sci.* **20**: 609 (1976).

33. J. S. Vrentas and J. L. Duda. Diffusion of large penetrant molecules in amorphous polymers. *J. Polym. Sci., Polym. Phys.* **17**: 1085 (1979).

34. E. L. Cussler. *Multicomponent Diffusion*, Elsevier, Amsterdam, 1976.

35. P. Meares. The physical chemistry of transport and separation by membranes. In P. Meares (ed.), *Membrane Separation Processes*, Elsevier, Amsterdam, 1976, p. 1.

36. H. B. Hopfenberg and K. C. Hsu. Swelling-controlled, constant rate delivery systems. *Polym. Eng. Sci.* **18**: 1186 (1978).

37. W. R. Good. Diffusion of Water Soluble Drugs from Initially Dry Hydrogels. In R. Kostelnik (ed.), *Polymeric Delivery Systems*, Gordon and Breach, New York, 1976.

38. R. W. Korsmeyer and N. A. Peppas. Effect of the morphology of hydrophilic polymeric matrices on the diffusion and release of water soluble drugs. *J. Membr. Sci.* **9**: 211 (1981).

39. R. W. Korsmeyer and N. A. Peppas. Swelling-Controlled Delivery Systems for Pharmaceutical Applications: Macromolecular and Modeling Considerations. In S. Z. Mansdorf and T. J. Roseman (eds.), *Controlled Release Delivery Systems*, Marcel Dekker, New York, 1983, p. 77.

40. N. A. Peppas, R. Gurny, E. Doelker, and P. Buri. Modeling of drug diffusion through swellable polymeric systems. *J. Membr. Sci.* **7**: 241 (1980).

41. C. K. Colton. Permeability and Transport Studies in Batch and Flow Dialyzers with Applications to Hemodialysis. Dissertation, M. I. T., 1969.

42. T. G. Kaufmann and E. F. Leonard. Studies of intramembrane transport: A phenomenological approach. *AIChE J.* **14**: 110 (1968).

43. D. R. Paul and S. K. McSpadden. Diffusional release of a solute from a polymer matrix. *J. Membr. Sci.* **1**: 33 (1976).

44. J. C. Fu, C. Hagemeier, and D. L. Moyer. A unified mathematical model for diffusion from drug–polymer composite tablets. *J. Biomed. Mater. Res.* **10**: 743 (1976).

45. T. Higuchi. Rate of release of medicaments from ointment bases containing drugs in suspension. *J. Pharm. Sci.* **50**: 874 (1961).

46. T. J. Roseman and W. I. Higuchi. Release of medroxyprogesterone acetate from a silicone polymer. *J. Pharm. Sci.* **59.**: 353 (1970).

47. T. J. Roseman. Release of steroids from a silicone polymer. *J. Pharm. Sci.* **61**: 46 (1972).

48. W. D. Rhine, V. Sukhatme, D. S. T. Hsieh, and R. S. Langer. A new approach to achieve zero-order release kinetics from diffusion controlled release polymer matrix systems. In R. Baker (ed.), *Controlled Release of Bioactive Materials*, Academic Press, New York, 1980, p. 177.

49. P. I. Lee. Diffusional release of a solute from a polymeric matrix—approximate analytical solutions. *J. Membr. Sci.* **7**: 255 (1980).

50. J. Cobby. Mathematical models for the release of drugs from matrix tablets. *J. Biomed. Mater. Res.* **12**: 627 (1978).

51. T. Higuchi. Mechanism of sustained-action medication. *J. Pharm. Sci.* **52**: 1145 (1963).

52. H. Fessi, J. P. Marty, F. Puisieux, and J. T. Carstensen. The Higuchi square root equation applied to matrices with high content of soluble drug substance. *Internatl. J. Pharmac.* **1**: 265 (1978).

53. S. J. Desai, P. Singh, A. P. Simonelli, and W. I. Higuchi. Investigation of factors influencing release of solid drug dispersed in inert matrices. II. Quantitation of procedures. *J. Pharm. sci.* **55**: 1224 (1966).

54. R. Langer, W. Rhine, D. Hsieh, and R. Bawa. Polymers for the sustained release of macromolecules. In R. Baker (ed.), *Controlled Release of Bioactive Materials*, Academic Press, New York, 1980, p. 83.

55. E. A. Swan and N. A. Peppas. Drug release kinetics from hydrophobic porous monolithic devices. *Proc. Symp. Controlled Rel. Bioact. Mater.* **8**: 18 (1981).

56. R. Gurny, E. Doelker, and N. A. Peppas. Modeling of sustained release of water-soluble drugs from porous, hydrophobic polymers. *Biomaterials* **3**: 27 (1982).

57. E. S. Lee, S. W. Kim, S. H. Kim, J. R. Cardinal, and H. Jacobs. Drug release from hydrogel devices with rate controlling barriers. *J. Membr. Sci.* **7**: 293 (1980).

58. H. Lapidus and N. G. Lordi. Drug release from compressed hydrophilic matrices. *J. Pharm. Sci.* **57**: 1292 (1968).

59. M. Bamba, F. Puisieux, J. P. Marty, and J. T. Carstensen. Release mechanisms in gel-forming sustained release preparations. *Internatl. J. Pharm.* **2**: 307 (1979).

60. M. Bamba, F. Puisieux, J. P. Marty, and J. T. Carstensen. Model for drug release from gel-forming sustained release matrices. *Proceedings of the International Conference on Pharmaceutical Technology*, 1980, p. 127.

61. N. A. Peppas and R. Korsmeyer. Polymers for sustained release of macromolecules. *Polym. News* **6**: 149 (1980).

62. J. Heller. Controlled release of biologically active compounds from bioerodible polymers. *Biomaterials* **1**: 51 (1980).

63. D. O. Cooney. Slow dissolution of implanted beds of spherical particles as a method for prolonged-release medication. *AIChE J.* **17**: 754 (1971).

64. D. O. Cooney. Effect of geometry on the dissolution of pharmaceutical tablets and other solids: Surface detachment kinetics controlling. *AIChE J.* **18**: 446 (1972).

65. H. B. Hopfenberg. Controlled Release from Erodible Slabs, Cylinders and Spheres. In D. R. Paul and F. W. Harris (eds.), *Controlled Release Polymeric Formulations*, ACS Symposium Series, Vol. 33, American Chemical Society, Washington, D. C., 1976, p. 26.

66. F. W. Harris, A. E. Aulabaugh, R. D. Case, M. K. Dykes, and W. A. Feld. Polymers Containing Pendent Herbicide Substituents. In D. R. Paul and F. W. Harris (eds.), *Controlled Release of Polymeric Formulations*, ACS Symposium Series, Vol. 33, American Chemical Society, Washington, D. C., 1976, p. 222.

67. H. Ringsdorf. Synthetic Polymeric Drugs. In R. J. Kostelnik (ed.), *Polymeric Delivery Systems*, Gordon and Breach, New York, 1978, p. 197.

CHAPTER 8

Design of Experiments and Statistical Analysis of Biological Studies

VIRGIL L. ANDERSON

Department of Statistics
Purdue University
West Lafayette, Indiana

ROBERT A. McLEAN

Statistics Department
University of Tennessee
Knoxville, Tennessee

CONTENTS

1. BACKGROUND

One approach to designing experiments in the last decade considers three essential ingredients of a well-designed experiment expressed in the book by Anderson and McLean (1). These three ingredients, in order of importance, are (1) inference space, (2) randomization, and (3) replication. The term "inference space" replaces the term "population" usually used by statisticians. It has been our experience that the term "inference space" demands more attention from the research worker.

The phrase "inference space" means the limits to which the investigator may use the results of the experiment. Common practice at present is for the research worker to indicate how extensively the results are to be applied before the experiment is set up. This requires that the experimental units (such as "white rats of a certain size" to represent all rats of this type) are to be used in the research and that this will be the basis for the inferences. The researcher must also define the time interval and the geographic extent in which the results are to be applied and then decide which levels of all factors are to be controlled in the experiment. Ordinarily more time should be spent on this phase of designing the experiment than either of the other two (randomization and replication) because without the inference space clearly defined, the best so-called "designed experiment" may be worthless to the investigator. We define this ingredient (inference space) as a part of the designed experiment. Hence there can be no "best-designed experiment" without a carefully defined inference space.

Randomization is the next most important ingredient in designing experiments. It must be present in the experiment for probability statements to be made. Fisher (2) expressed the idea that it is the physical basis of the validity of the test. It is also the basis of validity of confidence intervals.

Included in the ingredient, randomization, is another concept, "restriction" on randomization. To understand restriction on randomization, let us first explain "completely randomized," which means no restriction on randomization. This concept can be seen by considering a factor t with five levels and three experimental units treated with each of the five levels of factor t completely at random.

Assume that there are 15 randomly drawn experimental units from the inference space to be used for the entire experiment. One way to obtain a completely randomized design is to select a random number between 1 and 5—say 2. Then the first experimental unit must receive treatment 2 or the second level of factor t. Another number between 1 and 5—say, 5—is selected, and then the second experimental unit must receive treatment 5. Sampling or drawing random numbers is continued in this manner until the 15 experimental units have all been "treated." This sampling procedure requires that each level of factor t be represented three times in the experiment, and the design of this experiment is called "completely randomized."

The mathematical model for analyzing the data from such an experiment is

$$y_{ij}=\mu+T_i+\epsilon_{(i)j}: i=1,2,\ldots,5; \qquad j=1,2,3 \tag{1}$$

where y_{ij} = the response from experimental unit j treated with level i of factor t

μ = overall mean

T_i = effect of the ith level of factor t

$\epsilon_{(i)j}$ = the experimental error caused by the jth experimental unit nested in the ith level of factor t

The assumptions for the analysis of the data in a model such as this are:

1. The term y_{ij} is a random variable.
2. The variances of the responses within levels of factor t are equal.
3. The model is additive.
4. The experimental error is $NID(0, \sigma^2)$, normal and independently distributed with mean zero and variance σ^2.

This complete randomization assures the experimenter that the experimental units from the inference space have three opportunities for selection for each treatment. These three experimental units for each treatment then allow a measure of the variation within the treatments. It follows then that the test of significance on treatment effects (T_i in equation 1) must be based on the excessive amount of variation among the means of the treatments over the amount of variation obtained from within the treatments where the variation within the treatments is accounted for by the variance due to $\epsilon_{(i)j}$ in equation 1. Hence in equation 1 we can indicate that $\epsilon_{(i)j}$ is the correct error for evaluating T_i.

If, however, the sampling procedure was such that the first random draw, level 2, was used on the first three experimental units, then the second draw, level 5, was used on the next three experimental units, and so on, we would have a "restriction" on randomization because the randomization procedures were allowed only five times, not 15 as is required for complete randomization. If, as is frequently the case, there tends to be similarity between adjacent units in space or time, the variation within the group of three is smaller than the variation between the groups of three. In this design, then, the variation due to treatments is not separable from the variation between groups of three units (treatments confounded with groups). Thus if there is a source of error variation between groups, it will not be possible to test for treatments, and the following model depicts this:

$$y_{ij} = \mu + T_i + \delta_{(i)} + \epsilon'_{(i)j} \tag{2}$$

where $\delta_{(i)}$ is the "restriction" error or that random component due to the ith group of units (note how the subscript is identical to the subscript to T_i indicating complete confounding) and $\epsilon'_{(i)j}$ is $NID(0, \sigma^2_{\epsilon'})$, the error due the jth unit in the ith group. It is the variation due to $\delta_{(i)}$ that is representative of the variation across the inference space, whereas the variation due to the $\epsilon'_{(i)j}$ in equation 2 represents only a small portion across the inference space. Hence one needs an estimate of σ^2_δ to test for the effect of treatments. Of course, $\delta_{(i)}$ has no degrees of freedom, which indicates this is a poor design and should not be used.

Using the algorithm for deriving the expected mean squares described in Chapter 2 of Anderson and McLean (1), we can show that the correct error term for testing treatments is $\delta_{(i)}$. However, there is no estimate of this error in equation 2 unless the whole experiment is repeated. Hence the "restriction" on the randomization has caused $\delta_{(i)}$, which, in turn, tells the experimenter that this sampling procedure is not a good one even before the first observation is made. This, then, allows the experimenter to change the design early, to avoid collection of data that will not give a good analysis.

Before explaining the third ingredient of designed experiments, namely, replication, a few words should be stated about special cases where randomization may not be required. If an investigator can show by actual experimentation that the results are the same regardless of whether randomization takes place, it may not be necessary to randomize. This will happen on extremely well controlled experiments only. We are familiar with an example on a one-cylinder engine gasoline consumption laboratory experiment in which it did not matter whether speeds were randomized or taken in order. The reason for this was that the controls on speed were so precise and the setups so repeatable that the errors were identical within the capabilities of the recording equipment. We have not experienced such control, however, in biological experiments.

Keeping this nonrandom possibility in mind and knowing that an experiment cannot be designed well without knowledge of the inference space, we rank inference space above randomization in importance when considering ingredients of a well-designed experiment.

Finally, the third ingredient, replication, is quite often required for an estimate of an error term or to provide the basis for making decisions on the importance of factors contributing to the response variables. In addition, as the number of observations increases on a given treatment, the more precise the estimate of the effect of the treatment becomes, or the smaller its variance becomes. For example, in estimating the mean of the response from a treatment, the variance of the estimated mean $\bar{y}$ is

$$s_{\bar{y}}^2 = \frac{s^2}{n}$$

where s^2 is the variance estimated from the sample and n is the number of observations randomly obtained from the entire inference space for $\bar{y}$.

If, however, previous experimentation has shown certain information is available, for example, the variance is known or that higher-order terms in the model are zero, it may not be necessary to replicate the entire experiment. In fact, there are many good experiments run with fewer than the total number of combinations of levels of the factors in a "factorial" experiment. These experiments are called "fractional replicated factorials," which are described later.

With the various well-designed experiments without complete replications in mind, the ingredient "replication" is placed in third position behind inference space and randomization.

Before going into designs and analyses it should be understood that the readers of this material should understand (1) basic statistical concepts, (2) distributions such as the mean $\bar{y}$, t, χ^2, and F, and (3) analysis of variance [ANOVA, including expected mean squares (EMS)] and regression models.

2. DESIGNS

A definition of a designed experiment is an arrangement of the experimental material, including randomization of experimental units to the treatments so that statistical tests of significance (and confidence intervals) on the effects and interactions of the factors being studied can be made. To accomplish this, care must be taken to set up the arrangement efficiently (keep the cost reasonably low) and, at the same time, cover the inference space. For coverage of designs, major headings are used to indicate designs encountered by us in bioavailability studies.

2.1 Block Designs

2.1.1 *Importance of Blocking (Handling Extraneous Variables)*

Many authors of books on design of experiments express the importance of "blocking," that is, placing all treatments or all combinations of the levels of all factors of interest in a homogeneous group (thereby removing some of the effect of an extraneous variable from the experimental error) and repeating this group or block in time and/or space with different experimental units.

To show this concept, we use mathematical equations that are to be used as the basis for analyses of the data from the designed experiment.

Returning to the concepts of setting up equations 1 and 2, it follows that another design of the experiment could be to arrange three blocks of five treatments each, where the five experimental units were randomized onto the five treatments per block. Pictorially, one could have the arrangement shown in Table 1.

Table 1. Block Design—Three Blocks of Five Treatments Each

Blocks		
Treatments	Treatments	Treatments
5	2	3
2	4	1
3	1	5
1	5	4
4	3	2

It follows that the equation to be used as the basis for the analysis is

$$y_{ij} = \mu + B_i + \delta_{(i)} + T_j + \varepsilon_{ij} \tag{3}$$

where Y_{ij} and μ have the same meaning as they did for equation 2, B_i is the effect of block i, $\delta_{(i)}$ is similar to $\delta_{(i)}$ in equation 2, T_j is the effect of the jth treatment, and ε_{ij} represents the error due to the jth treatment in block i (assuming that there is no interaction).

Since the experimenter is interested in testing for treatment effects only, this is an excellent design because ε_{ij} is the basis for the test of T_i since the variation across treatments is compared to the variation due to ε_{ij} values. If it should turn out that the effects of B_i and $\delta_{(i)}$ are zero, B_i, $\delta_{(i)}$, and ε_{ij} may be pooled and equation 3 becomes equation 1. This completes the demonstration that, in general, blocking is always worthwhile in experiments and should be used whenever possible.

To show the effectiveness of blocking, the following simple example is provided. In case 1 the block effect is large. The block effect is zero in case 2. The effectiveness of blocking is shown in case 1 (Tables 2 through 4) by observing the differences in the error mean square when the data are analyzed as a randomized complete block design as compared to a completely randomized design (4.42 vs. 7.53; Tables 3 and 4, respectively). Note that the mean square for treatments is the same in both tables in case 1 and that

Table 2. **Block Design for Case 1: Experiment with Large Block Effect**[a]

Blocks					
1		2		3	
Treatment	y	Treatment	y	Treatment	y
5	1	2	9	3	2
2	7	4	3	1	8
3	5	1	8	5	5
1	4	5	8	4	3
4	1	3	10	2	10
	18		38		28

[a]Treatment 1: 4+8+8=20
2: 7+9+10=26
3: 5+10+2=17
4: 1+3+3=7
5: 1+8+5=14

Table 3. ANOVA for Case 1[a]

Source	*df*	SS	MS	F^b	EMS
Blocks	2	40.00	20.00		$\sigma^2+5\sigma_\delta^2+5\sigma_B^2$
δ	0	—	—		$\sigma^2+5\sigma_\delta^2$
Treatments	4	66.27	16.57	3.7 NS[c]	$\sigma^2+3\phi(T)$
Error	8	35.33	4.42		σ^2

[a]Refer to Table 5.1.3 on p. 129 of Anderson and McLean (1).
[b]$F_{4,8}(.05)=3.8$.
[c]NS, Not significant at $\alpha=.05$.

Table 4. Analyzed as a Completely Randomized Design (Ignoring Block Effects)

Source	*df*	SS	MS	F	EMS
Treatments	4	66.27	16.57	2.20 NS	$\sigma^2+3\phi(T)$
Error	10	75.33	7.53		σ^2

treatments are very close to being significant when analyzed properly, that is, as a randomized complete block design.

The initial model used for case 2 (Tables 5 through 7) is

$$y_{ij}=\mu+B_i+\delta_{(i)}+T_j+\varepsilon_{ij}$$

It is seen, however, that since $B_i+\delta_{(i)}=0$, one can now write the model as

$$y_{ij}=\mu+T_j+\varepsilon_{ij}$$

which gives the results shown in Table 7, where the F for treatments is now 4.7 as compared to 3.7 for the initial model (Table 6).

Table 5. Block Design for Case 2: Experiment with Zero Block Effect[a]

Blocks					
1		2		3	
Treatment	y	Treatment	y	Treatment	y
5	3	2	7	3	2
2	9	4	1	1	8
3	7	1	6	5	5
1	6	5	6	4	3
4	3	3	8	2	10
	28		28		28

[a]Treatment 1: 6+6+8=20
2: 9+7+10=26
3: 7+8+2=17
4: 3+1+3=7
5: 3+6+5=14

Table 6. ANOVA for Case 2

Source	df	SS	MS	F[a]
Blocks	2	0	0	
δ	0	—	—	
Treatments	4	66.27	16.57	3.7 NS[b]
Error	8	35.33	4.42	

[a]$F_{4,8}(.05)=3.8$.
[b]NS, Not significant at $\alpha=.05$.

Table 7. Analyzed as a Completely Randomized Design (Pooling Block and Error Effects)

Source	*df*	SS	MS	F^a
Treatments	4	66.27	16.57	4.7^b
Error	10	35.33	3.53	

[a] $F_{4,10}(.05) = 3.5$.
[b] Significant at $\alpha = .05$.

In both the above examples the data were analyzed by using the models for the randomized complete block design and completely randomized design. In the first case the effect of blocking is clear and illustrates the power of blocking. In the second case blocking was used to no avail, but the indication of no block effects was seen in Table 6, and then, by pooling block and error effects, the power of the significance test was again increased.

The point of all of this is to demonstrate that one does *not* lose by blocking in the original experiment because if the block effects are very small, one can pool to obtain an error term that would have been the same as if complete randomization had occurred.

2.1.2 *Incorrect Use of Blocks (Treatments Used as Blocks)*

In the previous example the effect of $\delta_{(i)}$, the restriction error caused by blocks, did not decrease the importance of blocking because the experimenter was interested in the effect of blocking plus the restriction error in reducing the estimated experimental error ε_{ij}. In that case ε_{ij} was the basis for testing treatment effects only.

Now one must consider the case in which the blocking concept is used incorrectly. Consider an example in manufacturing drugs in tablet form. The interest here was in studying disintegration of the tablets. The experimenter wanted to use five drugs compressed with three different pressures in the experiment.

The suggested design of the experiment was to use 15 batches of tablet mixture, one batch (or block) for each combination of the five drugs and three pressures. After the tablets were compressed from each batch of about 500 tablet, five were to be pulled at random from each 500-tablet batch and the time to disintegration was to be measured in seconds. This procedure would be carried out for all 15 batches, making 75 tablets to be tested for disintegration time.

The analysis of the data may be summarized with the following degrees of freedom (*df*) and model:

$$df: \quad 75 = 1 + 4 + 2 + \; 8 \; + \; 0 \; + \; 60$$

$$\text{Model:} \quad y_{ijk} = \mu + D_i + P_j + DP_{ij} + \delta_{(ij)} + \varepsilon_{(ij)k} \tag{4}$$

$$i = 1, 2, 3, 4, 5; \quad j = 1, 2, 3; \quad k = 1, 2, 3, 4, 5$$

where y_{ijk} = disintegration time of the kth tablet with the jth pressure using drug i

μ = overall mean

D_i = effect of ith drug

P_j = effect of jth pressure

DP_{ij} = effect of interaction of drug i at pressure j

$\delta_{(ij)}$ = restriction error caused by all the tablets in (i, j)th drug, with pressure combination manufactured under the same conditions (this is the only error appropriate for testing D, P, and DP)

$\epsilon_{(ij)k}$ = experimental error caused by kth tablet in (i, j)th cell

Equation 4 points out [by using $\delta_{(ij)}$] that one should *not* run the experiment in this manner because there will be no degrees of freedom for the appropriate error to test drugs, pressures, and their interaction. That error, of course, is the $\delta_{(ij)}$. This is a demonstration of using blocks incorrectly; that is, the blocks (batches) are completely confounded with treatments (drugs and pressures) of interest. One could not test for blocks separately in the previous example, but the interest there was not in blocks per se. When the experimenter is interested in testing for treatments (drugs and pressures), the individual should not use treatments as blocks.

The correct way to handle this problem is to run at least two batches for each of the 15 combinations of drugs and pressures. Then take one tablet per batch (some experimenters may demand to take two, but for this demonstration assume only one was used) and analyze the results of these tablets. The two batches provide the correct error for between "batch treatments" (drugs and pressures), and the inference space is sampled much more effectively because there are two samples (batches) from each combination rather than only one. The equation for the analysis of the data from this design is

$$y_{ijk} = \mu + D_i + P_j + DP_{ij} + B_{(ij)k} + \varepsilon_{(ijk)} \tag{5}$$

where $i = 1, \ldots, 5$; $j = 1, 2, 3$; and $k = 1, 2$.

The analysis of variance is shown in Table 8,

Table 8. ANOVA

		f		*r*	
		5	3	2	
Source	*df*	*i*	*j*	*k*	EMS
D_i	4	0	3	2	$\sigma^2+\sigma_B^2+6\phi(D)$
P_j	2	5	0	2	$\sigma^2+\sigma_B^2+10\phi(P)$
DP_{ij}	8	0	0	2	$\sigma^2+\sigma_B^2+2\phi(DP)$
$B_{(ij)k}$	15	1	1	1	$\sigma^2+\sigma_B^2$
$\varepsilon_{(ijk)}$	0	1	1	1	σ^2

Table 9. Time Used as Treatment on Experimental Units

	Drugs (Fixed)							
	1		2		3		4	
	People (Random)		People (Random)		People (Random)		People (Random)	
Time (Fixed)	1	2	3	4	5	6	7	8
1								
2								
3								
4								
5								
6								

where the arrows (↶) indicate the *F* tests; D_i, P_j, DP_{ij}, and $\varepsilon_{(jk)}$ are defined as for equation 4; and $B_{(ij)k}$ is the error caused by the *k*th batch within treatment combination (*ij*), the correct error for testing *D*, *P*, and *DP*.

2.2 Designs with Treatments on Same Experimental Units

2.2.1 *Repeated Measures*

The following examples use time as the treatments on the same experimental units (see Table 9), but this is not the only type of treatment used in bioavailability studies. Quite frequently in this type of experiment the research worker wants to compare the efficacy of only those four drugs used in the experiment on a population of people. To establish the experimental units in the inference space, the people may be defined in terms of age, sex, race, and so on with the sample for the experiment assumed to be random from the indicated population. The efficacy is then investigated over six periods of time.

One of the statistical dangers in this type of designed experiment is that the assumption of equal correlation between responses may not be met for the same person over the time periods. This has been recognized by statisticians and methods to handle the problem are discussed by various authors, including Greenhouse and Geisser (3), Cole and Grizzle (12), Winer (4), and Anderson and McLean (1).

The model appropriate for analysis of data from the drug experiment above if all assumptions are met is

$$y_{ijk} = \mu + D_i + P_{(i)j} + \delta_{(ij)} + T_k + DT_{ik} + PT_{(i)jk} + \epsilon_{(ijk)} \qquad (6)$$

where y_{ijk} = response of jth person in kth time period using ith drug
μ = overall mean
D_i = effect of ith drug (fixed)
$P_{(i)j}$ = effect of jth person using ith drug (random)
$\delta_{(ij)}$ = restriction error caused by the same person responding over time, $NID(0, \sigma_\delta^2)$
T_k = effect of ith time period (fixed)
DT_{ik} = effect of interaction of ith drug in time period k
$PT_{(i)jk}$ = effect of interaction of jth person using drug i in time period k
$\epsilon_{(ijk)}$ = random error caused by jth person using drug i in time period k, $NID(0, \sigma^2)$

The ANOVA for this model is shown in Table 10.

Table 10. ANOVA for Experimental Design of Table 9

Source	*df*	SS	MS	EMS
Drugs D	3	72.25	24.08	$\sigma^2+6\sigma_\delta^2+6\sigma_P^2+12\phi(D)$
People in $D(P)$	4	7.00	1.75	$\sigma^2+6\sigma_\delta^2+6\sigma_P^2$
δ	0	None		$\sigma^2+6\sigma_\delta^2$
Time T	5	105.42	21.08	$\sigma^2+\sigma_{PT}^2+8\phi(T)$
DT	15	38.25	2.55	$\sigma^2+\sigma_{PT}^2+2\phi(DT)$
PT	20	15.00	0.75	$\sigma^2+\sigma_{PT}^2$
ε	0	None		σ^2

Table 11.

	Drugs								
	1		2		3		4		
	People		People		People		People		
Time	1	2	3	4	5	6	7	8	Totals
1	2	3	4	2	6	5	7	5	34
2	4	4	4	4	5	5	5	4	35
3	5	7	4	3	5	6	6	5	41
4	3	5	5	3	8	10	9	10	53
5	7	7	8	5	9	9	10	11	66
6	6	6	6	7	7	8	8	9	57
Totals	27	32	31	24	40	43	45	44	286
	59		55		83		89		

Anderson and McLean (1) show that if there are very unequal correlations between observations from time to time within people, the *df* for testing time and DT should be 1 and 3, respectively, for the numerator of the F and 4 for the denominator. The actual mean squares calculated from the data should be used, however. Hence for testing hypotheses:

1. $H_0: \phi(T)=0$, use $F_{1,4}=\dfrac{\text{MS time}}{\text{MS } PT}$,

2. $H_0: \phi(DT)=0$, use $F_{3,4}=\dfrac{\text{MS } DT}{\text{MS } PT}$.

Let us consider a small experiment (for demonstration purposes only) of this type and show the calculations one usually follows to analyze the data (see Table 11).

The first calculation should be to run a homogeneity of variance test on all the data unless the experimenter knows the distribution of the errors for the variable to be analyzed. In this case the investigator may immediately transform the data appropriately. For example, if it is known that the variable y is exponential in nature, the log y may be run without bothering to investigate the homogeneity of the variances or the distributional properties of y.

For these data, let us assume that the distributional peculiarities are not known. To recognize the two errors in the nested factorial design, one should run two different tests for homogeneity of variances as follows:

1. Between people within drugs. (In this case there are six time periods for each person. Hence there is a divisor of 6.) For the four drugs

$$s_1^2 = \frac{(27-32)^2}{6 \cdot 2 = 12} \cong 2.08, \qquad s_2^2 = \frac{(31-34)^2}{12} \cong 4.08$$

$$s_3^2 = \frac{(40-43)^2}{12} = .75, \qquad s_4^2 = \frac{(45-44)^2}{12} = .08$$

$$q_{(1,4)} = \frac{4.3264 + 16.6464 + 5624 + .0064}{(2.08 + 4.08 + .75 + .08)^2} \cong .44$$

$$q_{(1,4)}(.01) = .92$$

Thus, accept homogeneity of the variances between people for the four drugs.

2. Interaction of people × time for the four drugs:

Example. Drug 1

	People		
Time	1	2	Total
1	2	3	5
2	4	4	8
3	5	7	12
4	3	5	8
5	7	7	14
6	6	6	12
Total	27	32	59

a. Drug 1

SS time: $\dfrac{5^2 + 8^2 + \cdots + 12^2}{2} - \dfrac{59^2}{12} = \underline{23.42}$

SS people: $\dfrac{(27-32)^2}{12} = 2.08$

SS total: $2^2 + \cdots + 6^2 - \dfrac{59^2}{12} = 323 - 290.08 = 32.92$

SS int^n: $32.92 - 25.50 = \underline{7.42}$

b. Drug 2

$$\text{SS time: } \frac{6^2+8^2+\cdots+13^2}{2}-\frac{55^2}{12}=\frac{551}{2}-252.08$$
$$=22.42$$

SS people: 4.08
SS total: $285-252.08=32.92$
SS int″: $32.92-26.50=\underline{6.42}$

c. Drug 3

$$\text{SS times: } \frac{11^2+\cdots+15^2}{2}-\frac{83^2}{12}=33.42$$

SS people: .75

SS total: $6^2+\cdots+8^2-574.08=36.92$

SS int″: $36.92-.75-33.42=\underline{2.75}$

d. Drug 4

$$\text{SS time: } \frac{12^2+\cdots+17^2}{2}-\frac{(89)^2}{12}=58.42$$

SS people: .08

SS total: $7^2+\cdots+9^2-660.08=62.92$

SS int″: $62.92-.08-58.42=\underline{4.42}$

$$q_{(5,4)}=\frac{55.06+41.22+7.56+19.54}{(7.42+6.42+2.75+4.42)^2}=\frac{123.38}{(21.01)^2}\simeq\underline{.280}$$

$q_{(5,4)}(.01)=.498$

Thus accept the homogeneity of the interaction variances.

Next, if the number of people per drug were 5 or greater, one could run a Shapiro–Wilk W test (1) to test for normality. Here there are only two people per drug so no test for normality can be made.

Next one may calculate the sums of squares by use of the original data because no transformation is indicated from the preliminary test on the homogeneity of variance and there is no theory to tell the experimenter that a transformation should be made.

Using equation 6, where $i=1, 2, 3, 4$; $j=1, 2$; and $k=1, 2, \ldots, 6$, one can calculate the sums of squares for the sources as

$$SSD_i = \sum_{i=1}^{4} \left[\frac{\left(\sum_{j,k}^{2,6} y_{ijk} \right)^2}{2 \cdot 6} - \frac{\left(\sum_{i,j,k}^{4,2,6} y_{ijk} \right)^2}{4 \cdot 2 \cdot 6} \right]$$

$$= \frac{59^2 + 55^2 + 83^2 + 89^2}{12} - \frac{286^2}{48}$$

$$= 1776.33 - 1704.08$$

$$= 72.25$$

$$\text{SS } T_k = \sum_{k=1}^{6} \frac{\left(\sum_{i,j}^{4,2} y_{ijk} \right)^2}{4 \cdot 2} - \frac{\left(\sum_{i,j,k}^{4,2,6} y_{ijk} \right)^2}{48}$$

$$= \frac{34^2 + 35^2 + \cdots + 57^2}{8} - \frac{286^2}{48}$$

$$= 1809.50 - 1704.08$$

$$= 105.42$$

$$\text{SS } P_{(i)j} = \sum_{i,j}^{4,2} \left[\frac{\left(\sum_{k}^{6} y_{ijk} \right)^2}{6} \right] - \sum_{i=1}^{4} \left[\frac{\left(\sum_{j,k}^{2,6} y_{ijk} \right)^2}{2 \cdot 6} \right]$$

$$= \frac{27^2 + 32^2 + \cdots + 44^2}{6} - \frac{59^2 + 55^2 + 83^2 + 89^2}{12}$$

$$= 1783.33 - 1776.33$$

$$= 7.00$$

$$\text{SS } DT_{ik} = \sum_{i,k}^{4,6} \left[\frac{\left(\sum_{j=1}^{2} y_{ijk} \right)^2}{2} - CT \right]. - \text{SS } V_i - \text{SS } P_{(i)j}$$

$$= \frac{5^2 + 6^2 + 11^2 + \cdots + 17^2}{2} - \frac{286^2}{48} - \text{SS } V_i - \text{SS } P_k$$

$$= 1920.00 - 1704.08 - 72.25 - 105.42$$

$$= 38.25$$

$$\text{SS } PT_{(i)jk} = \sum_{i} [\text{SS } PT(D_i)]$$

where

$$\text{SS } PT(D_1)=\left[\sum_{i=1}^{4} y_{ijk}^2-\frac{\left(\sum_{j,k}^{2,6} y_{ijk}\right)^2}{12}\right]-\left[\sum_{k=1}^{6}\frac{\left(\sum_{j=1}^{2} y_{ijk}\right)^2}{2}-\frac{\left(\sum_{j,k}^{2,6} y_{ijk}\right)^2}{12}\right]$$

$$-\sum_{j=1}^{2}\left[\frac{\left(\sum_{k=1}^{6} y_{ijk}\right)^2}{6}-\frac{\left(\sum_{j,k}^{2,6} y_{ijk}\right)^2}{12}\right]$$

$$=\left[2^2+3^3+\cdots+6^2-\frac{59^2}{12}\right]$$

$$-\left[\frac{5^2+8^2+\cdots+12^2}{2}-\frac{59^2}{12}\right]-\left[\frac{27^2+32^2}{6}-\frac{59^2}{12}\right]$$

$$=2.42$$

$$\text{SS } PT(D_2)=\left[4^2+2^2+\cdots+7^2-\frac{55^2}{12}\right]$$

$$-\left[\frac{6^2+8^2+\cdots+13^2}{2}-\frac{55^2}{12}\right]-\left[\frac{31^2+24^2}{6}-\frac{55^2}{12}\right]$$

$$=5.42$$

$$\text{SS } PT(D_3)=\left[6^2+5^2+\cdots+8^2-\frac{83^2}{12}\right]$$

$$-\left[\frac{11^2+10^2+\cdots+15^2}{2}-\frac{83^2}{12}\right]-\left[\frac{40^2+43^2}{6}-\frac{83^2}{12}\right]$$

$$=2.75$$

$$\text{SS } PT(D_4)=\left[7^2+5^2+\cdots+9^2-\frac{89^2}{12}\right]$$

$$-\left[\frac{12^2+9^2+\cdots+17^2}{2}-\frac{89^2}{12}\right]-\left[\frac{45^2+44^2}{6}\ \frac{89^2}{12}\right]$$

$$=4.41$$

Therefore,

$$\text{SS } PT_{(i)jk}=\sum_{i=1}^{4}\text{SS } PT(D_i)=15.00$$

and

$$\text{SS total} = \sum_{i,j,}^{4,2,6} y_{ijk}^2 - \frac{\left(\sum_{i,j,k} y_{ijk}\right)^2}{48}$$

$$= 323 + 285 + 611 + 723 - 1704.08 \text{ (from our work above)}$$

$$= 237.92$$

This completes the discussion on repeated-measures-type designs here. It must be understood that time is not the only treatment on the same experimental unit that an experimenter may encounter.

2.2.2 *Crossover Designs*

Another design frequently used by biological research people for non-curative drugs is the crossover design (5). The basic structure of the design comes from a 2 × 2 square called a *Latin square* because the treatments are represented by Latin letters inside the designated row and column combinations. Latin square design is discussed in Box et al. (9).

The overall structure of the crossover design is portrayed in the following layout:

		Groups of People 1	Groups of People 2
Time of Administering Drug	1	Drug A	Drug B
	2	Drug B	Drug A

where it is assumed that a random group (Group 1) of people were given drug A and blood measures taken and then a washout period was allowed before the same group was given drug B and a final blood measure was taken. Similarly, another group (group 2) was given drug B first, measured, and allowed a washout period and was then given drug A and measured again. Hence the two drugs (treatments) are used on the same person (experimental unit).

This method allows an evaluation of carry-over effects by accounting for time in the analysis. The necessary assumption, however, is that there is no interaction of groups by time because the effect of drug A versus drug B is completely confounded with that interaction. To demonstrate this, consider Table 12 (assume that the design is completely randomized with one observation per group so that the concept of calculating interaction (sums of squares) may be shown easily).

Since $G \times T$SS = 240.25 and (A vs. B)SS = 240.25, this demonstrates the complete confounding of the interaction of groups × time with (A vs. B) drug

Table 12.

		Groups 1	2	Total
Time	1	A = 25	B = 10	35
	2	B = 7	A = 23	30
	Total	32	33	65

ANOVA

Source	*df*	SS
Groups G	1	0.25
Time T	1	6.25
Interaction $G \times T$	1	240.25
	3	246.75

Group SS: $\dfrac{(32\text{-}33)^2}{4} = 0.25$

Time SS: $\dfrac{(35\text{-}30)^2}{4} = 6.25$

Total SS: $25^2 + 7^2 + 10^2 + 23^2 - \dfrac{(65)^2}{4} = 246.75$

$G \times T$ SS: $246.75 - 0.25 - 6.25 = 240.25$

(A vs. B) SS: $(48\text{-}17)^2/4 = 240.25$

Table 13.

Time	Subjects 1	2	3	4	5	6	7	8	9
					Formula 1				(351.7)
1	51.9	35.1	38.6	36.1	34.6	39.7	37.8	38.8	39.1
					7-Day Washout Period				
					Formula 2				(376.1)
2	43.5	45.4	35.4	43.7	49.8	39.9	41.4	37.5	39.5
Total	95.4	80.5	74.0	79.8	84.4	79.6	79.2	76.3	78.6

Time	Subjects 10	11	12	13	14	15	16	17	18
					Formula 2				(332.0)
1	50.8	41.1	39.1	35.7	33.7	31.2	34.3	31.8	34.3
					7-Day Washout Period				
					Formula 1				(316.6)
2	44.2	33.4	32.7	33.1	33.4	27.1	33.1	39.5	40.1
Total	95.0	74.5	71.8	68.8	67.1	58.3	67.4	71.3	74.4

$$\text{SS time} = \frac{(683.7)^2 + (692.7)^2}{18} - \frac{(1376.4)^2}{36} = 2.25$$

$$\text{SS formula} = \frac{(668.3)^2 + (708.1)^2}{18} - 52{,}624.36 = 44.00$$

$$\text{SS subjects} = \frac{(95.4)^2 + (80.5)^2 + \cdots + (74.4)^2}{2} - 52{,}624.36$$

$$= 717.79$$

$$\text{SS total} = (51.9)^2 + (35.1)^2 + \cdots + (40.1)^2 - 52{,}624.36$$

$$= 1093.98$$

$$\text{SS error} = \text{SS total} - \text{SS time} - \text{SS formulas} - \text{SS subjects}$$

$$= 1093.98 - 2.25 - 44.00 - 717.79 = 329.94$$

Table 14. ANOVA

Source	*df*	SS	MS	EMS
Subjects S_i	17	717.79	42.22	$\sigma^2+2\sigma_\delta^2+2\sigma_S^2$
Subject restriction error $\delta_{(i)}$	0	—	—	$\sigma^2+2\sigma_\delta^2$
Time T_j	1	2.25	2.25	$\sigma^2+18\phi(T)$
Formulas F_k	1	44.00	44.00	$\sigma^2+18\phi(F)$
Residual $\varepsilon_{(ijk)}$	16	329.94	20.62	σ^2
	35	1093.98		

effect. Hence one must assume that there is no interaction of $G \times T$ before (A vs. B) drug effect can be interpreted in these designs.

The usual approach to analyze crossover designs utilizing the Latin square and repeated-measures concepts is described in the following example.

Example An illustration of the crossover design occurred in a problem for a drug manufacturing company. Two formulas of a drug were given to 18 human beings selected at random from a population to which the drug would be given. Nine random subjects were given formula 1, and the other nine were given formula 2. The amount of the drug in the blood of each of the 18 subjects was measured 8 hours after administration of the drug, and that amount was recorded.

After 7 days of "washout" period in which the drug supposedly was excreted, another blood sample was taken and all 18 subjects had zero amount of the drug in their blood samples. The experimenter then had the group of nine who took formula 1 take formula 2 and vice versa for the other group. This part of the experiment is called the "crossover" part of the design.

A model for the analysis of this experiment is

$$y_{ijk}=\mu+S_i+\delta_{(i)}+T_j+F_k+\epsilon_{(ijk)} \qquad (7)$$

$$i=1,2,\ldots,18 \qquad j=1,2 \qquad k=1,2$$

where y_{ijk} = amount of drug in the blood of ith subject after 8 hours given order j and formula k

μ = overall mean

S_i = effect of subject i

$\delta_{(i)}$ = restriction error on ith subject due to all observations on orders and formulas coming from ith subject

T_j = effect of jth time plus any effect due to restricting randomization at jth time

F_k = effect of kth formula

$\varepsilon_{(ijk)}$ = error, $NID(0, \sigma^2)$, estimated from the remaining effects assuming that all interactions are zero

The data from this experiment are given in Table 13. The corresponding ANOVA is Table 14.

To find the error with the most degrees of freedom from these data, we may test for time

$$H_0\colon \phi(T)=0$$

$$F_{1,16}=\frac{2.25}{20.62}<1$$

Hence accept H_0 at $\alpha>0.25$ and pool mean squares, which actually results in a *RCBD* where subjects act as blocks and formulas are treatments. The error mean square with 17 *df* is

$$\text{Error mean square}=\frac{(1)(2.25)+(16)(20.62)}{17}=19.54$$

Subjects are random and of no interest other than to provide the inference space. The test on formulas is

$$F_{1,17}=\frac{44.00}{19.54}=2.25$$

$$\text{Tabulated } F_{1,17}\begin{cases}(\alpha=.10)=3.03\\(\alpha=.25)=1.42\end{cases}$$

Hence the effect of formulas is not significant at $\alpha=.10$ level.

Take the same example and consider the layout of the experiment to be:

	Groups	
	1	2
	Subjects	Subjects
Time	1, 2, . . . , 9	10, . . . , 18
1	Formula 1	Formula 2
2	Formula 1	Formula 2

This design may be considered in such a way that the following model can be used:

$$y_{ijk}=\mu+G_i+S_{(i)j}+\delta_{(ij)}+T_k+GT_{ik}+ST_{(i)jk}+\epsilon_{(ijk)} \tag{8}$$

Table 15. ANOVA

Source	*df*
Groups G	1
Subjects in groups $S_{(i)j}$	16
$\delta_{(ij)}$	0
Time T_k	1
Formulas GT_{ik}	1
$ST_{(i)jk}$	16
$\varepsilon_{(ijk)}$	0

where y_{ijk}, μ = the same as for equation 7
G_i = effect of ith group of subjects
$S_{(i)j}$ = effect of jth subject in ith group
$\delta_{(ij)} = \delta_{(i)}$ of equation 7
$T_k = T_j$ of equation 7
GT_{ik} = effect of interaction of ith group by kth time and/or formulas (confounded with effect of formulas) equal to F_k of equation 7
$ST_{(i)jk} = \varepsilon_{(ijk)}$ of equation 7 or effect of interaction of ith group by kth time
$\varepsilon_{(ijk)}$ = error, $NID(0, \sigma^2)$ (not estimable in this model)

The ANOVA for the analysis of the data using equation 8 is given in Table 15.

One can see that this ANOVA using equation 8 explains the error $ST_{(i)jk}$ to be used to test formulas and the details of the workings of the design on formulas and time effects much better than the analysis from equation 7, the traditional approach. The amalgamation of the two designs, Latin square and repeated measures, becomes apparent in this presentation by showing that the interaction of groups by time is really represented by formulas (Latin square) and time by subjects within groups is the real error for testing formulas (repeated measures).

Now we are ready to expand on a more recent concept in design of these experiments. This type of design was described by Albert et al. (6). Consider an experiment in which three drugs, A, B, and C, are to be compared. All six sequences of A, B, and C may be considered when administering the three drugs to a given person. The minimum number of subjects one should consider in an experiment of this type is 12, two for each sequence.

If one measurement is taken for each subject–drug combination and a sufficient washout period is allowed between drugs, one possible layout of the experiment is that given in Table 16 (where subjects are assigned at random to the sequences). Another possible layout of the experiment is that

Table 16.

	Sequence 1 Subjects		2 Subjects		3 Subjects		4 Subjects		5 Subjects		6 Subjects	
	1	2	3	4	5	6	7	8	9	10	11	12
Time 1.	B	B	A	A	B	B	C	C	C	C	A	A
	Washout period →											
Time 2.	C	C	B	B	A	A	A	A	B	B	C	C
	Washout period →											
Time 3.	A	A	C	C	C	C	B	B	A	A	B	B

Table 17.

	Sequence 1 Subjects		2 Subjects		3 Subjects		4 Subjects		5 Subjects		6 Subjects	
Drugs	1	2	3	4	5	6	7	8	9	10	11	12
A	t_3	t_3	t_1	t_1	t_2	t_2	t_2	t_2	t_3	t_3	t_1	t_1
B	t_1	t_1	t_2	t_2	t_1	t_1	t_3	t_3	t_2	t_2	t_3	t_3
C	t_2	t_2	t_3	t_3	t_3	t_3	t_1	t_1	t_1	t_1	t_2	t_2

given in Table 17. To arrive at a satisfactory method of calculating the sums for the data from such an experiment, let us consider the model for the layout given in Table 16 and compare the model with the appropriate one for Table 17.

The model with the corresponding degrees of freedom *df* for analyzing the data from Table 16 is

$$df\text{: } 36 = 1 + 5 + 6 + 0 + 2 + 10 + 12 + 0$$

$$\text{Model: } y_{ijk} = \mu + Q_i + S_{(i)j} + \delta_{(ij)} + T_k + QT_{ik} + ST_{(i)jk} + \epsilon_{(ijk)} \tag{9}$$

where y_{ijk} = response from kth time, for subject j following sequence i (note nothing is associated with the drug)

μ = overall mean

Q_i = effect of ith sequence (fixed)

$S_{(i)j}$ = effect of jth subject (random) following ith sequence

$\delta_{(ij)}$ = restriction error due to times and drugs on same subject

T_k = effect of kth time (fixed) plus any effect due to restricting randomization at kth time

QT_{ik} = effect of interaction of ith sequence and kth time (includes drug effect) similar to GT_{ik} of equation 8 except that there are 2 *df* for drugs here with a total of 10 *df* for QT (hence there are 8 *df* remaining)

$ST_{(i)jk}$ = effect of interaction jth subject following ith sequence by kth time

$\epsilon_{(ijk)}$ = error associated with observation on jth subject following ith sequence at kth time; $NID(0, \sigma^2)$

It follows that the corresponding degrees of freedom and model for analyzing the data from an experiment with the layout given in Table 17 is

$$df\colon 36 = 1 + 5 + 6 + 0 + 2 + 10 + 12 + 0$$

$$\text{Model: } y_{ijk} = \mu + Q_i + S_{(i)j} + \delta_{(ij)} + D_k + QD_{ik} + SD_{(i)jk} + \epsilon_{(ijk)} \qquad (10)$$

where y_{ijk}, μ, Q_i, $S_{(i)j}$, $\delta_{(ij)}$, and $\epsilon_{(ijk)}$ are the same as in equation 9; D_k is the effect of the kth drug; QD_{ik} is the effect of the interaction of the ith sequence by the kth drug (embedded in this component is the effect of time with 2 *df*); and $SD_{(i)jk}$ is the effect of the interaction of the jth subject following the ith sequence by the kth drug.

Since the design can be interpreted as two Latin square designs (sequences 2, 1, and 4 make up one Latin square and sequences 6, 3, and 5 make up the other one), the terms in equations 9 and 10 may be broken up in a manner that allows one overall model. To show this, in equations 9 and 10 we need look only at the *within*-subject effects because the sequences and subjects are identical in the two equations. From equation 9, $T_k + QT_{ik} = D_k + QD_{ik}$ from equation 10. It follows that $ST_{(i)jk}$ of equation 9 = $SD_{(i)jk}$ of equation 10. Now, if D_k is removed from QT_{ik}, the remainder is exactly equal to the remainder from equation 10 of T_k is removed from QD_{ik}.

As a result of all the above, equation 11 and corresponding degrees of freedom *df* can depict a preferred model as follows:

$$df\colon 36 = 1 + 5 + 6 + 0 + 2 + 2 + 8 + 12 + 0$$

$$\text{Model: } y_{ijkl} = \mu + Q_i + S_{(i)j} + \delta_{(ij)} + T_k + D_l + R_{ikl} + n_{ijkl} + \varepsilon_{(ijkl)}$$

where y_{ijk}, μ, Q_i, $S_{(i)j}$, $\delta_{(i)}$, and T_k are defined as they are in equation 9; $D_l = D_k$ in equation 10; R_{ikl} is the effect of the remainder interaction of Q_i, T_k, and D_l (fixed and testable); η_{ijkl} represents the error for testing T_k, D_k, and R_{ikl}, composed of parts of interactions of $ST_{(i)jk}$ from equation 9 and/or $SD_{(i)jk}$ from equation 10; and $\varepsilon_{(ijkl)}$ is the same as $\varepsilon_{(ijk)}$ from equations 9 and 10.

To show how equation 11 can be evolved from data laid out be equations 9 and 10, the following examples are presented:

1. Layout for equation 9 is given in Table 18, where the letters A, B, and C indicate the drugs used.

a. SS sequences: $\dfrac{28^2+31^2+\cdots+24^2}{6}-\dfrac{(169)^2}{36}=17.80$

b. SS subjects in sequences: $\dfrac{(14-14)^2}{6}+\dfrac{(14-17)^2}{6}+\cdots+$

$\dfrac{(11-13)^2}{6}=11.83$

c. SS time: $\dfrac{52^2+56^2+61^2}{12}-\dfrac{(169)^2}{36}=3.39$

d. SS sequences × time (from Table 19):

SS subtotal: $\left[\dfrac{5^2+12^2+\cdots+7^2}{2}-\dfrac{(169)^2}{36}\right]=98.14$

SS sequences × times = SS subtotal − SS sequences − SS time = 98.14 − 17.80 − 3.39 = 76.95

e. SS subjects in sequences by time:

(1) SS in sequence 1 (subjects × time) (from Table 20):

$3^2+2^2+6^2+8^2+5^2+4^2-\dfrac{(28)^2}{6}-\dfrac{(14-14)^2}{6}-$

$\left[\dfrac{5^2+14^2+9^2}{2}-\dfrac{(28)^2}{6}\right]=3.00$

(2) SS sequence 2 (subjects × time)

$5^2+7^2+4^22^25^2+8^2-\dfrac{(31)^2}{6}-\dfrac{(14-17)^2}{6}-$

$\left[\dfrac{12^2+6^2+13^2}{2}-\dfrac{(31)^2}{6}\right]=7.00$

Table 18.

	Sequences 1		2		3		4		5		6		
	Subjects												
Time	1	2	3	4	5	6	7	8	9	10	11	12	Total
1	3 B	2	5 A	7	3 B	5	5 C	6	7 C	4	4 A	1	52
2	6 C	8	4 B	2	6 A	7	2 A	5	3 B	1	5 C	7	56
3	5 A	4	5 C	8	9 C	6	4 B	3	6 A	4	2 B	5	61
Total	14	14	14	17	18	18	11	14	16	9	11	13	169

Table 19[a].

	Sequences						
Time	1	2	3	4	5	6	Total
1	5	12	8	11	11	5	52
2	14	6	13	7	4	12	56
3	9	13	15	7	10	7	61
Total	28	31	36	25	25	24	169

[a]Taken from Table 18.

(3) SS sequence 3 (subjects × time) = 7.00

(4) SS sequence 4 (subjects × time) = 4.00

(5) SS sequence 5 (subjects × time) = 0.333

(6) SS sequence 6 (subjects × time) = 10.333

SS subjects in sequence by time = 3.00 + 7.00 + 7.00 + 4.00 + 0.333 + 10.333 = 31.67. From all these calculations, one obtains Table 21.

2. Layout for equation 10 is given in Table 22, which is the data table from the design given in Table 17. The sums of squares for sequence, subjects in sequence, time, drugs, and (subjects by time) in sequence, which may be called (subjects by drugs) in sequence, are the same. To show the calculations of the sums of squares when drugs replace time, one may set up Table 22.

The product $Q \times T$ in Table 21 is really a mixture of many sources of variation because of the Latin square peculiarities of this design [refer to

Table 20[a].

Time	Subjects 1	2	Total
1	3	2	5
2	6	8	14
3	5	4	9
Total	14	14	28

[a]Taken from Table 18.

Table 21. ANOVA Using Equation 9

Source	*df*	SS	MS
Sequence Q	5	17.80	3.56
Subjects in sequence S	6	11.83	1.97
δ	0	—	—
Time T	2	3.39	1.70
$Q \times T$	10	76.95	—
Drugs	2	63.39	31.70
Remainder ($Q \times T$)	8	13.56	1.70
$S \times T$	12	31.67	2.64
	35	141.64	

Table 22.

	Sequence 1		2		3		4		5		6		
Drugs	Subjects 1	2	3	4	5	6	7	8	9	10	11	12	Total
A	5	4	5	7	6	7	2	5	6	4	4	1	56
B	3	2	4	2	3	5	4	3	3	1	2	5	37
C	6	8	5	8	9	6	5	6	7	4	5	7	76
Total	14	14	14	17	18	18	11	14	16	9	11	13	169

Table 23.

Drug	Sequence 1	2	3	4	5	6	Total
A	9	12	13	7	10	5	56
B	5	6	8	7	4	7	37
C	14	13	15	11	11	12	76
Total	28	31	36	25	25	24	169

Table 24. ANOVA Using Equation 10

Source	*df*	SS	MS
Sequence Q	5	17.80	3.56
Subjects in sequence S	6	11.83	1.97
δ	0	0	—
Drugs D	2	63.39	31.70
$Q \times D$	10	16.95	—
Time	2	3.39	1.70
Remainder $Q \times D$	8	13.56	1.70
$S \times D$	12	31.67	2.64
	35	141.64	

Table 25. ANOVA (Preferred)

Source	*df*	SS	MS
Sequence Q	5	17.80	3.56
Subjects in sequence S	6	11.83	1.97
δ	0	—	
Time T	2	3.39	1.70
Drugs D	2	63.39	31.70[a]
Remainder interaction	8	13.56	1.70
Error	12	31.67	2.64
	35	141.64	

[a]Significant at the .01 probability level.

Table 8.1.3, p. 215 of Anderson and McLean (1)], but the one source of interest is drugs (refer to Table 16 for the original design of the experiment and to Table 18 for the data arrangement associated with drugs A, B, and C):

$$\text{SS drugs (Table 21)} = \frac{(\Sigma A)^2 + (\Sigma B)^2 + (\Sigma C)^2}{12} - \frac{(\Sigma \text{ all})^2}{36}$$

$$= \frac{56^2 + 37^2 + 76^2}{12} - \frac{(169)^2}{36} = 63.39$$

SS sequence × drugs (Table 23) = SS subtotal − SS sequence − SS drugs = 98.14 − 17.80 − 63.39 = 16.95

The analysis of variance for this new arrangement of the responses is given in Table 24. The product $Q \times D$ in Table 24 is really a mixture of many sources of variation because of the Latin square peculiarities of this design. In fact, after removing time from this source, the remainder has the same SS as for the remainder ($Q \times T$) in Table 21. This remainder has $D \times T$, $Q \times T$, $Q \times D$, $Q \times T \times D$ pieces of interactions. The product $S \times D$ is also a mixture of $S \times D$, $S \times T$, and $S \times D \times T$ because of the Latin square arrangement.

It is seen that Tables 21 and Table 24 give the same analysis. The preferred way to write the ANOVA is given in Table 25.

In general, for this type problem one should use equation 11, which will lead to the correct analysis as demonstrated in Table 25. The results of Table 25 could be further analyzed by using an accepted multiple comparison test on the drug means.

If the number of sequences is too large for the experimenter to run, a balanced incomplete block design (BIBD) may be used (7). Two other approaches to evaluate bioequivalence are (a) to use confidence bands on differences of means (8) and (b) to use a Bayesian method (13). Mandallaz and Mau (14) compare different methods for decision making in bioequivalence evaluation. Kirkwood (15) and Westlake (16) also present cases for and against the bioequivalence method.

2.3 Other Designs

Biological research personnel should also be aware of designs of experiments that may be used when many factors must be evaluated simultaneously. Only factors with two levels are described here to give the reader a synopsis of the techniques. A detailed coverage of designs with different number of levels of the factors and with more than two equal number of levels of factors is given in Box et al. (9).

For demonstration purposes only, consider an experiment in which there are two factors (a, b) each at two levels (0, 1), where 0 represents the lower level and 1 represents the upper level of each factor. One possible layout for this completely randomized design is

		b 0	1
a	0	00 or (1)	01 or b
	1	10 or a	11 or ab

which allows the reader to use two notations to describe the factorial treatment combinations. In this case 00, 01, 10, and 11 represent the treatment combinations ab as

00 = low level of a, low level of b
01 = low level of a, high level of b
10 = high level of a, low level of b
11 = high level of a, high level of b

The second notation (1), b, a, ab, defines the treatment combinations in the same order identically as the other notation. Note that this notation, however, uses (1) when all factors are at the low level; the letter is missing when the low level of one factor is used in the treatment combination, and the letter is present when the high level of the factor is present.

The ANOVA of the data from such an experiment is shown in Table 26.

The usual method for calculating sums of squares is

$$\text{SSA} = \frac{(a+b)^2 + [(1)+b]^2}{2} - \frac{[a+ab+(1)+b]^2}{4}$$

which is identically equal to

$$\frac{[a+ab-(1)-b]^2}{4}$$

which is a much more efficient procedure.

It follows that SSB and SSAB may be calculated directly as

$$\text{SSB} = \frac{[b+ab-(1)-a]^2}{4},$$

$$\text{SSAB} = \frac{[(1)+ab-a-b]^2}{4}.$$

Table 26. ANOVA of 2×2

Source	*df*
A	1
B	1
AB	1
	3

Table 27. Treatment Combinations and Effects in 2^2

	Treatment Combination			
Effect	(1)	*a*	*b*	*ab*
A	−	+	−	+
B	−	−	+	+
AB	+	−	−	+
Mean	+	+	+	+

This idea of using plus and minus signs on the yields comes from expecting the high levels of the factors to have the higher yields. It does not matter, however, whether the yields actually reverse because the SS will still account for the effects of the treatments in all cases and all estimates of the treatment effect will have the correct sign. The nicety of this method of obtaining SS is that interactions may be calculated directly from the data, not subtracting the main effects (ME) SS from the subtotal SS to obtain the two-factor interaction (2 FI) SS as is the usual practice. It must be understood, however, that this differencing process is applicable only for two-leveled factorials. Whenever the number of levels is 3 or larger, one must resort to the usual procedure to find the SS.

Table 27 summarizes the plus, minus notation. Note that the mean uses all pluses and, of course, would require a division of the total yield by 4 here. Also note that *AB* signs are obtained by multiplying the signs of *A* by those of *B* for each column or treatment combination. This methodology generalizes for any number of factors if all have two levels.

The most important value of this notation is to allow easy investigation of experiments with several factors in which the number of treatment combinations is too large to be run under one condition. This situation demands blocks of treatment combinations that do not contain all the combinations for the experiment or "incomplete" blocks. Also, if the number of factors is large enough and certain higher factor interactions can be assumed zero, fewer than all the treatment combinations may be run and still allow a very good experiment. This type of design is called a "fractional factorial" design.

For demonstration purposes, let us show the incomplete block and fractional factorial concepts using 2^3 factorial. If only four of the eight treatment combinations can be run under homogeneous environmental conditions, there must be two blocks of four treatment combinations in each block. The experimenter must recognize that for this condition, the *df* for blocks must be confounded with one of the seven main effects or interactions from the factorial because each of *A*, *B*, *AB*, *C*, *AC*, *BC*, and *ABC* has 1 *df* and adds to the total of 7 *df*. In other words, there must be a loss of information if fewer than all treatment combinations are run at one time or place.

The experimenter must now decide which of the 7 *df* to lose. Since *ABC* should be of least interest, let us confound *ABC* with blocks. Table 28 shows the plus, minus notation one may use to select the correct treatment combination for each block when *ABC* is confounded with blocks. To obtain the SS for *ABC*, one subtracts the four "minus" treatment combination yields from the four "plus" treatment combination yields, squares that difference, and divides by 8. If blocks are to be confounded with *ABC*, that is, if the exact information on *ABC* is to be mixed with that of blocks, the SS for blocks will be calculated identically to that of *ABC*. It follows that the makeup of one block is the minuses of *ABC* and the pluses of *ABC* must be in the other block. Hence from Table 28 one can construct the two blocks to be run in the experiment as:

Blocks

1	2
Minus	Plus
(1)	*a*
ab	*b*
ac	*c*
bc	*abc*

The ANOVA for the analysis of the data from this experiment is given in Table 29. Note that there is no error for testing the MEs and 2 FIs in this case. This is why this experiment should be considered a demonstration of the technique.

Of course, if a few treatment combinations (at least one) were repeated in each block, a few degrees of freedom could be available for an error estimate.

Table 28. Treatment Combinations and Effects in 2^3

Effects	(1)	*a*	*b*	*ab*	*c*	*ac*	*bc*	*abc*
A	−	+	−	+	−	+	−	+
B	−	−	+	+	−	−	+	+
C	−	−	−	−	+	+	+	+
ABC (multiply)	−	+	+	−	+	−	−	+

Table 29. ANOVA (2^3 in 2 Blocks of 4, *ABC* Confounded)

Source	*df*
Blocks and/or *ABC*	1
δ	0
A	1
B	1
AB	1
C	1
AC	1
BC	1
	7

Using this same 2^3 experiment for demonstration purposes, one can show how a fractional factorial experiment can be constructed. If block 2, $\boxed{a, b, c, abc}$, is used, only four treatment combinations instead of eight would make up a one-half replicate or fractional factorial. To find out what effects may be estimated from only those four treatment combinations, Table 30 is set up.

Note that the mean $= ABC$, $A = BC$, $B = AC$, and $C = AB$. These equal effects may be indicated as aliases or completely confounded with each other. Furthermore, the mean may be called I or identity, and one has $I = ABC$. If we multiply each side of the equality by A, we obtain $A = A^2BC$, but the levels of the factors are only 0 or 1 and any even number becomes 0 or any odd number becomes 1 (modulo 2). Hence $A^2 = A^0 = 1$ and $A^2BC = BC$, or $A = BC$. Similarly, the ANOVA for the one-half fractional factorial of 2^3, $B = AB^2C = AC$ and $C = ABC^2 = AB$, is given in Table 31.

It must be understood that this is *not* a good design and is given here to demonstrate a methodology for handling fractional factorials.

A good example of a fractional factorial is a one-fourth replicate of a 2^9,

Table 30. Treatment Combinations and Effects for One-Half Replicate of 2^3

	Treatment Combinations			
Effects	*a*	*b*	*c*	*abc*
A	+	−	−	+
B	−	+	−	+
AB	−	−	+	+
C	−	−	+	+
AC	−	+	−	+
BC	+	−	−	+
ABC	+	+	+	+
Mean	+	+	+	+

Table 31. ANOVA (One-Half Replicate of 2^3

Source	*df*
A and/or *BC*	1
B and/or *AC*	1
C and/or *AB*	1
	3

where the factors are *a*, *b*, *c*, *d*, *e*, *f*, *g*, *h*, and *j*. If three-factor and higher interactions are zero, the effects can be identified as

$$I = ABCDEF = DEFGHJ = ABCGHJ$$
$$A = BCDEF = ADEFGHJ = BCHJ$$
$$AB = CDEF = ABDEFGHJ = CGHJ$$
$$ABC = DEF = ABCDEFGHJ = GHJ$$

Hence, in general, MEs are confounded only with 5 FI and higher: 2 FIs are confounded with 4 FIs and higher, and 3 FIs (assumed zero) are confounded with other 3 FIs and higher. This allows the ANOVA shown in Table 32.

Details of fractional factorials may be found in Anderson and McLean (1). A list of almost all usable 2^n fractionals is included in reference 10.

Another design that is occasionally of interest to bioavailability research

Table 32. ANOVA (One-Fourth Replicate of 2^9)

Source	*df*
ME	9
2 FI	$\binom{9}{2}=36$
(Residual) error	82
	127

Table 33.

Treatment Combination	Factors *A*	*B*	*C*
1	10	40	50
2	12	40	48
3	10	35	55
4	12	35	53

people is the *composite* design. This design allows estimation of curvature in experiments that have many factors, whereas the fractional factorial of 2^n designs does not. The composite design is built around the factorial (or fractional), and center points are used on all the faces of the hypercube from the factorial plus one point in the center of the entire design.

If there are k factors, there are only 2^k+2k+1 treatment combinations needed for the whole experiment. This is a tremendous savings relative to 3^k factorial (the smallest complete factorial allowing curvature estimation) when $k \geqslant 4$. For example, if $k=5$, then $2^5+2.5+1=43$, whereas $3^5=243$. Both of these designs allow estimates of all linear and quadratic ME plus the linear × linear 2 FIs. A thorough coverage of this design is given in Chapter 13 of Anderson and McLean (1).

One final type of experimentation that is encountered in drug biological studies is that called *mixture experiments*. The basic indicator of this type of experiment is the fact that all factors' levels must add to a constant. The usual constant is 100%, and the factor levels are certain percentages of the total. An illustration of a few treatment combinations for an experiment involving factors *A*, *B*, and *C* and presented in Table 33 (the levels of *A*, *B*, and C are percentages). Note that to lay out a 2×2 factorial experiment involving factors A and B, one must adjust the level of C has to make up the total composition to 100%.

Designs for this type of experiment are quite involved and are not included here. One type of design that is good when the number of factors is no greater than 5 is the extreme vertices design, the details of which are given in Chapter 13 of Anderson and McLean (1). A good review of the existing literature on mixture experiments is given in Cornell (11).

REFERENCES

1. V. L. Anderson and R. A. McLean. *Design of Experiments: A Realistic Approach.* Marcel Dekker, New York, 1974.
2. R. A. Fisher. *The Design of Experiments*, 7th ed., Hafner, New York, 1960.
3. S. W. Greenhouse and S. Geisser. On methods in the analysis of profile data. *Psychometrika* **24**: 95 (1959).
4. B. J. Winer. *Statistical Principles in Experimental Design*, 2nd ed., McGraw-Hill, New York, 1971.
5. J. E. Grizzle. The two-period change-over design and its use in clinical trials. *Biometrics* **21**: 467 (1965).
6. K. S. Albert, S. W. Brown, Jr., K. A. DeSante, A. R. DiSanto, R. D. Stewart, and T. T. Chen. Double Latin square study to determine variability and relative bioavailability of methylprednisolone. *J. Pharm. Sci.* **68**(10): 1312 (1979).
7. W. J. Westlake. The use of balanced incomplete block designs in comparative bioavailability trials. *Biometrics* **30**: 319 (1974).
8. W. J. Westlake. Statistical aspects of comparative bioavailability trials. *Biometrics* **35**: 273 (1979).
9. G. E. P. Box, W. G. Hunter, and J. S. Hunter. *Statistics for Experimenters*, Wiley, New York, 1978.
10. *Fractional Factorial Experiment Designs for Factors at Two Levels.* Statistical Engineering Laboratory of the National Bureau of Standards Applied Mathematics, Series 48, 1957.
11. J. A. Cornell. Experiments with mixtures: An update and bibliography. *Technometrics* **21**(1): 95 (1979).
12. J. W. L. Cole and J. E. Grizzle. Applications of multivariate analysis of variance to repeated measurements. *Biometrics* **22**(4): 810 (1966).
13. M. R. Selwyn, A. P. Dempster, and N. R. Hall. A Bayesian approach to bioequivalence for a 2×2 changeover design. *Biometrics* **37**(1): 11 (1981).
14. D. Mandallaz and J. Mau. Comparison of different methods for decision making in bioequivalence assessment. *Biometrics* **37**(2): 213 (1981).
15. T. B. L. Kirkwood. Bioequivalence testing—a need to rethink. *Biometrics* **37** (3): 589 (1981).
16. W. J. Westlake. Response (to Kirkwood Sept. 1981 Note). *Biometrics* **37**(3): 591 (1981).

CHAPTER 9

Marketing in a Generic Environment

JOHN P. MATHEU

Vice-President
Pfizer Pharmaceuticals
Pfizer, Inc.
New York, New York

CONTENTS

Rarely, if ever, has a pharmaceutical marketer faced as many changes as are now occurring in the marketplace. Changes in government policies, consumer education, and technologies as well as changes in the influence and relationships among members of the health care team are not new; however, they have become more intensified in recent years. And now, a new change is challenging major manufacturers of prescription drugs—in fact, several larger manufacturers have already been impacted whereas others will be by the end of the decade.

By 1990 over 100 of the leading dollar volume prescription drugs will have lost their patent protection. Approximately 60 have reached this position already with the balance due to expire during the next 7 years. Of the remaining 40 products there are 19, shown in Table 1, with sales in 1981 ranging from $70 million to $325 million. A more generalized breakdown of single source drugs whose patents expire in the 1980s can be seen in Table 2. Their availability to other manufacturers and distributors will only serve to stimulate the growth of the generic segment of the market.

1. MARKET PROFILE

The United States pharmaceutical market consists of prescription drugs and over-the-counter (OTC) products for therapeutic use by humans. Prescription drugs fall under three "labels"—the brand name or trademark assigned by the manufacturer, the generic name assigned to the compound by the government, and the chemical designation of the drug. Vibramycin, an antibiotic developed and marketed by Pfizer, is an example of this system:

Brand name	Vibramycin
Generic name	Doxycycline
Chemical designation	α-6-Deoxy-5-oxytetracycline

Prescription drugs can be single-source or multisource. A single-source drug is usually patent protected and available from one manufacturer, whereas a multisource drug is not under patent and is available from two or more manufacturers and is usually classified as generic. A generic drug can carry a brand name or can be nonbranded. Currently, branded and nonbranded generics and, in fact, all nonpatented drugs competing in the marketplace account for approximately 40% or $5.4 billion of 1981 estimated total sales of $13.5 billion at manufacturer's prices. With the market's annual growth projected at 14% through 1989, the industry would approximate $33.3 billion in total sales, of which $14.2 billion (40%) would be generated by nonpatented products. This projection assumes adjustment for inflation

Table 1. Top-Selling Drugs with Patents Due to Expire in the Next Few Years

1981 Rank	Product Launched	Manufacturer	1981 Sales (in Million $)	Therapeutic Class	Patent Expires
1	Tagamet 1977	Smith Kline	325	Antispasmodic; antisecretory	1993
2	Inderal 1957	Ayerst	225	Beta blocker	1984
3	Valium 1966	Roche	200	Ataractics	1985
4	Motrin 1974	Upjohn	190	Antiarthritic	1985
7	Keflex 1971	Lilly	150	Antibiotic	1984
8	Aldomet 1963	MS&D	140	Antihypertensive	1984
11	Clinoril 1978	MS&D	110	Antiarthritic	1989
12	Naprosyn 1976	Syntex	100	Antiarthritic	1989
13	Mandol 1978	Lilly	95	Antibiotic	1989
14	Mefoxin 1978	MS&D	90	Antibiotic	1990
16	Cleocin 1970	Upjohn	80	Antibiotic	1987
17	Adriamycin 1974	Adria	75	Anticancer	1988
18	Lopressor 1978	Ciba-Geigy	70	Beta blocker	1989
19	Diabinese 1958	Pfizer	70	Antidiabetic	1984

Table 2. Number of Single-Source Drugs Whose Patents Expire in the 1980s

Patent Expires	Number of Drugs	Estimated 1981 Sales at Manufacturing Level (in Million $)
1980	2	210
1981	7	300
1982	5	150
1983	4	132
1984	8	820
1985	6	450
1986	2	46
1987	2	60
1988	2	135
1989	4	340
	42	2643

in drug prices, bringing the real growth to about 8%. Also assumed are new product introductions and patent expirations.

According to a study by SRI International, the major prescription drug categories in 1981 were antibiotics, central nervous system, and cardiovascular—in that order, whereas in 1989 drugs for treatment of cardiovascular disease should be first followed by the central nervous system category and then by (in third position) the neoplastic, endocrine–metabolic agents.

2. PRESCRIPTION VOLUME

The April 1982 issue of *Pharmacy Times* reports that during 1981 the total number of prescriptions—new and refills—were 3.8% over 1980 levels, with branded drug prescriptions increasing 2.8% and generically written prescriptions advancing 10.8%. Since 1966 generically written new prescriptions have risen from 29.7 million (6.4%) of the total to 111.1 million (14.7%) and, for the first time, according to data compiled by IMS America, nine generic drugs appear among the top 50 new and refill prescribed products. The ranking of these drugs and the number of new prescriptions is given in Table 3. Another and final comparison of prescription volume in 1981 to 1980 is seen in the number of branded and generic prescriptions filled at the retail pharmacy level (Table 4). The significant shift in the refill category (an increase of 28.4% for generics compared to 4.9% for branded drugs) more than likely is a reflection of the pharmacists making decisions on the manufacturers' products that they dispense. On the other hand, the data reflect the point that pharmacists dispense new prescriptions as written.

Table 3. Generic Drugs in Top 50 New and Refill Prescribed Products

Rank	Generic Drug	Number of New Prescriptions (in Millions)
8	Ampicillin	15.6
10	Tetracycline	10.7
11	Penicillin VK	12.6
16	Amoxicillin	11.5
17	Hydrochlorothiazide	4.0
21	Erythromycin	9.1
33	Prednisone	5.3
39	Phenobarbital	2.6
47	Thyroid	1.7

Table 4. Comparison of Number of Branded and Generic Prescriptions Filled in 1980–1981

Category	Number of Prescriptions (in Millions)		Percentage
	1981	1980	1981 vs. 1980
New prescriptions	756	750	+0.8
Branded	645	640	+0.9
Generic	111	110	+0.6
Refills	691	644	+7.3
Branded	608	580	+4.9
Generic	83	64	+28.4
Total prescriptions	1447	1394	+3.8
Branded	1254	1220	+2.8
Generic	194	175	+10.8

3. FACTORS AFFECTING THE MARKET

A number of key factors are seen as stimulants to the growth of generic drug sales and market share:

1. There are 49 states (Indiana is the exception) with some form of substitution law. Even though there are variations in state laws resulting in confusion among pharmacists, physicians, and patients, the enactment of these laws places the pharmacist in a decision-making position. Implicit to the development is a weakening of the physician's position.

2. State laws are becoming more stringent, mandating substitution and making prohibition of substitution by physicians more difficult. Two states with strong laws are New York and Florida. In Florida a pharmacist is required to substitute a generic equivalent unless the physician specifically states that no substitution be made. In New York, pharmacists have no alternative—they must fill the prescription with a generic equivalent if it is less expensive, is available, and is approved by the state. Other states such as Kentucky, New Jersey, and California also have enacted strong substitution laws.

3. Consumer awareness and confidence in generic drugs has grown during the past several years and will continue to grow. In support of this change, the government has endorsed generics and, with the help of consumer groups,

media attention, the support of generics by opinion leaders, and the featuring of generics by major drug chains, has succeeded in educating the consumer to their benefits.

4. Several major pharmaceutical companies have entered the generic market with full lines, resulting in more marketing power for their products. Branded generics are manufactured and/or distributed by such companies as Smith, Kline and Beckmann, Dista (Lilly), Pfipharmecs (Pfizer), Wyeth, and Robins. The leading company of nonbranded generics among major manufacturers is Lederle, followed by Parke-Davis and Squibb. Additionally, small non-research-oriented manufacturers and many distributors of non-branded drugs have entered the market.

5. With the expiration of patents currently protecting single-source drugs, the market has a potential expansion of more than $2.6 billion. New and innovative dosage form techniques offer manufacturers of generic products an opportunity to maintain a strong position in the marketplace. Of course, this would be softened with the introduction of significant new single-source drugs.

Selected negative factors that could impact the future growth of generic drugs include the following:

1. It is an established fact that generic competition breeds price erosion. Examples of this are seen in the antibiotic market where ampicillin, amoxicillin, and penicillin VK have been subjected to price erosion of up to 80% from the original price. A paradoxical fallout of this erosion is the fact that unit volume of these drugs is up whereas dollar volume is down.

2. A marketing effort by manufacturers to curtail generic prescribing and substitution by pharmacists has been growing with major firms like Roche and Hoechst. The use of field representatives to promote brand name prescribing employing such tactics as preprinted prescription forms, special pricing to retailers, and the use of trade advertising have had limited success. At best, they are a holding action against generic prescribing and substitution.

3. The introduction of new single-source drugs, under patent protection, could be a deterrent to the growth of generics. These new drugs—especially those that compete directly with older, non-patent-protected products—may be superior in effectiveness and safety and could take market share from older drugs.

4. Recently there has been a decline in physician promotional activity following the expiration of a drug patent. Initially this phenomenon leads to an increase in the number of manufacturers and distributors of the drug. Eventually, however, because of the reduction in promotional activity by the

original manufacturer, the use of the drug declines to the point where it is no longer a major factor. Eventually generic manufacturers and distributors delete the drug from their line.

Weighing the assumptions that support the growth of generics against those pointing to a decline, it seems more likely that the generic market growth will become a reality. As previously noted, the market share captured by generics before the end of the 1980s could approximate 40%. This means that generic drugs would account for $12.0 billion. *Big volume*? Certainly it is! Will it be profitable? The answer depends on strategies established by each company doing business in a highly competitive commodity market. At this time, the generic drug business is characterized by lack of product differentiation, price competition, and significant pressure on profit margins, all of which could and probably will change.

4. DISTRIBUTION OF GENERIC DRUGS

Most large manufacturers tend to follow their traditional distribution policy. The smaller companies usually distribute through the wholesaler or by mail order utilizing catalog mailings to retail pharmacies and dispensing physicians. The sale of generic drugs has been and will probably continue to be concentrated in the retail class of trade as seen in Table 5. Since wholesale and retail pharmacy purchases account for the bulk of the volume and since selling activity to the other classes of trade is primarily the function of a bidding process, the focus will be on the retail pharmacy, regardless of whether the pharmacist purchases direct or from a wholesaler. Since the retail pharmacy is the primary source of business for wholesalers, these two classes of trade can be viewed as one. The retail pharmacy, branded and nonbranded generic market, accounted for $3.59 billion in 1981 (Table 6).

The market is dominated by branded drugs because even though the patent has expired on a particular drug, physicians have a tendency to continue prescribing by brand name. Even if the prescription is written generically, the pharmacist will in most cases fill the prescription with a branded product.

Companies involved in the complex generic market often play different roles. They are simultaneously customers, suppliers, and competitors. They can be grouped into three areas of activity: (1) manufacturers; (2) manufacturers and distributors; and (3) distributors. These interrelationships are illustrated in Table 7.

Smith, Kline manufactures and distributes several branded generics as well as distributing other branded generics manufactured by Mylan. Mylan

Table 5. Class of Trade of Generic Sales During 1981

1981 Generic Sales

Class of Trade	Percentage (%)	Amount ($Billion)
Wholesalers	53.7	2.53
Pharmacies	14.9	1.06
Private hospitals	14.9	0.70
City, county, and state hospitals	4.0	0.19
Federal hospitals	2.3	0.11
Other federal government	1.4	0.07
Physicians	1.2	0.06
	100.0%	4.72[a]

[a]$4.72 billion represents 35.0% of the total ethical pharmaceutical market.

Table 6. Retail Pharmacy Generic Market

	Amount ($Billion)	Percentage (%)
Nonbranded	0.255	7.1
Branded	3.335	92.9
	3.590	100.0

is involved in manufacturing only and then selling its generic products to distributors under a brand name or as a nonbranded drug.

Most distributors of nonbranded generics to the retail trade are small, marginal firms with sales in the $1–$2 million range. However, there are several, such as Purepac, with sales above that level. The branded market is dominated by major manufacturers. These major companies are becoming increasingly active, often in conjunction with third-party tollers in the development of comparatively extensive product lines along with the support needed to promote them. There is little question that major drug producers are concerned as an increasing number of their brand name products become vulnerable to generic competition.

Lederle Laboratories probably has the most extensive nonbranded line among major companies with approximately 100 products, whereas Purepac, among the smaller companies, offers the most complete nonbranded line and manufactures most of its own products.

Table 7. Interrelationships Between the Three Areas of Activity in the Generic Market

Manufacturer	Brand	Nonbranded	Manufacturers and Distributors	Distributors
Purepac		×	×	×
Mylan		×		
Pfizer	×		×	
Abbott	×		×	
Lederle	×	×	×	×
Lilly	×		×	
Bolar		×		
Barr		×		
Wolins				×
Vanguard				×
Robins				×
Smith, Kline	×	×	×	×

Table 8. Differences Between Single-Source Drug and Generic Drug Manufacture

Entry Parameters	Single-Source Drug	Generic Drug
Preentry		
research and development	$40,000,000	$300,000
Marketing expertise	Superior	Minimal
Competitive activity	Minimal	Substantial
Level of risk	Substantial	Minimal
Months to FDA approval	60–120	12–24
Other considerations		
Clinical studies	Substantial	Minimal, if any
Bulk material source	Required	Not required
Finished goods production	Required	Not required
Bioavailability	Not required	Required
Promotional costs	Substantial	Minimal

Among the nonbranded manufacturers, Mylan makes finished dosage forms for most distributors (listed in Table 7), plus several others (not listed). They also supply branded products to major companies. Some nonbranded companies are strictly distributors such as Wolins and Vanguard. Unlike major companies in the industry, nonbranded generic manufacturers do very little research and development of drugs. They generally do a minimum amount of testing to obtain bioavailability data to obtain FDA approval. New products, at lower prices, are added to their line by copying existing products made by major companies or other generic manufacturers. This is an industry with easy entry. Only a small amount of resources is required before one can become established as a supplier with someone manufacturing the drug. Conversely, considerably more is necessary before one can become a manufacturer of generic drugs. It seems appropriate to show the entry parameters for a single-source drug and a generic drug. The differences are obviously significant and revealing (Table 8).

5. INDUSTRY STRATEGIES

As previously noted, nonbranded generics account for a relatively small portion of the current generic market, and as major manufacturers enter the market, the small firms will find it difficult to survive. The greater resources of the major manufacturers could drive them out of business. On the other hand, the longer the generic companies have to cement their new marketing gains (e.g., Purepac and Key Pharmaceuticals), the more difficult it will be to upset them. And it is important to understand that nonbranded generic manufacturers have a clear advantage in production cost efficiencies and lower overheads. At Purepac, for example, $26 million in annual sales is the result of an effort by a six-person sales force and a headquarters team of six people. To support their branded line, major firms are employing the old strategy of trying to build a better mousetrap. Some are succeeding and a typical example is the effort Abbott made in protecting its erythromycin franchise. The company actually broadened its sales base when the patent expired in 1976 by introducing a variety of dosage forms that focus on specific segments in the hospital market as well as in physician's private practice. Other firms are *repackaging* their brand name products for easier use. Some are *reformulating* to reach new markets. Some are utilizing large field forces to sell the retail pharmacist while detailing single-source products to the physician. And then there is the effort to sell the value of being the original developer of the product and to convey the company's quality control and research orientation.

Other advantages stressed to the pharmacist in the promotion of branded generics include product liability insurance and a liberal return goods policy, including out-dated products and partial bottles. The availability, the service, and the reliability of a firm are important to many customers and are, therefore, stressed accordingly in promotional programs as well as service items for the pharmacist (e.g., bioequivalency data, instruction courses, abbreviated package insert information for consumers). And some companies are utilizing prescription product cooperative advertising, especially with chains. The "hard sell" to the pharmacist includes an offer of the best price (negotiable), quantity discounts, extended dating terms from 30 extra days up to 240 days on reorders as well as the initial order (that's 7 months working on the manufacturers money), semiannual or annual rebates ranging as high as 12% based on purchases, special 30–60-day deals involving two free packages with the purchase of 10 or one with 11, feature pricing or lost leader pricing to sell a "package deal," and on and on and on.

When competing in the generic market place, there is one inescapable fact of life—it is the same fact that dominates all commodity markets, and you can't get away from it—price is the bottom line in the decision-making process of retail customers. Sure, there are exceptions, but these are few and far between. It is hoped that this will change through innovative product and marketing strategies.

The price of the first generic product entry following patent expiration is usually established at 25–30% below the single-source drug price. As subsequent generic products enter the market, the price continues to fall to levels as low as 60–70% below that of the original product. Gross profit margins drop proportionately. The vast majority of pharmacists look for the best product at the best price. They much prefer to buy a major manufacturer's product, and to this end many retail pharmacists and chain store buyers "play" one manufacturer's representative against others to drive the price down. They often succeed. They become the only winner, whereas the manufacturers become the losers because their bottom line seldom shows any profit. Every decline in price reduces an already slim profit even more.

6. LOOKING TO THE FUTURE

A recent study by SRI International characterizes the decade of the 1980s as the "dosage-form rejuvenation decade," because of the veritable explosion of commercial, scientific, and professional interest in the development and use of different dose–form delivery systems. It is almost as though the pharmaceutical industry has rediscovered what are essentially new packaging methods. This innovation has emerged slowly during the past few years and has been highlighted by such development as (1) significant scientific advances and a better understanding of what is really going on in the human body, (2) the emergence of companies such as Alza Corporation, Key Pharmaceuticals, and KV Pharmaceuticals and their development of innovative drug delivery systems that optimize therapeutic response with the least amount of the drug over a long period of time with a minimum of side effects and patient inconvenience, (3) new delivery systems that represent an extension of the potential life cycle of a single-source drug, thus protecting the franchise of the original manufacturer. Obviously, these innovations represent the opportunity to reestablish generic drugs to a position of importance in the physician's armamentarium and patient acceptance. New and innovative drug delivery systems have a bright future across a wide range of therapeutic agents in the generic market. To bolster the quality image and capability of smaller manufacturers of generics, the former vice-president of medical affairs for Parke-Davis, Dr. Arthur D. Flanagan, has formed The Institute for Generic Drugs (IGD). In effect, the IGD will serve as the medical affairs department for those generic manufacturers who do not have one. It will provide independent professional services so that "members'" products receive the confidence of prescriber, seller, and user. It seems that Dr. Flanagan's goal is to change the perception that brand name drugs of larger manufacturers are seen as more desirable, often for reasons that can't be considered truly relevant. The organization is viewed as having great possibilities.

To build a dominant position in the generic marketplace, there are four key steps for a manufacturer to consider:

1. Select products:
   a. Where patents have recently expired or are due to expire in the 1980s and that have a high probability for introduction on the day the patent expires
   b. Where market size exceeds $12 million
   c. That are used in the treatment of chronic disorders
   d. That have a high probability for substitution
   e. That capitalize on the Company's image in a particular field
   f. That require minimal "selling" activity to the medical community

2. Become a basic manufacturer of the product by:
   a. Becoming a contract manufacturer to other companies
   b. Ensuring the availability of the product for itself
   c. Controlling the price
   d. Maximizing return on investment
   e. Developing new dosage forms and/or delivery systems

3. Capitalize on the Company's distribution system to establish dominant market share. Distribution is a major factor in establishing position on the pharmacist's shelf, particularly when introducing a product that has just gone off patent.

4. Develop unique promotional programs to build product preference at the retail pharmacy level.

As noted, the pharmaceutical market is in a state of great change. From the mid-1940s through most of the 1950s the market evolved from a generic product profile to a single-source profile as a result of substantial investments in research and development by major manufacturers. The industry enjoyed a relatively high degree of freedom in the introduction of new drugs, varieties of dosage forms and package sizes during the late 1950s, and for most of the 1960s. During the 1970s, however, a combination of restraining forces appeared and impacted the market negatively. FDA regulatory controls, inflation, pricing controls, and a slowdown in the introduction of new single-source drugs were major in their impact. The demand for generic drugs has grown substantially in recent years with the effort of government to educate the physician and public on the quality and low cost of generics being successful. Furthermore, socioeconomic conditions have all but forced the consumer to seek out the lowest-priced generic products. With patent expirations adding to the situation, the drug industry was faced with major problems and the need to change was clear.

For those companies with few, if any, single-source products coming out of research, the signal should be clear—they will probably enter the generic market with innovative marketing, a supplement to their remaining single-source products, and try to hold the line until research pays off with a new drug. For those with a stable full of new single-source products, scheduled for introduction through the 1980s, the road to success never looked better. On the other hand, the fact that generic drugs have produced substantial economic benefits to society and will continue to be a major factor in the market for years to come should not be overlooked.

Index